MEDIA

THIRD

EDITION

**CLIFFORD G.
CHRISTIANS**
University of Illinois

**KIM B.
ROTZOLL**
University of Illinois

**MARK
FACKLER**
Wheaton College

ETHICS

CASES & MORAL REASONING

Longman
New York & London

COMMUNICATIONS
George Gerbner and Marsha Siefert, Editors
The Annenberg School of Communications
University of Pennsylvania, Philadelphia

Media Ethics: Cases and Moral Reasoning, Third Edition

Copyright © 1991 by Longman Publishing Group

Longman, 95 Church Street, White Plains, N.Y., 10601

Associated companies:
Longman Group Ltd., London
Longman Cheshire Pty., Melbourne
Longman Paul Pty., Auckland
Copp Clark Pitman, Toronto

Executive editor: Gordon T. R. Anderson
Production editor: Camilla T. K. Palmer
Cover design: Kevin Kall
Production supervisor: Anne Armeny

Library of Congress Cataloging in Publication Data
Christians, Clifford G.
   Media ethics : cases and moral reasoning / Clifford G. Christians,
Kim B. Rotzoll, Mark Fackler.
      p.   cm. — (Communications)
   Includes bibliographical references.
   ISBN 0-8013-0650-7
   1. Mass media—Moral and ethical aspects.   I. Rotzoll, Kim B.
II. Fackler, Mark.   III. Title.   IV. Series: Communications
(Annenberg School of Communications (University of Pennsylvania))
P94.C45   1990
170—dc20   90-34033
                                                                     CIP

   ISBN 0-8013-0666-3 (csd.)
   ISBN 0-8013-0650-7 (pbk.)

ABCDEFGHIJ-HA-99 98 97 96 95 94 93 92 91 90

CONTENTS

CASES

FOREWORD

How American journalism has changed in the last quarter century!

When I started with the old *Chicago Daily News*, almost none of the reporters had university degrees, but they knew how to report brilliantly and honestly, and they had mastered the art of having more fun than any other group of people. Journalism was considered a "craft" of comrades, but it was not a particularly fashionable one. (Would you want your daughter to marry a journalist?) The task of journalism then was quite simple and unassuming: day after day, we patiently conveyed to our readers the announcements of the institutions of our society; that, in turn, made it quite easy to be "objective." Most reporters then were naturally ethical—it came with the parents—and the big ethical questions seemed always to revolve about such big questions as whether to take a bottle of whiskey from a Chicago alderman at Christmastime. (You mustn't.)

And, today?

Today, journalism is more fashionable than Hollywood, more powerful much of the time than the U.S. Congress, and more influential than most of the churches and synagogues of America. The State Department and the White House routinely watch American television coverage to see what is happening in world crisis moments. Journalists are well-educated and flush. The "fun" is to be had, most often, in setting oneself up in the most unrelievedly adversarial relationships with the other powers in our society and "getting" as many public figures as one can. Does this mean that this new, powerful, prepotent American journalism of today is more "ethical" than the one I saw pass by these last 25 years?

My answer, unfortunately, would be "No." My respected colleague, the great editor and writer Hoddings Carter III, wrote in his foreword to the earlier edition of this fine book, "To put the matter in plain language, the domain of the mass media today is an ethical jungle in which pragmatism is king, agreed principles as to daily practice are few, and many of the inhabitants pride themselves on the anarchy of their surroundings."

I would add that we have in our own minds not become a craft that realistically sees itself as dealing with what I call the "little relative truths that keep society relatively sane day after day." Too many of us now see ourselves in a self-styled "profession," one without the rules of any real profession and one that sees itself in theological terms as involved in some impossible "search for truth." On top of this self-righteousness and grandiosity, we then also refuse to be guided by— much less involve ourselves in—any serious moral and ethical discussion of our actions. That such an exercise is the basis of all real professions seems to bother no one.

What are the major ethical problems that our modish "in" profession faces—or refuses to face—today in place of the hoary old Christmas whiskey bottle?

In my own mind, I sum up the biggest problem as being "adversary journalism at the service of personal ambition." Too many young journalists (perhaps most, I add bleakly) are in journalism to get ahead fast and without having to deal with such nasty constraints and accountability as having to run for office, respond to a professional association, or listen to the judgment of the market. They are in it for uniquely quick and unfettered power. Journalism has become the Wizard of Oz' Golden Road to celebrity, and the highway is as jammed with upward-striving wayfarers as the road from the Red Sea to Mecca during Haj season. I came into journalism to explain the world to myself (and to have more fun along the way than anyone is entitled to have in one lifetime). Most of the new generation came into journalism to use it for power (and not have any fun at all.)

On top of all of that, you see the syndrome of displaced functions. The fashionable press today is judge and jury, prosecutor and inquisition, new reverend and Mother Superior. Librarian of Congress James Billington told me one day, "No system survives without some mythological and mythical system. If the end is there and it is not filled by authoritative men and real values, it will be filled by artificial myths and demagoguery. The media has replaced the church. It now provides the value mediators for people's lives. It is the validator of politics. It is where the power is. It is a kind of spiritual power, together with corrosive cynicism."

Eugene McCarthy argues further that journalism is becoming no less than the New Religion, complete with inquisitions and infallibility. "Media power," he writes, "now is acknowledged as having moved beyond the Index to the Inquisition, whereby the media decide who is to be sustained, who is to be elevated, who is to be rejected, who is to live and die in the public eye." On the positive side, the process is not unlike the Catholic Church's beatification and canonization; on the negative side, it approaches censorship, interdict, and condemnation.

One example: the spring of 1989 in Washington was a classic moment of revelation of the press-as-prosecutor and judge. Cynics and kind folk called what the press was doing in Congress an "ethics probe." In reality, it was a kind of witchhunt, whose noble words were, "Let's get him." It had started with "getting" Robert Bork, and it led that ugly spring to the amusing fun of "getting" Gary Hart, Joseph Biden, John Tower, Tony Coelho, Jim Wright. . . . The Vietnam War Memorial at least has an ending to the listing of names of the fallen. One had to wonder in the horror of it all whether there would be one to this "Lord of the Flies" children's war?

Jim Wright, in his dramatic resignation that spring, called the bloodletting "mindless cannibalism," and he used the interesting word "propitiation," which is a gesture that appeases a deity of sorts, particularly an evil one. Howard Fineman of *Newsweek* called it a "collective nervous breakdown" in Congress. New Speaker of the House Thomas Foley derided it with concern as a "Roman-games spirit abroad in the land." But perhaps the analyst who best captured the Savonarola spirit of these times was Jim Glassman, editor of the newspaper of Congress, *Roll Call.*

"It is a sort of coming together of a lot of different strains," he said. "One is the cultural 'zeitgeist' of the times—it is the end of the century, no big issues. Oh, there are issues, but they are not perceived as being of immediate danger to people. Also, there is no question that the press feels it owes no allegiance at all to institutions. On the one hand, we shouldn't have sacred cows; but to go about destroying all of this, it is just devastating to Americans. Finally, you have the baby boom generation. They were obsessed with morality—Vietnam was an immoral war. This we now see translated into this 'ethics' concern."

I personally came out of that unsettling spring, which amused me not a bit, feeling that we had become juvenilized, infantilized, as a nation, and that we in the press (particularly the Washington press) were more than doing our share at this reverse growth. In our decline, we were becoming like a Third World nation, going so far as to exhibit and even flaunt such typical Third World characteristics as vendetta in place of civil compromise, piousness in place of real morality, and envy ruling over community—and then we called it "ethics."

How on earth did the freest and supposedly most responsible press in the world get to this point?

The major changes can be traced to the 1960s, when the whole safe and secure (and supposedly righteously moral) United States of America for the first time faced the same problems that other, less isolated nations have always known and suffered. In Vietnam, with Watergate, with frontiers that were moving in upon us, American journalism changed. The old straight-news "coverage of the announcements of the institutions of society" that I had known gave way to the most savage of adversarial journalism in Vietnam. We became not just objective reporters but, as I call it, the "arbiters of truth." Younger journalists soon began talking about ominous things like the "search for truth," which is exactly the contrary to journalism—journalism is the search for what can be known; the search for truth is the search for what cannot be known. Out of those days came adversary journalism and advocacy journalism, and in the 1970s the "me generation" swept journalism into what all of American society was and still is suffering: the death of community and the rise of the indulged, the adversarial, the totally personally ambitious journalist.

One sees the debris from the war everywhere. "Bang-bang" television journalism has left what political scientist William Schneider calls a "vast inadvertent audience for news" which in effect comes out of the onslaught of conflict on television, not more pugnacious, but more terrified of involvement in the world. Spates of news reports about criminal investigations that resulted in no indictments, but were simply the result of overly adversarial journalism, have become the play of the day, as veteran TV journalist Daniel Schorr has pointed out—"simulated facts," he calls it. On top of this, simulation of actual news events has become a staple of the new news/entertainment shows.

TV's Roger Mudd calls this "disheartening because it's becoming increasingly clear in television that the wall between the news business and show business is getting lower; disheartening because the internal mechanism—the newsroom gyroscopes—that used to keep TV news operations on an even keel are starting to malfunction." He summed up at a conference of journalism educators: "The old guidelines are not up for today's competition. That unbreachable wall between news and the rest of television is now being breached every day by owners and managers who want bigger ratings and by news producers themselves who say such things as 'News recreations are an idea whose idea has come.'"

Actually, the idea whose time has come is that we desperately need an ethics underpinning for American journalism today. We need to think about the consequences of our now random actions. We need to take the brilliant American journalism that we still (thank God) find among so many journalists (David Broder, Hugh Sidey, Bill Moyers) and learn from it, and from them, what morality and ethics in journalism is all about.

But we also need to think consciously and deliberately about what we are about. We need to define—and to redefine—press and media and "image" ethics in a complex time, a time in which one's personal ambitions and whims of the moment self-serving cries of "the people's right to know" are too cynical a measure for the mission we perform. For if we are going to be a church, there is going eventually to have to be a catechism; if we are a courtroom, we are going to have to be accountable to some greater institution; if we are going to pretend to speak in the name of the people as their representatives, we will have to offer the American people some proof of our honor beyond what we have.

As to this fine book, combining as it does practical case studies with the ethical spirit of mankind and the centuries, I can think of no better place to begin to relearn what we must, as craftspeople, relearn—what honorable journalism is really about.

Georgie Anne Geyer

Syndicated columnist, author,
TV news analyst, educator.

Media ethics has been traveling a rough road at the junction of theory and practice. Occasionally textbooks will include an ethics chapter at the beginning but will not integrate it with the workaday problems that follow. Principle and practice do not merge well in such endeavors, nor in our daily actions. The rush of events forces us to make ethical decisions by reflex more than by reflection, like drivers wheeling around potholes, mindful that a blowout sends them into a courtroom at one ditch and into public scorn at the other.

Two different mindsets are involved, making fusion difficult. The study of ethics requires deliberation, careful distinctions, and extended discussion. The newsroom tends to emphasize other virtues: toughness and the ability to make rapid decisions in the face of daily crises. Advertising and public relations professionals are expected to be competitive and enterprising. Entertainment writers and producers value skepticism, confident independence, and hot blood. For the teaching of ethics to be worthwhile, the critical capacity must emerge; reasoning processes need to remain paramount. Yet executives of media firms tend to value people of action, those who produce in a high-pressure environment. If media ethics is to gain significance, the gap between daily media practices and serious study must be bridged creatively.

Like the first and second editions, this revision attempts to integrate ethics and media situations by using cases and commentaries. Communication is a practice-oriented field. Reporters for daily newspapers tend to work with episodes, typically pursuing one story after another as they happen. Advertisers ordinarily deal with accounts and design campaigns for specific products. Public relation professionals advocate a specific cause. Actors and writers move from program to program. Communication is case oriented and media ethics is uninteresting and abstract unless practical experiences are addressed. However, media ethics ought to be more than a description of practitioners' ethics. Therefore, in this book, cases are analyzed and connected with the ethical guidelines set forth in the Introduction. Those who work through these pages will be prodded and stimulated to think ethically. Considering situations from a systematic framework advances our

problem-solving capacity; it prevents us from treating each case in-
dependently and thereby reinventing the wheel too often. The commentaries pinpoint some crucial issues and introduce enough salient
material to aid in resolving the case responsibly. Much of the book's
inspiration originally came from Robert Veatch's award-winning *Case
Studies in Medical Ethics*, published in 1977 by the Harvard University
Press. Veatch mixed his commentaries, and we have followed suit—
raising questions for further reflection in some, introducing relevant
ethical theories in others, and pushing toward closure where doing so
seems appropriate.

All the cases are taken from actual experiences. In order to ensure
anonymity and increase clarity, names and places are changed in many
of them. Though our adjustments do not make these cases timeless,
they help prevent them from becoming prematurely dated and shop-
worn. We attempted to find ongoing issues that occur often in ordinary
media practice and did not select only exotic, once-in-a-lifetime encounters. In situations based on court records or in a few instances of
historic significance where real names aid in the analysis, the cases
have not been modified.

As the integration of theory and practice in ethics is important,
so is the integration of news with other aspects of the information
system. The three sections of this book reflect the three major media
functions: reporting news, persuading, and entertaining. Since we want
readers to do ethics rather than puzzle over their immediate experience, we have chosen a broad range of media situations. Many times
when similar issues are encountered in several phases of the communication process, new insights can be gained and sharper perspectives result. As the Cases by Issue list in the Appendix indicates, deception, economic temptation, and sensationalism, for example, are
common in reporting, advertising, public relations, and entertainment.
The issue of how violence is handled can be explored in reporting as
well as in entertainment. Stereotyping is deep seated and pervasive in
every form of public communication; cases dealing with this issue
occur in all three sections. Moreover, the wider spectrum of this book
allows specialists in one medium—television, newspapers, or magazines, for example—to investigate that medium across all its uses. The
Cases by Medium list in the Appendix organizes the cases according
to the major media involved. Often practioners of journalism, advertising, public relations, and entertainment are part of the same corporation and encounter other media areas indirectly in their work. As
a matter of fact, the Supreme Court has specifically included all three

media functions—information, persuasion, and entertainment under First Amendment protection.

The Potter Box is included in the Introduction as a technique for uncovering the important steps in moral reasoning. It is a model of social ethics, in harmony with our overall concern in this volume for social responsibility. It can be used for analyzing each case and reaching responsible conclusions about it. This book is intended for use as a classroom text or in workshops for professionals. We are especially eager that communication educators and practitioners read and think their way through the book on their own. Whether using this volume as a text or for personal reading, the Introduction can be employed flexibly. Under normal circumstances we recommend that the Potter Box be studied first and the theoretical perspective at the beginning be learned thoroughly before readers proceed to the cases. However, readers can fruitfully start elsewhere in the book with a chapter of their choosing and then return to the Introduction for greater depth.

Whether used in an instructional setting or not, the book has two primary goals. First, it seeks to develop analytical skills. Ethical appraisals are often disputed; further training and study can improve the debate and help lay aside rationalizations. Advancement in media ethics requires more attention to evidence, more skill in valid argument, and more patience with complexity. Without explicit procedures, as Edward R. Murrow reportedly complained on occasion: "What is called thinking is often merely a rearranging of our prejudices."

Second, this book aims to improve ethical awareness. Often the ethical dimension goes unrecognized. The authors are not content merely to exercise the intellect; they believe that the moral imagination must be stimulated until real human beings and their welfare become central. Surprising as it may seem, improving ethical awareness is in many ways more elusive than honing analytical skills. In stark cases, such as the Janet Cooke affair, we realize instantly the cheating and deception involved.* But often the ethical issues escape our notice. What about the Abscam coverage cited in case 15? The legal questions regarding entrapment are relatively clear, but what is unethical about using leaked information from the Justice Department outside the courts and jury? Or naming a shoplifter, photographic coverage of grieving parents whose children just died in a fire, writing about the sexual escapades of a senator, exposing a prominent right-to-lifer concealing an abortion, or revealing secret information about

* For a thoughtful analysis of this historic case, see Lewis H. Lapham, "Gilding the News," *Harper's*, July 1981, pp. 31–39.

government policy that contradicts public statements. Identifying the ethical issues here is not always self-evident; thus actual and hypothetical cases become a primary tool for firing the moral imagination.

Improving analytical skills and raising moral sensitivity are lifelong endeavors that involve many facets of human behavior. Studied conscientiously, the terms, arguments, and principles introduced in these chapters may also improve the quality of discourse in the larger area of applied ethics. We trust that using the Potter Box motif for the 86 cases in this volume will aid in building a conceptual apparatus that facilitates the growth of media ethics over the long range.

We are fully aware of the criticism from various kinds of radical social science that ethics is an euphemism for playing mental games while the status quo remains intact. That objection warrants more discussion than this preface permits. However, it should be noted briefly that we find this charge too indiscriminate. Much of the current work in professional ethics is largely a matter of semantics and isolated incidents, but this volume does not belong to that class. The social ethics we advocate wrestles forthrightly with organizational structures. Many of the commentaries, and even entire chapters, probe directly into significant institutional issues. Certainly that is the cumulative effect also. Reading the volume through in its entirety brings into focus substantive questions about economics, management and bureaucracy, allocation of resources, the press's *raison d'être*, and distributive justice. While raising and addressing these fundamental questions, we also have felt constrained to communicate effectively. The case and commentary combination, we believe, has instructional benefits—allowing us to dissect issues into their understandable dimensions without slipping into tiny problems of no consequence on the one hand, yet discouraging a complete dissolution of the democratic order on the other.

Serious students will recognize that we maintain the traditional distinction between ethics and morality. Ethics we understand as the liberal arts discipline that appraises voluntary human conduct insofar as it can be judged right or wrong in reference to determinative principles. The original meaning of *eethos* (Greek) was "sent," "haunt," "abode," "accustomed dwelling place," that is, the place from which we start out, the "home base." From *eethos* is derived *eethikos*, meaning "of or for morals." This word came to stand in the Greek philosophical tradition for the systematic study of the principles that ought to underlie behavior.

On the other hand, morality is of Latin origin. The Latin noun *mos* (pl. *mores*) and the adjective *moralis* signify a way, manner, or customary behavior. The Romans had no word that is the exact equivalent of the Greek *eethos*. Unlike the Greeks, they paid less attention to the inner disposition, the hidden roots of conduct, the basic principles of behavior, than they did to its external pattern. This perspective accords with the Roman genius for order, arrangement, and organization and with its generally unphilosophical bent of mind. The Romans looked to the outside more than to the inside. The Latin *mores* has come into the English language without modification (meaning folkways, how people behave). However, in English usage, the ethics of a people are not the same as its morality. Morality refers to practice and ethics to a basic system of principles.

We incurred many debts while preparing this volume. The McCormick Foundation generously supported our research into ethical dilemmas among media professionals; many of the cases and the questions surrounding them emerged from this research. Ralph Potter encouraged our adaptation of his social ethics model. Louis Hodges wrote the initial drafts for the commentaries in cases 2, 4, 6, 10, 12, 15, 16, 20, 23, 25 and 26 and read earlier editions of the Introduction and Part I. Richard Streckfuss prepared the first draft of cases 2, 4, 10, 12, 13, 15, 16, 20, 23, and 25. David Protess wrote case and commentary number 8. Robert Reid provided a detailed response to a previous version of the manuscript and spared us several inadequacies. James Haefner wrote the first draft of cases 54–60. Dick Christian and Jim Fish appraised many of the advertising cases from the wealth of their practical experience, and many advertising practitioners, in a limited survey in 1989, provided insights into current ethical confrontations. Vinita Hampton compiled material for the entertainment cases. Jay Van Hook and John Ferré edited the Introduction along with other chapters. Diane Weddington recommended the Potter Box as the organizing idea and wrote the original draft applying it to the Cinema theater. Several teachers, students, and professionals who used the first and second editions provided worthwhile suggestions that we have incorporated into this revision. The growing interest in public relations required that we include two chapters on that subject this time. Throughout the editorial process, Gordon Anderson of Longman has demonstrated integrity and good judgment. We absolve these friends of all responsibility for the weaknesses that remain.

Clifford G. Christians
Kim B. Rotzoll
Mark Fackler

Ethical Foundations and Perspectives

The Cinema, a metropolitan movie theater, was gutted by fire. Advertised as "the best spot in town for gay film buffs," the Cinema fire killed 16 men, including a minister, a politician, and a banker. The police did not release the names of the casualties until three days later. One victim's next of kin could not be located before then. Another carried false identification and was finally recognized through a dental examination.

Both city newspapers, the *News-Print* and the *Sentry-Citizen*, normally reported the names and addresses of disaster victims after the official investigation and the release of information. On the day of the fire, each newspaper printed a brief account of the disaster and an explanation for withholding the names. On the third day the *News-Print* published the names and addresses of the deceased; the *Sentry-Citizen* dropped the story completely. This event aroused the curiosity of media ethicists across the country. Both editorial staffs may be appropriately asked to defend their decisions.

The *News-Print* editor claimed "legitimate reader interest." The fire was obviously a significant local event, and the newspaper had always carried complete accounts of public disasters. The editor reasoned that this fire was no exception. The *Citizen* claimed to be protecting the interests of the survivors. "We are not sure the victims were homosexuals, and we do not wish to plant that suggestion in the public mind."

Both editorial staffs gave a specific reason for justifying opposite decisions. Why? Who was right?

When this case is presented to a media ethics seminar for discussion, the students usually argue passionately without making much

1

headway. Analysis degenerates into inchoate pleas that suffering survivors deserve mercy or into grandiose appeals to the privilege of the press. Judgments are made on what Henry Aiken calls the evocative-expressive level, that is, with no justifying reasons.[1]

Too often communication ethics follows such a pattern. Students and practitioners argue about individual sensational incidents, make case-by-case decisions, and do not stop to examine their method of moral reasoning. Instead, a pattern of ethical deliberation should be explicitly outlined in which the relevant considerations are isolated and given appropriate weight. Those who care about ethics in the media can learn to analyze the stages of decision making, focus on the real levels of conflict, and make defensible ethical decisions. This test case can illustrate how competent moral justification takes place.

THE POTTER BOX

Moral thinking should be a systematic process. A judgment is made and action taken. One newspaper concludes that survivors of the victims ought to be protected and withholds names. What steps are used to reach this decision? How does a paper decide that an action should be done because it is right or should be avoided because it is wrong? The second newspaper considers it immoral to withhold news from its readers and prints the names.

Any single decision involves a host of values and they must be sorted out. These values reflect our presuppositions about social life and human nature. To value something means to consider it desirable. Expressions such as "her value system" and "American values" refer to what a woman and a majority of Americans, respectively, estimate or evaluate as worthwhile. We may judge something according to esthetic values (harmonious, pleasing), professional values (innovative, prompt), logical values (consistent, competent), sociocultural values (thrift, hard work), and moral values (honesty, nonviolence). We often find both positive and negative values underlying our choices, pervading all areas of our behavior and motivating us to react in certain directions.[2]

Newspeople hold several values regarding professional reporting; they prize immediacy, skepticism, and their own independence, for example. In the case of the Cinema fire, readers, family members, and reporters all value homosexuality in varying ways. These values taken in combination with ethical principles yield a guideline for the newspaper such as, in the case of the *Sentry-Citizen*, "protect the innocent." The good end, in this instance, is deemed to be guarding an innocent person's right to privacy. The means for accomplishing this end is withholding information about the victims.

Likewise the *News-Print* came to a decision and based an action on that decision. The public has a right to know public news, the newspaper concluded; we will print the names. What values and ethical principles determined this decision? This paper strongly values the professional rule that important information should be distributed without hesitation. The staff argues that everyone ought to be told the truth. Professional values may be stated in positive or negative terms. In fact, in debates about values, an ethical principle might be invoked to help determine which values are preferable. In *News-Print*'s case, the moral rule "tell the truth under all conditions" is particularly relevant.

If we do this kind of analysis, we can begin to see how moral reasoning works. We understand better why there can be disagreement over whether or not to publicize this case. Is it more important to tell the truth, we ask ourselves, or to preserve privacy? Is there some universal end of actions that we can all respect, such as truthtelling, or do we choose to protect some persons, tempering the truth in the process? Thus we do ethical analysis by looking for guidelines and we quickly learn to create an interconnected model: we size up the circumstances, we ask what values motivated the decision, we appeal to a principle, and we choose loyalty to one social group instead of another. Soon we can engage in conflicts over the crucial junctures of the moral reasoning process, rather than argue personal differences over the merits of actual decisions. One disagreement that appears to be at stake here is a conflict between the norm of truthtelling and the norm of protecting the innocent. But differing values and loyalties can be identified too.

Creative ethical analysis involves several explicit steps. Dr. Ralph Potter of the Harvard Divinity School formulated the model of moral reasoning introduced in our analysis of the Cinema fire. By using a diagram adapted from Professor Potter and therefore conveniently labeled the "Potter Box," we can dissect this case further (see Figure 1.1). The Potter Box introduces four dimensions of moral analysis and aids us in locating those places where most misunderstandings occur.[3] Along these lines we construct action guides.

Note how this box has been used in our analysis of the Cinema fire: (1) We gave a definition of the situation, citing newspaper policy,

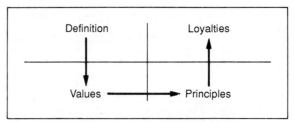

Figure 1.1 *The Potter Box.*
Permission to reprint was granted by Ralph Potter, Center for Population Studies, Harvard University.

police activity, and possible options. One newspaper printed the names when the police completed their investigation; the other did not. Both always followed the policy of printing the names of disaster victims, but in this case they chose differently. (2) Why? We have examined some of the values that might have been operative. But we clearly see that we have not exhausted all the possibilities. We could have stressed that public persons—in this case, the banker, politician, and minister—must be reported consistently in news dissemination or readers will not trust the paper's integrity in other situations. Nor may we suppose that a person is a homosexual simply because he dies in a gay theater. Even though we may personally value heterosexuality, we ought not simplemindedly assume that being caught in a theater catering to gays is embarrassing to everyone. Each value influences our discourse and reasoning on moral questions. (3) We named at least two principles and could have listed more. One paper invoked truthtelling as an ethical imperative. The second concluded that the principle of other-regarding care meant protecting the victims' right to privacy. But other principles could have been summoned: Do the greatest good for the greatest number or do the just action. One newspaper feels obligated to print the truth, even if some innocent people get hurt or are misunderstood. The other newspaper will not print the names, even at the risk of losing some credibility. (4) From the outset a conflict of loyalties is evident. The *News-Print* claims it is acting out of sympathy to its readership in general. The *Citizen* claims to act sympathetically toward the victims of the fire.

Moving from one quadrant to the next, we finally construct our action guides. But the problems can be examined in more depth. Conceive of the box as a circle and go one step further. This time concen-

trate on the ethical principles. Next time in the cycle, focus on the
definition of loyalties. If the major source of disagreement is over
professional values, for example, concentrate on that area the second
time around. Often we value certain things without thinking about
them; debating them with those who are not easily convinced will
make us more critical of ourselves in the positive sense. The/ *News-
Print* values release of information and properly so. But is that an absolute overriding all other considerations? Our sexual mores are often
honestly held, but having them periodically challenged leads to maturity. In such a process of clarification and redefinition, each element
can be addressed in greater detail and then the deeper insight can be
connected to the other quadrants.

The matter of choosing loyalties usually needs the closest scrutiny. The Potter Box is a model for social ethics and consequently forces
us to articulate precisely where our loyalties lie as we make a final
judgment or adopt a particular policy. And in this domain we tend to
beguile ourselves very quickly.

Examine the *Citizen*'s decision once again: Protect the innocent;
publish no names. Who is the staff thinking about when they make
that decision? Perhaps they are considering only themselves. They say
they do not wish to increase the suffering of survivors and the grief of
the victims' families. They claim they do not want to inflict pain. They
contend they do not want to lead people to label the victims as homosexuals when the victims might not have been gay. They seem to
be saying that they could not live with their conscience if they were
to print the news. But on additional reflection their loyalties may actually be different. Are they really protecting the innocent, or protecting themselves? Certainly, not reporting names is a means to an
end, but the end could be their private comfort. The staff members
appear to be interested in a gain for society. They appear to protect the
innocent, maximizing their privacy and minimizing scandalous gossip.
But the crucial question must be faced once more: For whom did they
do all this? If they do not return to the top right-hand quadrant of the
diagram and inquire more deeply where their allegiances lie—for
whom they did it—they have not used the Potter Box adequately.

Probe the *News-Print*'s decision in the same manner. Tell the
truth; print the names, it was decided. If the paper had always printed
the names of victims, why should it make an exception this time? If
it excludes them now, will exceptions be necessary again and again
until the paper's credibility is ended? The *News-Print*'s readers have
certain expectations; must these not be met, the staff seems to be
asking. If decisions are made that undermine credibility, has the news-

paper's long-range ability to contribute to society been damaged? What is more important: the welfare of the community's citizens at large or the welfare of those in the fire accident? Even if the rumors are untrue, will some of the stigma of homosexuality be removed by the implication that certain prominent people might have been homosexuals?

In the initial analysis, the *News-Print* did not seem to be concerned for the survivors. Its imperative was to tell the truth or lose the trust of advertisers, readers, and employees. But maybe this newspaper's loyalties to its readers can actually benefit the Cinema victims also. It could be reasonably argued that if the truth is told often enough, the public will be less shocked about homosexuality and less curious about private affairs. In time the survivors of the tragedy could become more than objects of curiosity. The truth of the tragedy may finally outweigh idle speculation and gossip. Important issues such as these are encountered and clarified when the loyalty quadrant is considered seriously, either in the first round of decision making or in more intensive analysis later.

Choosing loyalties is an extremely significant step in the process of making moral decisions. As the preceding paragraphs indicate, taking this quadrant seriously does not in itself eliminate disagreements. In this arena, honest disputes may occur over who should benefit from our decision. For media personnel who are sincere about serving society, choices must be made among various segments of that society: subscribers and viewers, sources of information, politicians, ethnic minorities, children, and so forth. Our calculations need to consider that flesh-and-blood people known by name cannot be sacrificed for euphemisms and abstractions such as the public, clients, audience, or market. In any case, the Potter Box is an exercise in social ethics that does not permit the luxury of merely playing mental games. Conclusions must be worked out in the rough and tumble of social realities. Often professional ethics makes a final appeal to moral principles and rests content if a decision can be justified according to some reasonable guideline arising from that body of scholarship called ethics. As developed in the next section, ethical principles are crucial in the overall process of reaching a justified conclusion. However, in the pursuit of socially responsible media, clarity over ultimate loyalties is of paramount importance.

In addition to considering each step carefully, the box must be seen as a circle, an organic whole (see Figure 1.2). It is not merely a random set of isolated questions, but a linked system. We have moved from first impressions to explaining various aspects of what is hap-

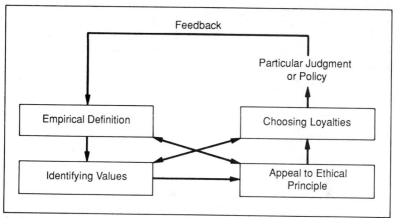

Figure 1.2

pening in the situation. Each newspaper has declared its loyalties. It now has a mechanism to assess further its values and principles. A decision about the Cinema fire is now possible. But the Potter Box can also be used to adopt policy guidelines that will govern future behavior in similar circumstances. On the basis of this episode, the papers might decide to alter their policy regarding names. At least the editorial staffs will be aware that there is a system for reaching a comprehensive policy regarding similar events. Through the four steps, institutions can establish or strengthen company policy regarding anonymous sources, suicide coverage, confidentiality, trial coverage, advertising to children, and so forth.

But we are still left with the initial question: Which newspaper made the right decision? This returns us to a central inquiry raised by this exercise: Is there a universal ground for making ethical decisions, an overarching theory from which we can choose among competing alternatives? Or, is ethical decision making a process of adjusting to the mores and commitments of a given community? Potter's circular model, with its potential for continual expansion, takes both aspects seriously (see Figure 1.3). Community mores are accounted for when we elaborate in step two on the values people hold and when we separate out our loyalties before making a final choice. But these sociological matters are tempered in the Potter Box by an appeal to an explicit ethical principle. Without such an appeal, a conclusion is not

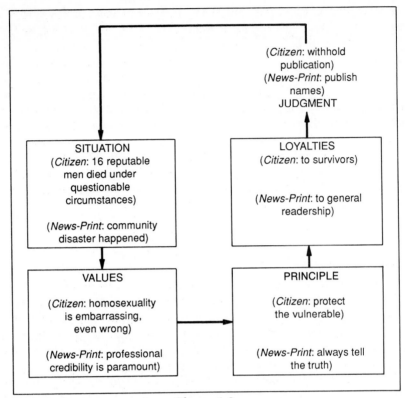

Figure 1.3

considered morally justified. Unfortunately, under the press of circumstances, the media tend to move directly into action from quadrant two, ignoring meticulous concern with three and four.

In this situation, both papers made a morally defensible decision. Both modes of argument are consistent and coherent. In this particular case, either choice can be made with integrity and defended. Both aim toward a good that is widely held in our society, though these goods are defined differently. Often one media company will adopt a morally enlightened option and the other will choose to break promises, cheat, and deceive. Such immoral behavior cannot be justified by serious attention to the Potter Box cycle. Happily there are situations in which two different choices are ethically credible. The Potter Box process does allow competing goods to stand. These conflicts can then be addressed by an appeal to ultimate values, metaphysics, or theology.[4]

For our purposes in this volume, the process by which choices are made is of the greatest importance. Media professions are demanding, filled with ambiguous situations and conflicting loyalties. The practitioner must make decisions quickly and without much time for reflection. Knowing the elements in moral analysis sharpens our vocabulary and thereby enhances our debates in media ethics. By understanding the logic of social ethics, we improve the quality of our conceptual work and thereby the validity of the choices actually made in media practice over the long term. The four dimensions introduced with the Potter Box, in effect, instruct media practitioners and students in developing normative ethics for situations of crisis or confusion.

USING ETHICAL PRINCIPLES

The Potter Box can help guide us through the various cases presented in this book. In the Cinema situation, the relevant empirical matters are reasonably few and simple. There may be some dispute over the theater's clientele—whether or not the 16 who died were homosexuals—but the essential details are fairly easy to list. The Potter Box insists that we always treat the specifics very carefully.

Our disagreements often result from our seeing the actual events differently. When a newspaper purchases a building secretly, sets up a bar, and records city officials on camera, a host of details must be clear before a conclusion can be reached, before we can decide whether the paper is guilty of entrapment, an invasion of privacy, or deception. When debating a television station's responsibility to children, much of the disagreement involves the station's profits and how much free programming of high quality it can contribute without going broke. The question of controlling advertising usually is divided over the effect we consider advertising to have on buyer behavior. Often we debate whether we must overthrow the present media system or work within it. Actually these quarrels are usually not genuine moral disagreements. Regarding the need to destroy the system or work within it, for example, both sides may appeal to a utilitarian principle that institutions must promote the greatest amount of good possible. The debate might simply be over facts and details, over conflicting assessments of which strategy is more effective, and so forth.[5]

Our values need to be isolated and accounted for also. In this straightforward Cinema episode, the values held regarding homosexuality probably had the greatest influence on people's attitudes about what ought to be done. People having the most positive commitments to gay rights, for example, would see no reason not to publish the victims' names. But several other values entered and shaped the decision-making process. No exhaustive list of the values held by participants is ever possible, but attention to them helps prevent us from basing our decisions on personal biases or unexamined prejudices.

Our values constitute the frame of reference in which theories, decisions, and situations make sense to us. Sometimes our moral values correspond favorably to carefully articulated ethical theories. We may value gentleness and compassion so highly, for example, that our attitudes and language mesh with a stringently systematic pacifism. It is more likely, however, that stepping into quadrant three will serve as a critique of the values which may cloud our judgment. Journalists, for instance, sometimes defend the smoking-out process—making public an accusation about a politician under the assumption that guilt or innocence will emerge once the story gets played out fully in public. This professional value is usually contradicted by ethical principles regarding truth and protecting privacy.

Cases and commentaries, as they appear in this book, attempt to clarify the first two squares in the Potter Box. Case studies, by design, describe the relevant details and suggest the alternatives that were considered in each situation. The cases themselves, and the commentaries particularly, explicate the values held by the principal figures in the decision-making process. Usually in conversations, speeches, memos, and animated defenses of one's behavior, a person's important values become clear. Ethicists examine rhetoric very carefully in order to determine what material is relevant for quadrant two. The manager of an advertising agency, for example, may value innovation so highly that other dimensions of the creative process are ignored. Efficiency may be so prized in a film company that only subordinate types survive. A reporter's commitment to the adversary relationship may distort her interpretation of a politician's behavior.

Occasionally the commentaries extend even further and offer ethical principles by which the decision can be defended. Yet, on the whole, these norms or principles must be introduced by readers themselves, and to aid this process, the following pages summarize five major options. As the Potter Box demonstrates, appealing to ethical principles which illuminate the issues is a significant phase of the moral reasoning process. Often one observes newspapers and broadcasters shortcircuiting the Potter Box procedures. They typically act on the basis of professional values, in effect deciding while in quadrant two what their action will be. In the Pentagon Papers (case 13), for example, the *New York Times* decided to publish the story because it valued First Amendment privileges so strongly that no other considerations seemed necessary. However, on the basis of the Potter Box we insist that no conclusion can be morally justified without a clear demonstration that an ethical principle shaped the final decision. The two quadrants on the left side, including values, explicate *what* actually happens. The two on the right side, including ethical principles, concern *why* we would conclude something ought to happen. The left half of the box is descriptive and the right half normative.

In this regard, we follow the standard definitions that locate the act of valuing deep within the human will and emotions, while ethics involves critical reasoning about moral questions. As Sigmund Freud argued in *Totem and Taboo*, all societies, as far as we know, raise up certain ideals to emulate and they also separate themselves from other cultures by establishing boundaries or taboos. A totem pole may indicate that a tribe values supremely the strength of a lion or the craftiness of a weasel. Rituals are maintained to pronounce a curse on behaviors considered totally unacceptable. Valuing, in other words, occurs as an aspect of our human condition as moral beings; it automatically comes to expression in everyday circumstances.[6] Values pervade all dimensions of human experience; even scientific experiments are saturated by value components. On the other hand, ethics involves an understanding of theology and philosophy as well as debates in the history of ideas over justice, virtue, the good, and so forth. Ethics emphasizes reasoning ability and adequate justification.

However, while the ethically appropriate options can be outlined, the imposing of ethical principles by teachers and authors is normally counterproductive in that it undercuts the analytical process. The purpose of sound moral reasoning is to draw responsible conclusions which yield justifiable actions. Therefore, several ethical norms are introduced below. In analyzing the cases, these principles can be incorporated where appropriate and beneficial to given situations. Historically ethicists have established many ethical principles.[7] The five ethical guidelines described below have achieved a significant hearing in the Western tradition, and together they represent a reasonably wide scope of time-tested alternatives. Readers acquainted with other theories from across the globe are encouraged to substitute them instead.

1. *Aristotle's Golden Mean*: "Moral virtue is appropriate location between two extremes."

The golden mean is a middle-level principle which emerged at the earliest beginnings of Western philosophy in fourth-century B.C. Greece. An ethical norm of enduring quality, the theory of the mean—more exactly rendered as "Equilibrium and Harmony"—was developed before Aristotle by the grandson of Confucius in fifth-century B.C. China.

By his "Principle of the Mean" Aristotle meant that moral virtue is a mean between two extremes, the one involving excess and the other deficiency.[8] From Aristotle's predecessor, Plato, the Greeks inherited the four cardinal virtues: justice, courage, wisdom, and temperance. When doing his ethics, Aristotle emphasized moderation or temperance and sharpened it. Just as wisdom is reasoning well, so moderation is living well. In moral virtue, excellence is regarded as a mean between excess and defect. Courage is a mean between cowardice and temerity; a generous person follows a mean between stinginess and wastefulness; modesty is a mean between shamelessness and bashfulness; righteous indignation stands between envy and spite. Propriety is stressed rather than sheer duty or love. As a biologist, Aristotle noted that both too much food and too little spoil health. While most Western theories focus on behavior, Aristotle emphasizes character rather than conduct per se. Outer behavior, in his view, reflects our inner disposition. Virtuous persons have developed habits in terms of temperance; in order for them to flourish as human beings, the path they walk is the golden mean.

One begins operating with this principle by identifying the extremes—doing nothing and exposing everything, for example, in a question of how to report some event. In case number 2, "Employment and Civic Duties in Lewiston," two competing obligations can be resolved through the mean. The newspaper rejects both the excess of excluding all outside involvements and the defect of paying no attention to external affiliations. In this situation, the application of Aristotle's principle leads a paper to publish a financial disclosure of the publisher's holdings, to withdraw from potential conflicts of interest such as local industry boards, to report all staff connections, and so forth, while allowing other civic involvements.

The basic idea is prominent in several diverse areas. In journalism, the sensational is derided and the virtues of balance, fairness, and equal time are recognized. When faced with a decision of whether to prohibit all raising of tobacco or to allow unregulated promotion, the Federal Trade Commission (FTC) took the golden mean—banning cigarette ads from television and placing warning labels on cigarette packages. The Strategic Arms Limitation Treaty (SALT) and Strategic Arms Reduction Talks (START) are a classic political example. Those who want an arms build-up without restrictions on the one hand and those who favor dismantling of nuclear weapons on the other are bound to be unhappy with SALT, START, and other negotiations on the nuclear summit. But in extremely complicated situations, Aristotle would contend, the golden mean is the most fair and reasonable option. This ethical principle may be the only intelligent appeal when one is negotiating between the legitimate claims of two legally appropriate entities.

The point for ethics is that virtue stands between two vices. That such vices are not always easy to locate is true enough, though virtuous persons can discern them with a precision unavailable to those without character. In considering action regarding a hostile editor, a reporter cannot say, "The two ends of the scale are to murder him or burn down his house, so I will take the mean and merely pummel him senseless in a back alley." Bank robbers cannot justify themselves by operating at night so customers will not be hurt, and by taking only $10,000 instead of $100,000. Finding excess and defect involves honesty and imagination before their mean—that is, responsible behavior—becomes clarified. Moreover, some issues are not amenable to a center. A balanced diet positioned between famine and gluttony is undoubtedly wise, but occasionally our health requires drastic surgery also. There were slaves in Greece; Aristotle opted for treating them well and fairly but not for the radical change of releasing them altogether.

Bear in mind, though, that Aristotle does not advocate a bland, weak-minded consensus or the proverbial middle-of-the-road. The mean is not isolated action reduced to political compromise or bureaucratic fixing. We say of an artistic masterpiece, "nothing can be added or subtracted without spoiling it," and this is Aristotle's intent with the golden mean as well. Moreover, while the word "mean" has a mathematical flavor, a sense of average, he explicitly denies that a precise equal distance from two extremes is intended. He speaks of the "mean relative to us," that is, to the individual's status, particular situation, and strong and weak points.[9] Thus, if we are generally prone to one extreme, we ought to lean toward another this time. Affirmative action programs thereby can be justified as appropriate since they help correct a prior imbalance in hiring. The mean is not only the right quantity, but at the right time, toward the right people, for the right reason, and in the right manner. The distance depends on the nature of the agent as determined by the weight of the moral case before him. Think here of the Greek love of esthetic proportion in sculpture. The mean in throwing a javelin is four-fifths of the distance to the end, in hammering a nail nine-tenths from the end.

2. *Kant's Categorical Imperative*: "Act on that maxim which you will to become a universal law."

Immanuel Kant, born in 1724 in Königsberg, Germany, influenced eighteenth-century philosophy more than any other Western thinker. His writings established a permanent contribution to epistemology and ethics. Kant's *Groundwork of the Metaphysic of Morals* (1785) and *Critique of Practical Reason* (1788) are central books for every serious student of ethics.

Kant gave intellectual substance to the golden rule by his categorical imperative, which implies that what is right for one is right for all. As a guide for measuring the morality of our action, Kant declares: "Act only on that maxim whereby you can at the same time will that it should become a universal law."[10] Check the underlying principle of your decision, he says, and see whether you want it applied universally. The test of a genuine obligation is that it can be universalized. The decision to perform an act must be based on a moral law no less binding than such laws of nature as gravity. "Categorical" here means unconditional, without any question of extenuating circumstances, without any exceptions. Right is right and must be done even under the most extreme conditions. What is morally right we ought to do even if the sky should fall, that is, despite whatever consequences may follow.

Kant believed there were higher truths (which he called *noumena*) superior to human beings' limited reason and transcending the physical universe. Conscience is inborn in every person and it must be obeyed. The categorical imperatives, inherent in human beings, are apprehended not by reason but through conscience. By the conscience one comes under moral obligation; it informs us when we ought to choose right and shun evil. To violate one's conscience—no matter how feeble and uninformed—brings about feelings of guilt. Through the conscience, moral law is embedded in the texture of human nature.

The moral law is unconditionally binding on all rational beings. Someone breaks a promise, for example, because it seems to be in his or her own interest, but if all people broke their promises when it suited them, promises would cease to have meaning and societies would deteriorate into terror. Certain actions, therefore, are always wrong: cheating, coveting, stealing, dishonesty, for example. Benevolence and truthtelling are always and universally right. These moral duties are not abrogated by the passage of time nor superseded by such achievements as the Bill of Rights. Even if one could save another's life by telling a lie, it would still be wrong. Deception by the press to get a good story or by advertisers to sell products cannot be excused or overlooked in the Kantian view. Violent pornography in entertainment is not just one variable among many, to be explained away by an appeal to the First Amendment.

Kant's contribution is called deontological ethics (*deon* from the Greek word for duty). The good will "shines like a jewel," he writes, and the obligation of the good conscience is to do its duty for the sake of duty.[11] Ethics for Kant is largely reducible to reverence for duty, and his work is like a hymn on its behalf. For Kant, categorical imperatives must be obeyed even to the sacrifice of all natural inclinations and socially accepted standards. Kant's ethics have an austere quality, but they are generally regarded as having greater motivating power than subjective approaches that are easily rationalized on the basis of temporary moods. Kant's dictum encourages obedience and faithful practice.

3. *Mill's Principle of Utility*: "Seek the greatest happiness for the greatest number."

Utilitarianism is an ethical view widespread in American society and a notion well developed in philosophy. There are many different varieties, but they all hold in one way or another that we are to determine what is right or wrong by considering what will yield the best consequences for the welfare of human beings. The morally right alternative produces the greatest balance of good over evil. All that matters ultimately in determining the right and wrong choice is the amount of good promoted and evil restrained.

Modern utilitarianism originated with the British philosophers Jeremy Bentham (1748–1832) and John Stuart Mill (1806–1873). Their traditional version was hedonistic, holding that the good end is happiness or pleasure. The quantity of pleasure depends on each situation; it can be equal, Bentham would say, for a child's game of kickball as for writing poetry.[12] Mill contended that happiness was the sole end of human action, and the test by which all conduct ought to be judged.[13] Preventing pain and promoting the pleasurable are for Bentham and Mill the only desirable ends.

Later utilitarians, however, have expanded on the notion of happiness. They have noted that if pleasure is upheld as the one object of desire (in the sense of "wine, women, and song"), then all people do not desire it (Puritans do not) and it cannot be the only desired goal. Thus, these utilitarians argue that other values besides pure happiness possess intrinsic worth—values such as friendship, knowledge, health, and symmetry. For these pluralistic utilitarians, rightness or wrongness is to be assessed in terms of the total amount of value ultimately produced. The press's role in Watergate, for example, did not yield a high amount of pleasure for anyone except enemies of Mr. Nixon. Yet in a utilitarian perspective, the overall consequences were valuable enough so that most people considered the press's actions proper, even though pain was inflicted on a few.

Worked out along these lines, utilitarianism provides a definite guideline for aiding our ethical choices. It suggests that we first calculate in the most conscientious manner possible the consequences that would result from our performing the various options open to us. In making this estimation we would ask how much benefit and how much disvalue would result in the lives of everyone affected, including ourselves. Once we have completed these computations for all relevant courses of action, we are morally obligated to choose the alternative that maximizes value or minimizes loss. Knowingly to perform any other action would result in our taking an unethical course.

The norm of utility actually becomes a double principle. It instructs us (1) to produce the greatest possible balance of good over evil and (2) to distribute this as widely as possible. Hence utilitarianism is often defined as promoting the greatest good for the greatest number. In this sense, the principle directs us to distribute a good consequence to more people rather than to fewer, when we have a choice.[14]

Two kinds of utility are typically distinguished: act and rule utilitarianism. For act utilitarians the basic question always involves the greatest good in a specific case. One must ask whether doing this particular act in this circumstance will result in a balance of good over evil. Rule utilitarians, also attributing their view to Mill, construct moral rules on the basis of promoting the greatest general welfare. The question is not which act yields the most utility, but which general rule does. The principle of utility is still the standard, but at the level of rules rather than specific judgments. The act utilitarian may conclude that in one specific situation civil disobedience obtains a balance of good over evil, whereas rule utility would seek to generate a broadly applicable moral rule such as "civil disobedience is permitted except when physically violent."[15]

While happiness is an end few would wish to contradict, utilitarianism does present difficulties. It depends on our making accurate measurements of the consequences, when in everyday affairs a blurred vision often emerges from the results of our choices, at least in the long term. Who can possibly calculate the social changes that will occur in the wake of computer technology in future decades, for instance. Moreover, the "greatest public benefit" principle applies only to societies in which certain nonutilitarian standards of decency prevail. In a society of ten people nine sadists cannot justly persecute the tenth person even though it yields the greatest happiness. In addition, utilitarians view society as a collection of individuals, each with his or her own desires and goals; the public good is a sum total of private goods. These ambiguities, while troublesome and objectionable, do not by themselves destroy the utilitarian perspective, at least for an intellectually sophisticated audience. For our purposes in this volume, no moral norms can be considered free of all uncertainties, and the obvious difficulties with utilitarianism can be addressed in round two or three when the Potter Box technique is used.[16] Occasionally in resolving the cases in the following pages, utility is the most productive principle to include in the lower right-hand quadrant. In the classic case of Robin Hood accosting the rich in order to provide for the poor, act utility appropriately condones his behavior as morally justified.

4. *Rawls's Veil of Ignorance*: "Justice emerges when negotiating without social differentiations."

John Rawls's book, *A Theory of Justice*, is widely quoted in contemporary work on ethics, and from his perspective fairness is the fundamental idea in the concept of justice.[17] He represents a return to an older tradition of substantive moral philosophy and thereby establishes an alternative to utilitarianism. He articulates an egalitarian perspective that carries the familiar social contract theory of Hobbes, Locke, and Rousseau to a more fundamental level.

In easy cases, fairness means quantity. Everybody in the same union doing similar work would all fairly receive a 10 percent raise. Teachers would give the same letter grade to everyone who had three wrong. All the children at a birthday party should have two cookies. Eliminating arbitrary distinctions expresses fairness in its basic sense. However, Rawls struggles more with inherent inequalities. For example, players in a baseball game do not protest the fact that pitchers touch the ball more times than outfielders do. We sense that graduated income taxes are just, though teachers pay only 22 percent and editors, advertisers, public relations staff, and film producers perhaps find themselves in the 50 percent bracket!

When situations are inherently unequal, blind averages are unfair and intuitional judgments too prone to error. Therefore, Rawls recommends his now classic "veil of ignorance," asking that all parties step back from real circumstances into an "original position" behind a barrier where roles and social differentiations are gone.[18] Participants are abstracted from such individual features as race, class, sex, group interests, and other real conditions and are considered equal members of society as a whole. They are men and women with ordinary tastes and ambitions, but each suspends these personality features and regains them only after a contract is in place. Behind the veil, no one knows how he or she will fare when stepping out into real life. The participants may be male or female, 10 years old or 90, a Russian or a Pole, rookie or veteran, black or white, advertising vice-president or sales representative for a weekly. As we negotiate social agreements in the situation of imagined equality behind the veil of ignorance, Rawls argues, we inevitably seek to protect the weaker party and to minimize risks. In case I emerge from the veil as a beginning reporter rather than a big-time publisher, I will opt for fair treatment for the former. The most vulnerable party receives priority in these cases and the result, Rawls would contend, is a just resolution.

Because negotiation and discussion occur, the veil of ignorance does not rely merely on intuition. Such individual decisions too easily become self-serving and morally blind. Nor is the veil another name for utility, with decisions based on what is best for the majority. Again, the issue is morally appropriate action, not simply action that benefits the most people. Rawls's strategy, in fact, stands against the tendency in democratic societies to rally around the interests of the majority and give only lip service to the minority.

Two principles emerge from the hypothetical social contract formulated behind the veil. These, Rawls declares, will be the inevitable and prudent choices of rational men and women acting in their own self-interest. The first principle calls for a maximal system of equal basic liberty. Every person must have the largest political liberty compatible with a like liberty for all. Liberty has priority in that it can never be traded away for economic and social advantages. Thus the first principle permanently conditions the second. The second principle involves all social goods other than liberty and allows inequalities in the distribution of these goods only if they act to benefit the least advantaged party. The inequalities in power, wealth, and income upon which we agree must benefit the worst-off members of society.[19]

Consider press coverage in the now-classic case of Edward Kennedy and Chappaquiddick. Normally such coverage is justified on the basis of the public's right to know superseding a person's right to privacy. But put Ted Kennedy and a newsperson such as Roger Mudd behind the veil of ignorance, not knowing who will be who when they emerge. Undoubtedly they would agree that the reporting of issues is always permissible but that Chappaquiddick itself, many years after the incident, is undue harassment in the absence of any new material. Rawls's principle precludes reporters from using their power to invade the privacy of innocent victims caught in a news story.

On a broader level, place politicians and journalists behind the veil and attempt to establish a working relationship agreeable to all after the veil is parted and space/time begins again. All stark adversary notions would disappear. It would not be agreed that elected officials as a class be called the enemy or liars since those who emerge as politicians would resent such labels. Independence, some toughness, and persistence seem reasonable for media professionals, but a basic respect for all humans would replace an unmitigated and cynical abrasiveness among those wielding instruments of power.

5. *Judeo-Christian Persons as Ends*: "Love Your Neighbor as Yourself."[20]

Ethical norms of nearly all kinds emerge from various religious traditions. The highest good in the Bhagavad-Gita, for example, is enlightenment. Of all the options, however, the Judeo-Christian tradition has dominated American culture to the greatest extent, and its theological ethics has been the most influential.

The ethics of love is not solely a Judeo-Christian notion. Already in the fourth century B.C., the Chinese thinker Mo Tzu spoke in similar terms: "What is the Will of Heaven like? The answer is—To love all men everywhere alike."[21] Nor are all Judeo-Christian ethics a pure morality of love; some ethicists in that tradition make obedience or justice or peace supreme. But the classic contribution of this religious perspective, in its mainline form, contends that ultimately humans stand under only one moral command or virtue: to love God and humankind. All other obligations, though connected to this central one, are considered derivative.

"Love your neighbor" is normative, and uniquely so in this tradition, because love characterizes the very heart of the universe. Augustine is typical in declaring that the supreme good is divine love.[22] The inexhaustible, self-generating nature of God Himself is love; therefore human love has its inspiration, motive, and ground in the highest reaches of eternity. Man is made in the image of God; the more loving humans are, the more like God they are. The Judeo-Christian norm differs from other ethical formulations at this very point. Love is more than a raw principle, stern and unconditional, as in Kant's categorical imperative. Regard for others is not based just on a contract motivated by self-interest, as in John Rawls. It remains personal at its very roots, and while rigorously dutiful, it is never purely legalistic. As Emil Brunner notes in summarizing the biblical exhortations:

> "Live in love." Or, still more plainly: "*Remain* in love." . . .
> It is the summons to remain in the giving of God, to return
> to Him again and again as the origin of all power to be good
> and to do good. There are not "other virtues" alongside the
> life of love. . . . Each virtue, one might say, is a particular
> way in which the person who lives in love takes the other
> into account, and "realizes" him as "Thou."[23]

The Old Testament already spoke of lovingkindness, but the Christian tradition introduced the more dramatic term *agape*—unselfish, other-regarding care and other-directed love, distinct from friendship, charity, benevolence, and other weaker notions. To love a human being in agapic terms is to accept that person's existence as it is given; to love him or her as is.[24] Human beings thus have unconditional value apart from shifting circumstances. The commitment is unalterable; loyalty to others is permanent, indefectible, in sickness and in health. It is unloving, in this view, to give others only instrumental value and use them merely as a means to our own ends. Especially in those areas that do not coincide with a person's own desires, love is not contradicted. In this perspective, we ought to love our neighbors with the same zeal and consistency with which we love ourselves.

Agape as the center of meaning in Judeo-Christian ethics raises significant issues which ethicists in this tradition continue to examine: the regular failure of its adherents to practice this principle, the relationship of love and justice and of the personal and institutional, the role of reason as distinguished from discernment, and whether agape is a universal claim or, if not, what is its continuity with other alternatives.[25]

However, all agree that loving one's neighbor in this tradition is far from sentimental utopianism. It is thoroughly practical, issuing specific help to those who need it. "Neighbor" designates the weak, poor, orphans, widows, aliens, and disenfranchised in the Old Testament. Even enemies are included. This love is not discriminatory: no black or white, no learned or simple, no friend or foe. While not denying the distinctions that characterize creaturely existence, agape stays uniquely blind to them. Love does not estimate rights or claims and then determine whether the person merits attention. The norm here is giving and forgiving with uncalculating spontaneity and spending oneself to fulfill a neighbor's well-being. Because of its well-developed understanding of humanness, the agape principle has been especially powerful in its treatment of social injustice, invasion of privacy, violence, and pornography.

To Whom Is Moral Duty Owed?

The Potter Box forces us to get the empirical data straight, investigate our values, and articulate an appropriate principle. These steps accomplished, the process faces us with the question of our ultimate loyalties. Many times, in the consideration of ethics, direct conflicts arise between the rights of one person or group and those of others. Policies and actions inevitably must favor some to the exclusion of others. Often our most agonizing dilemmas revolve around our primary obligation to a person or social group. Or we ask ourselves, is my first loyalty to my company or to a particular client?

To reach a responsible decision, we must clarify which parties will be influenced by our decision and which ones we feel especially obligated to support. When analyzing the cases in this volume, we will usually investigate five categories:

1. *Duty to ourselves.* Maintaining a sense of integrity and following our conscience may finally be the best alternative in many situations. However, careerism is a serious professional problem and often tempts us to act out of our own self-interest while we claim to be following our conscience.
2. *Duty to clients/subscribers/supporters.* If they pay the bills and if we sign contracts to work for them, do we not carry a special obligation to this class? Even in the more amorphous matter of a viewing audience that pays no service fee for a broadcast signal, a station's duty to them must be addressed when we are deciding which course of action is the most appropriate.
3. *Duty to our organization or firm.* Often company policy is followed much too blindly, yet loyalty to an employer can be a moral good. Whistle blowing is also an aspect here, that is, exposing procedures or persons who are harming the company's reputation. Reporters might even defy court orders and not give up records, under the thesis that in the long run the sources on which media

companies depend will dry up. Thus duty to one's firm might conceivably take priority over duty to an individual or to a court.

4. *Duty to professional colleagues.* A practitioner's strongest obligation is often held toward colleagues doing similar work. Reporters tend to prize first of all their commitments to fellow reporters and the standards of good reporting. Some even maintain an adversary posture against editors and publishers, without violating the standards of accepted etiquette. Film artists presume a primary obligation to their professional counterparts, and account executives to theirs. These professional loyalties, almost intuitively held, also must be examined when we are determining what ought to be done.

5. *Duty to society.* This is an increasingly important dimension of applied ethics and has been highlighted for the media under the term "social responsibility." Questions of privacy and confidentiality, for example, nearly always encounter claims about society's welfare over that of a particular person. The "public's right to know" has become a journalistic slogan. Advertising agencies cannot resolve questions of tobacco ads, political commercials, and nutritionless products without taking the public good fully into the equation. When a few Tylenol bottles were laced with cyanide, the public relations staff of Johnson and Johnson had its foremost obligation to the public. Violence and pornography in media entertainment are clearly social issues. In all such cases, to benefit merely the company or oneself is not morally defensible. In these situations, our loyalty to society warrants preeminence.

Throughout this volume the media practitioner's moral obligation to society is stressed as critically important. Admittedly the meaning of that responsibility is often ill-defined and subject to debate. For example, when one is justifying one's decision, particular social segments must be specified: the welfare of children, the rights of a minority, or the needs of senior citizens. As is emphasized throughout this introduction, in spite of the difficulties, precisely such debate must be at the forefront when we are considering the loyalty quadrant in the Potter Box. No longer do the media operate with a crass "public be damned" philosophy. Increasingly the customer is king and belligerent appeals to owner privilege have been lessened. However, these gains are only the beginning. They need to be propelled forward, so that a sincere sense of social responsibility and a genuine concern for the citizenry become characteristic marks of all contemporary media operations in news, advertising, public relations, and entertainment.

The version of the Potter Box described in this introduction furthers the book's overall preoccupation with social responsibility. Consider the upper tier of the Potter Box (empirical situation and ultimate loyalties), which stresses the social context and social order. As was noted earlier, the Potter Box as a schematic design is not just eclectic, a random gathering of several elements for justifying a decision or policy. The lower half (values and ethical principles) deals more with analytical matters than it does with sociological ones in everyday experience. But the lower tier feeds into the higher. Also the two levels are integrated at crucial junctures so that social situations initiate the process and the choice of cultural loyalties forces one toward the final decision. Thus the loyalty component especially provides a pivotal juncture in moral discourse and indicates that conceptual analysis can hardly be appraised until one sees the implications for institutional arrangements.

The line of decision making that we follow, then, has its final meaning in the social context. Certainly precision is necessary when we are dealing with ethical principles, and their relation must always be drawn to the values held and empirical situation described. But the meaning becomes clear when the choice is made for a particular social context or a specific set of institutional arrangements. Considered judgments, in this view, do not derive directly from normative principles but are woven into a set of obligations one assumes toward certain segments of society. In this scheme, debate over institutional questions is fundamental and ethical thinking is not completed until social applications and implications have been designated. In social ethics of this kind, the task is not just one of definition but an elaboration of the perplexities regarding social justice, power, bureaucracies, and cultural forms. Social theory assumptions are central to the task, not peripheral.[26]

WHO OUGHT TO DECIDE?

During each phase of ethical reasoning, some actor or group of actors is directly involved in deciding, determining values, selecting moral norms, and choosing loyalties. The cases in this book cannot be read or discussed fruitfully without constant attention to the question of who is making the decision. Applied ethics always considers seriously at every step the matter of who should be held accountable.

There are usually numerous decision makers involved. In simple cases, it is an organizational matter where an editor or executive decides rather than a reporter or sales representative. In more complicated areas, can producers of entertainment dismiss their responsibility for quality programming by arguing that they merely give the public what it wants? Are only parents to be held accountable for the television programs that children watch or do advertisers and networks carry responsibility also? If the latter, in what proportions? Does the person with the greatest technical expertise have the greatest moral obligation? We must be wary of paternalism in which laypeople and informal social networks are down-graded in the decision-making process. When is the state, through the courts, the final decision maker? Giving absolute authority or responsibility to any person or group is morally disastrous, yet insisting on accountability across the board is an important endeavor and helps to curb the human penchant for evading one's own liability.

For all the emphasis in this volume on social ethics, the individual practitioner ought not become lost. Only the individual is truly personal and therefore an authentic moral agent. It is true that a firm or institution, when infused and animated by a single spirit and organized into a single institution, is more than a mere sum of discrete entities and has a personality of its own. It is also true that such institutions can in a sense be held accountable for their deeds and become the object of moral approval or disapproval. But only in a limited sense. Such institutions are real enough, but they lack concreteness. Those we seek to call into account while reasoning morally are not organizations or generalities, but precisely individuals. These alone are existing and responsible agents and these alone can be praised or blamed.[27]

Certainly there is corporate obligation, and it is a meaningful notion. When individuals join an organization, and as long as they remain members, they are co-responsible for the actions taken by that organization. What is to be observed, however, is that guilt finally rests upon individuals. We wish in this volume to have all persons judged according to the measure of their responsibility and involvement.

It should be obvious that this is not a plea for a heavy-handed individualism; that would stand directly at odds with the social ethics of the Potter Box process. The point is that responsibility, to be meaningfully assigned and focused, must be distributed among the individuals constituting the corporation. Individuals are not wholly discrete, unrelated, atomistic entities; they always stand in a social context with which they are morally involved. But individuals they nevertheless remain. And it is with each person that ethics is fundamentally concerned. Gross attacks and broad generalizations about entire media systems usually obscure more than they enlighten. On most occasions such assessments are not normative ethics but hot-tempered moralism. The cases and commentaries in all four sections of this book, filtered through the Potter Box model, steer media practitioners toward socially responsible decisions that are justified ethically.

NOTES

1. Henry D. Aiken, *Reason and Conduct* (New York: Alfred A. Knopf, 1962), pp. 65–87.
2. For helpful background, see Richard L. Morrill, "Values as Standards of Action," in his *Teaching Values in College* (San Francisco: Jossey-Bass Publishers, 1980), chap. 3; David Boeyink, "What Do We Mean By 'Newspaper Values,' " unpublished paper, Southern Newspaper Publishers Association, editorial clinic, 8 February 1988, St. Petersburg, Fla.; and for values among artists, cf. Horace Newcomb and Robert Alley, *The Producer's Medium: Conversations with Creators of American TV* (New York: Oxford University Press, 1983).
3. The name "Potter Box" is a designation of Dr. Karen Lebacqz, Pacific School of Religion. The original version is described in Ralph B. Potter, "The Structure of Certain American Christian Responses to the Nuclear Dilemma, 1958–63" (Ph.D. diss., Harvard University, 1965). Potter assumes this framework in Ralph B. Potter, "The Logic of Moral Argument," in *Toward a Discipline of Social Ethics*, ed. Paul Deats (Boston: Boston University Press, 1972), pp. 93–114.
4. This is actually labeled the "ground of meaning" level in the original version. As Potter describes it in his dissertation, "Even when ethical categories have been explicated with philosophical exactitude it is possible for one to ask, 'Why ought I to be moral?' or 'Why ought I to consider your expressions of ethical judgment and your pattern of ethical reasoning to be convincing?' " Further inquiry "drives men ultimately to reflect on their more fundamental ideas concerning God, man, history, and whatever is behind and beyond history." Potter, "The Structure of Certain American Christian Responses," pp. 404–405.
5. While taking the empirical dimension seriously, this does not imply a commitment to neutral facts and what is called "abstracted empiricism" in C. Wright Mills, *The Sociological Imagination* (New York: Oxford University Press, 1959), chap. 3, pp. 50–75. W. I. Thomas's "definition of the situation" is actually a more sophisticated way of explicating the empirical dimension of moral questions. See W. I. Thomas, *Primitive Be-*

havior: An Introduction to the Social Sciences (New York: McGraw-Hill, 1937), p. 8.

6. Obviously the anatomy of values and their relation to beliefs and attitudes is a complex question both in psychology and axiology. In terms of the Potter Box, our concern is to identify the values invoked in various cases and to ensure that they are understood as only one phase of the decision-making process. In that sense, instead of the values-clarification approach of Louis Rath, Sidney Simon, and Merrill Harmin, we insist on the critical normative reflection represented in quadrant three.

7. Ethical egoism has not been included in the list despite its immense popularity. The authors stand with those who doubt its adequacy and coherence as an ethical theory. Furthermore, the view that everyone ought to promote his or her own self-interests does not synchronize with the social responsibility thrust of the Potter model. However, there are several formulations of ethical egoism, and students interested in pursuing this option should see Edward Regis's significant attempt to present a conception that overcomes the standard objections. Edward Regis, "What Is Ethical Egoism?" *Ethics* 91 (October 1980): 50–62. For a history of the debates in this area, see Tibor R. Machan, "Recent Work in Ethical Egoism," *American Philosophical Quarterly* 16 (1979): 1–15.

8. For example, *Nicomachean Ethics*, in *Introduction to Aristotle*, ed. Richard McKeon (New York: Modern Library, 1947), (1104a) p. 333, (1106a) p. 340, (1107a) p. 341, (1138b) p. 423.

9. Ibid. (1107a) p. 340.

10. Immanuel Kant, *Groundwork of the Metaphysic of Morals*, trans. H. J. Paton (New York: Harper Torchbooks, 1964), pp. 69–71, 82–89.

11. Ibid., p. 62.

12. Bentham suggests a scheme for measuring the quantity of pleasure in human acts in Jeremy Bentham, *An Introduction to the Principles of Morals and Legislation* (New York: Hafner, 1948), chaps. 3–7.

13. John Stuart Mill reached this conclusion in the last chapter of *A System of Logic* (London: J. W. Parker, 1843). He attempted 18 years later to expand and defend this conviction. See John Stuart Mill, *Utilitarianism* (London: J. M. Dent & Sons, 1861), esp. chap. 2.

14. For a significant discussion of these and related issues, see Samuel Gorovitz, ed., *Utilitarianism: Text and Critical Essays* (Indianapolis: Bobbs-Merrill, 1971), pp. 59–401.

15. The Potter Box can function without this distinction, but a working knowledge of act and rule utility increases the Box's sophistication. Students are therefore encouraged to read additional descriptions of these two forms of utilitarianism, such as William Frankena, *Ethics* (Englewood Cliffs, N.J.: Prentice-Hall, 1962), pp. 29–35; and Paul W. Taylor, *Principles of Ethics: An Introduction* (Encino, Calif.: Dickenson Publishing Co., 1975), pp. 63–72. A twentieth-century act-utility is presented in George

E. Moore, *Principia Ethica* (Cambridge, England: Cambridge University Press, 1954), chap. 5. Richard Brandt and J. O. Urmson are prominent rule-utilitarians. Cf. Richard Brandt, "Toward a Credible Form of Utilitarianism," in *Morality and the Language of Conduct*, ed. H. N. Castēneda and G. Nakhnikian (Detroit: Wayne State University Press, 1963), pp. 107–143; and J. O. Urmson, "The Interpretation of the Moral Philosophy of J. S. Mill," *The Philosophical Quarterly* 3 (1953): 33–39.

16. For an exceptional analysis of utilitarianism for beginners, see Arthur J. Dyck, *On Human Care: An Introduction to Ethics* (Nashville, Tenn.: Abingdon Press, 1977), pp. 57–71.

17. John Rawls, *A Theory of Justice* (Cambridge, Mass.: Harvard University Belknap Press, 1971), chap. 1, pp. 3–53.

18. Ibid., chap. 3, pp. 118–192.

19. For critique and elaboration of the two principles, see Norman Daniels, ed., *Reading Rawls: Critical Studies of A Theory of Justice* (New York: Basic Books, 1976), part III, pp. 169–281. For an effective classroom strategy to teach Rawls' theory, see Ronald M. Green, "The Rawls' Game: An Introduction to Ethical Theory," *Teaching Philosophy* 9:1 (March 1986): 51–60.

20. A rationalized and secularized account of this principle was developed by Kant, who centended that we ought to treat all rational beings as ends in themselves and never as means only. The Judeo-Christian version is included here because of its vast influence on the popular level. William Frankena judged Judeo-Christian ethics to be even more important to Western society than utilitarianism.

21. Cf. E. R. Hughes, *Chinese Philosophy in Classical Times* (London: J. M. Dent and Sons, 1942), p. 48.

22. Augustine, *The Confessions*, trans. J. G. Pilkington (New York: Liveright Publishing Corp., 1943), (2.2) p. 40, (4.10–4.13) pp. 71–75, (7.12) p. 150, (9.1) p. 188, (10.1) p. 218, (10.29) p. 249, (13.1–13.4) pp. 340–343. God's love is a basic theme throughout Augustine's writings. For a summary, see Frederick Copleston, "St. Augustine: Moral Theory," in his *A History of Philosophy*, vol. 2 (Westminster, Md.: Newman Press, 1960), pp. 81–86.

23. Heinrich Emil Brunner, *The Divine Imperative*, trans. Olive Wyon (Philadelphia: Westminster Press, 1947), pp. 165 and 167.

24. For a comprehensive review of this concept, see Gene Outka, *Agape: An Ethical Analysis* (New Haven, Conn.: Yale University Press, 1972); pp. 7–16 are particularly helpful in understanding the meaning of *agape*.

25. For the best available introduction to the historical and contemporary issues in Christian ethics, see Edward LeRoy Long, Jr., *A Survey of Christian Ethics* (New York: Oxford University Press, 1967); and his *A Survey of Recent Christian Ethics* (New York: Oxford University Press, 1982). James M. Gustafson develops a systematic approach to theological ethics in his

Ethics from a Theocentric Perspective, 2 vols. (Chicago: University of Chicago Press, 1981 and 1984).

26. The precise role of philosophical analysis and social theory is debated even among those who generally follow this decision-making paradigm. Potter himself emphasized philosophical analysis as the primary element in moral deliberation, highlighting, in effect, the principal quadrant as the key to a tough-minded social ethics. James Childress follows the spirit of Potter's apparent focus on philosophical ethics in the analytical tradition. See James Childress, "The Identification of Ethical Principles," *Journal of Religious Ethics* 5 (Spring 1977): 39–66.

    The desire for precision does war against the power of a comprehensive method. But the issue is not over the desirability of philosophical rigor versus the benefit of social theory. Both are indispensable forms of knowledge for ethical reflection. The question is which domain galvanizes the total process of reaching a justifiable moral decision. Which particular emphasis achieves the superior disciplinary coherence for applied ethics? Stassen argues for a "focus upon social theory which includes philosophical analysis but extends beyond it" (Glen H. Stassen, "A Social Theory Model for Religious Social Ethics," *The Journal of Religious Ethics* 5 [Spring 1977]: 9). This volume provides a streamlined version of Stassen's adaptation of Potter, a schematic model that seeks to be both useful and rigorous.

27. Henry Stob, *Ethical Reflections: Essays on Moral Themes* (Grand Rapids, Mich.: Eerdmans, 1978), pp. 3–6. For a distinction between task and collective responsibility, cf. Clifford G. Christians, "Can the Public Be Held Accountable?" *Journal of Mass Media Ethics* 3:1 (1988): 50–58.

PART 1

NEWS

Democratic theory gives the press a crucial role. In most mainline democracies, education and information are the twin pillars on which a free society is said to rest. Informed public opinion is typically heralded as a weapon of enormous power and, indeed, the cornerstone of legislative government. A free press is central to Jefferson's understanding of politics, for example, and Jefferson characteristically referred to an independent information system as "that liberty which guards our other liberties."[1]

Because of this privileged position—commonly called the enlightenment function—outside critics and inside leaders have persistently urged the press toward responsible behavior. Thomas Jefferson himself lamented how such a noble enterprise could degrade itself by publishing slander and error. Joseph Pulitzer worried that without high ethical ideals newspapers would fail as a public servant and even become dangerous. Early in the seventeenth century the French moralist LaBruyère chided newswriters for trivia, for demeaning their high obligation: "They lie down at night in great tranquility upon a piece of news . . . which they are obliged to throw away when they awake." John Cleveland a few years earlier cautioned against respecting diurnal makers, "for that would be knighting a Mandrake . . . and giving an engineer's reputation to the maker of mousetraps."[2]

Modern condemnations of journalism seem merely to echo complaints that are centuries old. Yet the number of today's cavilers and the bitterness of their attacks set the present decade apart. Open news remains our national glory in a complicated world, and expectations of journalistic performance are higher than ever before. In fact, the intense and widespread carping may have yielded a modest dividend in this decade. Never before have the media been so aware of their need for responsible behavior. A self-conscious quality hangs heavily over newsrooms and professional conventions. Aside from the bandits and the pompous who remain untouched by any attacks, some movement is evident. How can we fulfill our mission credibly? Should Pulitzer prizes be given to reporters who deceive to get a story? Why not form an ethics committee? Do journalism schools teach ethics courses or not? Such well-intentioned questions crop up more and more. Like the horsemen of old, one sees a stirring in the mulberry trees. Ezekiel's dry bones are revivifying. Only a little, perhaps, but a splendid little. As always, the smoke means at least a small fire somewhere. The cases in Part I represent the primary issues and problems that are being debated at present among those with a heightened awareness of journalism's ethical responsibility.

The fresh interest in ethics and whatever profit may be gained from working through these cases are threatened by the press's visceral commitment to independence. "Where the press is *free*," cried the prince of freedom, Thomas Jefferson. And others chime: "You cannot chain the watchdog." "The First Amendment guarantees the news media's independence." "Allowing controls by anyone makes us a mockery." Such is the common rhetoric. And in an environment where freedom is prized above all, accountability is not often understood clearly. Accounting, properly requested and unreservedly given, is alien territory. The belief in a free press is sincere and of critical importance, yet it often plays tricks on the press's thinking about ethics. Ethical principles concerning obligation and reckoning do not find a natural home within a journalism hewn from the rock of negative freedom. While advocating press freedom, Part I promotes an accountable news system and attempts to provide content for that notion.

Ethical questions concerning conflict of interest, truthfulness, privacy, social justice, confidentiality, and the other issues in this section must be considered in an environment of stress. The latest Gallup polls reveal press credibility at 13.7 percent, the lowest figure in decades and an alarming one by anyone's measure. For some it represents kicking the chair on which you stubbed your toe. The anxieties present in a nation downsizing its world leadership often provoke outbursts against the messenger. Nonetheless we must continue working on media ethics, even in these hard times. Restriction tends to make newspersons feel stifled, yet the contemporary cultural climate demands that journalism use restraint and sobriety. The five chapters in this section cannot solve all the problems, but the analysis and reso-

lution of the moral dilemmas presented here address matters of high
priority on the journalist's agenda.

NOTES

1. Thomas Jefferson, Address to Philadelphia Delegates, 25 May 1808, in Andrew J. Lipscomb, ed., *The Writings of Thomas Jefferson* (Washington, D.C.:
   The Thomas Jefferson Memorial Association, 1903), vol. 16, p. 304. For
   similar highly quoted passages see his Letter to Marquis De Lafayette, 4
   November 1823, and his Letter to Dr. James Currie, 18 January 1786, in
   Paul L. Ford, ed., *The Writings of Thomas Jefferson* (New York: G. P. Put-
   nam's Sons, 1894), vol. 4, p. 132. The Lafayette letter is also located in
   Lipscomb, vol. 15, p. 491.
2. LaBruyère and Cleveland are quoted in William Rivers, Wilbur Schramm,
   and Clifford Christians, *Responsibility in Mass Communication*, 3d ed.
   (New York: Harper & Row, 1980), p. 2.

CHAPTER 1

Business Pressures

William Peter Hamilton of the *Wall Street Journal* apparently argued at one time: "A newspaper is private enterprise owing nothing whatever to the public, which grants it no franchise. It is emphatically the property of the owner, who is selling a manufactured product at his own risk."[1] This is an extreme statement, yet over the last two centuries many American publishers and broadcasters have tended to approve its spirit. Based on the principles of classical democracy and traditional capitalism, the individual's right to publish has been a strongly held convention.

However, the mood may be shifting somewhat, at least in theory. Increasingly, enlightened owners and executives realize their special obligation precisely because news—and not widgets—is their business. In First Amendment perspective, journalism is in fact a business, but of a particular kind.

Nothing is more difficult in the mass media enterprise than promoting the public good even though the rewards professionally and financially do not depend on such altruism. In actual practice it becomes extraordinarily difficult to separate the media's financial interests from the public's legitimate news interests. American media are constitutionally protected from government constraint, but the news is under the perpetual risk of corporate control. Granted, a conflict between the public's need for unpolluted information and stockholders' profits is not inevitable. Earning a respectable income and deciding to stop a dead-ended investigation could both be appropriate; moral questions emerge when the two are connected as cause and effect. Without a press pool to help pay expenses for a charter, a minor party candidate could not conduct a modern campaign. One person serving in two potentially conflicting capacities—for example, as executive for Columbia Broadcasting and board member for Columbia University—may indeed be working ethically.[2] Not every owner or executive is automatically suspect.

Nonetheless, ever since mass communications took on a big business character at the turn of the twentieth century, built-in commercial pressures have vied for mastery. Upton Sinclair, the angry critic, cried out in 1920: "The Brass Check is found in your pay envelope each week . . . the price of your shame—you who take the fair body of truth and sell it in the market-place, who betray the virgin hopes of mankind into the loathsome brothel of Big Business."[3] As the ominous trend continues toward concentrated ownership of media properties, cost-conscious publishers threaten to overwhelm the press's noble mission.[4] The six cases that follow demonstrate how media practitioners are often caught in conflicting duties to the owners, to their readers or viewers, and to their own professional conscience. Together with examples in Part II regarding persuasion (advertising and public relations) and Part III involving media ownership, these cases illustrate some of the conundrums that occur regularly in today's news business. No wonder the public remains enormously concerned whether media enterprises spend money honorably.

The first case, "The Time Warner Colossus," illustrates a disturbing trend in cross-media ownership. The pattern toward concentration has been occurring for decades, but increasingly it is reaching dangerous levels of integration. While financially beneficial in this case—by combining the strengths of print and visual communications—Time Inc.'s acquisition of Warner raises ethical questions about independent artists and cultural imperialism.

The second case, "Employment and Civic Duties in Lewiston," considers potential conflicts between newspaper employment and activity in community affairs. It focuses on the owner's outside commercial affiliations as the most morally problematical.

The third case, "Ownership of Cable Television," addresses some of the financial issues that need to be considered in areas of new technology. The media are constantly changing through computers, minicams, teletext and videotex, satellites, and more. Their ownership patterns and organizational structures obviously involve important ethical questions that to date have been difficult to get on the public agenda.

The fourth case in this chapter, "Disney World's Fifteenth Birthday," addresses a common conflict of interest, where journalists are paid money by the agency being covered. This case involves freebies made available by Disney World; concrete situations such as the Super Bowl in football could have been selected just as easily. Every January hundreds of sportswriters enjoy a week of gala Super Bowl activity funded by the National Football League. The ethical issues—whether one is reporting for the leisure section or on sports or politics—are fundamentally the same. The Ethics Code of the Society of Professional Journalists is more explicit in this regard than on any other matter: "Nothing of value should be accepted."

Case 5, "Hispanics versus Suburbia," revolves around the expanding percentage of ethnic minorities in American cities. High-minded talk about social welfare and minority hiring clashes directly in this instance with the newspaper's profitability. Regrettably, the publisher reduced the issues to budgetary concerns only, assuming that when the time was ripe in the future, he could reconsider.

In the sixth case, "Antigambling Corporate Gift," the question is whether a specific newspaper ought to use its money to maintain an existing business climate favorable to its own sales position. A media company decides to wield its financial power to benefit itself directly—in effect, to use its position to expand its position.

Since biblical times, sages have warned against serving two masters. Nearly all professions, politics most notably, confront the same problem. Yet the issues cut especially deep in reporting. The conviction of former *Wall Street Journal* reporter R. Foster Winans is a highly publicized reminder that easy cash is always a temptation—for individuals as well as for companies. Leaking advance information from his "Heard on the Street" column to stockbroker Peter Bryant yielded a $30,000 under-the-table payment. Apparently even small amounts of money are occasionally worth more than our integrity as journalists. As some observers have noted, the issues of handling profits responsibly and spurning fattened pockets are not just one chapter in a book, they are the cornerstone of media ethics.

1. THE TIME WARNER COLOSSUS

In June 1989, Time Inc. acquired Warner Communications for $13 billion in cash and securities, after a ferocious struggle with Paramount's take-over attempt. The dramatic story over four months now fills 12,000 pages of sworn depositions on the legal entanglements which accompanied the clashes in the corporate boardrooms. The result is a business feat made in heaven. With assets of $25 billion, "it is awesome how impressive this company will become," says Dick Munro, one of Time Warner's new CEO's.[5]

When Time Inc. was a separate company, its magazines included *Time, Southern Living, Sports Illustrated, Fortune, Life, Money,* and *People.* The magazine division had long been wonderfully profitable, controlling nearly one-fourth of all U.S. magazine advertising revenue. However, in recent years Time's investment bankers could not project more than 6 percent revenue growth annually for the future. The corporate strategy began to focus investment on video programming, but, in spite of increasing involvement in video, the company considered itself underdeveloped here, given today's explosion in visual technologies. Since the early 1960s, Time Inc. had diversified into cable and book publishing in order to expand its growth potential. Most of these ventures had become household words—Book of the Month Club, HBO Video, Home Box Office, Time-Life Books, and Scott-Foresman. However, Warner's wildly successful records-and-music division, its film production capabilities, and extensive overseas marketing made merger an attractive way to prevent an unwelcome buy-out from a hostile company such as Paramount. Management also predicted that combining revenues and sales would jump-start the new Time Warner corporation into a growth cycle neither one would experience separately.

Critics have charged that executives from both companies were more interested in padding their income and stock holdings than in serving either stockholders or the public. According to *Fortune,* Steve Ross of Warner orchestrated a compensation package for himself with the new corporation "so abundant in dollars that, should the oilman fail to show this winter, Ross can shovel money into his furnace and have plenty left over in the spring." In addition to multi-million-dollar salary and pension packages, Ross received $193 million in cash and stock-based compensation.

Henry Luce III of Time Inc.'s Board of Directors, and former editor-in-chief Hedley Donovan, objected to the deal on the grounds that Time is primarily a journalistic enterprise and Warner's organizational culture is essentially entertainment. As a matter of fact, the management staff creating the acquisition turned the independence of the news–editorial component into one of Time's problems. Video and print had never been integrated, they said; putting *Sports Illustrated*'s swimsuit issue in video format had been one of Time's few meager attempts to exploit the company's resources. Warner's electronic and visual expertise was seen to overcome that "deficiency" forever.

The Time Warner merger illustrates a disturbing trend of the last decade toward media conglomeration.

> Five years ago (1983) I suggested that sooner or later a handful of corporations would control most of what the average American sees and hears. Today leaders of the media industry are themselves predicting this. . . . And many of them are engaged in trying to make the predictions come true, but none of them talk about the social consequences. . . . The public learns only of the stock market transactions, the building of dazzling empires, and the personalities of corporate leaders.[6]

Ten years ago, 50 firms controlled half the U.S. media whereas 25 firms—including Time Warner—now hold that distinction. Furthermore, the structure is currently in place for those corporations soon to be controlling it all. If the current trends continue, before the next century the mass media will be owned largely by a dozen major companies. The resultant unsettling political and economic questions are obvious for a nation that, in principle, prizes diversity of opinion and access to the marketplace. Obviously the independent decision making of practitioners becomes increasingly difficult as corporations expand into impersonal behemoths.

In terms of the agape principle in ethics, two issues arise from the Time Warner development: the rights of independent producers and cultural imperialism.

In spite of Time Inc.'s profitability and general corporate luster, its top executives complained that it did not own any important copyrights in the video sector of its business. Time's cable operations gave the company a distribution system, but software had to be purchased in the open market, where prices continued to climb. Thus Time concluded: "In the media and entertainment business of the future, the winners will own the copyrights to creative products, as well as avenues of distribution. We intend to increase our ownership of both."[7]

In order to own copyrights without violating the law, Time needed to own more creative talent. Thus, with the merger, it has expanded its copyright capabilities 100-fold, but in the process Time Warner no longer has a motivation to draw on the resources of independent writers and producers. Time Warner has solved its copyright problem by cutting itself off from the world's pool of ideas in favor of a creative staff that generally conforms to the values of the mainstream media. This is "repression by the bottom line," whereby enhancing a corporation's business position ironically diminishes the quality, flexibility, independence, and variety of the very programming it is designed to market.[8]

In addition to putting a squeeze on the creative sector, Time Warner views the international audience in an ethically inappropriate manner according to the agape principle. At a time when so-called foreign markets offer the greatest growth opportunities, only 10 percent of Time Inc.'s revenues have come from overseas. Warner Communications, however, has been a stunning financial success worldwide, with 40 percent of its profits outside the United States.

In the media business, Warner's concept is called "synergy" and it means that an article can be spun off as a book, movie, or TV show domestically and then sold abroad through an international distribution network. Warner's prowess in spinning off "Batman," "Superman," and "Wonder Woman" recommended it to Time executives as the standard by which their merged corporation would now compete with Sony of Japan, Bertelsmann of West Germany, Pearson PLC of England, and the handful of communications companies that control the world's media. As media analyst John Bauer put it, "This is a lot of empire building cloaked in terms of global international media competition."

The ethical problem is that throughout the planning and execution of the merger, the international audience was seen exclusively as a paying market, as an exploitable resource. No attention was given to indigenous programming and enhancing local talent. It is this one-way notion of information flow that carries over the colonial and paternalistic spirit no longer acceptable in politics or even in international economics. Increasingly since World War II, seeking to dominate another's culture is becoming as reprehensible as dominating another's government or business out of exploitative self-interest.

2. EMPLOYMENT AND CIVIC DUTIES IN LEWISTON

The *Lewiston* (Idaho) *Morning Tribune* recently took a look at the community interests of its staff. Staff member Cassandra Tate summarized the issue in the newspaper article that resulted: "Should the journalist exercise the rights and responsibilities of citizenship by participating in civic and political affairs? Or should he/she remain above the fray, a neutral observer? There is a danger of conflict in the first course, the potential for social isolation and sterility in the second."[9]

As would be expected, the *Morning Tribune*'s publisher had the lengthiest list of civic involvements. A. L. "Butch" Alford, Jr., was president of the Idaho Board of Education and a director of the Lewiston Roundup Association, the Lewis-Clark Boys Club, the Nez Perce National Historical Park Advisory Committee, and the Twin County United Way. He also served on the St. Joseph's Hospital Lay Advisory Board, the Bonneville Power Regional Advisory Council, and Potlatch Corporation's Foundation for Higher Education. He was active in the Lewiston Chamber of Commerce and was a director of the Idaho First National Bank and of the University of Idaho Foundation.

The newspaper's editorial-page editor, Bill Hall, had recently returned to the paper after 16 months as press secretary for Idaho Senator Frank Church. Night managing editor Perry Swisher was serving on the Governor's Blue Ribbon Committee on Taxation, the Idaho Manpower Board, and the Idaho Advisory Committee to the United States Commission on Civil Rights. He also was advisor to the Lewiston Downtown Beautification Committee and the Public Safety Building Committee. Executive editor James E. Shelley had held a position five years earlier as campaign coordinator for a Democratic Senate candidate. Reporter Thomas W. Campbell was chair of the Lewiston Historic Preservation Commission, a Democratic precinct committee member, and a member of the Civic Theater Board. Part-time writer Diane Pettis was a member of the County Planning and Zoning Commission. Business writer Sylvia Harrell chaired the Lewiston Planning and Zoning Commission. Harrell's husband worked for Potlatch, the area's largest industry and a frequent subject of pollution stories.

A similar list could be drawn up for the staffs on most newspapers, particularly the smaller ones. The *Morning Tribune* follows standard policy—staff members do not report on their own activities—but, of course, those who draw the assignments are aware they are reporting on the performance of their friend and co-worker or, in cases where editors or publishers are participants, on the performance of their bosses. For example, Gary Sharpe, a young reporter uninvolved in the community, encountered difficulties in covering the Roundup, Lewiston's annual rodeo, because the publisher served on its board. Said Sharpe, "I don't know how many times I've been confronted by a person aware of Butch's membership on the board who says, 'I think Butch would like to see this in the paper.' "

As one concrete result of the *Tribune*'s study, reporter Campbell was told he could no longer write about politics if he did not resign as a Democratic precinct committee member. Campbell took exception: "They're saying I won't give a fair interview to the Republicans because I'm a Democratic precinct committeeman. I'm saying that doesn't make one bit of difference."

Said publisher Alford of the story on external involvements of his staff: "It's the first time in my association with the paper that we've thought to look at ourselves. . . . I hope as a result of our editorial coverage of ourselves we can see the weaknesses in our own process."[10] Alford's newspaper departed from tradition in publishing an open examination of its own operation. Alford also broke another tradition. Copies of his complete income tax return were filed with the newsroom secretary to be examined by anyone interested.

Most of the problems in this case come from potential role conflicts. The journalist's role as practitioner may at times contradict the journalist's role as citizen. The good a journalist can achieve is the publication of news as free from bias as possible. The good a citizen can achieve, on the other hand, is the social service that comes from responsible citizenship. The question, then, in part, is whether journalists should sacrifice their role as contributing citizens in order to be journalists, or whether the conflicts in this case are more apparent than real. Publisher William Branen of the *Burlington* (Wisconsin) *Standard Press*, for example, calls it a "terrible mistake" when journalists refuse to become involved in their communities. "That's why many large newspapers are going down the drain," he says. "They've lost contact with their readers."[11]

It can be reasonably argued that organizational memberships themselves are not a significant source of biased journalism. In the present case, it is likely that a reporter who is a Democratic precinct committee member could not be entirely fair in an interview with a Republican candidate. That bias, however, would not be the consequence of committee membership. The reporter might show bias whether on the committee or not. Hence, resignation from that job would be essentially cosmetic, since the reporter would surely remain a Democrat with perhaps strong political views.

On the other hand, it is possible that the reporter with active political interests is much more likely to be well informed about political matters than a politically disinterested reporter. It may be that even with a Democratic bias, reporter Campbell could do a better job interviewing either Democrats or Republicans than would someone who had no political interests. Cassandra Tate is incorrect if she thinks that a human being can "remain above the fray, a neutral observer." Since humans are valuing creatures, neutrality is not possible. The moral obligation, then, cannot be to produce value-free journalists. The objective, as the Potter Box suggests, is to make clear at all times what values are operating.

Since bias-free reporting is not possible, another distinction becomes necessary. Note, for example, Alford's membership in United Way. A bias in favor of the ideals for which an institution stands must be distinguished from a bias toward the organization itself. Bias in favor of charitable giving is a proclivity that can be tolerated, but favoritism toward the United Way organization, its directors, and its paid employees cannot. Corruption or misuse of public funds by that organization should be reported vigorously and, indeed, can be if the journalist's bias is simply toward charitable giving and not in favor of the United Way as an institution. Moreover, Alford's affiliation with United Way ought not diminish publicity for other charitable organizations.

What kind of policy, then, should journalists adopt regarding membership in community organizations? Some would discourage membership in all organizations: religious, civic, country club, corporate, and so on. Such a policy, however, risks the isolation of journalists from community affairs. The damage would include loss of leads on important stories as well as frustration over the inability to pursue personal, nonjournalistic value commitments in an active, organized way. Thus a policy preventing all organizational memberships has little to commend it. On the opposite end of the spectrum, media companies could ignore the question of organizational memberships altogether. They might do so on the grounds that biased reporting stems not from memberships per se, but from underlying value systems, making journalists' memberships in organizations a superficial matter.

Using Aristotle's golden mean as an ethical guideline, it is not desirable to preclude all outside involvements, nor is it acceptable for the staff to have no restrictions at all. That leaves the problem of finding strategies for minimizing the conflicts that arise from community memberships. In this regard the *Morning Tribune*'s policy of not allowing reporters to cover their own activities is sound. Commendably, the *Morning Tribune* took a second step, alerting readers to the staff's external activities.

The boss's affiliations are another matter. His presidency on the Idaho Board of Education and his membership on the Historical Park Advisory Committee would not likely create unmanageable conflicts, but several of his positions in commercial firms are clearly problematical. Potlatch is the largest local industry and often under public scrutiny for pollution violations. Alford is also a director of First National Bank and a member of the advisory council for Bonneville Power. These commitments are very questionable. A reporter's interest in pleasing the boss would inevitably conflict with a concern for sound news reporting. Would the reporter be free to investigate discrimination in hiring, irresponsible service, or mishandling of company finances?

The hazards can be minimized. Alford can make it unmistakably clear to the staff that he is a newspaper owner first and a member of Potlatch Foundation second. He can also convey his priorities to Potlatch as a condition for serving. If the *Morning Tribune*'s staff is made up of competent journalists, the message will likely get across. If, however, the staff see themselves primarily as employees and only secondarily as responsible journalists whose obligations are to the public, the point will not get through. Thus, Alford's clarifying his commitments—even in the best of all circumstances—can only reduce the likelihood of damage. His employees could be better "watchdogs" if he would sever entirely his connections with Potlatch, First National, and Bonneville Power. Bitter experience has taught us, for example, that publishers sitting on the boards of utility companies often initiate pro-utility stories when rate increases are requested.

On a more fundamental level, Alford must consider whether he is caught up in a business mentality that subtly weakens his service to the community. William Allen White, an outstanding editor and publisher, once complained, "Too often the publisher . . . is a rich man seeking power and prestige. He has the country club complex . . . and the unconscious arrogance of conscious wealth. Therefore it is hard to get a modern American newspaper to go the distance necessary to print all the news about many topics."[12] Within the free enterprise system, owners of media institutions consider themselves entitled to order whatever policy they choose, provided such policies are legal. Ethically sensitive publishers and broadcast executives follow stronger guidelines, however, deliberately adopting specific safeguards against the bewitching power of business allegiances.

3. OWNERSHIP OF CABLE TELEVISION

The city of Hawthorne anticipated a new cable television system within two years. The city council had debated the matter for several months and had called for bids from cable companies who might be interested in the franchise. Bob Evans of the local radio station WCCR covered all phases of the discussion. Community interest was substantial and the city council seemed determined to negotiate an enlightened contract. Enough information carried through to the public so that over 75 percent of those interviewed in a survey knew the basic details: $10 per month service charge, 32 video channels and 4 audio; they knew the purpose of a local origination channel. When the city council selected the two finalists, Armco and Warners, the majority of those interviewed knew the names and national headquarters of both.

Two questions that surfaced during the council's proceedings and hearings continued to bother Bob Evans. For one thing, all the prospective cable companies had refused to cooperate in a regional plan without an increase of 40 percent in the monthly charge. Company representatives contended that in population areas of less than 1,000 per square mile, it is not cost efficient to provide cable service. Including the small towns in outlying areas would increase their equipment price so much as to make the investment unprofitable.

Second, Evans became curious about why the operators preferred to lay cable only according to market demand and did not insist that it reach every home in the city. Apparently companies realize their profit margin with two-thirds of the city and find that connecting the remaining one-third is cost inefficient. In a private conversation one company executive complained about the "poor in the ghetto" who cannot afford the $8 per month, or, at least, "will not pay their bills promptly."

Meanwhile, Evans had become an interested student of cable technology. He was especially intrigued by third-generation cable systems built on fiber optics and capable of 200 channels or more that would provide a complete range of information and cultural services. This two-way, broadband cable structure, as Evans understood it, would become as basic to the city of the future as water and electricity are now. Through these 200 channels, library material, police protection, retail shopping, public affairs, banking, mail delivery, voting, meter reading, and medical diagnosis would all be available.

Evans began wondering whether the distribution patterns of the current cable proposals were equitable. He understood the realities of marketplace economics but wondered whether Hawthorne's projected cable system was not just an added convenience for those already information-rich, and whether failure to include the ghettos and rural areas now would breed further inequities when the system was updated and expanded in the future.

He was aware that a few North American cities had chosen the path of municipal ownership for cable, by which every home was treated equally and all had hook-up potential. He also noted that the average price in municipal systems was two dollars below the Hawthorne proposals. Evans realized that municipal bonds would be necessary for equipment and that their payment would eventually increase taxes. He also rated the city administration as only slightly above average in competence and effectiveness. However, on balance, Evans considered a publicly owned system as more just, and he developed in his own mind a regional commission through which the citizens themselves would own and operate the franchise.

As part of a series on cable television in cities of similar size (350,000 population), Evans included one story on a neighboring municipal system. He felt compelled to do more, but frequent appeals to his station management were rebuffed. Station executives saw no useful purpose in advocating public ownership; they found it virtually impossible to appreciate Evans's concerns and were afraid that promoting this option would be heard by their listeners as a cause not of social justice but of socialism.

Six weeks later the city council adopted the Armco proposal. No discussion of the public ownership alternative had surfaced. Evans remained attracted to a nonprivate option, though he found himself discussing it only in personal conversations with friends.

Bob Evans correctly laments the dominance of engineering criteria to determine cable television policy. It gradually became clear to him that the city council was selecting a cable franchise in the same manner that they chose a contractor for building a new sewage system—on the basis of price, performance, and service. While not denying the relevance of such technical matters, Evans caught hold of the larger social dimensions and began wondering which ownership and control design best served the needs of all. The citizens, politicians, and company officials considered the issues within very narrow parameters and appeared satisfied with WCCR's facts-and-detail emphasis. Because he grasped a larger picture, Evans had an obligation to insist on covering the deeper dimensions, even though he was initially rebuffed by the management of his station and no one seemed particularly interested.

The overriding issue here is the concept of social justice that underlies the selection of Hawthorne's cable franchise. Evans appears to operate with some notion of fair distribution, but the principle never gets fully clarified in his mind and often becomes entangled with political realities such as city council competence and marketplace economics. The important ethical question in this case is whether one can justify allocation of this resource to all parties without discrimination. On what basis can one argue that it is morally desirable to ensure comprehensive information for every person regardless of income or geographic location? Evans implies at times that there is a plausible case for equal access. Can such a rationale be constructed? If so, then the leverage exists for a publicly owned medium designed to ensure equal participation by the entire resident population.

A view of social justice based on merit, to be sure, does not accede to Evans's concern.[13] There are several variants of this approach, but all of them judge on the basis of conduct or achievement and not solely on the inherent value of human beings. Thus, the argument goes, those who have expended the most energy or taken the greatest risk or suffered the most pain deserve the highest reward. Though not all differences in people result from varying amounts of their own effort or accomplishment, in this view, ability to pay is considered a reasonable basis for determining who obtains this service. In the same vein, it can be argued that citizens who produce more face a heavier obligation in ordinary affairs, a duty that can be facilitated by high-capacity technologies. Again, there are several elements in the perspective that equal access to certain resources is merited, but a prominent canon is whether consumers are at liberty to express preferences, to fulfill their desires, and to receive a fair return on their expenditures. The cable structure would be unjust only to the degree that supply and demand or honest dealings are abrogated.

However, another notion of social justice, "to each according to one's essential needs," does validate Evans's concern for equal access. The contention here is not that all felt needs or frivolous wants ought to be met, but that basic human requirements must be satisfied equally. The basis for judging is not activity or achievement, but our being human. While there is legitimate argument over which needs qualify, agreement is rather uniform on most fundamental issues such as food, housing, safety, and medical care. People as persons share generic endowments that define them as human. Thus everyone is entitled—without regard for individual success—to those things in life that permit his or her existence to continue in a humane fashion. One prominent version of this need conception of justice is the Judeo-Christian ethic of love whereby all deserve equal consideration as God's image bearers. Thus whenever a society allocates the necessities of life, the distribution ought to be impartial.

Evans was evidently grasping toward a need conception of justice. Within this framework, prognostications generate some dispute. What really is the future of the so-called wired city? Evans assumes that an industrialized economy such as Hawthorne's will eventually be based on an information network. In his view, information technologies combining computer storage, a video screen, and efficient transmission will eventually prove as necessary to the city as water and electricity are now. He bases his predictions on technologies already in place, not on an imaginary figment or utopian dream. As a student of such other media as cinema, radio, and television, he undoubtedly realizes that a media structure once in place is incredibly difficult to revolutionize. He feels that the system Hawthorne chooses in the early stages will probably not permit wholesale changes after the system matures and becomes more complex. Thus one could grant that cable's future course cannot be fully known, yet one ought to be morally bound to initiate the structure that best organizes cable according to the equal distribution principle. Otherwise there will be no guarantee of equitable dissemination of public services, nor equal participation in the political or educational process. Given the economics of monthly costs in urban poverty sections and in wiring rural areas, complete saturation will not be automatic in a view-data system established on profitability. Free competition among goods and services has been a historically influential rationale for media practice, but in the case of a monopoly performing a vital function, the need-based criterion appears to be the more fitting ethical standard.

4. DISNEY WORLD'S FIFTEENTH BIRTHDAY

To celebrate its fifteenth birthday, Walt Disney World invited 10,500 guests to a three-day party. Half of them were media representatives and the other half a personal guest of each. A financial group of the Walt Disney Company, airlines, Orlando-area hotels, convention bureaus, and state and local governmental agencies contributed approximately $8 million to underwrite the event.

Disney did not disclose how many of those attending paid nothing. A face-saving offer of $150 per person was billed to those requesting it. A few news organizations prohibit all gratuities and paid their own way. On the bus ride back to the hotels after the last party on Saturday night, one fan of central Florida's hospitality announced to all: "My wallet's been in hibernation all weekend. That ole Walt Disney is some party animal."[14]

Disney estimated that during their visit, crews from radio and television stations broadcast more than 1,000 hours of coverage to all parts of the United States. Also, as gifts from Disney's public relations army, media personnel left with material for months of possible stories. The three days featured spectacular parades, air and water shows, food extravaganzas, and Disney employees catering to every request. Some of the nation's top entertainers, such as country singer Dolly Parton, provided broadcast-quality material and meanwhile endorsed Disney World's glamour. Disney's management made no effort to shape the reporting but, given their expertise at generating publicity, it correctly presumed that the results would be overwhelmingly positive. As the *Chicago Tribune* reported: "One Orlando TV reporter interviewed a woman from a Colorado TV station and asked if she uncovered anything negative during the weekend. The Coloradan said she did find the weather very humid and might mention that in her next report."

Most of those in the crowd were talk show hosts, travel writers, station owners, radio disk jockeys, publishers, and magazine staff. A small percentage represented the working press, and news conferences for them dealt with Disney's future plans for its 28,000 acres and its international ventures. No one mentioned the dispensations given to Disney by the Florida legislature for developing its land, though a former Orlando newsman wryly observed, "They could have been building nuclear weapons for years at Disney World and nobody would have bothered them."

The problem is obviously to record faithfully both the good and bad associated with such a trip. However, to expect reporters on free trips to report carefully on both sides is to assume that reporters are willing to "bite the hand that feeds them." That is more than one should normally expect of mere mortals. Thus agreeing to free trips is tantamount to accepting the proposition that it is morally permissible to write puffery.

The question, then, turns on company policy regarding free trips for travel writers. To examine the matter of policy, one must inquire about the reasons for having a travel section at all. Since people are interested in traveling, the paper's self-interest encourages coverage of this subject. If the public's fascination with travel stories were purely one of entertainment, no journalistic question would be involved at all. There would be no need for balance or accuracy, and the more fanciful and entertaining the story the better. But some people are interested in reading about travel in order to determine where to go and how to do so most efficiently. Such readers turn to travel sections for important information on which they will depend rather heavily. The informing role of travel writing places special moral responsibility on reporters assigned to it.

What then should the media's policy be regarding the acceptance of free trips? The ethical problem is immediately apparent, because accepting free trips may involve a conflict of interest whereas refusing them does not. Certainly the logic of this Society of Professional Journalists' (SPJ/SDX) iron-clad guidelines is obvious: "Gifts, favors, free travel, special treatment or privileges can compromise the integrity of journalists and their employers. Nothing of value should be accepted."

In the final analysis, nothing in life is free. The agency or organization that picks up the tab expects some return on its investment. Sponsoring organizations such as Disney pay the bill in order to get relatively inexpensive and very effective publicity. That expectation converts the role of the reporter from journalist to public relations agent. The organization offering the free trip is fully aware that reports in travel columns can be more influential than a paid commercial advertisement. In light of those circumstances it seems clear that the media's policy should flatly prohibit participation. If a company cannot pay for the reporter's trip, the reporter should stay home.[15]

For some papers, however, such a policy would, in effect, eliminate stories on travel. The consequence would be to deprive readers and viewers of information in which they have a justifiable interest. The question then becomes whether it is possible to adopt a strategy to meet the legitimate public need for travel information while accepting the gift of trips from outside organizations. Can ways be found to minimize the likelihood of deceit?

Two things can be done. First, the editor or station manager can insist that reporters who take trips report as accurately as possible without considering the effect on possible future trips. Editors are more likely to be successful, of course, if the reporter is not just a travel specialist but a carefully trained journalist.

Second, an editor can notify the public that the trip was in fact underwritten by some outside organization. The specific name of the party need not be reported, but the article should identify the kind of enterprise it was (a travel agency, hotel, airline). The information enables the reader or viewer to assess the story more intelligently.

The decision to accept outside sponsorship of such trips does nevertheless run the risk of biased reporting that deceives the public. As travel writer Jeremy Alderson puts it, asking hard questions of travel industry executives when they are paying the bill "is considered as tasteless as . . . a television news anchor asking our vice-president about allegations of criminal conspiracy."[16] On the other hand, if the paper or station or magazine cannot pay for a trip, the decision not to accept it in effect deprives certain social groups. Thus the absolute policy of forbidding free trips is not always in the public interest.

It might be useful to examine a situation in which a free trip involves more serious journalism. Suppose Hotwire Electric is contemplating construction of a nuclear generating facility in your area. Your television station has been reporting carefully about the benefits and risk of that facility. The utility, rightly or wrongly, believes that reporters have not given an accurate picture of the alternatives. The utility operates a nuclear facility in a distant state and has asked the station to send a reporter to that area to get firsthand information on the operation of the facility and on public attitudes toward it. The station cannot pay the bill so the utility offers to pay it. Should the station send a reporter at the utility's expense?

"Yes" seems to be a reasonable answer. The station should send its best-informed reporter, and it should make clear that Hotwire Electric paid for the trip. In this case, the public has an overriding need for the most accurate information available. If that news story cannot possibly be obtained without the acceptance of the gift, the station should take Hotwire's financial assistance and find strategies for avoiding a deceptive report.

5. HISPANICS VERSUS SUBURBIA

As a conscientious publisher of a large-city newspaper, you want to print news that is meaningful to your city's residents. Your goal is information that citizens want to know because it illuminates their social, economic, and political affairs. Your newspaper, however, is losing its urban readers and gaining its customers from the suburbs. Over the years, your paper has followed these population shifts with content and advertising designed for suburban readers. You ask yourself, "Are we still fulfilling our obligations to our city? Ours historically is a city paper, and maybe we should try to regain our next-door readers."

Because you presume the necessity of your newspaper surviving economically, you seek the advice of your advertising and circulation experts. "The money lies in the suburbs," you are told. "If you gear a daily toward the poorer city residents, you risk alienating your suburban buyers. And that means losing substantial advertising revenue."

You specifically inquire about a Spanish-language edition for the city's burgeoning Mexican-American population. "I'm afraid you would lose too much money on that one," comes the reply. "The *Los Angeles Times* studied such a possibility a few years ago and concluded that it would be financially unfeasible because many Hispanics still suffer from economic deprivation.[17] Almost ten years later the *Times* was able to publish a bi-weekly insert, *Nuestro Tiempo*, in Spanish. By then it had become at least a reasonable venture because disposable income among the Hispanics had steadily increased. In your market, there is simply not enough economic strength among Hispanics to warrant any dramatic changes."

Meanwhile, you have become better acquainted with the powerful organization "U.S. English." Founded with the guidance of linguist S. I. Hayakawa, a former U.S. senator from California, the 350,000-member organization seeks a constitutional amendment making English the official language of the United States. Though Arizona's English-only law has recently been declared unconstitutional, 17 states, including your own California, still have this policy on their books. "Language is one of the very few things we have in common in the U.S.," says Steve Workings, the group's director of government affairs.[18] Therefore, the group advocates limiting bilingual education to transitional status and tightening English proficiency standards for all prospective citizens. Even Alfredo Estrada, publisher of the upscale monthly *Hispanic*, you learn, argues that "clinging to their native language holds Hispanics back."[19] And, after all, with a new Spanish-language television station in town, Hispanic culture and news are already available. At least in good conscience, you muse, we can continue the paper's focus on English as our state's official language.

A colleague teaching in a nearby journalism school insists that you are facing not a moral question at all but merely an administrative decision. Her argument goes something like this: Every medium develops a particular mission and audience. All media have built-in limitations; no matter how big a company is, it must choose what to present and which markets to reach. The fact that the readers of your paper have moved to the suburbs is not the fault of the paper's management. The paper's readers have not changed, only their address has. The situation is a strategic one of supply and demand. The newspaper, she contends, still fulfills its social responsibility by serving its long-standing readership, regardless of where subscribers choose to live. In fact, she reasons, it is paternalistic to think that your paper can offer something viable to this new urban audience. If they need a newspaper, they should fund, edit, and distribute one themselves.

Walking through the newsroom, you notice, as you have so many times before, the large proportion of white reporters and editors. This proportion reflects the present readership but hardly

resembles the city's population. Despite the city's large percentage of ethnic minorities, and your newspaper's policy of funding
minority scholarships and training programs, only 5 percent of
the full-time editorial staff is nonwhite. You feel embarrassed that
your newspaper has solved neither the circulation nor hiring dilemma. You point with pride to a few gains in both areas. Eight
years ago you had only one minority staff person and now there
are twelve. Your paper has run a series periodically on Hispanics
and other nonwhites that was rated sensitive and intelligent by
most readers. You do not tolerate blatantly segregationist practices, and most stereotyping has been edited out of the paper's
articles. You conclude that nothing can be done to alleviate the
problem right now—but in your mind's eye you see Pulitzer Prize-
winning Hispanics on your staff in the future, and enough afflu-
ence among this market to finally make a Spanish-language edition feasible somewhere down the road.

The publisher struggled with the demographic dilemmas within a very
explicit financial framework. A year earlier he had invested $1.5 mil-
lion to add an edition for readers in the southwest suburbs. With $96
million in net profits the previous year, the paper did have the capital
for continued expansion. A news bureau was then opened on the north
side and a special edition was proposed for white readers who were
flocking to the new housing sites in that area. The specific question
for him was whether a Spanish-language edition should also be initiated for the 700,000 Hispanics that now comprised 25 percent of the
city's population. The editor concluded that such a paper would not
make sense financially at this time because the Mexican-American
audience currently did not have enough purchasing power to attract
the massive advertising on which the paper depends.
    He realized also the magnitude of the editorial task. While most
Hispanics in his city were West Coast Chicanos, he recognized that
the Spanish-speaking population is a complex group composed of different nationalities. Even though Hispanics are expected to become
the country's largest minority early in the next century, their diversity—Cuban, Puerto Rican, Mexican, for example—makes them an
almost impossible audience to reach successfully. He wanted to watch
other Spanish-language newspapers, magazines, and radio and televi-

sion stations for a time to understand better how to manage this problem.

The publisher satisfied himself that his decision was not racist. "We are talking only about a certain demographic profile," he argued. "Race does not matter. The audience can be red, yellow, or brown. It just happens that our major advertisers have requested a certain type of person who happens to be affluent, white, and suburban."

The publisher thus based his rationale solely on economic criteria. Certainly he has a demographic dilemma, with the demands of the stockholders pushing in one direction and the city's population in another. But he lays out his agenda in profit-and-loss terms only. There is no evidence from his argumentation or conclusion that he thinks about the moral dimension of catering to ethnic changes in his city. As the chief officer for this firm, he could have used this occasion to show moral leadership, but he asks only about the paper's solvency. Heads of institutions are regularly tempted to use the structure to limit the range within which they consider issues. In this case, the profit-based character of his newspaper sets the parameters of the publisher's thinking. He missed a chance to shape company policy in a morally enlightened manner. He decided against a proactive position which would enable the resources of his paper to serve the Hispanic population even before doing so was financially rewarding. He wanted to see Hispanics taken seriously in government policy and education but believed it was premature for his private enterprise to become a crusading partner.

6. ANTIGAMBLING CORPORATE GIFT

Voters in Florida were being asked to legalize casino gambling in Miami Beach and other nearby resort communities. Hotel owners were contributing heavily to a campaign to sell the idea to the voters. Alvah E. Chapman, president of the *Miami Herald*, was concerned. He believed the introduction of gambling would damage the area's economy, change its image, and threaten a lifestyle worth preserving. Chapman was also worried about the effect casino gambling would have on his newspaper. "I was concerned," he said, "that the Las Vegas South image in Miami would make it difficult to attract and hold the bright, competent newspaper professionals who are so vital to the future and present success of the Miami Herald Publishing Company."[20] Chapman sensed that his paper's prospects were directly linked to Miami Beach's future as a commercial and cultural center.

Chapman decided to fight the proposal with money. The *Miami Herald* contributed $16,000 to anti-casino groups. Three other Knight-Ridder dailies in Florida contributed $9,000. Chapman and his family, as well as James L. Knight, the *Herald*'s board chairman, made personal contributions of more than $10,000. Chapman led a fund drive among other media owners. In all, $180,000 was raised from media sources to be used by "No Casinos, Inc.," a citizens' committee sponsored by the governor.

Before the November referendum, Chapman's action became the subject of a complaint before the National News Council. The charge: Financial backing by the media would taint its news coverage. Ironically, the complaint was filed by Jim Bishop, whose syndicated column appeared in the *Herald* and who headed the organization working for the passage of the casino proposal. Chapman told the News Council that he made his contributions with the confidence that the independence of the paper's editorial and news operations was so deeply established and widely understood that there was little danger of public misunderstanding.

According to the News Council staff, reporters and editors assigned to the story believed they had been put in an "uncomfortable position" by the *Herald*'s contribution to the governor's campaign. According to the investigative staff, the reporters decided to "strive even harder than they normally did to be fair," and, again according to the council's staff, "they succeeded admirably."[21] Because of the corporate donation, the top news executives kept themselves totally remote from the coverage, a stance that would have been unthinkable in the case of any other major story.

The News Council concluded that on the question of whether such a financial contribution affected the news coverage, the *Herald* "accquitted itself with distinction." But the council left open for further debate what it called the "more fundamental question of the appropriateness of such financial involvement by a newspaper on one side of an emotional and controversial issue before the voters."[22] The council was concerned that such corporate activity would undermine a newspaper's credibility—a disservice to the public faced with a referendum. Indeed, a statewide poll conducted by the *Herald* underscored the council's concern. It showed that both those favoring casinos and those opposed to them believed, by a substantial margin, that newspapers contributing financially to the referendum could not be fair in their news columns.

This case is primarily a problem in business ethics. Presidents of media corporations are ordinarily not journalists even though their corporations have journalism as their business. If Chapman were the president of a company that manufactured fishing nets, a decision by its president to make contributions to a campaign against gambling would hardly have received attention as a serious moral dilemma.

Chapman made a number of judgments about fact, some judgments about competing values (regarding lifestyle and the quality of his paper), and a number of decisions concerning what kinds of action would, under these circumstances, be morally justifiable.

He judged in the first instance that the impact of legalized casino gambling would change the area's economy, image, and lifestyle. He was convinced also that it would change the conditions under which his corporation and his newspaper conducted their business. When he evaluated those changes which seemed inevitable, he made some key value judgments and concluded that the legalization of casino gambling would threaten certain values that he held for the community and for the corporation. He then made a decision to take action, opposing the legalization of gambling in order to preserve a certain community lifestyle and to protect what he perceived as his corporation's self-interest. He further decided to use not merely his personal resources but also the resources of the corporation in an attempt to influence public thinking and policy.

Chapman's next choice was one of strategy—*how* to influence the vote. It is not clear what alternative strategies he considered. He might have used the editorial page of the *Miami Herald*; he might have sought to control the content of news columns. He could have sought to conduct his corporation's own campaign. In fact he chose to join forces with an existing organization, No Casinos, Inc. Perhaps there were alternative strategies toward morally acceptable ends. It would be useful in examining this case to brainstorm which possible strategies might arguably be better.

Chapman, as president of the Miami Herald Publishing Co., actually faces a serious set of competing obligations. In the first place he has a contractual obligation to investors to protect and advance both their short- and long-term financial interests. Second, he has an obligation to readers to disseminate unbiased news and editorials. If he makes a contribution to an agency designed to influence public policy, he risks polluting the news, and if he does not contribute, he risks—at least in the long run—loss to the corporation. If he made an anonymous donation, he could contribute financially without influencing the paper's content since the editorial staff would not be aware of his position. But since he did not choose anonymity, he risks biasing the news and editorial columns.

But what did Chapman's decision to contribute to No Casinos, Inc. actually do to the *Herald*'s coverage? Reporters and editors at the *Herald* believed they were put in an "uncomfortable position" by the contribution. They decided to "strive even harder than they normally did to be fair." Thus the News Council concluded that the contribution was a decision to risk effects that proved to be innocent in this case.

The bottom line is whether this media corporation should have made financial contributions to support one side in a matter of public policy. It seems obvious that siding with a partisan group does influence news coverage. Even if management does not directly interfere with reporters, the subtle pressures toward uniformity will be even greater than usual. While that effect in the *Herald*'s case may not have been detrimental, in general the risk of biased coverage is very high. A well-informed public is too important a matter to allow corporate interests this kind of power. The National News Council left that question open for further debate—a fact, incidentally, which seems irresponsible on the council's part.

NOTES

1. Fred S. Siebert, Theodore Peterson, and Wilbur Schramm, *Four Theories of the Press* (Urbana: University of Illinois Press, 1956), p. 72.
2. The question is whether one's dual obligation in this instance prevents the fulfilling of both contracts. See Joseph Margolis, "Conflict of Interest and Conflicting Interests," in *Ethical Theory and Business*, ed. Tom L. Beauchamp and Norman E. Bowie (Englewood Cliffs, N.J.: Prentice-Hall, 1979), pp. 361–372.
3. Upton Sinclair, *The Brass Check: A Study of American Journalism* (Pasadena, Calif.: published by author, 1920), p. 436.
4. For a useful overview of concentration in various media, see Benjamin M. Compaine, ed., *Who Owns the Media?*, 2d ed. (White Plains, N.Y.: Knowledge Industry Publications, 1982).
5. For the quotations and background negotiations summarized in this case,

see Bill Saporito, "The Inside Story of Time Warner," *Fortune*, 20 November 1989, pp. 164–185.

6. Ben H. Bagdikian, *The Media Monopoly*, 2nd ed. (Boston: Beacon Press, 1987), p. x.
7. Charles Thiesen and Barbara Beckwith, "Marketplace of Creative Ideas May Now Go to Highest Bidder," *Los Angeles Times*, 20 November 1989, p. B7.
8. For a description of this problem and the international audience issue which follows, cf. "Business: The Counterattack," *Newsweek*, 26 June 1989, pp. 48–54.
9. Cassandra Tate, "Conflict of Interest: A Newspaper's Report on Itself," *Columbia Journalism Review* 16 (July/August 1978): 44–48.
10. Ibid.
11. Karen Schneider and Marc Gunther, "Those Newsroom Ethics Codes," *Columbia Journalism Review* 23 (July/August 1985): 55.
12. Commission on Freedom of the Press, *A Free and Responsible Press* (Chicago: University of Chicago Press, 1947), pp. 59–60.
13. For elaboration of the issues see Clifford Christians and Leon Hammond, "Social Justice and a Community Information Utility," *Communication* 9 (June 1986): 127–149.
14. Quotations and details are from Charles Storch, "Disney Does Its Magic for the Media," *Chicago Tribune*, 8 October 1986, sect. 3, pp. 1, 7.
15. Additional examples and commentary on the importance of avoiding even the appearance of impropriety are in John L. Hulteng, *Playing It Straight* (Chester, Conn.: Globe Pequot Press, 1981), pp. 25–33. See also Charles W. Bailey, "Conflicts of Interest: A Matter of Journalistic Ethics," Report to the National News Council, at the Minnesota Journalism Center, Minneapolis, 1984.
16. Jeremy Weir Alderson, "Confessions of a Travel Writer," *Columbia Journalism Review* 26 (July/August 1988): 27–28.
17. See Felix Gutierrez and Clint C. Wilson II, "The Demographic Dilemma," *Columbia Journalism Review* 17 (January/February 1979): 53–55. For background see Clint C. Wilson II and Felix Gutierrez, *Minorities and Media* (Beverly Hills, Calif.: Sage, 1985).
18. "Only English Spoken Here," *Time*, 5 December 1988, p. 29.
19. Leslie Whitaker, "Dancing to the Latino Beat," *Time*, 23 October 1989, p. 114.
20. National News Council Report, "Should the Media Use Dollars to Sway Public Issues?" *Columbia Journalism Review* 17 (March/April 1979): 73.
21. Ibid., p. 74.
22. Ibid.

CHAPTER 2

Truthtelling

The press's obligation to truth is a standard part of the rhetoric. Virtually every ethics code begins with the newsperson's duty to tell the truth under all conditions. High-minded editors typically etch the word on cornerstones and their tombstones. Credible words are pivotal to the communication enterprise.

When Pontius Pilate asked "What is truth?" he posed the question people of every kind have struggled to define. And as ideas and world views shift, so does the definition of truthfulness. Newspeople must live within the larger ambiguities about truth in Western scholarship and culture today. Their situation is further complicated by budget constraints, deadlines, reader expectations, editorial conventions, and self-serving sources. Journalism is often referred to as history in a hurry, and providing a precise, representative account can rarely occur under such conditions. All the while, sophisticated technology generates unceasing news copy and the journalistic gatekeeper must choose from a mountain of options, often without the time to sift out the moral intricacies.

The cases that follow introduce several dimensions of the truthtelling issue. While not every conceivable aspect is offered, truth is enlarged beyond a simple facts-only definition.[1] One way to broaden our scope, for example, is to consider the antonym of truthfulness and to account for newsgathering as well as newswriting. The opposite of truthtelling is deception, that is, a deliberate intention to mislead. Outright deceit occurs infrequently in the newswriting phase; only rarely, if ever, does a reporter or editor specifically and consciously give the wrong story. But deception in newsgathering is a persistent temptation, because it often facilitates the process of securing information.

The first case in this section, "Prize-Winning Photo Electronically Altered," struggles with the ethical issues raised by the dramatic advances in media technology. While traditionally a sharp line has been drawn between truth and fiction, between news and entertainment, this boundary is impossible to maintain in an age of electronic images that can be manipulated mechanically.

The second case, "Abortion Profiteers," illustrates the high stakes sometimes involved in investigative reporting. While several ethical questions are woven through the case, deception is central in the analysis. Gathering news under false pretenses for a noble end is a typical issue occurring in small towns as well as in major cities. When newspapers or stations receive phone calls about violence in an orphanage, maggots in the bandages of patients at a nursing home, cheating on repairs, deception becomes one possible alternative for breaking the story.

The third case, "Sexism and Mayor Burns," represents one of journalism's most persistent agonies. Social groups suffering from discrimination are particularly sensitive to stereotyping. In this situation, even determined efforts from the media to avoid prejudicial language is not considered sufficient. Many instances of blatant sexism could have been chosen, but they present no moral dilemma; sexist language dehumanizes and is therefore wrong and unprofessional. The accounts contrasted in this case suggest the subtler forms of sexism that exist even among those of good purpose. The Christine Kraft dispute with KMBC-TV in Kansas City indicates that sexism or alleged sex discrimination is a point of contention in employment also, not just in message content.

The fourth case, "Tony Holds a Sawed-Off Shotgun," demonstrates the increasing use of media spectacle by hijackers, the mentally deranged, and the aggrieved. This case questions our conventional definitions of newsworthiness. Here a person's life is at stake and the moral problem is how to protect that life most effectively in the short term without encouraging more violence by others in the long term. Terrorism on a worldwide scale adds the further complexities of international law and politics. The Tony Kiritsis episode serves to establish the ethical parameters that ought to shape both domestic and international decision making in a convoluted and dangerous arena.

The fifth case introduces a discussion of Henrik Ibsen's *An Enemy of the People*. Ibsen, the great Norwegian playwright of the nineteenth century, wrote it out of concern for the future of democracy. In Arthur Miller's adaptation to a modern setting,[2] this vivid and troubling drama demonstrates how institutions respond to the painful truth of contaminated springs on which the city's livelihood depends. With skyrocketing public concern over environmental, health, and safety issues, *An Enemy of the People* is a powerful context in which to examine the press's role.

7. Prize-Winning Photo Electronically Altered

Ron Olshwanger was only an amateur photographer, but he took a powerful picture of a St. Louis firefighter trying to breathe life into 2-year-old Patricia Pettus. It was published on the front page of the *St. Louis Post-Dispatch* on 31 December 1988.[3]

When Olshwanger heard late in March that this photograph had received a Pulitzer Prize, he went with his wife Sally to the managing editor's office to celebrate. "I don't even drink. I hope they have a Diet Coke down there," he told a *Post-Dispatch* reporter before he arrived. The managing editor sent out for Diet Cokes on ice along with the champagne, and when the assistant director of photography shot a picture for the next day's story, the Coke can was on the desk beside the Olshwangers.

But Robert C. Holt III, director of photo technology, airbrushed the can away with the aid of the paper's new Scitex system. The managing editor insisted that there had merely been a miscommunication: he had told his staff that the picture would look better without the can and assumed it would be cropped accordingly. Holt remembers somebody suggesting, "Let's Scitex out the Coke can," but in retrospect, he thought that probably meant "Let's crop it out." "For some reason," Holt said, "I airbrushed it out. It was stupid. It was my fault."

The incident was hotly debated internally because Holt himself had a reputation for promoting Scitex but steadfastly opposing image altering. Three years earlier he had warned the American Newspaper Publishers Association not to misuse electronic imaging systems. He was especially chagrined that the Pulitzer Prize-winning photo was the first front-page picture in the *Post Dispatch* produced by Scitex. Even in retrospect, Holt is still not sure why he Scitexed away the can. "It was a more-than-usually hectic day and it was not until [I] went home that [I] realized what

Photo of Olshwanger and his wife at the office reception (top). In the photo that ran on the front page of the Post-Dispatch, *the Diet Coke Can had been removed electronically (below). Source: From the St Louis Post Dispatch* (March 31, 1989). Photograph by Ron Olshwanger. Reprinted by permission.

[I] had done." To photographers who became upset that the "mistake was made by the very same people who said it would not happen," Holt insists they should "do what I say, not as I do."

The *Post-Dispatch* staff have taken the incident seriously. They have discussed it openly with the public in terms of the technical advances that make abuses nearly impossible to detect. In fact, the staff was in the final stages of developing a company policy on electronic manipulation when the Olshwanger incident occurred.

In George Orwell's *1984* "there were the huge printing shops with their sub-editors, their typography experts, and their elaborately equipped studios for the faking of photographs."[4] Abuses have been common since 1857, when Oscar Gustave Rejlander combined thirty negatives to produce a single image in the "The Two Ways of Life."[5] On the whole, however, Orwell's wolf has been kept from the door. Since the earliest photographic history, the press has denounced manipulated images, and the media continue to draw a hard line in principle between untouched photography for news and documentary, and photo images used in features and advertising. Thus when *National Geographic* squeezes pyramids together to fit its cover's vertical format, the retouching does not stir the frenzy that accompanied a staged photo at the *St. Petersburg* (Florida) *Times* and *Evening Independent*. It was "a nothing event" in which a veteran photographer etched "Yea, Eckerd" on the bare feet of a teenage baseball fan. The photographer's seventeen years with the company was terminated abruptly, on the grounds, said the executive editor, "that there is simply no room for people who don't tell the truth."[6]

The news press operates on the assumption that a picture taken by a photojournalist ought to meet the same standards as does a reporter's stories. Just as reporters ought always to guard against misrepresentation, so photojournalists must not fabricate events. The moral obligation is to avoid deceiving the public with stories or pictures; both should carry the inherent meaning and present an accurate account. To assume otherwise makes photographers second-class members of the newsroom who need not operate with the same professional standards as writers; they are subtly demeaned as merely providing art or diversion for the printed copy.

Along the lines of this historic distinction between news and entertainment, the *Post Dispatch* news policy states: "To assure the integrity of our visual reportage, the Scitex system may not be used to distort or change the image in a way that misleads the reader." Scitex can remove dust particles and strike the correct color balance, but moving, eliminating, or adding elements is prohibited. If a picture is altered for a necessary reason, readers must be informed.

Sheila Reaves correctly argues that this traditional guideline protecting the distinctiveness of news can serve only as a temporary measure while ethicists scramble to develop a more adequate framework in light of the revolutionary technological changes introduced by digital processing. New computer technology based on pixels (a computer term derived from "picture elements") contradicts the 135-year-old view that photography is a slice of reality. "Because pixels are computer data," says Reaves, "they can be moved, cloned, and colored. This new technology turns all photographs into pixel-based images with a new precedent. Anyone with access to the computer has unlimited access to altering the original image."[7] As Hal Buell of the Associated Press explains, "There is not an original picture when you shoot an electronic photo. The changed picture becomes the original."[8] A photograph historically is a record of something that reflects light. As long as Scitex systems cost $2 million and therefore only the major firms invest in them, news photography may be protected in terms of the credibility with which it is seen to record that reflected image. But when pixel-based equipment becomes as common as personal computers, "Who will set the standards of digitized photography?" The old saw "technology changes, ethics don't" is a handy commonplace, but it is rapidly losing its applicability.

8. ABORTION PROFITEERS

In May 1978 the *Chicago Sun-Times* received information from a highly reliable source that women were undergoing unnecessary abortion procedures in four Michigan Avenue clinics. The source, a government official who insisted upon remaining anonymous, claimed that each year hundreds of women were being misinformed by clinic personnel that they were pregnant. Apparently over 60,000 abortions were performed at these for-profit clinics yearly.

Working with the Better Government Association (BGA), a citizens' watch-dog group, the *Sun-Times* began its investigation by sending female investigators into private agencies that referred women to the clinics. The investigators, pretending to seek pregnancy counseling, brought male urine specimens into the referral agencies for testing. On several occasions the pregnancy tests on the male urine were found to be positive, and the female investigators were referred for abortions to the Michigan Avenue clinics.

In order to pursue the story further, investigators attempted to obtain jobs at both the referral agencies and the clinics. Their employment resumés did not distort their background or qualifications for the jobs, but they did omit any journalistic connection. The first investigator to be hired worked as a receptionist at a swank clinic on Chicago's Magnificent Mile. As part of her job training, she quickly learned that women with negative pregnancy tests were told that the findings were positive or were simply not informed of the results. In the first few weeks of undercover work, she observed that more than 10 percent of the clinic's patients were given "abortions" even though their urine tests indicated that they were not pregnant.

The newspaper was able ultimately to obtain salaried jobs in all four clinics and two referral agencies. Several of the investigators worked as counselors or nurses' aides. None became involved in the operating room procedures, but they did have direct contact with patients both before and after the supposed abortions were performed. (At no time were the clinic operators or patients aware of the fact that these "health professionals" were really investigative journalists.) Over a period of four months, they also observed abortions being performed on women in advanced stages of pregnancy, anesthetics being improperly administered, clinic personnel practicing medicine without a license, evidence of Medicaid fraud, and other improper practices. Several deaths and frequent complications were documented.

In order to provide back-up support for their eyewitness observations, the undercover investigators photocopied more than 100 medical records from the clinics. The records were brought to the *Sun-Times*, where the names of the women were deleted. The act of photocopying the records without consent, however, was a violation of Illinois law.

The Abortion Profiteers series was published in November 1978. Subsequently, the state passed new laws to regulate outpatient abortion clinics. Two of the Michigan Avenue clinics were closed, one permanently, and several of the doctors involved left the state. One physician was ultimately sent to prison. One of the clinics sued the *Sun-Times* and the BGA; the suit was later dismissed.

The sensational charges in the Abortion Profiteers series were based largely on direct observations of undercover reporters. Throughout the investigation, the *Sun-Times* and the BGA used a variety of deceptive newsgathering techniques to verify the information supplied by the anonymous source. When, if ever, are journalists justified in lying to get a story? Does the abortion series provide a case of ethically acceptable deception? These are exquisitely complicated questions that have no easy answers in everyday practice.

One way to assess the use of deception is to examine the purpose that it serves. On Mill's utilitarian grounds, journalists could claim that the misrepresentation served a "greater good." After all, the newspaper series informed the general public about a dangerous and illegal scandal. While the newsgathering process may have prolonged some women's exposure to unscrupulous medical practitioners, ultimately the series enabled greater numbers of women to make more informed decisions about whether and where to seek an abortion. This was further ensured by the governmental crackdown that occurred in the wake of the series. Given these benefits, the costs of deception may be viewed as justifiable, at least in retrospect.

On the other hand, the newspaper's methods run counter to several philosophical traditions. To Kant, all deception is morally wrong. In this case, the newspaper became involved in a web of deception that prevaded its entire newsgathering process. It is certainly reasonable to question whether the ultimate truth of the findings is believable in light of the many falsehoods that were told in order to obtain it.

Moreover, Kant's categorical imperative and the Judeo-Christian ethic, which states that people should always be treated as ends and not means, would cast doubt on the use of deception in this particular case. For months, investigators observed nonpregnant women having "abortions." To protect their cover, the investigators rarely intervened to prevent these abuses; worse, they were at times at least indirect agents of the wrongdoing.

The decision to continue gathering information for the story was often agonizing, and always made on utilitarian grounds—the newspaper's justifiable need to back up its sensational allegations with solid information. Nonetheless, these justifications may be considered morally shaky in view of the known harm that was being inflicted on women during the months that the investigation was being conducted. Certainly, the sacrifice of scores of women to get a newspaper story would be rejected by the moral tradition of providing help to those in immediate need.

The categorical imperative is also useful for considering the appropriateness of the decision to photocopy illegally the abortion records. Kant's doctrine would not, of course, tolerate lawbreaking. Others would argue that lawbreaking is situationally tolerable, such as when it is necessary to speed to a hospital in order to save a life. But a special problem arises in the Abortion Profiteers case. Can journalists, who oppose government searches of newsrooms, justify their own decision to remove records from similarly private, professional institutions? Both law-enforcement agents and journalists would claim that their actions were motivated by a utilitarian concern for achieving a greater societal good. On the other hand, Kant's maxim that "what is right for one is right for all" should cause journalists who approve of media but not governmental intrusiveness to examine the consistency of their position.

What standards can the media use for making difficult choices in similar situations? In her book *Lying*, Sissela Bok proposes that honest alternatives be thoroughly considered and debated before any form of deception or impropriety is practiced.[9] In the Abortion Profiteers case, the newspaper began its undercover probe after its source was unwilling to go on record or provide sufficient documentation for his allegations. It may be reasonably argued that there was no way other than through undercover methods to obtain a story of this nature; clinic personnel would obviously deny any wrongdoing and patients were unaware of it.

Thus the journalists in this situation were left to choose between informing law-enforcement authorities of the allegations or engaging in deception to further document them. The selection of the former alternative would run counter to a journalist's professional values and loyalties and may not even have produced corrective action. However, the selection of the latter threatened to create a fabric of deception that was ethically unjustifiable.

Once undercover techniques were chosen as the least offensive alternative, what could have been done to minimize the ethical costs? If the newspaper had retained medical personnel (for example, nurses) to apply for jobs at the clinics, it would have limited the journalistic misrepresentation while increasing the newspaper's participation in the very wrongdoing it was trying to expose. Having journalists pose as patients in the clinics would have reduced the potential for inflicting harm on others while exposing the journalists to the possibility of harm.

Ultimately, the newspaper decided to accept the problems and the risks involved in working in the clinics. Some of the moral difficulty was relieved by the decision not to change the identities of the undercover investigators. Misrepresentation by "commission"—the creation of fictional names and backgrounds—was viewed as unnecessary and even dangerous in this case. The use of Aristotle's golden mean—misrepresentation by "omission" only—was the more ethically tolerable alternative. Although journalists were still going beyond their traditional professional role of openly and neutrally recording events, this use of passive deception enabled them to get the story while at least minimizing the potentially harmful consequences.

The Abortion Profiteers series had a dramatic impact on readers and policymakers. However, the newspaper failed to win a Pulitzer Prize, in part because of its use of deception, a problem similar to that raised by the Pulitzer judges in rejecting the *Sun-Times*'s "Mirage" tavern series that same year.[10] Nonetheless, undercover reporting remains a widely employed and accepted journalistic practice. As Bok directs us, when used as a last resort under restricted conditions to get an important story in a crisis situation, it can be a justifiable tool to inform the public about events it otherwise would not be aware of. When used with impunity, undercover reporting fuels the public's concerns about the power and morality of today's news media.

9. SEXISM AND MAYOR BURNS

Jean Burns's administration began with great promise. While on the city council for two terms she had gained a high profile. All signs of corruption in local government were mercilessly exposed. Burns had warred with the mayor, garbage collectors, taxi drivers, and funeral directors. Her productivity and her spirit earned the voters' respect and she won election to the mayor's office by a landslide.[11]

Before long, however, the acerbic mayor had the tough local press aiming at the jugular. In this extremely competitive two-newspaper city, reporters tended to be as scrappy as the mayor. The climax in a deteriorating relationship came six months after the mayor's inaugural, when the *Morning Tribune* gave front-page play to a report that Burns had shelved a study she had commissioned on the efficiency of local government and which had criticized waste and fraud in City Hall. The *Morning Tribune* saw self-serving politics suppressing the city's progress, and it blew the horn. The report in Sunday's paper included charts and detailed background studies from the shelved report—measurements of worker efficiency, size of departments compared with those in similar municipalities, number of secretaries and administrators per agency, pay scales, and so forth. It also included interviews with the university professor who headed the investigation: "The absence of action that has bothered me most," said the panel chief,

is our lady's failure to appoint the best and brightest administrators that this city deserves. Our report documents the severe weaknesses and incompetencies of [former mayor] Billing's appointees. With notable exceptions, Mrs. Burns has merely dismissed our recommendations and followed in the old ruts.

Her Honor took the newspaper's coverage personally. Her press office quickly issued a release accusing the paper of "innuendoes, lies, smears, character assassination, and male chauvinist tactics since Jean Burns became mayor." In fact, as the *Morning Tribune* hit the streets, Burns called the city desk to announce she would throw its reporter out of City Hall's press room on Monday morning. On Sunday James MacMillan, Burns's husband and press officer, called Rupert Davis, the reporter in question, telling him to remove his personal belongings from City Hall immediately. The *Morning Tribune* was paper non grata in the halls of power, and Burns indicated that city employees would be instructed not to speak to its reporters.

The reaction was fast and furious from both sides. The *Morning Tribune*'s managing editor, William Jones, said: "There is no vendetta and the mayor knows it. We will continue to publish the news without first seeking approval from the city administration." On the editorial page the *Morning Tribune* lamented:

If the city's image is being hurt, it is the mayor herself

who is hurting it, by her past record of impulsive and often inconsistent behavior, by her inability to obtain and keep qualified administrators, and now by a vindictive step that is bound to make her administration the laughing stock of the country. People have been good-naturedly jesting about her hats; now they will begin to scorn her politics. We hope that the mayor will reconsider her stand, because an attack on freedom of the press goes far beyond the cast of characters involved; it is a nationwide threat, especially to publications smaller than the *Morning Tribune* and less able to resist the arrogance of power.

In the news hole the paper reported Burns's reactions to reporters' questions about the incident. She "picked up her purse and hurried into an elevator, refusing to comment," the paper said.

On Monday the mayor backed down. Rupert Davis was at his desk, a momentary celebrity. Nevertheless Monday's *Morning Tribune* carried an editorial criticizing the "continued round of thoughtless and unproductive public outbursts by the chief executive. . . . Mayor Burns's antics would be more frightening if they were not so absurd."

Milton Rooster, a syndicated columnist for the competing newspaper, the *Daily Times*, was a minority voice on the mayor's side, sort of. Why all the fuss, he asked?

> The *Morning Tribune* can go on implying, without proof, that Burns is a tool of the crime syndicate, that she may be mentally unbalanced, and that she might destroy our city. It can go on dreaming up nonexistent scandals and fishing around for something—almost anything—that will make her look bad. And it can go on pompously pretending that all it is doing is covering the news fairly and impartially. That's really the fascinating thing about this silly flap—the thinness of the news media's skin.

Columnist Rooster was not alone on the mayor's side. The summer issue of *Feminique* featured a story on the mayor revolving around the *Morning Tribune* conflict. Claiming "repeated and continuing incidents of sexist treatment," the *Feminique* writer declared that the *Morning Tribune* had not attempted to understand the mayor. Contrary to her press image, *Feminique* de-

clared, Burns has attributes of "forthrightness and honesty in saying what she thinks, regardless of the consequences. She has been
known to take positions that no man would espouse, but she
sticks with them because she has drawn a line in her mind on
what is morally right and won't cross it." Her enemies are "ethnic
groups who feel slighted," and "her troubles stem from her liberal
views in a conservative city." For the future, "there's no telling
what goal the mayor can achieve. It is tempting to say that she
could be the first woman vice-president, but the latent sexism in
that prediction is too apparent. And Jean Burns probably would
impose no such limitation upon herself."

The *Feminique* article attempted to balance the record. The
author focused on "a job well done" and dismissed criticism by
a patronizing press. But that slant failed to convince all *Feminique*
readers. A subsequent letter to the editor condemned the "gee-
whiz, this woman did it first mentality" and pointed to some
subtleties:

> I can't agree with *Feminique* in applauding Mayor Burns
> for a job well done. We can't make examples of women
> in jobs . . . simply because they are women and we may
> need that morale boost. I think it's commendable that
> Mayor Burns believes and fights for [women's rights]—
> but it is not commendable that she lets every criticism
> of her behavior in office be labeled as sexism. You have
> totally ignored the person who is mayor. She had no busi-
> ness in City Hall and we have no business commending
> her for being a woman in a tough spot because she puts
> herself there time and time again. We don't want to en-
> courage women to continue in jobs just because they have
> them.

Several dimensions of this case warrant consideration: Did Mayor
Burns actually pose a "nationwide threat" to press freedom, as the
Morning Tribune claimed, when she told Rupert Davis he was no
longer welcome at City Hall? Did the *Morning Tribune*, as Milton
Rooster charged, suggest without proof that Mayor Burns "was a tool
of the crime syndicate"? Did the mayor's rejection of the efficiency
study indicate an ongoing wastefulness in her administration? Does it

represent a conflict of interest that James MacMillan, Burns's husband and press secretary, was at the time on leave from the *Morning Tribune*'s competitor, the *Daily Times*?

The specific moral issue, however, concerns unfair treatment of Mayor Burns as a human being. Is the *Morning Tribune* guilty of sexist bias as she charges? In contrast, has the *Feminique* article or the followup letter given the public a true account? What kind of portrait best emulates the ethical principle regarding respect of persons?

Women have been stereotyped regularly in the press. The problem has long historical roots. During the women's suffrage movement, for example, news accounts often distorted the issues; editorials regularly denounced women's "petty whims," spoke of "appalling consequences," and even used labels such as "insurrection." Sample twentieth-century writing of almost any kind (including journalism) and the failures become obvious: overemphasis on clothes and physical appearance, the glorification of domesticity, portrayal of women as empty headed or at least nonintellectual.

Even in recent years, Edward M. Miller used blatant sexism to defend the rules for women issued by the Associated Press Managing Editors Association (APME). Women, in his view, do well on people stories but cannot unravel complicated financial ones. Miller considers them excellent copy editors because of their disposition and because "repetitious work does not seem to bother them."[12] As this adaptation of Alma Graham indicates about our use of language in general:

> At every level of achievement and activity—from primitive man to the man of the hour—woman is not taken into account. Consider the congressman, fulfilling his position faithfully as intended by the founding fathers. He is a man of the people. To prove that he's the best man for the job, he takes his case to the man in the street. He is a champion of the workingman and the middleman. He speaks for the little man. He has not overlooked the forgotten man or the chairman. And he firmly believes: one man, one vote. He considers the policeman and fireman, the postman and milkman, the clergyman and businessman.[13]

Because the media generally reflect cultural mores and because male–female inequality does exist, a thorough content analysis of all the *Morning Tribune* copy regarding Mayor Burns is warranted. She quickly dismisses her male critics as chauvinists who refuse to admit that women can be successful politicians. Negative press coverage she likewise rejects as sex bias. Such claims are too sweeping to be believable, yet so many failures have occurred on so many levels that the *Morning Tribune* must ensure that all antifeminist bias has been purged from its stories. The staff should be forced to review every line of the story and editorial with the *Associated Press Stylebook* in hand (note such entries as "courtesy titles," "persons," "man, mankind," and "women"). Even in the few quotations selected for the case study above, several sexist words and phrases do appear. Or if the city editor wants even greater consciousness raising, Casey Miller and Kate Swift's *The Handbook of Nonsexist Writing* can be made required reading by the staff.[14]

It is pertinent to ask whether the *Morning Tribune* has provided any institutional safeguards for covering City Hall in the future. Under maximum conditions, one's behavior should be justifiable even to the accused. Would the mayor ever be able to admit, "they disagreed with my policies, but they did treat me fairly and represented my viewpoint accurately"? Given the emotional overtones surrounding sexism, such an expectation may be too strong. Additional measures by the *Morning Tribune*, however, could indicate its unalterable commitment to respecting all persons. Should women reporters not be assigned to City Hall, for example? Why should women editors not be appointed to scrutinize all mayoral coverage? Susan B. Anthony spoke prophetically in 1900: "As long as newspapers and magazines are controlled by men ... women's ideas and deepest convictions will never get before the public."[15] Admittedly dictionaries cannot be rewritten overnight and these corrections must be etched out of inherited usage. However, to prove their sincerity, editors at the *Morning Tribune* and other newspapers could adopt specific guidelines for the treatment of women, such as the list of 10 complied by Pat Corbine, editor of *Ms.*[16]

10. TONY HOLDS A SAWED-OFF SHOTGUN

Richard O. Hall, a 42-year-old mortgage company executive in Indianapolis, spent 63 hours with a sawed-off shotgun attached to his neck. Part of that time was on camera, Hall standing numbly in the glare of the television lights while his captor, Anthony G. (Tony) Kiritsis, told viewers how Hall's mortgage company had cheated him in a land transaction.

In some ways, the media helped keep Hall alive and may have

caught unnecessary criticism for so doing. But on two occasions
the media endangered Hall's life by following the principle that
the public ought to be informed. The media were Kiritsis's conduit for making public his grievances against the mortgage company. During the ordeal, the mortgage company aired a public
apology to Kiritsis and one radio news director allowed Kiritsis
air time to tell his side of the story. The news director, Fred Heckman, gradually assumed the role of a mediator. Heckman later
said his conversations with Kiritsis and the fact that he permitted
Kiritsis the microphone "set up a trust that eventually was cred-
ited as a major part in saving not only Dick Hall's life, but that
of Kiritsis." But, as critics pointed out, Heckman, in giving Kiritsis a platform, contributed to his becoming a folk hero. Many
viewers saw him as a good but frustrated man who had been
swindled by a loan company when in fact the courts were later
to judge him insane.

Heckman concedes the point. He explained his position at a
workshop of the Radio-Television News Directors Association:

> I didn't like it. There was a twenty-year development of
> credibility and integrity in the Indianapolis market that
> I had on the line and quite obviously some of it was lost.
> Yes, it did make Kiritsis a folk hero. . . . To a great extent
> I was probably the one responsible for that and I didn't
> like it, but felt that there was no other way, no other
> course to take.[17]

One of Heckman's most outspoken critics was Steven Yount,
director of news and public affairs for WIRE-AM/WXTZ-FM, Indianapolis. He charged that in general the Indianapolis media surrendered their independence "by basing news reports on a police
request that we not report anything that would upset the kidnapper. We became part of a police effort to fool a kidnapper instead of being an independent bystander there to inform the public." Yount insisted it was the news media's responsibility "to
gather and report facts," even if such reporting endangered the
life of a hostage or angered the police.[18]

One news organization did report the truth, and that report
could have heightened the danger to Hall's life. The truth concerned an offer of immunity made by the county prosecutor's
office, an offer intended as a last-resort, ace-in-the-hole strategy
reserved for an emergency. The emergency arose because of the

way Douglas O'Brien, a newsperson from Heckman's station, was describing the episode. At the scene he reported:

> The Army bomb squad that's here has begun to try and think of ways to somehow get in without setting off the explosives. We're told (here some words were indistinct) that they may be able to. . . . If Kiritsis could be incapacitated somehow, they could get in and defuse the explosives that are in the room, if they are in fact there, and they do believe they are.
>
> Announcer: Okay, but it hasn't really come to that and we'll anxiously await the next report from the scene.[19]

Kiritsis, who had his radio tuned to the station, interpreted the report to mean that the bomb squad was rushing the apartment. Ordering a brother and a friend to leave a nearby apartment, he angrily threatened to blow up Hall and himself. Officials decided the time had come to offer Kiritsis immunity. George Martz, a Marion County deputy prosecutor, broadcast the offer of immunity from state prosecution if Kiritsis would release Hall unharmed. Martz added that he understood that immunity from federal prosecution was "in the making."

Hearing the broadcast, a reporter at the Associated Press (AP) bureau called the U.S. Attorney for Southern Indiana. The attorney, speaking for the record, said immunity would not be offered. "The Justice Department won't bargain with gunmen." A reporter at AP's Washington bureau got the same answer from Justice Department officials. Should AP run the story? AP staffer Darrell Christian said the staff "had a severe conscience qualm. . . . What if we ran the story, Kiritsis hears it on TV and blows Hall's head off?"

AP decided to move the story. However, the decision was not made in Indianapolis, but rather by AP's managing editor in New York. This occurred, said Christian, "because no one here wanted to take responsibility involving two lives." When Kiritsis surrendered, it was unclear whether he had actually heard about the denial of federal immunity.

This case raises a number of fundamental issues. An analysis could begin with simple identification of the several decisions that were made. Then the issues involved in each of those decisions can be located and evaluated.

The following seem to be the central decisions: (1) Some journalists had to choose whether to put Kiritsis and Hall on camera. (2) Heckman had to decide whether to provide air time to allow Kiritsis to tell his side of the story. (3) Heckman had to decide whether to assume the role of mediator. (4) Someone had to decide whether to report an offer of immunity by the county prosecutor. (5) Reporter O'Brien had to decide whether to broadcast speculations by the army bomb squad about whether they could get in the building and incapacitate Kiritsis. (6) Someone at the Associated Press had to decide whether to report the fact that no immunity to Kiritsis would in fact be given by federal prosecutors.

As in all decisions to act, the moral dimension of human choice lies in the possible impact these conclusions will have on human well-being. The choices are complex because of the difficulty in predicting the likely outcome. Many people are involved here and some will be affected more seriously than others. Some will be hurt badly and others helped. The case has so many possible ramifications that a complete examination would require several chapters. Therefore, the focus will be on numbers 1, 2, and 5, with brief attention to the other decisions made.

Decision 1 is clearly the most complex in terms of both factual assessment and moral judgment. Should Kiritsis and Hall be allowed to go on camera? The very existence of the mass media makes such choices inevitable. In a sense the media's own definition of newsworthiness tends to make them a pawn in the hands of people like Kiritsis. We do not know what specific facts led to the decision to air this event, though its very nature made the story a natural victim of these circumstances. If Kiritsis demanded that he be put on the air with the threat of otherwise executing Hall, he would put both journalists and the authorities in a genuine moral bind. How could they assess the seriousness of his threats? How could they predict what his actions would be if they did put him on the air or if they did not? He might have executed Hall before an audience.

More important is the question as to who should decide when an individual is seriously deranged. Journalists by and large are not well equipped either by experience or by training to make predictive judgments concerning the behavior of such a person. Nor are the police well equipped to make such judgments. Both must depend upon consultations with professionals who deal with the mentally deranged. As a matter of fact, even after Kiritsis served ten years in Indiana's Central State mental hospital, psychiatrists debated before a judge the implications for society of what they diagnosed as his "paranoid personality."[20]

Should they put Kiritsis and Hall on camera? For Hall's sake it seems that they should decide on the basis of whatever the responsible public authorities determine. If the authorities in charge conclude that Kiritsis's going on television might save Hall's life, the station should put him on. There is a positive moral obligation not only to avoid harm but also to prevent harm to a fellow human being if doing so does not subject us to the risk of comparable harm. In this case the station does not risk serious loss. The journalists do indeed become pawns, not in the hands of the police, as Yount suggested, but in the hands of Kiritsis, who by holding Hall hostage manipulates both the media and the police. These same considerations apply to news director Heckman and his decision to provide air time for Kiritsis.

That brings us to Yount's criticism of Heckman, a response frequently heard. However, claiming that the media became a part of the police effort to fool the kidnapper is a criticism that does not recognize the fundamental realities of the situation. By Kiritsis's action the media were no longer able to remain independent bystanders. Kiritsis made them participants whether they wished to be or not. Yount's insistence that the news media's responsibility was only "to gather the facts" gives no guidance whatever in this situation. In this case, getting the facts interferes clearly with the responsibility for Hall's life. Anything that risks the life of an innocent human being is immoral by almost any standard. Or, to place the issue in terms of the Potter Box, professional values that we identify in the second quadrant cannot be our only guide to a morally justified conclusion. Step four asks us to investigate our loyalties, and in this situation saving innocent life is of paramount importance.

Regarding decision 5, reporter O'Brien had to decide on the spot whether to broadcast speculations by the bomb squad. Remote, on-the-scene, live broadcasting places very heavy responsibilities on reporters at the scene. These responsibilities are unavoidable. Live broadcasts put reporters in a position of having to make far-reaching news judgments and make them quickly. For that reason it is arguable that remote facilities should not be taken to such a scene at all! Yet to be there as a reporter is ipso facto to become a participant. In this case, since lives are at stake, and since O'Brien could report enough later to straighten out the entire situation, O'Brien should decide what to broadcast not by the typical criterion of newsworthiness, but by criteria applicable to his role as a participant. Once the crisis is over and he no longer participates, he can report the event without endangering life. It was morally irresponsible for him as a participant to broadcast speculations about the bomb squad since that quite predictably would further upset an already desperate and deranged kidnapper. He clearly compounded the risk to Hall. The same may be said, of course, of the AP decision to report the fact that no immunity would be given to Kiritsis by federal prosecutors. The public gained nothing by being told the facts *then*. Those facts could keep until the crisis was over.

The coverage of hostage taking in the international arena often requires even more savvy than reporting the Kiritsis story. On 7 October 1985, for example, four men hijacked the Italian ship *Achille Lauro*, which was cruising on the Mediterranean Sea with 400 passengers and crew aboard. The hijackers, claiming membership in the Palestine Liberation Front, threatened to kill all on board unless Palestinians imprisoned in various countries were released. After two days of negotiations, the hijackers surrendered to Egyptian authorities at Port Said. Italian officials reported soon afterward that an American tourist, 69-year-old Leon Klinghoffer, who was confined to a wheelchair, had been shot and thrown overboard—apparently because he was Jewish. On October 11, U.S. jets intercepted an Egyptian plane heading for Tunisia with the hijackers; the plane was forced to land at a NATO base in Italy, where the hijackers were charged with murder. This series of events triggered the involvement of six governments and the PLO, military forces and civilians, and incredibly complicated issues of international law. No matter how well trained and comprehensive a news staff happens to be, covering the *Achille Lauro* competently under such extremity is impossible.[21] Thomas W. Cooper argues correctly that "greater cooperation between and among international journalists" is crucial if we are to overcome the welter of cultures, religions, languages, and political systems which often become entangled in terrorism.[22] In addition to being subject to relentless pressure toward sensationalism, reporting of political violence on the international scene easily becomes trapped in ignorance or ethnocentrism.

Of course, not all hijackings make similar demands on the media. More than 60 died when Egyptair's 737 was stormed in Malta without direct negotiations through the media system. In Enniskillen, Ireland, during a memorial service, a bomb exploded, fatally injuring eleven gathered mourners; news coverage began after the fact. While cases of terrorism differ in form and none can be reduced to one issue, Tony Kiritsis, Egyptair, the Enniskillen bombing, TWA Flight 847, the Pan Am crash in Scotland, Iran's holding Americans hostage in 1978–79, and the *Achille Lauro* incident all center around the threat to innocent victims. "What is distinctively wrong or evil about terrorism . . . is that it harms or menaces innocent people to achieve its political ends."[23] Obviously, terrorists themselves do not usually use this distinction. Hall represented for Kiritsis an evil lending system; in terrorist acts, civilians are usually understood to bear moral complicity in the political regimes being opposed. Terrorists taking presumed injustice into their own hands, in Robert Fullenwider's view, see themselves "as appealing to a higher law, to morality itself." And he is correct in arguing that even though innocence and guilt are often debatable in the sociopolitical context, we cannot reject "the immunity of the innocent" as a moral notion.[24] For ethical journalists, the overriding goal ought to be increasing the chances of hostages' survival.

Undoubtedly inflammatory rhetoric from the news media endangers the lives of victims. In their study of newspaper coverage of political violence, Picard and Adams distinguish nominal terms (those intended to indicate what happened) from descriptive terms (those containing judgments). In the former category they include hijacking, bombing, shooting, attack, gunman, assassination, killing, commando, and abduction. As judgmental terms, Picard and Smith include murder, terrorism, criminal, freedom fighter, left-wing, sabotage, piracy, dissident, and extremist.[25] A journalist's never forgetting that hostage takers are humans, reporting events concisely, and refusing to speculate about motives keep the coverage from itself triggering a massacre.

British Prime Minister Margaret Thatcher strikes sensitive nerves when she demands that terrorists be starved of the "oxygen of publicity." In fact, however, studies implicating the media as a contagion for political violence are sparse and inconclusive.[26] Serious voices within the news enterprise did take to heart Edward Meese's suggestion when he was U.S. attorney general that guidelines be formulated controlling the press's behavior. As with the Kiritsis case, however, protecting innocent victims often entails cooperation with the authorities and experts. Clearly that cannot mean a knee-jerk acquiescence, and certainly the collaboration should never be done covertly. However, a set of voluntary guidelines focused on protecting victims can be established for news media performance, even though their precise role varies with each hijacker's plans and mental state.[27]

11. AN ENEMY OF THE PEOPLE

In Henrik Ibsen's *An Enemy of the People,* most of the important players appear in the opening scene. Peter Stockmann, the Mayor, stops at his brother's home and meets his dinner guests. Hovstad, editor of the local paper, arrives and tells the Mayor that the *People's Daily Messenger* is to print an article by Dr. Stockmann extolling the medicinal value of the town's baths, Kirsten Springs, in Norway. The Mayor, who implemented the idea, resents the credit lavished on his brother for founding the baths.

Dr. Stockmann enters his home with another guest, Captain Horster. In high spirits, Dr. Stockmann says that his days of living on starvation wages are over since his brother, the Mayor, obtained a position for him with the Health Institute set up by the baths. Peter Stockmann refers to the article to be published and Dr. Stockmann replies that he may no longer want it printed. The Mayor demands an explanation; when his brother declines to offer one, the Mayor upbraids him for not subordinating himself to authority and leaves in anger.

Petra Stockmann returns home and hands her father a letter. It reveals that the baths are contaminated by bacteria from the discharge of a tannery upstream. His suspicions had been aroused by an excessive number of visitors who suffered from typhoid and gastric disturbances the previous year. Samples of the water that he sent to the university's chemists for testing confirmed his fears. Dr. Stockmann now speaks disparagingly of the Health Institute's board of directors who originally refused to accept his recommendation on how to lay the water pipes to the baths; he condemns them as politicians who reject a doctor's advice. As a result, the entire water system will have to be relaid. He sends his report and the university's results to his brother who is on the Institute's board of directors. Hovstad realizes the scandalous nature of the news and states that he will print the story because the public ought to know it. He adds that the paper and the people should praise Dr. Stockmann for his discovery.

The following morning Morton Kiil, Mrs. Stockmann's father, drops by the Stockmanns' home. He is skeptical about Dr. Stockmann's report on the existence of "millions of tiny animals invisible to the eye," but gleefully thinks it is a good trick to play on the Mayor and the town council. Kiil is still bitter toward the Mayor, who was instrumental in removing him from the council.

Hovstad arrives as Kiil is leaving. Hovstad confides to Dr. Stockmann that he desires to use the story to rid the town council of "that smug cabal of old, stubborn, self-satisfied fogies." Aslaksen, the paper's publisher, calls on Dr. Stockmann and assures him of both his support and that of "the solid majority." He wants to stage a demonstration to compliment Dr. Stockmann, but stresses moderation. He brushes aside Dr. Stockmann's protestation that a simple issue is being overamplified. After Hovstad leaves, Dr. Stockmann tells his family that it feels good to have the majority of the townspeople on his side.

Peter Stockmann arrives and informs his brother that it will cost $60,000 to relay the pipes and take two years. In the meantime the news of the poisonous springs would irreparably devastate the town's financial fortunes. The Mayor dismisses his brother's report as hyperbolic; he advises him to be discreet and rectify the problem with his skills as a physician. Dr. Stockmann accuses the Mayor of treachery and an unwillingness to acknowledge his error. The Mayor admits his concern for his reputation and intends to prevent his brother's report from reaching the board. Dr. Stockmann retorts that the Mayor is too late, since the "liberal, free, and independent press will stand up and do its duty!" Peter Stockmann castigates his brother's irresponsibility for habitually expressing his thoughts before he fathoms their implications. Dr. Stockmann maintains that it is a citizen's duty to share new ideas with the public. The Mayor argues that the public is better off with traditional ideas. He demands, as his brother's superior on the board, that the report be withdrawn. When Dr. Stockmann refuses, the Mayor threatens his brother with dismissal from the Health Institute, points out the dire consequences for his family, and labels him a traitor to society. When the Mayor leaves, a distressed Mrs. Stockmann cautions her husband about his brother's political clout. When he states the truth is on his side, his wife warns him that truth without power is useless. Dr. Stockmann nevertheless is confident of victory in the end, and reminds her that the press and the majority are on his side. She urges him to live with injustice and provide for his family. Dr. Stockmann, however, insists on standing by his principles.

In the editorial office of the *Messenger*, Hovstad and his reporter, Billing, conclude that Dr. Stockmann's article will expose the Mayor's incompetence. Hovstad hopes that the town council will be replaced by a liberal administration. Aslaksen, the publisher and print shop owner, agrees to print it; but he cautions moderation. He distinguishes between the paper's attack on the national government and on local authorities. While it is all right to do the former, Aslaksen rejects the latter as questionable because of the local consequences when a town's administration is destroyed.

Peter Stockmann arrives at the newspaper office's rear entrance. He asks Hovstad about his brother's article and spots it in Aslaksen's hands. The Mayor tells them that if the article were printed and it became necessary to change the water system, then the people would have to be taxed. He adds that it will take two years to reconstruct the pipes and the town's businessmen would be without income during that time. Aslaksen, chairman of the Property Owners Association, is horrified by these revelations. The Mayor accuses his brother of vindictiveness. Hovstad is also swayed. The Mayor offers to provide Hovstad with an article presenting his side of the story.

Just then, Dr. Stockmann arrives and the Mayor hides in an adjoining room. He asks for the proofs and Aslaksen replies that they are not ready. Dr. Stockmann notices the Mayor's cane and hat on the table, opens the door to the next room and an embarrassed Mayor emerges. Dr. Stockmann realizes what his brother is attempting to do and mockingly tells him that he has the truth, the majority, and the press on his side. Aslaksen and Hovstad, however, say that they are not printing his article after all because it will ruin the paper and the town. Aslaksen asks Dr. Stockmann to consider the consequences for his family. Dr. Stockmann stands by his principles and insists on publicizing the truth at any cost.

In Act 2, Captain Horster offers his house for a public meeting called by Dr. Stockmann. Before Dr. Stockmann can present his case, the rowdy crowd votes on the Mayor's suggestion and Aslaksen is elected chairman of the meeting. He calls on the Mayor to speak first. Peter Stockmann accuses his brother of wanting to destroy Kirsten Springs and legitimate political authority. The Mayor argues that abusing the democratic right to free speech leads to revolution and chaos, and he moves that his brother be prohibited from reading his report. The hostile crowd punctuates the Mayor's tirade with uproarious shouts of anger at Dr. Stockmann.

Conceding defeat at the hands of the majority, Dr. Stockmann agrees to drop the subject of the springs and to address a more vital topic. He sarcastically refers to liberals and radicals, like Hovstad, who have fought for the principles of free speech. Hovstad interrupts him and says that he will not impose his will on the majority, especially if they are his readers. Dr. Stockmann passionately lashes out at the belief that the majority is always right, referring to Jesus' crucifixion and Galileo's solar system. When he attempts to read his report, a citizen threatens him with violence. Aslaksen moves a resolution that Dr. Stockmann be declared an enemy of the people when he threatens to publish his report in out-of-town newspapers. Only Captain Horster and a drunk vote against the motion.

Act 3, the following morning, brings a litany of disasters for the Stockmanns. The windows of their home have been shattered. The glazier refuses to fix the windows and they are also given an eviction notice by their home's owner. Dr. Stockmann decides to leave for the United States. Petra returns early; she has been fired from her job. Captain Horster comes with the news that he, too, is jobless. The Mayor arrives to hand his brother a letter of dismissal from the Health Institute Board, and informs him that the people are signing a petition not to seek his medical services. He urges his brother to retract his report on the poisonous waters in order to calm people's fears and be reinstated. When Dr. Stockmann refuses to do so, the Mayor charges him with conspiracy. He asserts that Dr. Stockmann has waged a destructive campaign against the springs in order that his father-in-law, Morten Kiil, could buy up Kirsten Springs stock at half its value. Dr. Stockmann is shocked. The Mayor threatens to arrest him if he publishes his report outside town.

As the Mayor leaves, Kiil enters and places on the table Kirsten Springs stock that he just bought. Kiil states that the polluted waters are coming from a tannery that has belonged to his family for generations. He wants Dr. Stockmann to retest the water and pronounce it clean so that his family reputation is not sullied and the stock will be inherited by Mrs. Stockmann. If his son-in-law refuses, he will give the stock to charity. They are interrupted by Aslaksen and Hovstad's arrival; Kiil leaves. They want to make Dr. Stockmann a hero for buying up stock to force the management to improve public health. They, however, require him to donate money to their paper to offset an anticipated short-term

loss of circulation for supporting him. Dr. Stockmann is attracted
by the offer to clear his name, but is aghast at the thought that
they are merely proposing that he sanctify the springs with medical respectability without rectifying the root cause of the problem. Hovstad excoriates Dr. Stockmann for his refusal, calling
him insane with egotism for wishing to put his family through
further suffering.

They are interrupted by the arrival of the Stockmanns' children,
Morten and Ejlif. Morten's head is bruised. While he was fighting
with another boy who called his father a traitor, he was attacked
by the whole group. Dr. Stockmann decides to accept the "enemy
of the people" label, condemns his opponents as "ambassadors
from hell," and resolves to stay. Maybe, he muses, he can teach
street kids to be free and independent seekers of truth. Dr. Stockmann tells his family that the reason they are alone is because
they are fighting for the truth. As he speaks, a hostile crowd gath-
ers outside his home for further harassment.

For democratic societies, truth is indispensable. Only when citizens know the facts, it is assumed, can they make responsible judgments about public policy. Along this line, Ibsen agrees that truth is
a powerful political force. The issue for him is what happens when the
truth is painful. When everyone hears good news that will benefit
them, the information is welcome and serves as a social lubricant. But
Ibsen is worried that when the truth hurts, when it disrupts the status
quo, the truth usually creates a crisis rather than promotes the general
welfare.

The play is a realistic depiction of the complex human reaction
to tragedy. It asks whether any persons or institutions can be depended
on when the spa is found to be poisonous and its profitability destroyed.
To answer that question, Ibsen examines several democratic mainstays
in their response to the scientific evidence. The Mayor refuses to take
responsibility since he would thereby admit the mistakes of his administration. The newspaper buckles once it learns that the majority
of its readers would not appreciate this revelation. The businessmen's
council opposes the higher taxes and lost revenue. Even Dr. Stockmann's last resort—the average citizen—refuses to listen in a town
meeting called to discuss the problem. Dr. Stockmann, as an individual
with conscience, does generally follow the truth out of principle. Yet

his own arrogance, his feuds with his brother, and his recalitrance are Ibsen's way of indicating that even the morally enlightened individual is not pure. Individuals may be the bastion of a democratic society, but even they are not a final and reassuring answer to disturbing truth. The play ends with uncertainty about democracy's future.

Ibsen's play features characters who are not despicable. On all levels, the democratic institutions involved (the press, medicine, politics, and business) are not outrageously evil. They are narrowminded, spiteful, and defensive, but not totally corrupt. Thus the resolution of Ibsen's concern is extremely difficult; it is not a simple matter of rejecting an immoral practice or two. The current debates—national, regional, and local—over water pollution, acid rain, toxic dumps, garbage landfills, chemicals, and oil spills illustrate the same complexities as Ibsen's drama. It suggests that our penchant for scapegoats and easy-fixes is not productive.

NOTES

1. For a classic statement of truthfulness-in-context, see Dietrich Bonhoeffer, *Ethics* (New York: Macmillan, 1955), sec. 5, pp. 363–372.
2. Arthur Miller, *An Enemy of the People: Adaptation of Henrik Ibsen's En Folkefriende.* New York: Penguin Books, 1984. A film version starring Steve McQueen is also available. The play is short enough to make a review essay assignment for students.
3. This case is adapted and quoted from Staci Kramer, "The Case of the Missing Coke Can," *Editor and Publisher,* 29 April 1989, pp. 18–19.
4. George Orwell, *1984* (New York: Harcourt, Brace and World, 1949), p. 43.
5. The history is reviewed by Paul Lester, "Faking Images in Photojournalism," *Media Development* 1 (1988): 41–42.
6. Jim Gordon, "Foot Artwork Ends Career," *News Photographer,* November 1981, p. 32; for details of this event see pp. 31–36.
7. Sheila Reaves, "Photography, Pixels and New Technology: Is There a Paradigm Shift?" Paper presented to Qualitative Studies Division, AEJMC, Washington, D.C., August 1989, p. 5. Cf. also her "Digital Retouching in Newspapers," *Journal of Mass Media* Ethics 2:2 (Spring/Summer 1987): 40–48.
8. Reaves, "Photography, Pixels and New Technology," p. 7.
9. Sissela Bok, *Lying: Moral Choice in Public and Private Life* (New York: Pantheon Books, 1978), pp. 123–126.
10. Zay N. Smith and Pamela Zekman, *The Mirage* (New York: Random House, 1979).
11. For the actual story on which this hypothetical account is based, see the *Chicago Tribune,* 22 June 1980, pp. 1, 6, and 8, sec. 1; 23 June 1980, p. 2,

sec. 4; *Chicago Sun Times*, 24 June 1980, p. 2; *Matrix* 65 (Summer 1980): 17; *Matrix* 66 (Winter 1981): 30.

12. Edward M. Miller, "APME's Guidelines a 'Sexist Document'? An Editor's Reply," *Columbia Journalism Review* 10 (September/October 1981): 62–63.

13. In Haig Bosmajian, *The Language of Oppression* (Washington, D.C.: Public Affairs Press, 1974), p. 92.

14. Practical suggestions for avoiding sexist language are compiled in Casey Miller and Kate Swift, *The Handbook of Nonsexist Writing* (New York: Harper & Row, 1981).

15. Quoted in Joan Behrmann, "How the Press Treats Women," in *Questioning Media Ethics*, ed. Bernard Rubin (New York: Praeger, 1978), p. 119.

16. Maurine Beasley and Sheila Silver, *Women in Media: A Documentary Source Book* (Washington, D.C.: Women's Institute for Freedom of the Press, 1977), pp. 163–169. For an analysis of where the issues stand currently in all phases of mass communications, including magazine, television, and public relations, see Pamela J. Creedon, ed., *Women in Mass Communication: Challenging Gender Values* (Beverly Hills, Calif.: Sage, 1989). For an examination of feminism in terms of social and political theory, see Seyla Benhabib and Drucilla Cornell, eds., *Feminism as Critique: On the Politics of Gender* (Minneapolis: University of Minnesota Press, 1987).

17. Walter B. Jaehning, "Journalists and Terrorism: Captives of the Libertarian Tradition," *Indiana Law Journal* (1977–1978): 735.

18. Ibid.

19. Ibid., p. 726.

20. Scott L. Miley and Linda Graham Caleca, "Ruling on Kiritsis' Freedom Monday," *The Indianapolis Star*, 4 December 1987, pp. A1, A10.

21. For an examination of the devastating impact on Klinghoffer's family, see Jack Lule, "The Myth of My Widow: A Dramatistic Analysis of News Portrayals of a Terrorist Victim," Terrorism and the News Media Research Project, Emerson College, n.d., pp. 4–15.

22. Thomas W. Cooper, "Terrorism and Perspectivist Philosophy: Understanding Adversarial News Coverage," Terrorism and the News Media Research Project, Emerson College, July 1988, p. 5.

23. "Terrorism," *Report from the Center for Philosophy and Public Policy*, University of Maryland, 7:4 (Fall 1987): 2.

24. Ibid.

25. Robert G. Picard and Paul D. Adams, "Characterizations of Acts and Perpetrators of Political Violence in Three Elite Daily Newspapers," Terrorism and the News Media Research Project, Emerson College, n.d., pp. 3–11.

26. Robert Picard, "News Coverage as the Contagion of Terrorism: Dangerous

Charges Backed by Dubious Science," *Political Communication and Persuasion* 3 (Fall 1986): 35–40.

27. For an example of proposed guidelines, see Robert L. Terrell and Kristina Ross, "Guidelines for U.S. Press Coverage of Terrorism," *Media Development* 3 (1987): 32–33.

CHAPTER 3

Reporters and Sources

Well-informed sources are a reporter's bread and butter, and dependence on them creates some genuine perplexities. A news medium's pledging to reveal frankly all its sources of information would be significant for the public; however, printing names usually results in the sources thereafter speaking guardedly or even drying up. Several tactics are used in confronting this dilemma so that audiences are served and sources remain content. As Hugh Culbertson writes, "The unnamed news source has been called a safety valve for democracy and a refuge for conscience, but also a crutch for lazy, careless reporters."[1] A *Washington Post* editorial captured some of the struggle in a recent description of "Source's" family tree:

> Walter and Ann Source (née Rumor) had four daughters (Highly Placed, Authoritative, Unimpeachable, and Well-Informed). The first married a diplomat named Reliable Informant. (The Informant brothers are widely known and quoted here; among the best known are White House, State Department, and Congressional.) Walter Speculation's brother-in-law, Ian Rumor, married Alexandre Conjecture, from which there were two sons, It Was Understood and It Was Learned. It Was Learned just went to work in the Justice Department, where he will be gainfully employed for four long years.[2]

The complications here are not easily resolved. Walter Lippmann noted this journalistic bind more than 50 years ago in his *Public Opinion* and, as a result, distinguished news from truth. News he saw as fragments of information that come to a reporter's attention; explicit and established standards guide the pursuit of truth.[3] The judicial process, for example, follows rigorous procedures when gathering evidence. Academics footnote and attribute sources so that knowledgeable people can verify or dispute the conclusions. Medical doctors rely on technical precision and expertise. Reporters, however, cannot compete with these other professions. They have found no authoritative way of examining, testing, and evaluating their information, at least not in a public arena and not under risky, hostile conditions.

The difficulties result primarily because a multitude of practical considerations need to be jockeyed under deadline pressures. On occasion reporters must be adversarial, at least skeptical; at other times, friendliness and cooperation work better. If newspeople become too intimate with important men and women, they lose professional distance or develop unhealthy biases protecting them. However, to the degree that powerful sources are not cultivated and reporters establish no personal connections, the inside nuance and perspective may be lost. At times written documents supplemented by public briefings are superior to information painfully dug out by a conscientious reporter. On most other occasions the official source is blinded by self-interest. But who can predict? Regarding sources the American Society of Newspaper Editors (ASNE) Statement of Principles correctly warns: "Journalists must be vigilant against all who would exploit the press for selfish purposes."[4] Little wonder that as Watergate documents came to light, for instance, several "scoops" proved to be stories leaked originally by Mr. Nixon's staff.

Most news operations have developed specific procedures to help prevent chaos and abuse. Certain conventions also hold together journalistic practice. It is typically assumed that all information must be verified by two or three sources before it can be printed. Most codes of ethics and company policies insist on attribution and specific identification whenever possible. A few news operations allow reporters to keep sources totally secret, but a majority openly involve editors as judges of the data's validity. The rules also include accurate quotation marks, correction of errors, and an account of the context. However, even with these safeguards, a responsible press must continually agonize over its treatment of sources in order to prevent lapses.

This chapter chooses five entangled aspects of the reporter–source relationship, all of them actual occurrences of some notoriety. The first case, from Watergate, concerns the question of tapping grand jury sources: members and documents. In the second case the debate

revolves around the use of stolen materials. While few journalistic
events have the historic significance of the Pentagon Papers, the decision whether or not to accept valuable stolen materials has to be
made frequently. The third case indicates that new understandings of
confidentiality are emerging in the courts, forcing media companies
to establish guidelines for promise keeping which are undergirded by
ethics rather than law. The fourth case, the Abscam episode, provides
a specific example of leaked sources and the journalist's responsibility
in turning leaks into public information. The last case in this chapter
treats the issue of familiarity and the boundary between exploiting
friendship and building on it legitimately in gathering news. Cheap
answers are not forthcoming, but at every point the ethical issues ought
to form a prominent part of the resolution.

12. Watergate and Grand Jury Information

After leading the pack on the Watergate story in the early going,
Washington Post reporters Carl Bernstein and Bob Woodward ran
into rough waters.[5] On 25 October 1972, a major coup had turned
into a major disaster. They had written that H. L. (Bob) Haldeman,
President Nixon's chief of staff, had been personally involved in
controlling espionage and sabotage. The charge moved the Watergate break-in to the door of President Nixon. But then, through
his attorney, their source for the report denied he had given such
testimony before a grand jury. The White House used the opportunity to respond with a vigorous counterattack on the *Washington Post.*

In an effort to discover how they had gone wrong, Woodward
and Bernstein revealed their primary source (an agent of the Federal Bureau of Investigation) to his superior. Back at the office the
two reporters and *Post* executives discussed revealing all five
sources of their erroneous information, but decided against it.

After that debacle, Woodward and Bernstein ran into more trouble; now the problem was not erroneous stories but no stories at
all. They had hit a lull. The timing was bad. The *Post*'s executive
editor, Benjamin Bradlee, became frustrated. The Nixon forces
were shooting at him. Charles Colson, speaking to a group of New
England editors, said, "If Bradlee ever left the Georgetown cocktail circuit where he and his pals dine on third-hand information
and gossip and rumor, he might discover out here the real Amer-

ica." Bradlee told an interviewer that he was "ready to hold both Woodward's and Bernstein's heads in a pail of water until they came up with another story." That dry spell was anguish.

Such was the pressurized atmosphere in the *Post* newsroom at the time that Woodward and Bernstein and their editors decided to seek information from members of the Watergate grand jury. They came to the idea by happenstance. One night late in November a *Post* editor told Woodward that his neighbor's aunt was on a grand jury, that judging from remarks she had made, it was the grand jury on Watergate, and that in the words of the editor, "My neighbor thinks she wants to talk."

The two reporters checked the Federal Rules of Criminal Procedure—grand jurors take an oath of secrecy. But it appeared that the burden of secrecy was on the jurors; nothing in the law directly forbade questioning them. The *Post*'s lawyers agreed with that interpretation but urged "extreme caution" in approaching the jurors. Bradlee, nervous, echoed that warning: "No beating anyone over the head, no pressure, none of that cajoling."

All the consultation and advice were for nothing. The woman, Woodward and Bernstein were to learn, was not on the Watergate grand jury after all. But the episode had "whetted their interest." The day after the abortive interview, Woodward went to the courthouse, found the list of Watergate grand jurors, and memorized their names; he had been forbidden to take notes.

After typing up the list of jurors, Woodward and Bernstein had a session with Bradlee, *Post* metropolitan editor Harry M. Rosenfeld, managing editor Howard Simons, and city editor Barry Sussman. They went over the list looking for members "least likely to inform the prosecutors of a visit." Eliminating civil servants and military officers, they sought, through occupation, jurors "bright enough to suspect that the grand jury system had broken down in the Watergate case" and "in command of the nuances of the evidence." "Ideally," Woodward and Bernstein wrote, "the juror would be capable of outrage at the White House or the prosecutors or both; a person who was accustomed to bending rules, the type of person who valued practicality more than procedure." *All the President's Men* describes the mental state of those in the room:

> Everyone had private doubts about such a seedy venture.
> Bradlee, desperate for a story, and reassured by the law-

yers, overcame his own. Simons doubted out loud the rightness of the exercise and worried about the paper. Rosenfeld was concerned most about the mechanics of the reporters not getting caught. Sussman was afraid that one of them, probably Bernstein, would push too hard and find a way to violate the law. Woodward wondered whether there was ever justification for a reporter to entice someone across the line of legality while standing safely on the right side himself.

Bernstein, who vaguely approved of selective civil disobedience, was not concerned about breaking the law in the abstract. It was a question of *which* law, and he believed that grand jury proceedings should be inviolate. The misgivings, however, went unstated, for the most part.[6]

The procedure for interviewing the jurors was agreed upon. The reporters were to identify themselves and say that through a mutual but anonymous friend they understood he or she knew something about the Watergate case. They would then ask if he or she was willing to discuss it. If the answer was no, the reporters were to leave immediately.

Visits to about half a dozen grand jurors yielded nothing but trouble. One of the jurors reported the visit to a prosecutor, who informed Judge John Sirica. *Post* attorney Edward Bennett Williams met with Sirica. After the meeting, he told Woodward and Bernstein he thought they would get off with a reprimand. He was right. The chiding came in open court, in a room packed with reporters. But Sirica did not identify them or the *Post*. The reporters present were out for the story, questioning each other, seeking the identity of the reporters mentioned by the judge. Woodward and Bernstein agreed they would make an outright denial "only as a last resort." A colleague caught up with them as they headed for the elevator. *All the President's Men* describes the scene and thinking of the two reporters:

> He (the reporter) caught up with Woodward near the elevator and asked point-blank if the Judge had been referring to him or Bernstein.
> "Come off it, what do you think?" Woodward answered angrily.

The man persisted. "Well, was it one of them or wasn't it? Yes or no."

"Listen," Woodward snapped, "Do you want a quote? Are we talking for the record? I mean, are you serious? Because if you are, I'll give you something, all right."

The reporter seemed stunned. "Sorry, Bob, I didn't think you'd take me seriously," he told Woodward.

The danger passed. The nightmare vision that had haunted them all day—Ron Ziegler at the podium demanding that they be the object of a full federal investigation, or some such thing—disappeared. They tried to imagine what choice phrases he might use ("jury tampering"?), and they realized that they didn't have the stomach for it. They felt lousy. They had not broken the law when they visited the grand jurors, that much seemed certain. But they had sailed around it and exposed others to danger. They had chosen expediency over principle, and, caught in the act, their role had been covered up. They had dodged, evaded, misrepresented, suggested and intimidated, even if they had not lied outright.[7]

This case involves a long sequence of ethical choices. It reveals many of the pressures on the *Post*'s staff. Bradlee's desire, for example, for a story, "any story," to take the heat off the *Post* could be examined as a nonethics of self-interest, principles be damned. In this way the case is realistic in its reflection of conditions under which journalistic decisions are frequently made. Under most circumstances these pressures are much less strong than they were for the *Post* in this instance. However, knowledge of these circumstances does not help resolve the ethics of the case. Surely, the existence of pressures, even intense ones, cannot itself justify a reporter's conduct. At best the reality of pressure may help one sympathize with a reporter who, feeling it strongly, made bad moral judgments. But that is not ethics in the sense of reaching justified decisions.

Perhaps the best way to begin examining this multisided situation is to identify some of the moral choices made along the way:

1. They decided to reveal the identity of a source to his superior "in an effort to find out how they had gone wrong." But they also

decided not to reveal all five sources. The decision to reveal their source likely involved the violation of promises, but the case does not tell us.

2.   They decided to seek information from the grand jury. Clearly they were aware of potential legal problems, as evidenced by their check into the Federal Rules of Criminal Procedure and by their conversation in the planning session.

3.   They decided to get the list of grand jurors by memorization rather than by taking notes. This is already a step in the direction of misusing the grand jury system and of violating the important ethical principles on which it stands.

4.   They decided to do everything possible to avoid being caught in interviews with grand jurors. This was not a case of deliberately violating the law toward the end of changing an unjust law; it was a case of violating the law in order to serve the interests of the newspaper at the moment.

5.   In their approach to the grand jurors they decided to deceive by saying that "through a mutual friend. . . ." This lie was told in order to open the possibility of getting jurors to talk, to use jurors toward the *Post*'s own ends.

6.   They decided to lie if they were identified by fellow reporters as those reprimanded by Sirica. Admittedly, they would stoop to that only "as a last resort."

Certainly the nation can be grateful to Woodward and Bernstein for the final result of their investigation (Nixon's resignation). The morality of their investigation is seriously flawed, however. They did nothing that could not be justified by utilitarian principles. If they had known at the time that issues of overriding national importance were involved, their improprieties could be considered outweighed by the enormous public benefits. Their lying and their serious tampering with the grand jury resulted in uncovering one of the biggest threats to American democracy in its history. That vital end could be used to justify the immoral means.

The ethical problem is that they employed these immoral means toward immoral ends, namely, the self-interest of protecting themselves and the *Post*. At the time that they chose to lie and to violate the grand jury system, they could not have known, and did not claim to know, the final dimensions of the story they would uncover. In this case, then, democracy was benefited, but not by their conscious intent to aid society. The benefit was an unforeseen, and unforeseeable, consequence of decisions to violate not only the law but basic moral principles. Their decisions cannot, therefore, be justified ex post facto in light of the fortunate results. Evil choices do sometimes unwittingly evoke good ends. But such results do no more than place us in the awkward position of being glad that immoral people were at work on this case.[182] Journalists cannot morally follow in the *Post*'s footsteps as a general rule. Lying must always be justified in terms of some higher value; truthtelling need never be justified.

13. THE PENTAGON PAPERS AS STOLEN DOCUMENTS

The Pentagon Papers, a confidential report detailing American involvement in Vietnam since World War II, had been commissioned by Robert McNamara when he was secretary of defense. The account of their publication, begun in the *New York Times* on 13 June 1971, reads like a spy story. The *Times* would say only that it received 7,000 pages of the document through investigative reporter Neil Sheehan sometime in March 1971. (It was a former *Times* reporter, speaking on a radio show, who named Daniel Ellsberg as the man who supplied the document to the *Times*.)

The *Times* set about publication with a secrecy worthy of a security agency, according to *Times* writer Jules Witcover. Preliminary work was done in two rooms of the Jefferson Hotel in Washington, D.C. Then the operation was moved to a three-room suite in New York's Hilton, and eventually it commanded nine guarded rooms on two floors. Staffers working on the story were told to stay away from the *Times*'s main office. In late May, key production people were told of the project. In a vacant office building, these employees set up a secret composing room to handle the special copy and included a paper shredder to destroy extra proofs. On June 10, the first segment of the finished copy was brought from the hotel and punched on tapes. The pages were made up in the secret composing room. At 1:30 P.M. on Saturday, June 12, the first page of the *Times*'s report was sent to the presses "amid a mood of exultation. . . . One of the great journalistic coups had been achieved with hardly a whisper of suspicion anywhere," Witcover wrote.[9]

The second installment appeared on Monday, June 14. That evening U.S. Attorney General John N. Mitchell requested that the *Times* stop publication, arguing that the papers contained "information relating to the national defense of the United States" whose publication was "directly prohibited" by the Espionage Law. Two hours later the *Times* read a statement addressed to Mitchell that it also published: "The *Times* must respectfully decline the request of the Attorney General, believing that it is in the interest of the people of this country to be informed of the material contained in this series of articles."[10] Later that day the *Times* was enjoined from further publication, pending a hearing on the government's plea.

On Thursday, June 17, the *Washington Post* obtained 4,000 pages of the document, and plans were made for publication. Ben Bagdikian, then assistant managing editor for national news, said the *Post*'s management and lawyers were wary of publishing stories based on the document. The lawyers, posing a question of "propriety," said it would be "wiser to establish the right to publish by allowing the *Times* case to run its course, avoiding indication of a contempt for the court in that case." But, Bagdikian said, "The editors and writers saw it strictly in terms of freedom of the press and journalistic responsibility to the public—if it is authentic and significant, publish it."[11] The editors and writers prevailed. The *Post* began publication on Friday, June 18. It, too, was enjoined.

While the cases of prior restraint were in the courts, partial copies of the Pentagon Papers cropped up elsewhere: The *Boston Globe*, for example, began publication and was enjoined. The *St. Louis Post-Dispatch* began a series on Friday, June 25. Contacted by the Justice Department, the *Post-Dispatch* executives said they did not plan to publish an article on Saturday (because of the size of that day's edition) but would resume on Sunday. Before it could do so, it too was required to desist from further publication. Finally on June 30, the Supreme Court in a 6–3 decision ruled in favor of the newspapers.

Three questions must be answered satisfactorily before publication of the Pentagon Papers can be justified morally. The issues are too complicated to allow us to emphasize such professional values as freedom from government interference and then presume no further debate is necessary.

First, was it ethically permissible to publish classified material?

The legal battles centered entirely on that issue and were finally resolved by the Supreme Court in favor of First Amendment guarantees regarding the free press. Nor would typical moral systems contradict this type of decision. Nearly all ethical frameworks permit civil disobedience under certain circumstances. Obeying legally constituted authority is promoted as a moral good under normal circumstances (and in this instance the Espionage Law invoked by the attorney general had been duly enacted). However, this act of conscience against the state cannot be dismissed in itself as immoral by any typical set of ethical principles.

Second, ought the *New York Times* and the other papers use stolen documents as their source? Daniel Ellsberg had taken the material without authorization. The decision to publish stolen goods is a fundamental ethical issue.

From a Kantian perspective, theft is always wrong. The categorical imperative suggests that we not permit for ourselves what we do not wish to make a universal law. Obviously, from this viewpoint, societies cannot exist if stealing is allowed. A Kantian would point to the double standard involved, arguing that newspapers do not want government officials stealing their property so why should they condone theft for themselves? Justice Warren Burger reflected this ethical perspective:

> To me it is hardly believable that a newspaper long regarded as a great institution in American life would fail to perform one of the basic and simple duties of every citizen with respect to the discovery or possession of stolen property or secret government documents. That duty, I had thought—perhaps naively—was to report forthwith to responsible public officers. This duty rests on taxi drivers, Justices, and the *New York Times*.[12]

An opposing point of view over stolen property can be built on a utilitarian basis. The various editors who published the Pentagon Papers appealed to the historic circumstances and enormous consequences of the material. Fifty-five thousand Americans had already died in Vietnam, tens of billions of dollars had been spent militarily, and the nation was acrimoniously divided. Thus, when A. M. Rosenthal, managing editor of the *Times*, gave his paper's rationale, he dismissed simplistic declarations and contended that publication was within the *Times*'s

constitutional rights and in the best interests of our country. . . . Can you steal a decision that was made three years
ago and that has caused consequences that a country now
pays for, good or bad? How can you steal the mental processes of elected officials or appointed officials? . . . I never
thought that Americans would buy the argument that you
can steal information on public matters.[13]

Unfortunately, in all the lengthy arguments defending the
Times's actions, no attention is explicitly paid to ethical theory. Apparently, decisions were based on professional values and legal rights,
rather than on a struggle over step three in the Potter Box process.

Third, were the contents of the Pentagon Papers treated fairly and
accurately? Not all the documents were printed, since they totaled
more than 7,000 pages and covered a 25-year period. Substantial sections were complex and academic. The *Times* staff chose the theme
of duplicity, that is, American leaders were saying different things
about the Vietnam War in public and private. Edward Jay Epstein did
not score the *Times* very highly in meeting their editorial obligations:

To convert this bureaucratic study into a journalistic exposé
of duplicity required taking certain liberties with the original history. Outside material had to be added, and assertions
from the actual study had to be omitted. For example, to
show that the Tonkin Gulf resolution resulted from duplicity, the *Times* had to omit the conclusion of the Pentagon
Papers that the Johnson Administration had tried to avoid
the fatal clash in the Tonkin Gulf, and had to add evidence
of possible American provocations in Laos which were not
actually referred to in the Pentagon Papers themselves.[14]

Clearly this case represents an important legal triumph for the
press. Even though of ancient vintage, it remains as well known in
the press as any incident other than Watergate. It takes on historic
proportions because the Anglo-American tradition, in principle, has
condemned all kinds of prior restraint for nearly three hundred years.
The ethical questions of "Ought the *New York Times* and the other
papers use stolen documents as their source?" and "Were the contents
of the Pentagon Papers treated fairly and accurately?" warrant consideration nonetheless. The media generally do not traffic in stolen property and this celebrated situation ought not to dim their conscience.

As was suggested before, a utilitarian defense is possible here but not compelling. Did the editors unequivocally serve the public interest or merely use a noble end to justify desultory means? Ethicists remain uneasy about the duplicity theme also, wondering whether that characterization honestly represents official Department of Defense decision making. Impugning evil motives is not permitted by any moral system that respects human beings. To justify their action, the *New York Times* would have to demonstrate that its presentation faithfully tells the Pentagon Papers story and does not piece together a story of its own.

14. CONFIDENTIALITY IN MINNESOTA

Dan Cohen was director of public relations for the advertising agency handling the political campaign of Wheelock Whitney, an Independent Republican campaigning for governor of Minnesota.[15] One week before the election, Gary Flakne, a county attorney and former Independent Republican legislator, unearthed documents which showed that the Democratic-Farmer-Labor candidate for lieutenant governor, Marlene Johnson, had been arrested and convicted of a six-dollar theft thirteen years earlier.

A group of Independent Republican supporters agreed that Cohen should release these documents because he had the best rapport with the local media. Cohen immediately contacted four journalists: Lori Sturdevant of the *Minneapolis* (Minnesota) *Star Tribune*, Bill Salisbury of the *St. Paul Pioneer Press Dispatch*, Gerry Nelson of the Associated Press, and David Nimmer of WCCO Television. All four subsequently agreed to Cohen's proposal:

> I have some documents which may or may not relate to a candidate in the upcoming election, and if you will give me a promise of confidentiality, that is, that I will be treated as an anonymous source, that my name will not appear in any material in connection with this, and that you will also agree that you are not going to pursue with me a question of who my source is, then I will furnish you with the documents.[16]

The *Star Tribune* editors assigned four or five reporters to follow up the story by contacting members of the two gubernatorial campaigns. The reporter who was directed to verify the authenticity of the court records discovered Gary Flakne's name on the list of persons recently reviewing the records. Flakne admitted to the reporter that he had obtained the documents for Cohen.

The *Star Tribune* editor responsible for the final decision decided that the newspaper would be guilty of suppressing information if the story were not run. Sturdevant was asked to see whether Cohen would release the *Tribune* from its promise of anonymity. She telephoned Cohen twice but he refused to agree to include his name in the story. Sturdevant adamantly objected to reneging on her promise to Cohen and withdrew her name from the article. On 28 October 1982, the *Star Tribune* ran the story on the bottom half of the front page, entitled "Marlene Johnson Arrest Disclosed by Whitney Ally." The article described Johnson's arrest and conviction, named Cohen as the source, and identified him as the agent handling advertising for the opposition campaign. The article did not mention Sturdevant's promise of anonymity. This was the first time the *Star Tribune*'s management had overturned a reporter's pledge to keep the source confidential.

The *Dispatch* also ran an article similar to the *Tribune*'s in both October 28 editions. The Associated Press upheld its promise of confidentiality by stating that the court documents "were slipped to reporters." WCCO-TV decided not to broadcast the story at all.

Later in the day, Cohen's employer confronted him and, after a heated discussion, fired him.

On October 29, the *Star Tribune* published a column criticizing Cohen for his self-righteousness and unfair campaign tactics. The next day it ran an editorial cartoon of a trick-or-treater named Dan Cohen. On November 7, four days after the election, Cohen initiated a breach of contract and misrepresentation suit against the *Tribune* and the *Dispatch*.

Eight months later, a jury awarded Cohen $200,000 in actual damages and $500,000 in punitive damages, with payment divided equally between the two papers. The jury found that both newspapers had entered into binding contracts with Cohen and that they had breached those contracts. The case is currently being appealed on the grounds that a reporter's relationship with a source is not contractual; the newspapers contend that the issue can be understood only in terms of the press's First Amendment freedom.

In response to Cohen's lawsuit, the *Star Tribune* has issued a set of guidelines for using anonymous sources. It has concluded that eliminating them totally would make newsgathering virtually impossible, muzzling the dog rather than leashing it. The newspaper's editors now make a categorical pledge to uphold its promises of confidentiality, just short of a Kantian absolute. Sources will never be revealed, says company policy, with only three exceptions: (1) if the newspaper subsequently discovers that the source lied or unknowingly gave bad information—on the grounds that even if some stories must be unattributed they never can be unsubstantiated; (2) if it turns into a life-and-death situation, life will be protected; and (3) if ordered to reveal sources by a court of law, the paper will relent. "We will fight an order all the way to the U.S. Supreme Court if necessary," says executive editor Joel Kramer, "but if the Supreme Court upheld it, the newspaper would comply; we're not above the law."[17]

The *Star Tribune's* executive editor, Joel Kramer, believes that "anonymity is granted too freely. The problem is that certain promises should not be made." The heart of the issue is not making promises. The paper recognizes that turning back on its word undermines its credibility; therefore, in order to minimize the number of its commitments, the *Star Tribune* has established such written policies as the following:[18]

> Reporters must inform editors of the names of anonymous sources. Sources must understand that the right to commit the newspaper to a pledge of confidentiality lies with the management and not solely with individual reporters. Therefore, newspersons must always explicitly review the conditions and not make vague statements, such as "I probably won't use your name."
>
> Anonymous quotations should ordinarily not be used to express negative opinions about individuals or organizations, and never without the approval of the managing editor or executive editor. In other words, personal attacks by unnamed sources are forbidden, such as smear tactics in a political campaign.

If, on rare occasions, anonymous sources appear to be the only alternative, both reporters and editors must be satisfied that the material could not be obtained on the record. In addition, its news value must be significant and the newspaper must have no reason to doubt the information's reliability. When the story is run, it must include the rationale for protecting the source's identity.

Even after promising anonymity, reporters should make every effort to get the information attributable before publication, even if that means asking the anonymous source to reconsider. Should the source refuse, editors retain the option of declining to publish a story if they believe anonymity should not have been granted in the first place.[19]

Historically, anonymous sources have infected nearly all aspects of the news-gathering enterprise. When legal frameworks dominated our thinking about anonymity, the concerns revolved around tighter shield laws and around jail sentences for those disobeying court orders to reveal names. For example, reporter Myron A. Farber of the *New York Times* spent 40 days in jail during a 34-week murder trial in which Farber categorically refused to surrender his notes and names for private inspection by the judge. In fact, Clark R. Mollenhoff concludes his rules on confidentiality with this advice: "If litigation is initiated to force you to disclose your source with threats of jail and fines . . . you should be prepared to serve a substantial jail term, to pay a fine, and to pay legal fees. Your publisher can pay your fine and your legal fees but he cannot serve your jail term for you."[20]

Shifting to an ethical framework, the debates center on the nature of promises. When "keeping one's promise" is recognized as a moral rule, news professionals become far less enamored of anonymity, on the grounds that no one should make promises lightly. On the other hand, when promises are given, the media's integrity suffers deeply unless they are kept in good faith. What is true about the significance of promise keeping in the general morality governing everyday affairs holds for news reporting as well.

15. A LEAKING ABSCAM

A United States senator and nine representatives were informed that the Arab businesspeople with whom they had been dealing were not Arabs at all; they were undercover agents of the Federal

Bureau of Investigation. The Abscam (Arab scam) case was breaking. The elected officials learned through information leaked to
the press that they were suspected on bribery charges. The secrecy
of the two-year-old operation had not been officially lifted by the
FBI itself, but the curtain had been rent by inside informers. The
New York Times story was filled with details: how much each
suspect was alleged to have accepted from the "Arabs" in return
for promising political favors, where and when the transactions
occurred, even the type of containers used (for one a briefcase, for
another a paper bag). The *Times* story, written by Leslie Maitland,
said the results of the investigation would soon be presented to
a federal grand jury, which, according to the account, "would be
asked to consider bringing criminal charges against some of the
officials." The attribution given in the first paragraph—"law-enforcement authorities"—was repeated dozens of times in the
lengthy story.[21]

Three days later, one of the *Times* stories included the announcement that the Justice Department would "seek to determine if department employees deliberately disclosed information" on the Abscam case. Further, an editorial on that date took
up the matter of naming names prior to indictment and formal
charges. That editorial read, in part:

> Our first reaction is to marvel at the scale of the greed
> attributed to the alleged bribe-takers. . . . Our second re-
> action—perhaps it should be our first—is to caution that
> none of the implicated individuals has been indicted,
> much less convicted of any crime. . . . It is unfortunate,
> though perhaps hard to avoid in so large an investigation,
> that political reputations may suffer before guilt or in-
> nocence can be legally established.[22]

The next edition of the *Times* carried a short article reporting
that the American Civil Liberties Union (ACLU) accused the Justice Department of misconduct in leaking to the press "prejudicial details of bribery allegations." Ira Glasser, ACLU executive
director, complained: "Justice by press release and summary political punishments are methods we should have learned by now
to avoid." Another story in this edition noted that news reports
"have attributed accounts of the investigation to 'law enforce-

ment officials' rather than to either the Justice Department or the Federal Bureau of Investigation."

Two days later, a story by David E. Rosenbaum asked the question: Why would law-enforcement authorities disclose information on an investigation to reporters before it was presented to a grand jury? The answers given:

> One reason is the belief of some law-enforcement officers in the field that charges against politicians tend to be watered down or negotiated away by high-priced legal talent once they reach the Justice Department's headquarters in Washington. If the case is known to the public, it is felt, there will be pressure on the Department for strong action. More ominous, some law-enforcement officers may have a grudge against a politician and want to punish him with publicity even if an indictment is not warranted.
>
> Another reason is the desire of some investigative units for public credit for their work and the belief that, unless they put the story out themselves, officials in Washington will receive all the glory.
>
> In short, law-enforcement officers talk to reporters for the same reasons that politicians, publicists, corporate executives and others do. That is, they have a story to tell, and they want it to be based on their point of view, not someone else's.[23]

The exact motive of the Abscam leakers is not known, but one *New York Times* article might be a clue. The day after the original story, the *Times* reported that the U.S. attorney for New Jersey had recommended against prosecuting Senator Harrison A. Williams, Jr. The prosecutor was reported to have said the evidence against Williams was insufficient.

Because of the morally valid principle that we should assume innocence until guilt is proved, mere allegations of criminal conduct ought never be published. The *New York Times* editor concedes it is "unfortunate" and "hard to avoid" that political reputations may suffer before guilt or innocence can be legally established. That result is a good deal more than "unfortunate," and instead of being hard to avoid it is easy to avoid.

Three basic ethical principles are germane to this case. The first is the principle of protecting the innocent. In publishing allegations by unnamed sources against public figures, the *Times* harmed people who were possibly innocent. The *Times* damaged individuals before knowing whether they were guilty or innocent.

Second, the *Times* violated the ethical guideline that a person's right to a fair trial ought not be jeopardized. Given the current American propensity to assume guilt until innocence is proved, and given the current high level of public distrust of politicians, the likelihood of a fair trial is significantly reduced by published allegations of wrongdoing in high places.

The third moral principle relevant to this case is the Judeo-Christian principle that one should treat other people always as ends and never as means. The corollary is that no one should allow himself to be treated as a means to someone else's ends. By publishing the allegations leaked to the paper, the *Times* became a pawn in the hands of law-enforcement agents who were merely using the newspaper as a means to their ends, whatever those ends might be.

The focus of this case, then, should not be on the motives of the law-enforcement authorities in disclosing information. David Rosenbaum's speculations on the matter are interesting but not really germane to the *Times*'s decision to publish the leaked information. Rosenbaum does raise an important issue for the *Times*, however. He notes the belief of some law-enforcement officers that charges against politicians tend to be watered down or negotiated away by high-priced legal talent before they reach the Justice Department. That theme would have given the *Times* a good story, and it could have been pursued in a morally responsible manner.

Suppose the *Times* editors, instead of publishing the details of the allegations against these officials, had published the fact that they possessed such details and would print them if they were significantly watered down for purposes of a public hearing. The *Times* had news of accusations made against top officials. Once the matter came to a public hearing, if the original accusations were reduced, the *Times* would be in a superb position to investigate the matter further and see what happened. By holding the details of the allegations, the *Times* could still have rendered a critical public service by comparing the first charges with the later ones.

What then ought the *Times* have contained in its release? It should have reported the fact of the leak, the general character of the allegations, some details of the alleged methods of payment (the brown bag and briefcase), and the fact that names were included. There is no reason initially to reveal the identity of the person who leaked the information, or to publish the name of any official against whom the allegations were made.

16. A TELEVISION REPORTER AS FAMILY FRIEND

Marjorie Margolies, a television reporter in Washington, D.C., found herself doubting her own motives while covering a story of a missing 12-year-old boy. Early in the story, she became an ally of the boy's family. The boy's mother, Rose Viscidi, knew that television publicity might help in the search for her son. She gave television interviews, offering friendship in return. Marjorie Margolies had gained an entree. She suspected that the nature of her work helped cultivate the friendship. "It is a fact of television newscasting," she wrote, "that we reporters are known to the public already—in effect, we've already been in their homes, as non-drinking guests at cocktail time."[24]

So she and her camera crew were well treated. "The Viscidis welcomed us—they fed us, gave us places to rest out of the hot August sun, and talked." Then came a report that 12-year-old Billy's body had been found—buried in the Viscidis' garden. Margolies recorded her reaction: "Oh, darn, the worst has happened— Billy's not coming back." But there was also a big side of me that said, "Geez. I've been with the story for so long and this has to happen on a day I was off it."

She and her camera crew rushed to the hospital where Rose Viscidi's husband was being treated for a kidney infection. Reporters were barred. But Margolies decided she could still act as a friend. She persuaded an administrator to allow her to pay her condolences to Rose Viscidi (the administrator was subsequently fired). She found Rose sitting alone in a small room. "I bent down and patted her on the shoulders, and planted a kiss on her forehead. 'Do you have any idea how this happened?' I asked her— as a friend."

Developments in the case were to change Margolies's relationship with Rose Viscidi. Police suspected that another son, 15-year-old Larry, had killed his younger brother and buried his body in the garden. The Viscidis consulted a law firm and were advised to give no more information to the press. Margolies writes: "I was torn. I had grown to like Rose very much. But if I did my job as a reporter, the Viscidis would see me as a traitor. It was a no-win situation."

The news media, which had been focusing on the case of the missing boy, now concentrated on his 15-year-old brother. "Hordes of newspeople and photographers congregated on the Viscidi lawn and on the neighbors' lawns." Margolies wrote, "At times it took on the air of a picnic, people eating sandwiches and drinking Cokes. I felt uncomfortable."

Margolies and her camera crew, outmanned by members of the print media, attempted to capitalize on their strength—the impact of pictures.

> We would wait hours for the chance to get five seconds of usable tape. Some might think this overkill—that especially in a story of this tragic nature we were intruding too deeply. A number of letters to me complained of this. They said we were all too hungry, but others said we were holding back information. There were times when I would say to myself, "I wish I were not going out there again." But every time, we would come back with something newsworthy. There was incredible public interest in the story. It was news. And we had to report it.[25]

Margolies covered the funeral of Billy, being "careful not to disturb the services," but not before delivering a potted plant to the Viscidi home.

Officially, the story hit a lull. Neither the police nor the Viscidis were releasing information. The fact that the suspect was a juvenile further hindered the flow of information. Margolies developed sources and pieced together parts of the story. She explained:

> When you are one-tenth of a television news team, you are expected to produce. There is continual pressure either to produce on that story, or to go on to something else. I couldn't leave the Billy Viscidi story, so I spent every night—after a long day covering other assign-

ments—calling, working sources, into the small hours of the morning.[26]

Margolies found out that the police were sure Larry buried his brother's body, but they were not so sure he did the killing. Billy may have smashed his skull in a fall and Larry, in shock, may have hidden the body to spare his mother grief. Margolies learned that Larry passed a lie detector test. She also learned that Larry was being given a truth serum. Larry's father inadvertently confirmed that report. Margolies told the prosecuting attorney she had the information and was going to use it. She did. The Viscidis concluded she was feeding information to the prosecutor. Margolies asked herself, "Was I crossing the line, inflicting pain on this family with my revelations?"

Finally, police arrested Larry—identified only as "a juvenile." Wrote Margolies:

> I resisted pressure to rush to the Viscidi house that evening to take shots. Another station did have someone out there, knocking on the door and attempting to get pictures of the family. It is a matter of taste—and that, I told my superiors, was something I wouldn't do. When the other channel aired its shots, I took some flak for not being on top of the story—when I clued them in on my scoop that Larry was with a psychiatrist taking a truth serum, they wanted me to camp outside the doctor's office and get some pictures. I refused. My bosses began to wonder whether I had gotten so involved with the family that I could not aggressively go after the story.[27]

When Larry was brought to court, the news media had assembled. Margolies called it a "madhouse scene." But she and her crew scored a coup—they got the only pictures of Larry leaving the courthouse through a back door. "I couldn't feel very proud," Margolies writes. "I felt like a vulture."

Daily the press and television crews waited outside the courthouse for the entrance and exit of the Viscidi family. A bailiff provided Larry with a large bag to wear over his head. On one occasion Rose Viscidi shoved Margolies's soundman and sent him sprawling to the ground. The father, Burton, once passed Margolies's crew and said under his breath, "What do you want me to do—a little jig for you?" Eventually, a county court judge dismissed the manslaughter charge against Larry, holding that the death could as easily have been caused by an accident as by homicide.

And so the case ended. Six months of publicity came to a conclusion, or nearly so. There was one more interview. Rose Viscidi wanted to tell the family's side of the story. She mended her differences with Margolies, and she and her husband gave an interview. It was aired as a five-part series.

The most telling phrase appears after the boy's body is discovered. In Margolies's own words: "Hordes of newspeople and photographers congregated on the Viscidi lawn and on the neighbor's lawn. At times it took on the air of a picnic with people eating sandwiches and drinking Cokes. I felt uncomfortable."

Well she might have felt uncomfortable. The reporters in this scene seemed oblivious to the grief of the Viscidis. The Viscidis were—to everyone but Margolies—merely objects to be reported on; they were not people. Because of Margolies's relationship to the family, she saw them as real people. She could identify with their needs and could be sympathetic to their feelings and frustrations. Thus, according to the principle that we should always treat others as ends and not merely as means, her attachment to the family inclined her to morally responsible conduct—that of restraint and compassion.

Her discomfort stemmed from what she perceived as a confusion of roles: reporter (aggressive, analytical, above the fray) and friend (sympathetic, concerned, involved). It is therefore pertinent to ask whether the attributes usually associated with responsible reporting apply under some conditions and not under others. When a journalist is functioning as a "watchdog" over a government agency, something of an adversary relationship exists. Under these circumstances a hard-nosed, aggressive, assertive, observer stance may be both necessary and good. When, however, these attributes become so ingrained that they spill over into the reporter's job of covering the story of a family's tragedy, they are altogether inappropriate. Under these conditions they only add to the family's grief.

Margolies was torn between the roles of reporter and friend. She gained access to Mrs. Viscidi at the hospital, but she did not exploit that occasion to get special information for the broadcast. In fact, she never used her friendship to get the story. At the end, the interview with the Viscidis benefited the family as well as the station. The friendship served both quite well.

Did she intrude too much into family privacy? There is no evidence in the case that she did. She wonders about that in connection with the information concerning the lie detector and truth serum. But using that information does not necessarily inflict pain. Moreover, there is reason for the public to know that the authorities are administering such tests to a juvenile.

Overall Margolies made no bad moral choices in this episode. Throughout the drama, she continued to define the situation as a family tragedy and not as a "great news story." It is a case where a reporter felt a deep internal, personal conflict. Since she did not use her friendship with the family to get private information, she did not behave unethically. Margolies did not permit her career to determine her actions. In justifying her behavior before a court of reasonable people, Margolies could rightfully claim that in handling the complexities of the two legitimate roles, she followed Aristotle's golden mean. The question, then, is: Should reporters allow themselves to become personally involved with the people on whom they report? Yes, when the situation is essentially one of family tragedy. No, when the situation is essentially adversarial, as in monitoring the performance of public officials.

But these comments only probe into the reporter's responsibility. It could be argued that prurient factions of the public are blameworthy also. At least some news directors perceived the viewing audience as clamoring for every detail. That thirst forced Margolies into a predicament. The institutional pressures were obvious too—either generate some footage and do your share or turn to another assignment. But such inhouse demands cannot obscure the public's apparent fascination with all the details—even though it is not a mad killer or rapist on the loose and thereby does not require up-to-the-minute coverage.

NOTES

1. Hugh M. Culbertson, "Leaks—A Dilemma for Editors as Well as Officials," *Journalism Quarterly* 57 (Autumn 1980): 402–408.
2. Editorial in the *Washington Post*, 12 February 1969. Quoted in John L. Hulteng, *The Messenger's Motives* 2nd ed. (Englewood Cliffs, N.J.: Prentice-Hall, 1985), p. 79.
3. Walter Lippmann, *Public Opinion* (New York: The Free Press, [1922] 1949), part 7, pp. 201–230.

4. John L. Hulteng, *Playing It Straight* (Chester, Conn.: The Globe Pequot Press, 1981), p. 15.

5. Quotations for this case are taken from Robert Woodward and Carl Bernstein, *All the President's Men* (New York: Simon and Schuster, 1974), pp. 205–224.

6. Ibid., p. 210.

7. Ibid., p. 224.

8. This commentary focuses on the contribution of journalists in uncovering Watergate, though measuring the size of that contribution is debatable. Judge Sirica attempts to document that the judiciary (including special prosecutors) were primarily responsible for developing the case and securing the resolution. See John Sirica, *To Set the Record Straight* (New York: W. W. Norton, 1979).

9. Jules Witcover, "Two Weeks That Shook the Press," *Columbia Journalism Review* 10 (September/October 1971): 9.

10. Ibid., p. 10.

11. Ibid., p. 11.

12. Cf. Ben H. Bagdikian, "What Did We Learn?" *Columbia Journalism Review* 10 (September/October 1971): 47.

13. A. M. Rosenthal, "Why We Published," *Columbia Journalism Review* 10 (September/October 1971): 17–18.

14. Edward Jay Epstein, "Journalism and Truth," *Commentary* 57 (April 1974): 36–40.

15. This case is taken from the *Media Law Reporter*, 2209.

16. Ibid., p. 2210.

17. Andrew Radolf, "Anonymous Sources," *Editor and Publisher* 27 (August 1988): 17.

18. Ibid., pp. 17, 19, 33; cf. also Felix Winternitz, "When Unnamed Sources Are Banned," *The Quill*, October 1989, p. 40.

19. A majority of news sources believe that reconsidering an agreement is understandable when journalists are under pressure; cf. Bob M. Grassway, "Are Secret Sources in the News Media Really Necessary?" *Newspaper Research Journal* 9:3 (Spring 1988): 69–77.

20. Clark Mollenhoff, "Rules for Thoughtful Dealing with Confidential Sources" available from the author at Washington and Lee University, Lexington, Va. 24450.

21. Leslie Maitland, "High Officials Are Termed Subjects of a Bribery Investigation by FBI," *New York Times*, 3 February 1980, pp. 1, 26.

22. "Abdul's Sting," *New York Times*, 5 February 1980, p. A22.

23. David Rosenbaum, "The Federal Corruption Inquiry: Questions on FBI Techniques," *New York Times*, 8 February 1980, p. B6.

24. Quotations for this case are taken from Marjorie Margolies, "The Billy Viscidi Story," *The Washingtonian* 14:8 (May 1979): 125–128.

25. Ibid., p. 127.

26. Ibid.

27. Ibid., p. 128.

CHAPTER 4

Social Justice

Historian Charles Beard once wrote that freedom of the press means "the right to be just or unjust, partisan or nonpartisan, true or false, in news columns and editorial columns."[1] Historically the media have been conceived as reflecting the world on their own terms and telling the particular truth the owners preferred.

Very few still have confidence in such belligerent libertarianism. There is now substantial doubt whether the truth will emerge from a marketplace filled with falsehood. The contemporary mood among media practitioners and communication scholars is for a more reflective press, one conscious of its significant social obligations. But servicing the public competently is an elusive goal and no aspect of this mission is more complicated than the issue of social justice. The Hutchins Commission mandated the press to articulate "a representative picture of the constituent groups of society." The commission insisted that minorities deserved the most conscientious treatment possible and chided the media of its day for tragic weaknesses in this area.[2]

Often a conflict is perceived between minority interest on the one hand and unfettered freedom of expression on the other. The liberty of the press is established in the First Amendment and this freedom continues to be essential to a free society. Practitioners thereby tend to favor an independent posture on all levels. Whenever one obligates the press—in this case to various social causes—one restrains its independence in some manner. Obviously the primary concern is government intervention, the argument goes, but all clamoring for special attention from the press ought to be suspect.

In spite of such debate over the precise extent of the news media's obligations to social justice, there have been notable achievements. Abolitionist editors of the nineteenth century crusaded for justice though the personal risks were so high that printing presses were thrown into rivers and printing shops burned by irate readers. A symbiosis between television and the black movement aided the struggle for civil rights in the 1960s. This chapter introduces five problems of social justice on a lesser scale, but involving typical issues of justice nonetheless. In all cases, a responsive press is seen to play a critical role. All five situations assume that genuine social concerns are at stake, and not just high-powered special-interest groups seeking their own selfish ends. Each of the five examples pertains to the poor or disenfranchised—the malnourished in the first case, the racially stereotyped in the second, the homeless in the third, victims of bureaucratic agencies in the fourth, and Native Americans who had run out of options in number five. In all cases, the reporters sense some measure of obligation. Though press response is sometimes extremely weak, no cause is dismissed out of hand by journalists in these situations.

Social ethicists typically show a strong commitment to justice. We assume that principle here and try to apply it in complicated situations. The heaviest battles usually occur in this chapter over questions in the middle range, issues that media personnel confront along with the larger society. For example, don't the media carry a particular mandate from subscribers and audiences, in the same way a politician may sense a special obligation to represent the people who voted for him or at least live in his district? And further, does the press have a legitimate advocacy function, or does it best serve democratic life as an intermediary, a conduit of information and varying opinions? In a similar vein, should the press mirror events or provide a map that leads its audience to a destination? The kind of responsibility for justice that a particular medium is seen to possess often depends on how we answer these intermediate questions about the press's proper role and function.[3]

17. PRESIDENTIAL COMMISSION ON WORLD HUNGER

On 26 April 1980, the Presidential Commission on World Hunger called a press conference. After months of deliberation, its bleak report was being presented to an aide of then President Carter:

> Millions of human beings live on the edge of starvation—
> in conditions of subhuman poverty that . . . must fill us
> with shame and horror. We see this now most poignantly
> in famine conditions, but it is a fact of life every day for
> half a billion people. At least one out of every eight men,
> women and children on earth suffers malnutrition severe
> enough to shorten life, stunt physical growth, and dull
> mental ability.[4]

The commission surrounded its study with chilling accounts of
hunger and distress from Latin America to Africa and Asia. It
emphasized that all other problems are academic if people cannot
eat adequately. Sadly enough, the commission argued, even if food
production should increase 100 percent by the year 2000, expanding populations and harvests going to those already fed will
result in twice the number of malnourished by the turn of the
century. Therefore, the commission recommended that eliminating hunger become the primary aim of the United States' foreign policy in the next two decades. Already, with 35,000 dying
each day from hunger and hunger-related causes, in two days more
die of hunger than the total destroyed by the atomic bomb at
Hiroshima.

The television networks were silent. One White House cor-
respondent attended the briefing, but no story was filed with the
nightly news. The national news magazines ignored it also and
only 6 newspapers out of 1,750 dailies were known to include
wire service copy, and none on page one.

When criticized for the network's callous refusal to carry the
commission's report, ace television news official Tom Jape might
have retorted:

> Issuing a government report is not news. This is a dead-
> letter study which will surely make no difference what-
> soever in political and economic policy. President Carter
> did not even appear personally to receive it. Public aware-
> ness about world hunger may be dim, but repeating ele-
> gant phrases from this document reaches no one. The
> press is not responsible for making world hunger a na-
> tional issue, government officials are. Meanwhile, as we
> report on the world scene, real poverty and hunger will

be shown whenever they are newsworthy and relevant. But don't make pious demands that we hold up paper and ink.

Conventional definitions of news undoubtedly precluded press interest in the report. Studies have no visual impact. Had the president shown up, he might have been photographed with virtually no reference to the report's content. Hunger and poverty will be reported occasionally as actual events, in the context of fleeing refugees, or bloodshed by vicious dictators, or bloated bodies in the Sahara drought. But background, argumentation, political strategy, and ethical debates are scarcely considered news. More wire service lines appeared in 1977 on a South American boy flown to the United States for surgery than on massive hunger in his country. In 1976 more news space went to a live elephant sculpture in Kenya than to reporting starvation on the African continent. Veteran reporter Wesley Pippert kept a log while he was UPI Washington overnight editor, and noted that this penchant toward the visual and immediate is a long-standing practice. He has documented how "newspaper wire editors [prefer] to use the more traditional political stories, many of which, upon examination a decade or more later, proved to have had little lasting impact."[5]

Undoubtedly the president expected little to be done. In that sense the commission issued a dead letter. But could we not argue that the press had an opportunity here to put the president on public record and call him to action should nothing materialize? Otherwise the press's inaction becomes a self-fulfilling prophecy, a conspirator in a pious charade. The report issued a specific recommendation regarding policy—that eliminating hunger become the cornerstone of U.S. foreign relations since malnutrition is seen as a greater threat to world stability than Soviet aggression. Rather than pessimistically contending that nothing will happen anyhow, the press could monitor that recommendation and demand an explanation should it be rejected or fall into disuse.

No ethical system can reasonably hold the press accountable for world hunger. However, to argue as the television reporter did that only government officials are responsible is not defensible either. Assuming that individuals and agencies are answerable within the range of their capacity to effect just policies, the press certainly plays a role in making world starvation a national issue. Studies indicate that

American citizens are not very knowledgeable about hunger and tend to rate their own country's performance much more strongly in this area than is warranted by the facts. Journalists cannot be blamed for all the lack of information and for the ineffective public concern. During the 1980s, millions died from famine in Ethiopia and Sudan; but the causes are enormously complex, including vicious civil wars. However, the press could at least attempt comprehensive presentations on undernutrition rather than showing bits and pieces only. Obviously it aids no one to spurn occasions, such as a commission report, for a full inquiry into the relevant issues and government policy. Paulo Freire notes that social conditions can be transformed only to the extent that reality be codified in symbols that strike our critical consciousness.[6]

The *Christian Science Monitor*, although a slender paper averaging 25 pages, has been an exception to media neglect of world hunger. Its coverage is thoughtful and analytical. The *Washington Post*, while burying the commission report in a brief note in page 18, has achieved a notable record in well-researched front-page articles on hunger in various countries. Other notable exceptions can be cited too. The disturbing ethical question is why such coverage does not appear more regularly, given the magnitude of the problem.

18. BOSTON'S BIZARRE MURDER

On 23 October 1989, the Boston police received an emergency message from a car phone in the reputedly dangerous Mission Hill district: "My wife's been shot. I've been shot. . . . Oh, man, it hurts and my wife has stopped gurgling. She's stopped breathing." The caller broke down crying before police dispatcher Gary McLaughlin could get any clues on his exact location: "You can't blank out on me, I need you, man. Chuck? Chuck? Can you hear me? Chuck . . . Chuck, pick up the phone. I can hear you breathing there, Chuck. Come on, buddy."[7] The police and emergency medical crews had to follow sirens audible over the open phone to find him.

Earlier that evening, Charles and Carol Stuart had left a childbirth class at the Brigham and Women's Hospital.[8] According to Charles, on the way home a raspy-voiced black man jumped in the back seat of their Toyota Cressida at a red light, forced them onto a side street, killed Carol at point-blank range, shot Charles through the abdomen, and made off with her jewelry. Carol's seven-month unborn child was delivered by emergency Cesarean

section but lived only 17 days. Politicians attended Carol's funeral
out of sympathy for this starry-eyed "Camelot" couple destroyed
by an urban savage. Hospitalized himself for over a month, Stuart
sent a farewell letter to be read at his wife's burial: "I will never
again know the feeling of your hand in mine, but I will always
feel you. I miss you and I love you. . . . We must know that God's
will was done. In our souls, we must forgive the sinner, because
He would." He also pulled himself out of bed to kiss his dying
son goodbye.

Boston Mayor Raymond Flynn ordered all available detectives
on the case. Following their only lead, they routinely stopped and
frisked black men in the Mission Hill area surrounding the crime.
Three weeks after the murder, William Bennett, a 39-year-old
paroled convict with a record of violence, was arrested and held
on an unrelated charge. Stuart tentatively identified him from
police photographs, though he could not single him out in a later
police line-up.

Ten weeks later Stuart's younger brother, Matthew, told Boston
police that he had met Stuart right after the childbirth class and,
at his brother's instructions, took Carol's Gucci bag, wallet, and
makeup kit tossed to him from the car's open window, and dis-
posed of them in the Pines River outside Boston. Matthew also
turned over Carol's diamond ring that supposedly had been stolen.
His lawyer claimed that the belated disclosure was prompted by
Matthew's concern that an innocent man might be prosecuted.

On 4 January 1990, Stuart reportedly jumped to his death from
the Tobin Bridge into Boston's Mystic River, having probably
heard that the District Attorney had directed the police to arrest
him. The prior night he had checked in at the Sheraton-Tara hotel
in Braintree, a Boston suburb, and supposedly sometime after 4:30
A.M. he left the hotel, drove ten miles in his new Nissan Maxima,
and jumped. A brief note found on the passenger seat said: "I love
my family. . . . The last four months have been hell; . . . all the
allegations have taken all my strength." In the hotel room, police
found an uncalled list of defense attorney numbers and a colos-
tomy bag Stuart was forced to wear after his surgery.[9]

A Boston television station reported that on the night before
he committed suicide, Charles confided to a family friend that
he had killed his wife for the insurance money. Other reports
based on an anonymous source suggested he was involved with
another woman. Three days after his wife's murder, Stuart col-

lected a $182,000 insurance payment. As a matter of fact, he had taken out extra life insurance on his wife, and in addition to using it for a new car, he purchased a $1,000 pair of diamond earrings. Apparently Charles had shot himself inadvertently in the stomach when a plan to wound himself in the foot went awry. Reportedly he wanted the cash to begin a new restaurant business and believed that his wife and fathering role would deter him.

Boston's mayor was extremely reluctant at first to face up to the issues. But under tremendous pressure, he devoted half of his State of the City message to what he called "a giant fraud on this city. . . . It turned out that we were all victims of a sinister hoax, especially the residents of the good Mission Hill community." And he brought an apology to Bennett's mother: "I've been on this earth 50 years, and I've read a lot of suspense stories, but I've not heard anything as bizarre and troubling as this." Carol Stuart's parents and brother established a memorial fund in her name to underwrite educational scholarships for Mission Hill children.

In the aftermath, a prominent black pastor accused local news media of overkill that whipped up racial tensions with prejudiced stories "of the worst of what black people are supposed to be." And, indeed, the butchery was often sensationalized, beginning with endless repetition of Stuart's desperate pleas over the car phone. Even the generally circumspect *Boston Globe* oozed over the Stuarts as "rich with potential" and a marriage "so loving it warmed even those at its edge." The media's typical interpretive framework had martyred saints set upon by scum, an epic struggle between good and evil. The Stuarts and their tragedy became symbols in a moral tragedy that confirmed stereotypes while the tears flowed. The Boston police, pressured by national headlines, pursued their only lead with a vigor that led to 200 friskings a day in the heavily black areas of Roxbury and Dorchester.

However, the important ethical question centers on the way the issue should be handled once the ruse has been exposed. When the police recovered Charles Stuart's body from the Mystic River, a police spokesman said of his story, "It is not true." Bennett was no longer a suspect and the revelation was greeted with "one part relief and 99 parts outrage." "I'm still outraged," writes columnist William Raspberry, "that Stuart fingered a black man for the murderous deed. Black America is still angry, and our anger is not moderated by the fact that we aren't quite sure where to direct it."[10] The debate is complicated, of course, by the fact that everyone was duped at first.[11] Now, during the embarrassment of having been taken in by Stuart's damnable lie— itself grounded in a perceived Boston racism—what should commentators and news editoralists do to enable the public to put this tragedy in a morally appropriate framework?

Many leaders demanded the resignation of government officials, police administrators, and news editors. But Raspberry himself points in a possible direction. He calls for a response in the Aristotelian mode, quoting, in fact, from the *Nicomachean Ethics*: "It is easy to fly into a passion—anybody can do that. But to be angry with the right person to the right extent and at the right time and with the right object and in the right way—that is not easy, and it is not everyone who can do it." In that spirit, he recognized that the Boston police ten weeks later actually came to doubt Stuart's account and began a stake-out on him as the chief suspect. "Can't we give them credit for not being content to find a credible black scapegoat for the murder? Can't we muster a little gratitude for their refusal to fall for a carefully concocted tale?" Lawyer Howard Alan Dershowitz noted that physical evidence naturally led the police on the trail of a black male: "They don't want the defense later saying they were looking at other people because they had doubts about your case." And Paul Leary, assistant district attorney of Suffolk County, indicated that black residents themselves—though perhaps under police pressure—had led the police to Bennett as the primary suspect. Presumably if the assailant had been described as "John Smith," the police would have searched for him.

Even though it is unfair to do psychoanalysis at a distance, the trail of Stuart's spectacular behaviors, beyond his blaming a black gunman, indicates that Boston is dealing with psychopathic behavior and not merely with a white supremacist who tricked a city with a history of racism into believing his story. Perhaps if Aristotle's mean governs our rhetoric in the aftermath, around the nation we will be more judicious when we call for swift justice without waiting for the facts of a crime with racial overtones. A swirl of questions remain, and ethical theorists will play a vital role in resolving them. At least Raspberry's appeal to Aristotle suggests a place to start.

19. THE HOMELESS STORY

When the weather turns cold in the northern climates, and elsewhere on cue around Thanksgiving and Christmas, the homeless show up in the news.[12]

On 17 December 1986, *USA Today* spread 50 mug shots across two pages, one homeless person from each state. A short quotation from each tried to stir emotions and add individuality to an otherwise bland and nameless group.

During a frigid February Pat Harper of New York's WNBC-TV dressed as a bag lady and spent a week on the streets of Manhattan. With concealed cameras, she filmed a series featuring herself— huddled in a doorway, crying when someone gave her $15, and sitting on park benches next to homeless "friends" drinking alcohol.

In 1968 on New Year's Eve, NBC included poverty as one of four major issues facing America, with 12.8 percent of its people statistically poor. On New Year's Eve twenty years later, however, none of the networks included the poor in its summaries of the year's important stories, even though the poverty rate had increased to 14 percent. Michael Moss, indicating that perhaps there is a compassion fatigue in this country, concludes that reporting on poverty in the United States totals a mere one percent of our news coverage each year—and homelessness is only a fraction of that larger issue. The *Washington Post*, for example, put 28 of its 540-person newsroom staff on the Iran–Contra story but has yet to probe the welfare system in depth.

The *USA Today* spread, "like most other homeless stories in most other papers and broadcasts," ignored the causes and reduced its coverage to the plight of isolated individuals. The WNBC-TV segment exploited "the homeless by not going beyond the pitiful portraits to explore and explain the politics and economics of homelessness."[13] Government policy during the 1980s on public housing, ineptitude in the welfare system, unemployment compensation rules, mainstreaming the mentally retarded, rampant chemical substance abuse, the increasing social disorganization of urban ghettos, and other long-term social issues has not been integrated successfully into homeless reporting.

The occasional serious attempt indicates that such public media as newspapers, magazines, radio, and television can be used to communicate homelessness more comprehensively. The *Dallas Morning News* published a sixteen-page story on Thanksgiving Day 1986 that clarified the kinds of homeless people in their city and connected one segment of them with the state's mental health hospital system. The

PROFILES FROM THE SHELTERS AND

FACES OF THE USA's HOMELESS

Homelessness — once a big city problem — now plagues all 50 states. Oil Belt joblessness, prohibitive rents, housing shortages . . . the reasons vary. The dimensions are tough to track: Birmingham, Ala., estimates from 2,000 to 12,500; Michigan counts 30,000 to 90,000. In many states, the gnawing problem is suddenly made worse by the "new homeless" — families and people under 40. Thursday in USA TODAY: a report on homeless children. These two pages measure the toll on 50 states — and on 50 human beings: (Story, 1A)

ALABAMA

Homelessness is "so visible now," says Karen Carney of Health Care for the Homeless. "There are more people just wandering around."

By Kim Kulish

Sylvia Towns, 44, left her home and 6-year-old son in Cincinnati 12 years ago. "It was something I had to do. I needed a job, and I was tired of Cincinnati." On the road ever since — Atlanta, Chicago, Cleveland, Detroit, Mobile, Ala., Montgomery and now Birmingham. Has high school degree, typing skills. "But I'm a little rusty."

ALASKA

Rising unemployment and falling oil prices have sent many job-seekers packing, while other residents have lost jobs and homes. Estimated homeless in Anchorage: 600-1,200.

By Dan Smith, AP

Don R. Hughes, 44, from Gaston County, N.C., says he is "just an old hobo who came up

between mental institutions and group homes for the past four years. Now, she's on the streets of Norwich — waiting for the state to find her a home. "I don't know what I'll do if these people don't have an answer. I know they said it takes time to do this stuff. I want an apartment and job. I can't live off Social Security the rest of my life. Thank God for all the people that have helped me."

DELAWARE

A new study found far more mothers with children (27 percent) and persons under age 35 (65 percent) among the state's estimated 800-1,000 homeless than in neighboring states.

USA TODAY

Matthew Colatriano, 28, has been living at the Wilmington Salvation Army for two months with his wife and daughter. Family was in an accident in Atlanta two months ago. Colatriano left his construction job to be with them. When he returned, his apartment was gone.

D.C.

In 1986, $7.6 million spent for 10 emergency shelters with 1,113 beds, a 17 percent increase in beds available in '85. For 1987, $8.2 million OK'd for emergency shelter, plus another $7 million for preventive programs.

By Ken Sakamoto, USA TODAY

Dancette Yockman, 33, who lives with her five children in a tent off Waimanalo Beach. Had problems finding home since she was divorced 13 years ago. The children — ages 4 to 14 — sleep on one mattress. She and her boyfriend sleep on another. "I'd die before I would separate my children. I wish my mother were alive. She would never let me stay like this."

IDAHO

Troubles in farming and timber are blamed for worsening homelessness. No statewide estimates. In Boise, homeless sometimes live along the Boise River and in cars.

By Greg De Ruiter, USA TODAY

Don Moseley, 64, in Washington, D.C., remembers when he had an apartment in the shadow of the U.S. Capitol. But since the breakup of his marriage 20 years ago, Moseley has lived on the streets, doing yard work, day labor and housecleaning when he can. He sleeps in a parking garage rather than at a shelter because "people are either drinking, gambling or playing their radios loud."

By Mark Jeremy Karell

William Hyde, 24, says he's turned to alcohol and marijuana because it's so tough on the streets. Now homeless in Atlanta, he gets most of his clothes and food at the Samaritan House shelter. He sleeps there when there's space. "I have a dream that I'll eventually find me a permanent job. I pray a lot. I talk to God. He's the only one I can really trust."

HAWAII

Even though unemployment is low, high cost of living and poor tourist industry wages have led to estimated 1,000 homeless. In Honolulu, families now living on beaches.

INDIANA

Estimate: 20,000 hor in Indianapolis a 4,000 low-cost housi to demolition, rem gentrification in 4]

By Me

David Haddon, 29, c paint, hang sheet houses, fix plumbin weld, wax floors ai — but can't find a Gary shelter, Hadd off 18 months ago, ment a year ago. own place: "I want TV, listen to musi things a man can do private place."

IOWA

Des Moines has ar 1,200 homeless; i shelter in abandor In rural towns, fi families aid displace

By Ann Klose,

Ron Canaday, 51 Moines: "I'm sitting sion waiting to die. living. There's nothi If a car runs ove freeze to death, I People don't unders think we're proud t here, to be winos ani We ain't proud. If I my life over, I wou have hung on to that married. She was thing God ever sent

KANSAS

Wichita estimates less; jobs scarce. A dustry laying off a who failed to find oil to the south are retu

CALIFORNIA

Estimated 50,000-70,000 homeless, most in L.A. and San Francisco. Over past three years, $17.2 million spent on 211 emergency shelter programs.

By Doug Menuez

Victoria Douglas, 37, has a Ph.D., but is on the streets of East Oakland because she has Huntington's disease. "I'm not crazy. But the police think I am. They take me to the hospital where the doctors strap me down and then they shoot me with Haldol."

COLORADO

Energy bust, airline woes and high rents have led to estimated 6,000 homeless. Half are in

Source: USA Today, copyright 1986. Reprinted by permission

By Jeff Mitchell, USA TODAY

122

Nashville Tennessean in March 1984 crusaded professionally and competently for weeks until the state legislature finally acted on behalf of a critical matter for the homeless poor and raised welfare payment levels. Nicholas Lemann wrote a powerful account in the *Atlantic Monthly* of the middle-class emigration from black ghettos, which created a social chaos in its wake that jobs, public housing projects, and welfare reform cannot overcome.[14] The *Chicago Tribune* ran a brilliant "American Millstone" series exploring the socioeconomic upheavels that have been creating a permanent underclass.[15] The *Los Angeles Times* did a front-page story on California's new earthquake law and the prospect that landlords would abandon 34,000 low-income apartments rather than meet the safety standards.[16]

The major news weeklies, networks, PBS, and newspapers—in addition to occasional small-town media—have occasionally moved readers and viewers beyond sentiment to city hall and Congress. But Moss's conclusion suggests how the press must improve to become morally acceptable:

> It's hard to prove that the press's generally superficial coverage of the homeless results in superficial political decisions. It's harder still to link news to public opinion. But it stands to reason that if the public associates the homeless merely with a need for emergency shelter, that's what the homeless will get—a band-aid, and no prescription to cure the illness. . . . By and large, the emphasis is on temporary beds in a dorm. And it's a political truism that, as the weather warms up, the homeless issue will melt away.[17]

In addition to engaging the political and economic infrastructure, reporting on homelessness ought to present authentic human beings and not pathological fragments. Leon Dash of the *Washington Post* needed 17 months in a ghetto apartment to earn the confidence of six families and learn local culture well enough to write precisely about the people and their circumstances. Denis Hamill of New York's *Newsday* could write credibly about Manhattan's Third Street Men's Shelter because he regularly immerses himself in reporting on the disenfranchised. From the days of journalism training in largely middle-class institutions, reporters on the whole find it difficult to experience underclass society on its own terms rather than reducing it to a hotbed of human-interest stories.

The agape principle insists on treating human beings with equal dignity, regardless of their merit or achievements. Persons are valued for their own sake, because they exist, and whether they benefit anyone else or not. Reinhold Niebuhr has elaborated the agape principle in terms of justice, demonstrating that it does not simply signify the commitment of one person to another. Agape in its fullest meaning must be understood as righteous institutions also, both in their policies and structures. In the way governments, schools, businesses, and social agencies are organized, the human beings they serve must have unconditional value—not just instrumental value—for these organizations to be considered just in both their structure and their policies.[18] Therefore, for the press that seeks to be socially responsible, the litmus test is whether it takes the most alienated seriously. Coverage of the homeless that is politically astute and humanly authentic provides a barometer of the press's overall integrity in serving the public.

20. INVESTIGATING PUBLIC AGENCIES

The police detective was passing his outrage on to the reporter. He pointed to the file on his desk. "See how thick the file on that kid is!" he exclaimed. "And look where it all ended. A nice girl is dead and this young creep is in the lockup. But too late."

The reporter took notes. The file did, indeed, seem to indict the community's social service and juvenile agencies. The young man behind bars had been charged that morning with the sex-motivated slaying of a 20-year-old college woman, and he had built quite a dossier in his 18 years. In trouble at age 12, he had been referred to the county mental health agency for counseling. Then came arrests and contact with juvenile agencies, then probation, then the county detention center, and finally a state prison facility. Then came parole, including referral back to the mental health center for therapy. "Every one of those people in the agencies had to smell this coming," the detective fumed, "but they just mealy-mouthed around and wrote up reports with big words in them."

The reporter nodded. "What sort of case do you have against him?" she asked. "I can't give you details," said the detective, "but it's a good case—a damn good case."

Back at the office, the reporter talked with the city editor. She wanted to do a case-study story on the man, a detailed look at what the agencies had done and had not done. At first the city editor objected. "The kid's still presumed innocent, you know. His case has not even gone to a grand jury yet. And we do not report past criminal records—most of his arrests were as a juvenile, too."

"That's just it," the reporter persisted. "We hardly ever examine the performance of juvenile courts and juvenile probation officers—or the mental health center either."

The city editor shook his head. "It smacks of sensationalism."

"No," the reporter argued, "it's not a crime story, really. I'm talking about a public service story. The community should be aware of how these things are allowed to happen. It's a social issue, not a crime story."

"Why don't we wait till after the trial?" the city editor suggested. "It would still be the same story."

"No, it wouldn't," said the reporter. "By the time the case comes to trial, the murder will have left people's minds. They are stirred up now. They'll read every word. Besides that, the detective is really hot right now—he'll let me get into the records. Later he might think better of it."

The city editor liked the reporter's motives. "Okay," he said. "Go to it. But be thorough."

The editor made the morally responsible choice in this case by letting the reporter see what she could get on the story. He did not decide to publish the story, nor was it a decision on which story to write. There are obviously two stories. One involves the individual's life history, and the other concerns the performance of public agencies that deal with juveniles.

This case points to a very real problem. It is extraordinarily difficult to let the public know about the performance of key public agencies—especially those that deal primarily with juveniles—and at the same time to preserve the anonymity and the confidence of minors. Since that problem is very real and very complex, it puts enormous pressure on the journalist. When, as here, there is an opportunity for examining the performance of these agencies, the temptations are all the greater and the possible gain all the more significant.

In this particular circumstance, journalists should pursue simultaneously and vigorously four important goals or values. The first is that of informing the public about public agencies and about individual crimes. The second is the protection of juvenile anonymity. The third goal is that of monitoring public agencies. The public needs to know how the agencies perform. The fourth goal is a critical one for all citizens, namely to guard the Sixth Amendment rights of the accused. The problem is this case, then, is to find strategies that would allow the pursuit of all four goals at once. Most everyone would agree that the goals are valid. Disagreements would come over strategies and tactics for pursuing them together.

It seems obvious that the reporter should not publish a case study on this man before the trial. That would be a serious violation of the journalist's moral obligation to protect the Sixth Amendment rights of the accused and to avoid potentially damaging pretrial publicity, such as the prior record of the accused. If the reporter is correct in arguing that by the time the case comes to trial the murder will have left people's minds, then so be it. She is almost surely wrong in that judgment, however. Regardless of the verdict, this man's story will be timely when the verdict is announced and, in the case of a guilty verdict, may be more timely at that point than before the trial. She should therefore, before the trial, get all the information on him she can obtain responsibly.

Should the paper publish this man's life story after the trial is over, including identifying him by name? Probably so, if doing so can be done discretely. It is a story about a life turned sour, about the forces which impinged on that life, about its tragic consequences. For the local audience, after a guilty verdict, the name would add poignancy to the story without doing significant harm to the convicted. If the verdict is not guilty, there is probably no life story at all. Only the issue of juvenile records would be relevant material, and these do not involve the accusation of murder.

Should she gather and publish the second story, the public service story on the performance of public agencies? Yes. Though it will be a difficult story to do well, the public needs to know about these agencies. The case of this 18-year-old provides an important sense of immediacy (and perhaps a lever for gaining access to the agencies) for the public service story. In order to avoid a wholesale indictment of all public agencies dealing with juveniles on the basis of one failure, the life story of this individual could well *not* be published unless the second story can be written and published simultaneously.

In order to write either story, it is important that this reporter gather information prior to the trial, that is, immediately, while the detective may be inclined to provide it. The really difficult issue here is that of the possible violation of the moral and legal rights of an accused individual to get access to his past record. The fact that he is a juvenile adds yet another ethical dimension. Laws governing access to juvenile court records, while they may help cover incompetence in juvenile judges, are socially significant since they are designed to help in juvenile rehabilitation. Our society simply has not found a tactic for monitoring trials by juvenile judges while still preserving the privacy of juveniles. Though that is another matter, lawyers who practice before juvenile judges likely carry the heaviest moral obligations to monitor judicial performance.

That raises the difficult question of whether the reporter has a special obligation to the irate detective. She wants to gain access to records that in some jurisdictions are protected by law and in virtually all jurisdictions are regulated by law-enforcement agencies. She herself recognized that it is the detective's state of mind that might prompt him to give her access to the documents now—an act that upon further consideration and in a calmer moment he might be unwilling to perform.

Thus important moral considerations arise in the relationship of the reporter to the detective as a key source of information. What kinds of conduct are acceptable in her strategies for encouraging the detective to give her access to restricted records? Should she, for example, stop short of bribing the detective? Yes, since the public need is not that powerful and overriding. Should she ask the detective for the documents? To do so would be to encourage him to violate the rules of his agency (and perhaps to violate the law). If he gives them to her and she uses them, he may later be identified as the source of the leak and thus risk the loss of his job and possible prosecution under the law. How far should she go in encouraging him to incur that risk? If she thinks his state of mind (anger) is such as to blind him to the risk he would be taking, she does have an obligation to let him cool off or to remind him of his risk. Such a claim would be based on the proposition that we not only have a moral obligation to others to prevent harm, but we also have an obligation not to entice others unwittingly to risk incurring harm to themselves.

Thus she and the detective should agree before the documents exchange hands just what obligation each has to the other. In order to enable him to assess his degree of risk, she should tell the detective whether she would go to jail if it were necessary in order to protect his identity as her source. The point is that the detective is the key person in her search for information and that she has special obligations to him.

If the reporter does gain access to the records, then she has an obligation to the accused to treat them as confidential documents. She and the paper must not use them in such a way as to jeopardize the chance for a fair trial for the accused.

There is no genuine moral dilemma in this case. Though this case involves different moral goals and principles, they do not fundamentally clash. Strategies can be identified that enable the simultaneous pursuit of several worthwhile goals in order to meet various moral obligations.[19]

21. TEN WEEKS AT WOUNDED KNEE

One of this century's leading civil libertarians, Zechariah Chafee, Jr., once wrote: "Much of our [national] expansion has been accomplished without attacking our neighbors. . . . There were regrettable phases of our history, such as breaches of faith with the Indians, but these are so far in the past that they have left no running sores to bother us now. . . . We have not acted the bully."[20]

If a distinguished Harvard law professor, a man considered a champion of oppressed minorities, can write so casually about the plight of American Indians, little wonder a tight circle of American Indian Movement (AIM) leaders thought they needed a major event to publicize their concerns. And what better event than an old-fashioned "uprising" complete with teepees, horses, rifles, war paint, and television cameras.

On 27 February 1973, some 200 Indians seized the hamlet of Wounded Knee on the Pine Ridge Sioux Indian Reservation in the southwest corner of South Dakota. Tension had been growing steadily for three weeks, ever since a group of Indians clashed with police in Custer, South Dakota, protesting the light charge (second-degree manslaughter) returned against a white man accused of stabbing and killing an Indian there. Thirty-six Indians were arrested in that melee, eight police were injured, and a chamber of commerce building was burned.

But the problem at Wounded Knee was of a different magnitude. Indians had taken hostages (11 townspeople who later declared they were not being held against their will and who refused to be released to federal authorities) and were prepared to hold their ground by violence if need be. They sensed considerable public support as they traded on sympathy for Chief Big Foot's warriors who were slaughtered there in 1890 by the U.S. Seventh Cavalry. That morbid raid had been the last recorded instance of open hostilities between American Indians and the U.S. government— until February 1973.

As the siege began, news crews rushed to cover the developing story. On February 28, Indians demanded that the Senate Foreign Relations Committee hold hearings on treaties made with Indians and that the Senate begin a full-scale investigation of the government's treatment of Indians. George McGovern, a liberal democrat and South Dakota senator at the time, flew home to try negotiations, but to no avail. Meanwhile, FBI agents, federal marshals, and Bureau of Indian Affairs (BIA) police surrounded Wounded Knee, hoping to seal off supplies and force a peaceful surrender.

But the siege turned violent. On March 11, an FBI agent was shot and an Indian injured as gunfire erupted at a roadblock outside town. On the same day, AIM leader Russell Means announced that Wounded Knee had seceded from the United States and that federal officials would be treated as agents of a warring foreign power. A marshal was seriously wounded on March 26, and two Indians were killed in gunfire as the siege wore into April. Finally on May 6, with supplies and morale nearly expended, the Indians negotiated an armistice and ended the war.

An incredible 93 percent of the population claimed to follow the strike through television. Indian attorney Roman Roubideaux did not think they were seeing the real story:

> The TV correspondents who were on the scene filmed many serious interviews and tried to get at the essence of the story, but *that* stuff never got on the air. Only the sensational stuff got on the air. The facts never really emerged that this was an uprising against the Bureau of Indian Affairs and its puppet tribal government.[21]

Television critic Neil Hickey summarized the feelings of many:

> In all the contentiousness surrounding the seizure of Wounded Knee last winter, a thread of agreement unites

the disputants: namely, the press, especially television, performed its task over a quality spectrum ranging from "barely adequate" to "misguided" to "atrocious." For varying reasons, no party to the fray felt that his views were getting a decent airing.[22]

The lack of sufficient evidence foiled prosecutors at the subsequent trial of AIM leaders Russell Means and Dennis Banks. Defense attorneys Mark Lane and William Kunstler argued that the Indians were not guilty since they were merely reclaiming land taken from them by treaty violations. But the real defense was an inept offense. In September 1974, U.S. District Judge Fred Nichol accused the FBI of arrogance and misconduct and the chief U.S. prosecutor of deceiving the court. After an hour's lecture to the government, he dismissed the case.

The occupation at Wounded Knee was deliberately staged for television. AIM leaders knew that the legends of Big Foot and the recent popularity of Dee Brown's *Bury My Heart at Wounded Knee* would virtually guarantee a good press. Yet no one can reasonably contend it was not a newsworthy event. The Indians at Pine Ridge had just witnessed what they perceived as a breakdown in the judicial system at Custer. The American Indian Movement had tried other forums for airing their argument that 371 treaties had been violated by the U.S. government. The Ogalala Sioux were Western Plains horsemen pushed off their land during Western expansion. And while the tribal militants actually precipitated the siege—though numbering only a small percentage of the Pine Ridge population—traditional grievance procedures through the Bureau of Indian Affairs had been tried and to date had failed. While the event produced several excesses, sympathy for it was aided by heavy doses of folklore and liberal guilt. Yet it was based on a defensible civil disobedience. Joe Ledbetter, a painter in Custer, did not represent the prevailing opinion: "Them Indians learned from the niggers. They got the same tactics." Assuming the distinction between Ledbetter's neurotic behavior and AIM's understandable frustration, media coverage seems warranted.

The moral issue concerns the degree to which the conflicting voices were fairly represented. In fact, the ten weeks of siege produced so many aggrieved parties that fairness to all protagonists became totally impossible. How accurately did reporters cover the law officials ordered to the scene, for example? After the event, FBI agents and marshals were hissed by hostile crowds near Wounded Knee and ordered to leave lest another outbreak occur. And how could the press treat fairly the Bureau of Indian Affairs? Its policies became the lightning rod of attack, catching all the fury born from 200 years of exploitation. An inept Justice Department, abuses from ranchers and storekeepers, racism from area whites, and inadequate congressional leadership also contributed to the situation but received only a minor part of the blame. How does one evaluate where accusations are appropriate and yet recognize legitimate achievements in a raucous setting? The Bureau contended, for example, that it was not responsible for every conceivable abuse and that it had sponsored nearly all the vocational training and employment on the reservation.

But the hardest questions concern the fair treatment of the Ogalala Sioux grievances. According to the ethical principle that human beings should be respected as ends in themselves, the moral ideal entails an account that clearly reflects the viewpoint of these aggrieved. And even a minimum definition of fairness certainly includes all avoidance of stereotypes. A young Ogalala Sioux bitterly scourged some members of the press in this regard for giving their stories the stilted cast of "wild West gunfights between the marshals and Indians." On 30 December 1890, the *New York Times* warped its news account of the original Pine Ridge battle with biased phrases about "hostiles" and "reds." The story concluded: "It is doubted if by night either a buck or squaw out of all Big Foot's band is left to tell the tale of this day's treachery. The members of the Seventh Cavalry have once more shown themselves to be heroes of deeds of daring."[23] After 85 years, many newspapers and broadcasters had still not eliminated clichés, prejudices, and insensitive language.

Russell Means himself complicated the press's rhetorical task with his penchant for quotable but stinging discourse. Years later, in fact, Means was working to erect a monument at the site of the 1876 Battle of the Little Big Horn. In the process, he called for razing the statue of the "mass murderer" General George Custer. "Can you imagine a monument to Hitler in Israel?" he demanded in a news conference. "This country has monuments to the Hitlers of America in Indian country everywhere you go."[24] Means called for a fitting memorial to a battle that "continues to epitomize the indigenous will to resist oppression, suppression, and repression at the hands of European parasites.[25]

Fairness, at a minimum, also requires that the coverage reflect the degree of complexity inherent in the events themselves. Admittedly, when events are refracted through the mirrors of history, separating fact from fiction becomes impossible. Moreover, the Pine Ridge Indians themselves disagreed fundamentally about the problems and the cure. Richard Wilson, president of the tribal council, despised the upstarts of AIM: "They're just bums trying to get their braids and mugs in the press." He feared a declaration of martial law on the reservation and considered the militants Means and Banks to be city-bred leaders acting like a "street gang," who destroy the tribe in the name of saving it.

"No more red tape. No more promises," said Means in response. "The federal government hasn't changed from Wounded Knee to My Lai and back to Wounded Knee." Raymond Yellow Thunder, after all, had been beaten to death earlier by whites and the charges limited to manslaughter by an all-white jury in Custer. Investigations demanded by Congress, the Justice Department, and Senator McGovern had been to no avail. The average annual wage at Pine Ridge was $1,800, with alcoholism and suicide at epidemic rates. Why not action now? Why were the AIM occupiers, speaking for thousands of Indians, unable to get a hearing for themselves? Maybe the BIA had instituted a corrupt, puppet government after all. Where is the truth in all the highly charged rhetoric?

Some reporters did break through the fog with substantive accounts. NBC's Fred Briggs used charts and photos to describe the trail of broken treaties which reduced the vast Indian territory to a few small tracts. CBS's Richard Threlkeld understood that AIM really sought a revolution in Indian attitudes. ABC's Ron Miller laid vivid hold of life on the Pine Ridge reservation itself by "getting inside the Indian and looking at what was happening through his eyes." But, on balance, journalists on the scene did not fully comprehend the subtleties of tribal government nor the historical nuances. Reporters covering Wounded Knee complained that their more precise accounts were often reduced and distorted by heavy editing at home. In any case, after 71 days the siege ended from weariness, not because the story was fully aired or understood. During that period the press largely became an accomplice of the guns and spectre, a victim of media politics rather than an agent whereby a political complaint was sensibly discussed.

Maybe the principle of fairness can operate only before and after a spectacle of this kind, when the aggrieved knock on doors more gently. If that is true, owners of news businesses in the Wounded Knee region carry an obligation to develop substantial and balanced coverage of Indian oppression over the long term, even though such coverage may threaten some of their established interests. Often reporters sensitive to injustice receive little support and thus have no choice but to break stories of injustice when they fit into traditional canons of newsworthiness.

This regrettable weakness in Native American coverage did not end with Wounded Knee. A decade later, 100 miles east of the Grand Canyon, the federal government began the largest program of forced relocation since the internment of Japanese-Americans during World War II. Thousands of Navajos are being taken from a million acres awarded to the neighboring Hopi tribe. The Navajo–Hopi turmoil is the biggest story in Indian affairs for a century, and "a still-evolving issue of national significance." But, Jerry Kammer complains, major newspapers have hurried past "the way some tourists hurry across the reservations en route to the Grand Canyon. They have regarded the dispute and its people as little more than material for colorful features."[26] Violence is a likely possibility even for years after the resettlement is completed—given the sacred burial grounds involved, disputes over oil and minerals, Navajo defiance, and so forth. Periodically banners emblazoned with "WK 73" (Wounded Knee 1973) appear to remind everyone that a battle to the death may be at hand with authorities.

> . . . if federal marshals sent to evict Navajos do battle with an unlikely guerrilla force of AIM members, Navajo veterans of Vietnam, and grandmothers in calico skirts, the press will descend like Tom Wolfe's fruit flies, just as they did at Wounded Knee. They would feast on the violence of a tragedy that was spawned by competing tribes, compounded by the federal government, and neglected by the national press.

And the beat goes on. Because of this historic pattern of failure, observers predict that the confrontations will move to the state and county level during the nineties. Seventy-two Wisconsin counties, for example, have formed an association to resolve the costly and complex jurisdictional disputes between the Oneida Indians and local governments over fishing rights, timber, minerals and water, property taxes, welfare, and education. Jumbled federal policies, many of them as old as the U.S. Constitution, fan the disputes rather than clarify them. Increasingly local journalists face the same contentious issues of social justice brought to a head on the national level at Wounded Knee.

Notes

1. Charles Beard, "*St. Louis Post-Dispatch* Symposium on Freedom of the Press," 1938. Quoted in William L. Rivers et al., *Responsibility in Mass Communication*, 3d ed. (New York: Harper and Row, 1980), p. 47.
2. The Commission on the Freedom of the Press, *A Free and Responsible Press* (Chicago: University of Chicago Press, 1947), pp. 26–27.
3. For further development of the issues, see Clifford Christians, "Reporting and the Oppressed" in *Responsible Journalism*, ed. Deni T. Elliott (Beverly Hills, Calif.: Sage, 1986).
4. *Overcoming World Hunger: The Challenge Ahead*. Report of the Presidential Commission on World Hunger, March 1980, p. 3.
5. Wesley G. Pippert, *An Ethics of News: A Reporter's Search for Truth* (Washington, D.C.: Georgetown University Press, 1989), p. 32; cf. chap. 3.
6. Paulo Freire, *Pedagogy of the Oppressed*, trans. Myra Bergman Ramos (New York: Seabury, 1970), chap. 3, pp. 75–118.
7. Conversations reported by Associated Press writer George Esper, "Death and Deceit," *Champaign-Urbana* (Illinois) *News-Gazette*, 14 January 1990, p. A9.
8. The details and quotations that follow are summarized from Margaret Carlson, "Presumed Innocent," *Time*, 15 January 1990, pp. 10–14; also p. 30.
9. This case was written while revelations continued to unfold. Professors Thomas Cooper and David Gordon of Emerson College are continuing to master the ongoing details. Write them for a copy of their latest work on it; 100 Beacon St., Boston, MA 02116.
10. For William Raspberry's analysis, see his "Death and Deception in Boston: Anger in Search of a Target," *Chicago Tribune*, 11 January 1990, sect. 1, p. 11.
11. Apparently Michelle Caruso of the *Boston Herald* was suspicious of Charles Stuart from the beginning. However, she could not uncover enough evidence to justify a news story identifying him as the assailant. Cf. Christopher Lyon, "The Boston Hoax: She Fought It, He Bought It," *Washington Journalism Review*, March 1990, pp. 56–61.
12. For the examples used below and an overview, see Michael Moss, "The Poverty Story," *Columbia Journalism Review* 25 (July/August 1987): 43–54.
13. Ibid., p. 44.

14. Nicholas Lemann, "The Origins of the Underclass," *The Atlantic Monthly*, June 1986, pp. 31–68.
15. *Chicago Tribune*, "The American Millstone," 16 September 1985, 1 October 1985, 20 October 1985, 30 October 1985, 18 November 1985.
16. Penelope McMillan, *Los Angeles Times*, 23 November 1986.
17. Moss, "The Poverty Story," p. 45.
18. For example, Reinhold Niebuhr, *Moral Man and Immoral Society* (New York: Charles Scribner's Sons, 1932); his *Beyond Tragedy* (New York: Charles Scribner's Sons, 1937); and his *Love and Justice*, ed. D. B. Robertson (Cleveland: Meridian Books, [1957] 1967).
19. Several legal questions overlap with the moral concerns noted in this case. The reporter would, in some jurisdictions, face possible prosecution for even possessing these documents. In nearly all jurisdictions, there are penalties for enticing. This situation is based on a study of ways to avert damaging confrontations between the bar and press. See "Protecting Two Vital Freedoms—Fair Trial and Free Press," *Columbia Journalism Review* 18 (March/April 1980): 75–84.
20. Zechariah Chafee, Jr., "Why I Like America" (Commencement Address at Colby College, Waterville, Maine, 21 May 1944).
21. Neil Hickey, "Only the Sensational Stuff Got on the Air," *TV Guide*, 8 December 1973, p. 34. For details on which this case and commentary are based, see the other three articles in Hickey's series: December 1, "Was the Truth Buried at Wounded Knee?" pp. 7–12; December 15, "Cameras Over Here!" pp. 43–49; December 22, "Our Media Blitz Is Here to Stay," pp. 21–23.
22. Ibid.
23. Arnold Marquis, "Those 'Brave Boys in Blue' at Wounded Knee," *Columbia Journalism Review* 13 (May/June 1974): 26–27; and Joel D. Weisman, "About That 'Ambush' at Wounded Knee," *Columbia Journalism Review* 14 (September/October 1975): 28–31.
24. Daniel Wiseman, "Indians Will Erect Own Monument Over Defeat of 'Murderer' Custer," *Casper* (Wyoming) *Star-Tribune*, 23 June 1988, p. A1.
25. "Statement of Russell Means, Lakota Nation," *Akwesasne Notes*, Summer 1989, p. 12.
26. For details on this story and the quotations, see Jerry Kammer, "The Navajos, the Hopis, and the U.S. Press," *Columbia Journalism Review* 24 (July/August 1986); 41–44.

CHAPTER 5

Invasion of Privacy

The right of individuals to protect their privacy has long been cherished in Western culture. Samuel Warren and Louis D. Brandeis gave this concept legal formulation in their famous essay "The Right to Privacy" in the December 1890 *Harvard Law Review*. Thirty-eight years later, Brandeis still maintained his concern: "The makers of our Constitution undertook to secure conditions favorable to the pursuit of happiness. . . . They conferred, as against the Government, the right to be let alone—the most comprehensive of rights and the right most valued by civilized man."[1] Since that time the protection of personal privacy has received increasing legal attention and has grown in legal complexity. While the word "privacy" does not appear in the Constitution, its defenders base its credence on the first eight amendments and the Fourteenth Amendment, which guarantee due process of law and protection against unreasonable intrusion. The many laws safeguarding privacy now vary considerably among states and jurisdictions. Yet the general parameters are being defined as proscriptions "against deep intrusions on human dignity by those in possession of economic or governmental power."[2] Privacy cases within this broad framework are generally classified in four separate, though not mutually exclusive, categories: (1) intrusion upon seclusion or solitude, (2) public disclosure of embarrassing private affairs, (3) publicity that places individuals in a false light, and (4) appropriation of an individual's name or likeness for commercial advantage.

However, for all of privacy's technical gains in case law and tort law, legal definitions are an inadequate foundation for the news business. Merely following the letter of the law—presuming that that can even be reasonably determined—certainly is not sufficient. There are several reasons why establishing an ethics of privacy that goes beyond the law is important in the gathering and distribution of news.

First, the law that conscientiously seeks to protect individual privacy excludes public officials. Brandeis himself believed strongly in keeping the national business open. Sunlight for him was the great disinfectant. While condemning intrusion in personal matters, he insisted on the exposure of all secrets bearing on public concern. In general, the courts have upheld that political personalities cease to be purely private persons and First Amendment values take precedence over privacy considerations. In recent years, court decisions have given the media extraordinary latitude in reporting public persons. The U.S. Supreme Court in a 1964 opinion (*New York Times* v. *Sullivan*) concluded that even villifying falsehoods relating to official conduct are protected unless done with actual malice or reckless disregard of the facts. The Court was profoundly concerned in its judgment not to impair what they considered the press's indispensable service to democratic life. In 1971 the Court applied its 1964 opinion to an individual caught up in a public issue—a Mr. Rosenbloom arrested for distributing obscene books. Subsequent opinions have created some uncertainties, though continually reaffirming broad media protection against defamation suits. Thus, even while adhering to the law, the press has a nearly boundless freedom to treat elected officials unethically.

Second, the press has been given great latitude in defining newsworthiness. People who are catapulted into the public eye by events are generally classified with elected officials under the privacy law. In broadly construing the Warren and Brandeis public-interest exemption to privacy, the courts have ruled material as newsworthy because a newspaper or station carries the story. In nearly all important cases, the American courts have accepted the media's definition. But is not the meaning of newsworthiness susceptible to trendy shifts in news values and very dependent upon presumed tastes and needs? Clearly, additional determinants are needed to distinguish gossip and voyeurism from information necessary to the democratic decision-making process.

Third, legal efforts beg many questions about the relationship between self and society. Democratic political theory since the sixteenth century has debated that connection and shifted over time from a libertarian emphasis on the individual to a twentieth-century version much more collectivistic in tone. Within these broad patterns, several narrower arguments have prevailed also. Thomas Jefferson acquiesced to the will of the majority, whereas John Stuart Mill insisted that individuals must be free to pursue their own good in their own way. Two of the greatest minds ever to focus on American democracy, Alexis de Tocqueville and John Dewey, both centered their analysis on this matter of a viable public life. Walter Lippmann likewise worried about national prosperity in his *Public Opinion* and *The Public Philosophy*. Together these authors and others have identified an enduring intellectual problem that typically must be reduced and narrowed down in order for legal conclusions to be drawn. Professor Emerson's summary is commonly accepted:

> The concept of a right to privacy attempts to draw a line between the individual and the collective, between self and society. It seeks to assure the individual a zone in which to be an individual, not a member of the community. In that zone he can think his own thoughts, have his own secrets, live his own life, reveal only what he wants to the outside world. The right of privacy, in short, establishes an area excluded from the collective life, not governed by the rules of collective living.[3]

Shortcuts and easy answers arise from boxing off these two dimensions. Glib appeals to "the public's right to know" are a common way to cheapen the richness of the private/public relationship.

Therefore, sensitive journalists who struggle personally with these issues in terms of real people lay on themselves more demands than the technically legal. They realize that ethically sound conclusions can emerge only when various privacy situations are faced in all their complexities. The cases that follow illustrate some of those intricacies and suggest ways of dealing with them responsibly. The privacy situations selected below involve a drinking senator, uncovered spy data, small-town gossip, petty thievery, and a drowning accident. They represent typical dilemmas involving both elected officials and persons made newsworthy by events beyond their control. The information-gathering and disseminating functions are included also.

Woven through the commentary are three moral principles which undergird an ethics of privacy for newspeople. The first guideline promotes decency and basic fairness as nonnegotiable. Even though the law does not explicitly rule out falsehood, innuendo, recklessness, and exaggeration, human decency and basic fairness obviously do. The second moral principle proposes "redeeming social value" as a criterion for selecting which private information is worthy of disclosure. This guideline eliminates all appeals to prurient interests as devoid of news-worthiness. Third, the dignity of persons ought not be maligned in the name of press privilege. Whatever serves real people best must take priority over some cause or slogan.

As a minimum, this chapter suggests, private information in news accounts must pass these three tests to be ethically justified, though the commentaries introduce the subtleties involved. Clearly, privacy matters cannot be treated sanctimoniously by ethicists. They are among the most painful that humane reporters encounter. Often they surface among those journalists with a heart in a recounting of battles lost.

22. THE DRINKING COMMITTEE CHAIRPERSON

Ellen Steenway had covered Washington for 16 years. From the beginning Washington intrigued her. Already as a journalism student she had spent her internship on the president's press secretary's staff. She had accepted a position with the State Department's public relations unit after graduation, until the urge for newswriting sent her to a Washington magazine and then a Washington paper before switching six years ago to her latest assignment on the Washington bureau of a New York paper.

During these professional years she had observed heavy drinking by several public officials, heard well-documented reports on extramarital affairs by members of Congress, watched a cabinet secretary ridicule his wife, and personally knew a photographer who had followed a senator around gay bars. She had never reported any of these private episodes because she believed that these personal affairs were private business as long as they did not interfere with public duties. She also refused to pursue several of these stories for fear she might jeopardize her access to the parties and offices of various politicians.

Then one day Steenway covered the hearings of the Senate Banking Committee when its chairperson was visibly drunk at 10 A.M. He asked rambling questions, interrupted the proceedings, maintained no semblance of parliamentary procedure, and had to be helped from his chair for the noon luncheon. As before, Steenway made no mention of his drinking, even though it clearly interfered with the quality of his committee work and was not merely an after-hour activity. A month later, when the Banking

Committee presented a new bill on the Senate floor, Chairperson Williams was again visibly drunk and Steenway explicitly reported his drinking habits rather than use euphemisms such as "the Chairman did not defend the bill successfully." By any standard of fairness, Williams had now crossed over the line. A major complicated tax bill was involved and its enactment near.

However, Steenway's editor refused to include any reference to Williams's drunkenness. For decades, the paper had a policy that sex and drinking were not mentioned unless there had been arrests with documented evidence available in a public record. In the editor's view, the bill's path through the Senate certainly did not depend on how eloquently Williams defended it. He reasoned that presidential drunkenness might be reported since presidents are responsible for the nuclear trigger, but banking committees could not lead us to World War III. In addition, the editor felt that references to Williams's drinking would sensationalize the story; it was not serious news and he preferred to focus on the issues. The merit and weakness of the proposed legislation were all that really counted to him. And how did she know for sure? Maybe Williams just had a high fever that day.

Steenway reminded the editor that in 16 years she had not included personal matters nor had she reported Williams's behavior during the hearings. "Then why change your practice now," the editor demanded. "Or are you weakening just because so many cheap papers are printing that drivel." Steenway was upset but did not feel strongly enough to resign. In fact, when the same incident occurred several days later, she did not even mention it, knowing that her editor would reject the story anyhow and might even consider her insubordinate.

Both decision makers take their responsibilities seriously. Neither can be faulted for outright carelessness or brazen disregard for standards. There is no evidence that the editor is merely protecting an old crony or is concerned about a possible libel suit. Perhaps the editor harbors an artificial reverence for important officials, but his crusty manner makes that doubtful. Steenway does not appear to want to report the senator's drunkenness simply because this will move a page-12 story to page 1.

In fact, Steenway could be held blameworthy for not reporting the incident. Senator Williams, in her judgment, had allowed his personal habits to affect seriously his acumen. Many readers of her newspaper were from New Jersey, the senator's home state, and they had a right to know. No sensational language had been included, though his incoherent speech, tottering, and occasional belligerence were mentioned in a matter-of-fact tone. Given Williams's long record of drinking, Steenway was convinced the cause could not have been a temporary physical ailment.

The editor also could be considered blameworthy if he chose to do nothing. His company policy was explicit and he upheld the same long-standing reservations, as Steenway had, about reporting on private matters. He understood the press's vast legal rights regarding public officials, but sincerely felt that the content of the bill and its potential effect were the only relevant story here. Not to overrule his reporter would mean violating his conscience and ignoring his paper's definition of newsworthiness.

In the first phase of this case, both the editor and reporter could justify their actions before reasonable people. The reporter has not wantonly invaded the senator's privacy, but limited her account to his behavior on the Senate floor. The editor, meanwhile, invokes a defensible company policy. Given the fact that the senator is not a personal friend of either the paper's owner or editor whom they were protecting, the reporter's story and the editor's rejection can be considered morally acceptable. In fact, both of them appear quaint, given the current climate. The press reported every detail about Gary Hart's liaison with Donna Rice in his Washington, D.C., townhouse and on a boat ride to Bimini; his campaign for the Democratic presidential nomination was finished. Senator John Tower's scandalous personal life was dramatized in the news, and his appointment as Secretary of Defense was defeated. While all boundaries of restraint disappeared with Hart and Tower, the struggle between Steenway and her editor still represents the morally appropriate way to treat the personal affairs of public officials.

The issue for debate concerns phase two—Steenway's behavior after the editor's decision. The fourth step in the Potter Box process now became inescapable. Where were her ultimate loyalties? Steenway was upset, but she did not resign. When Williams was subsequently drunk on the Senate floor, she made no reference to it. As an employee, she chose not to contradict company policy. Her perceived duty to the paper overrode her concern for her New Jersey readers and her own conscience.

23. SPY DATA AND SUICIDE

On Saturday night, 28 February 1976, the editors of the *Dallas Times-Herald* had a decision to make before the 10 P.M. press time. The Sunday edition would feature an exposé that investigative reporter Hugh Aynesworth had been working on for three months. The article would disclose that Norman J. Rees, a former oil engineer who was retired and living in Connecticut, had been a Soviet spy from World War II until 1975. Since 1971 Rees had been a double agent working for the Federal Bureau of Investigation.

Rees had twice flown to Dallas and allowed himself to be interviewed by the *Times-Herald*. According to executive editor Ken Johnson, Rees admitted accepting money from the Soviets for technical information and had "voluntarily undergone polygraph examinations" to substantiate his account.[4] But on that Saturday afternoon before publication, Rees had called the *Times-Herald*. He asked if the story would be printed and if he would be identified. Told yes, Rees responded that such a disclosure would leave him "no choice but suicide."

On Sunday morning the story appeared. On Sunday morning Rees's wife found her husband's body. He had shot himself in the head at his home in Connecticut.

That afternoon an Associated Press reporter talked with Rees's son, John, a 31-year-old junior-high-school teacher. He told the reporter he had informed his mother, Ann, of the story and she was "acting like it's unreal. She didn't know the story was coming out."

After Rees's death, the *Times-Herald* issued a statement:

> From time to time, newspapers receive threats about stories from people attempting to protect their identities. In our judgment, if a story is newsworthy and supported by the facts it is our policy to publish. In this instance it was decided that the story could not be suppressed, even in the face of Mr. Rees's threats.[5]

On March 13, the *New York Times* printed a letter from a reader questioning the *Times-Herald*'s judgment. Wrote Nancy Boardman Eddy of Chevy Chase, Maryland:

I cannot comprehend the thinking of newsmen who, when told that Mr. Rees would kill himself if the story identified him, excuse themselves by saying "the story could not be suppressed."

I'd like to ask, Why not? To what higher moral code do newsmen adhere than we mortals do? The First Amendment may give them the freedom to print the news, but why are they somehow obligated to print knowingly a story that may lead to a man's death, and, indeed, what purpose is served? The arrogance displayed is beyond belief.[6]

On March 31, a second letter was printed, defending the press. John Pyle of Brooklyn wrote: "The threat of just such disclosure has prevented many people from committing just such infamy, knowing that possible disclosure is the price they might be asked to pay. This is possibly a greater deterrent to spying and treason than the law."[7]

Three major choices were made by people at the *Times-Herald*: (1) someone decided the story merited investigation and publication; (2) someone decided to publish it on the Sunday morning originally scheduled; and (3) someone decided to ignore Rees's suicide threat.

What considerations are relevant to each of these decisions? The *Times-Herald* policy was to publish if a story is deemed newsworthy and is supported by the facts. Someone decided that both criteria were met in this case. Presumably the *Times-Herald*, because of two interviews with Rees, had the details straight and judged them newsworthy. It might have reminded readers that when Rees first began working with the Russians in World War II, Russia was an ally! It might have contained publicly useful reports on the forces and reasons that compelled Rees to continue to supply the Russians with secrets long after World War II was over. It might therefore have given a measure of guidance to some other public official who was contemplating disloyal conduct. Thus, judged by the criterion that it contained information that might conceivably work toward the public good, it is arguable that the story may have been newsworthy. It also is arguable that the story contained nothing that the public *needed* to know but only something the public might *want* to know in the form of an entertaining spy thriller.

On the second question (the decision to publish on schedule), several relevant factors enter the picture. This story is clearly one that would keep. Postponing publication would allow time for negotiation with Rees in order to see what part of the information he had given voluntarily in interviews that he now would prefer to keep off the record. Further conversations with Rees might well have protected those things he wished to conceal while simultaneously serving the public's need to know. In any case, the decision to publish now a story that could have been delayed, and to do so under the threat of suicide, appears on its face to be made in indifference to Rees's well-being. The *Times-Herald*'s statement about its reason for publication does not address this question, though in an interview 13 years later, reporter Hugh Aynesworth elaborates on the *Times-Herald* decision: "I was willing to give him time to tell his wife, to move, and the editors agreed to give him time as well. . . . At that point, he said that if you use it, I will have to kill myself."[8]

The third matter—ignoring Rees's threat altogether—provides solid evidence of the editors' disregard of Rees's relatives or the authorities who might seek to prevent him from carrying out his threat. The failure of the *Times-Herald* to apprise someone of the threat is remarkable. Any high-school sophomore should have picked up on Rees's apparent instability, and yet the paper ignored his threat even to the point of not alerting anyone that it had been made. Rees's suicide may not have been ultimately preventable if the story appeared, but it could have been obstructed through several possible actions by the *Times-Herald*. These editors demonstrated a callous disregard for the life of a human being, a life that almost certainly could have been saved simply by some editor's decision not to publish. The paper violated the basic moral principle that we not only should not cause harm, but should prevent it when doing so does not subject us to a risk of comparable harm. As a minimum, the staff should have done everything possible to negotiate with Rees. Sometimes changing the emphasis or clarifying the information removes the objection that triggered the suicide threat. Laurence Jolidon, the metro editor of the *Times-Herald* in 1973 and the last person from the newspaper to see Norman Rees, has concluded correctly that "threats of suicide are extreme examples of what happens when sources feel that the newspaper isn't treating them fairly. . . . You have to keep the dialogue going."[9] He now believes the newsroom has a responsibility to communicate to sources who are threatening suicide that their interests are being taken seriously.

It is obvious, however, that our duty to prevent harm does not mean that every threat of suicide ought to be honored automatically. As Hugh Aynesworth asks: "If newsworthy information was withheld every time somebody [threatened suicide], what would we have in the papers?"[10] The source's reaction is one component but not the exclusive one in deciding whether to publish. One could imagine another kind of case in which Rees is a wealthy community leader respected for his charity, but he controls a blind trust owning slum property in violation of city codes. A poor family dies in a fire. Rees is unstable and distraught; he threatens suicide if his ownership is ever disclosed. If this situation were considered in terms of Rawls's veil of ignorance, publishing the story would be justified. Or, giving the issues an even harder twist, assume this Rees dies of natural causes and there had been no fire. Should his obituary indicate how this rich tenement owner amassed his wealth?

24. A PROSTITUTE ON PAGE 12

Cindy Herbig was a model teenager. A high-school student and the only daughter of a prominent family in Missoula, Montana, she had won a scholarship to Radcliffe. On 17 January 1979, she was murdered in downtown Washington, D.C.[11]

The *Missoulian*, a daily with a circulation of 32,000, carried a page 1 story the following day—a tragedy for the community and grief to her family. The sordid details of Cindy's life in Washington were not part of that first local obituary; indeed, managing editor Ron Deckert knew little until his paper was contacted by the *Washington Post*, which was developing the story to its dramatic hilt: promising, talented teenager turned prostitute stabbed on the streets, presumably in the course of plying her trade.

Cindy's reorientation from gifted musician to streetwalker was first manifest in an uneasy adjustment to the pressures of Ivy League competition and urban Northeastern impersonality. By Thanksgiving of 1976 she was out of college and back in Missoula, soon discontented there as well, unable to find interesting work. Six months later she met a recruiter in a Missoula bar, traveled with him to Washington, and entered the seedy world of 15th and K streets NW. The pimp was known to police, though never arrested. In December 1977, Cindy was convicted of solicitation for prostitution.

All this became clear when a *Post* reporter called the *Missoulian* on Monday, January 22, the day of Cindy's funeral, to get information from the published obituary. In return for the help, the *Post* writer agreed to dictate his story over the phone on Tuesday night.

Cindy's parents, Hal and Lois Herbig, first caught wind of the *Post*'s intentions late Monday when they too were called by a Washington reporter. They were appalled by this encroachment on their privacy and the senselessness of publicizing their daughter's problems. Family friend and Missoula attorney Jack Mudd agreed to help the Herbigs squelch the story. On Tuesday morning Mudd called the *Post* to request a kill. The family had suffered enough, Mudd argued. Further publicity would endanger the parent's health. At least the story should be softened, Mudd contended. The *Post* declined.

Meanwhile, Mudd learned that the *Missoulian* planned to use the story in Wednesday morning's edition. Mudd appealed to Deckert, even making vague references to suicide if the story were printed locally. Deckert told Mudd that a decision to publish would have to wait until the *Post* called to dictate its story later that evening. Deckert hoped the *Post* would not go for the jugular on this one, and he was disappointed when the story came in at about 9:00 P.M. The *Post* lead read: "In the 21 years of Cynthia Herbig's life, she received honors and accolades at a Montana high school, mastered the cello, won a scholarship to Radcliffe College, and finally, came to Washington to work as a $50-a-trick prostitute."

Other parts of the story also bothered Deckert. For example, the fifth paragraph read: "Herbig used to talk freely about her work, telling an acquaintance at a party here recently, 'I'm a prostitute.' " After 19 paragraphs describing Cindy's musical gifts and general modesty, the story flipped abruptly into details of her bizarre other life. The *Post* had actually interviewed prostitutes near Cindy's corner and summarized their comments in the twentieth paragraph: "Several women . . . described her as a bright young woman whose dress was 'conservative' and whose manner with customers was 'very sweet.' 'She charged the going rate of

$50,' they said. A police officer who knew Herbig said he once remarked to her that 'she didn't seem like the type to be working out on the street.' 'She responded with a giggle,' he said."

And finally Deckert came to the last paragraph—the chilling quotation from Cindy herself, as recalled by an unidentified male acquaintance: "'You see, you didn't believe that I worked the street, and now you know that I'm a pro,' said Herbig."

Deckert finished reading the copy and knew that his paper would have to print the story. It had news value, after all, since much of Cindy's death was still a mystery in Missoula. Deckert also believed that her story would serve as a warning to other Missoulian teenagers. The pimp who had recruited her in a bar was still doing business, along with thousands like him. Perhaps Cindy's story would prevent a similar tragedy. Finally, Deckert knew that the story would certainly be distributed nationally and around the region through the *Washington Post/Los Angeles Times* News Service; if he printed nothing, his community would question how often he suppressed other information and on what basis.

In eleven years of journalism, Deckert had never faced this intense a quandary. Local citizens were sure to protest, and in a town of 30,000, it might be hard to find many friends. He decided to run an edited version of the *Post* story on page 12, with local news. The *Post* headline ("A Life of Promise that Took a Strange, and Fatal, Turn") would be dropped in favor of something more sensitive: "Cindy Herbig 'shouldn't be dead,' friend says." Deckert also killed the *Post*'s fifth paragraph, added four original paragraphs from a telephone interview with a Washington detective, deleted the report of Cindy's giggle, and dropped the *Post*'s last paragraph, including the boast, "I'm a pro." Finally, Deckert put the best light on one minor detail near the end of the story. The *Post* had noted that Cindy kept "a book of regular customers, men she thought she could trust." Deckert's version had Washington police indicating that Cindy's "book of regular customers" was "a way for her to avoid the dangers of working the street when she could."

Decker called Mudd at 11 P.M. Tuesday to say that the story would run. Mudd voiced a final plea to hold the story until he could prepare the family.

The Herbigs and much of Missoula were shocked at the intrusion. Businesses pulled their advertisements and the *Missoulian*'s law firm dropped the paper as a client. An advertiser boycott was threatened, though it did not materialize. More than 150 letters appeared in the paper in two weeks, most of them bristling with outrage. *"The Missoulian* has shown the public once more what a tasteless rag it can be and is," wrote one reader. "Whether the story is fact or fiction, it should not have been printed in her hometown newspaper for friends and relatives to read. . . . The *Missoulian*, in my opinion, isn't fit for use in 'the little boys' room.'" At least 200 readers cancelled their subscriptions.

Yet Deckert's final embarrassment would come from his own staff. Editorial page editor Sam Reynolds, two days after the story, wrote his own letter, headed "A personal note," which began: "It was with shame that I read the story about Cindy Herbig—shame for the newspaper profession, shame for once to be a part of it, shame above all for inflicting additional hurt where hurt already had visited more than enough." Reynolds reviewed for readers the agony of the *Missoulian* decision, then blasted the *Post* story as "blatant sensationalism—the worst of journalism—and my sensation is disgust." Reynolds was also not happy (though he did not say so in print) that Deckert had edited his signed column to soften the mortar shells falling on his own position.

In the aftermath, businesses that had pulled advertising returned to the paper, Hal and Lois Herbig were given the privilege of a last printed letter on the subject, and the *Missoulian*'s publisher admitted that the paper could have handled the story better by honoring Mudd's request to postpone publication for a day. But Deckert insisted in a later interview that if he had that day to live over again, his decision would probably be the same. Under deadline pressure, journalists do the best they can to get the news out, even news that hurts.

The clash between the outrage of the Herbigs' supporters and Ron Deckert's news judgment arises from the disagreement about whether news value for the community outweighs the invasion of privacy for those personally involved. Deckert's utilitarian framework, in effect, argued that the benefit for the many outweighed the bite to the few. If one applied the agape principle, however, what would be considered

morally appropriate behavior? Agape is particularly suitable because
it has a strong view of human personhood, and in order to understand
the need for a private inner self in its deepest sense, it requires a sophisticated understanding of the human psyche.

Certainly the agapic mind would eliminate the "fallen angel"
story as totally unwarranted intrusion. Why should victims of circumstance endure punishment through a sensational account? The pimp-
in-Missoula angle received only eight words in Decker's edited version
of the *Washington Post* release. Most of the gory details about the stab
wounds were included—the number, size, and location on the body.
The small-town, rural-virgin-off-to-Ivy-League-and-big-city slant
framed the account. All of that was an indecent, sensational, obdurate
invasion of privacy. While Decker did nothing illegal, his willingness
to follow the timing and the reportorial framework of the *Washington
Post* was irresponsible.

However, the opposite extreme—reporting nothing—is ruled out
as well. Agape would suggest that the *Missoulian* had a social responsibility to advance citizen understanding, to investigate pimps and police in Missoula, to get that local story and take whatever additional
time might be necessary to do so. When dealing with Cindy Herbig,
there are public dimensions to the case; it is not solely a matter of
innocent victims of tragedy. A compassionate story would inspire readers to confront the community's problem with unwelcome pimps in
local bars and would give the police a public forum in which to fulfill
their role effectively. In the process of developing the larger context,
Cindy could conceivably be mentioned by name, if doing so were ma-
terially relevant to the bar-pimp focus and if it could possibly be judged
as a healing story by the Herbigs. But that substantive flavor contrasts
sharply with the street-walking prostitute tone which actually appeared.

The argument from agape can be summarized in this fashion:
Protecting privacy is a moral good. Being able to control information
about ourselves is essential to our personhood. However, while being
a precondition for maintaining a unique self-consciousness, privacy
cannot be made an absolute since we are cultural beings with responsibilities in the social and political arenas. We are individual beings,
therefore we need privacy; we are social beings, therefore we need
public information about each other. Since we are personal, eliminating privacy would eliminate human existence as we know it; since we
are social, elevating privacy to absolute status would likewise render
human existence impossible.[12]

25. NAMING A SHOPLIFTER

The caller's request was a familiar one; in fact, the editor turned down such requests every week or two. Sometimes callers shouted at him. Sometimes they spoke in a voice that trembled. This caller was one of the latter. The editor knew from experience that the conversation would end in tears.

The woman at the other end was repeating herself: "Really, I am *not* that sort of person," she said. "All my life, I've never done anything against the law; I've never even had a traffic ticket."

"I believe you," the editor said, "and it's a shame, but we'll have to use your name. Our policy is that we print the names of people arrested for shoplifting. We have to be consistent."

"But if you publish my name I won't be able to face anybody; I just won't ever. I have children in grade school and it would be terrible for them. And I've just been through a divorce; that was bad enough. Please, isn't there something you could do? Why is it so important to print my name?"

The editor always had a hard time answering that question. "Arrests are part of the public record," the editor began. "They are public because our justice system is conducted in the open—that protects everybody from secret arrests."

"But I *want* my arrest to be secret," the caller said. "Why would it hurt to leave out my name? No one would know."

"I would know," said the editor. "I would remember when I received another call like yours. And if I said okay to you, then to be fair I'd have to say okay to the next person, and the next one after that."

"But I've paid so much already," said the caller, her voice trembling more than ever. "I've never, never done anything like that. Never. I don't know what came over me. I just saw that little bear and my son collects bears and I didn't have any money and I put it in my purse. The minute I did, I felt just terrible. And then they arrested me and I was so ashamed and embarrassed. And if you run my name, then my friends will know, and the people I work with, and the teachers at school, and my children's friends. If you run my name I swear I'll have to move away from this town. I just couldn't stand it. Oh, please!"

The tears began.

"I'm really sorry," the editor said. "I really am."

The most obvious and immediate response is to consider this newspaper's practice harmful. Naming persons charged with lesser offenses
inflicts undue harm to the people involved. Publishing the final court
decision—if the initial story was reported at the time of arrest—would
be a useful step in protecting reputations; but even that is not an adequate solution. Readers might see only the original story and not the
final verdict. Meanwhile mere association with crime generates suspicion among acquaintances and fuels gossip. Not reporting routine
charges when they are filed eliminates trivia from the newspaper and
avoids an unfair presumption of guilt toward the accused. Why report
minor charges such as shoplifting, petty theft (under $50), trespassing,
traffic violations? On the grounds of compassion, why should coverage
not be restricted to trials and convictions where sentences include a
jail term?

This is a hard-luck story accompanied by an honest request to
prevent further pain. The children will be hurt and teased because of
the undesirable notoriety of their mother. Employment may become
more difficult since she now carries a social stigma. The editor justifies
his action by a general appeal to newsworthiness; however, it can be
reasonably assumed that he upholds the practice of publishing names
because such public gossip enhances the human-interest value and
attracts readers.

Probing more deeply, the ethical issue may not be as simple and
straightforward as inflicting unnecessary harm. The editor defends
himself somewhat weakly by claiming he must be consistent regarding
arrests and by noting that the judicial system ought to be conducted
in the open. Yet the seeds of an important principle in social ethics
lie underneath his comments. This case involves crime and therefore
leads us to a different line of argument than when dealing with innocent victims of tragedy, celebrities, or temporary heroes.

Does not the public interest demand that justice be administered
without favoritism? If names are suppressed, what will prevent society
from concluding that this paper acts arbitrarily? Selective reporting of
crimes can lead to abuses and, even if it is handled fairly, the public
does not have an accurate picture of crime as a social phenomenon in
its community.

Moreover, thorough publication safeguards the public from abuse
by officials and thus protects the general liberty. Knowledge by the
police that their arresting power is subject to public scrutiny provides
an important boundary for them. Society has an abiding interest in
knowing exactly who the police have arrested, why they have arrested

them, and what has happened to them. The public rarely goes to police stations and courts; its access to such information is through the eyes of the press. While risking unwarranted abuse of personal reputations, the larger concern should be that nothing brings the administration of justice into disrepute. An open system of justice suggests that publishing names, with extremely rare exceptions, is superior to the general rule of not publishing names. One could argue that reporters should do a more analytical reporting of crime in order to provide the public with an accurate account of the problems it faces. Such aggressive reporting, however, would inevitably include names even though the stories went beyond merely listing the bare details about the person and the offense. If they are to aid in protecting the general welfare, the channels of communication ought to be open and free, and in principle report all information without arbitrary selection.

26. Dead Body Photo

John Harte was the only photographer working on Sunday, July 28, at the *Bakersfield Californian*. After some routine assignments, he heard on the police scanner about a drowning at a lake 25 miles northeast of Bakersfield. When he arrived on the scene, divers were still searching for the body of five-year-old Edward Romero, who had drowned while swimming with his brothers.

The divers finally brought up the dead boy, and the sheriff kept onlookers at bay while the family and officials gathered around the open body bag. The TV crew did not film that moment, but Harte ducked under the sheriff's arms and shot eight quick frames with his motor-driven camera.[13]

The *Californian* had a policy of not running pictures of dead bodies, so managing editor Robert Bentley was called into the office on Sunday evening for a decision. Concluding that the picture would remind readers to be careful when kids are swimming, Bentley gave his approval. On Monday, Harte transmitted the picture over The Associated Press wire "after a 20-minute argument with an editor who was furious we ran the picture . . . and accused [Harte] of seeking glory and an AP award."[14]

Readers bombarded the 80,000 circulation daily with 400 phone calls, 500 letters and 80 cancellations. The *Californian* even received a bomb threat, forcing evacuation of the building for 90 minutes.

Source: The Bakersfield Californian, *29 July 1985, p. 1. Photo by John Harte. Reprinted by permission.*

Distraught by the intensity of the reaction, Bentley sent around a newsroom memo admitting that "a serious error of editorial judgment was made. . . . We make mistakes—and this clearly was a big one." He concluded that their most important lesson was "the stark validation of what readers—and former readers—are saying not just locally but across the country: That the news media are seriously out of touch with their audiences."[15]

For photographer John Harte, Bentley's contrition was "disappointing to me and many of my co-workers." And editorial page editor Ed Clendaniel of the *Walla Walla* (Wash.) *Union Bulletin* was not apologetic either about running it in his paper, even though it was out of context. "First, the foremost duty of any paper is to report the news," he argued. "One of the hard facts of life is that the world is filled with tragic moments as well as happy moments.... Second, we believe the photograph does more to promote water safety than 10,000 words could ever hope to accomplish."

Later Bentley entered Harte's photo in the Pulitzer Prize competition. "I really don't see any contradiction," he explained. "I think the photograph should never have been published.... But the Pulitzer Prize is given for journalistic and technical excellence. It is not given for reader approval."

Michael J. Ogden, executive editor of the *Providence Journal-Bulletin*, condemns photographs that capitalize on human grief:

I can understand the printing of an auto accident picture as an object lesson. What I can't understand is the printing of sobbing wives, mothers, children.... What is the value of showing a mother who has just lost her child in a fire? Is this supposed to have a restraining effect on arsonists? I am sure that those who don't hesitate to print such pictures will use the pious pretense of quoting Charles A. Dana's famous dictum that "whatever the Divine Providence permitted to occur I was not too proud to print." Which is as peachy a shibboleth to permit pandering as I can imagine.[16]

But Ogden is a rare editor. Every day in newspapers and on television, photographs and film footage emphasize grief and tragedy. Though Harte's photo did not win the Pulitzer, in fact, professional awards are regularly given to grisly pictures regardless of whether they pander to morbid tastes.

Defending photos of this type usually centers on newsworthiness. The broken-hearted father whose child was just run over, a shocked eight-year-old watching his teen-age brother gunned down by police, the would-be suicide on a bridge—all pitiful scenes that communicate something of human tragedy and are therefore to be considered news. Photojournalists sum up a news event in a manner the mind can hold, capturing that portrayal "rich in meaning because it is a trigger image of all the emotions aroused by the subject."[17] Harte in this case acted as an undaunted professional, fulfilling his role as reporter on everyday affairs including the unpleasantries. From the photographer's framework, to capture the newsworthy moment is an important self-discipline. Photographers are trained not to panic but to bring forth the truth as events dictate. They are schooled to be visual historians, and not freelance medics or family counselors.

On what grounds, however, can the photographer's behavior be condoned in the Bakersfield drowning? The principals at the scene tried to prevent him from intruding, though, it should be granted, the authorities' judgment is not always correct. The warning bell thesis was generally used by the picture's proponents, asserting that this photo will make other parents more safety conscious. However, this utilitarian appeal to consequences has no genuine basis in fact.[18] Perhaps in the name of reporting news, the photojournalist in this case is actually caught in those opportunistic professional values that build circulation by playing on the human penchant for morbidity.

No overarching purpose emerges that can ameliorate the direct invasion of privacy and insensitivity for these innocent victims of tragedy. In all jurisdictions, the reporting of events of public concern involves no legal issue of privacy invasion. But it is here that the photographer should consider the moral guideline—that suffering individuals are entitled to dignity and respect, despite the fact that events may have made them part of the news.

Photojournalism is an extremely significant eyewitness of our humanity and inhumanity. In pursuing its mission, the ethical conflict typically revolves around the need for honest visual information and for respecting a person's privacy. Bob Greene of the *Chicago Tribune* is only slightly hyperbolic in calling the Harte picture "pornography." "Because of journalistic factors they could not control," he wrote, "at the most terrible moment of their lives" the Romeros were exposed to the entire country.[19] The older brother's hysteria for not watching his little brother closely enough is presented without compassion before an audience who had no right to become a participant in this traumatizing event for a suffering family. And even those who find the photo acceptable are upset by the context; that is, by the *Californian's* printing it right next to a headline about teen killings by a satanic cult.

NOTES

1. *Olmstead* v. *United States*, 277 U.S. 438, 478 (1928). Brandeis dissenting.
2. *Briscoe* v. *Reader's Digest Association*, 4 Cal. 3d 529, 93 Cal. Reptr. 866, 869 (1971).
3. Thomas I. Emerson, *The System of Free Expression* (New York: Vintage Books, 1970), p. 545.
4. For a full account of this episode, see the *Dallas Times-Herald*, 29 February 1976, and the *New York Times*, 1, 2, 5, 13, 31 March 1976. For a similar suicide story, see Leslie Brown, "Seattle's Press and the case of the Judge Who Killed Himself," *Columbia Journalism Review* 27 (January/February 1989):31–33; in this case, reporter Duff Wilson did not face an explicit suicide threat from Judge Little over an investigation into his sexual activities with juvenile offenders.
5. "Spy Said He'd Kill Himself If Exposed, Then Did So," *New York Times*, 2 March 1976, p. 1.
6. Letter to the Editor, "Of News & Death," *New York Times*, 13 March 1976, p. 24.
7. Letter to the Editor, "Espionage's Price," *New York Times*, 31 March 1976, p. 40.
8. Deni Elliott, "How to Handle Suicide Threats," *Fineline* 1:7 (October 1989):1.
9. Ibid., p. 4.
10. Ibid., p. 1
11. Details in Jack Hart and Janis Johnson, "Fire Storm in Missoula," *Quill* 67 (May 1979): 19–24.
12. For further background on the ethics of privacy, see Louis Hodges, "The Journalist and Privacy," *Social Responsibility: Journalism, Law, and Medicine*, vol. 9 (Lexington, Va: Washington and Lee Monograph, 1983), pp. 5–19.
13. "Graphic Excess," *Washington Journalism Review* 8:1 (January 1986): 10–11.
14. For the quotations and details in this case, unless otherwise noted, see "Grief Photo Reaction Stuns Paper," *News Photographer*, March 1986, pp. 16–22.
15. H. Eugene Goodwin, *Groping for Ethics in Journalism*, 2nd ed. (Ames: Iowa State University Press, 1987), pp. 211–213.
16. John Hohenberg, *The News Media: A Journalist Looks at His Profession* (New York: Holt, Rinehart and Winston, 1968), p. 212.

17. Harold Evans, *Pictures on a Page* (Belmont, Calif.: Wadsworth, 1978), p. 5.

18. Obviously beneficent results do sometimes follow, as in Stanley Foreman's *Boston Herald-American* photos of two girls falling from a broken fire escape.

19. Bob Greene, "News Business and Right to Privacy Can Be at Odds," 1985–86 Report of the SPJ-SDX Ethics Committee, p. 15.

PART 2

PERSUASION

At its deepest level, all communication is persuasive. We do not speak unless we believe someone will listen. When we write or speak we assume our audience will pay enough attention to understand the meaning. Persuasion is a permanent dimension of every message. We always try to influence in at least some minimal form. In that sense, persuasion is unavoidable and cannot be a word of reproach.

The communication process is not the transmission of data from a source to receivers, akin to a railroad car hauling cargo from one destination to another. James W. Carey argues for a ritual view instead; he substitutes the behavioral effects mode for a transactional one in which communication is a complicated attempt to negotiate meaning.[1] Through the communication process we celebrate, draw and repel, spar with one another, create societies, and express our values. Given that richer definition, communication implies persuading, intention, the search for a listening ear.

In fact, the French social philosopher Jacques Ellul warns us against a simplistic distinction between information and propaganda.[2] We are beguiled, he suggests, into thinking that truthful and accurate information safely belongs to the news media, while advertising and public relations are propagandistic in character. We, therefore, are taught to resist attempts at indoctrination through the latter, while welcoming the respectable information of news which feeds our reasoning minds. Ellul refuses to accept this dichotomy and contends correctly that all communication faces the same problem, though in varying degrees—how to avoid manipulation and allow maximum freedom of response. Or, in Martin Buber's terms, how can communication

159

of every variety promote I-Thou relationships and minimize I-It coercion.[3] The issue is not eliminating persuasion, but ensuring that it is socially responsible.

While all communication is persuasive, certain genres exhibit this feature more intensely than others. In Chapters 6–12 following, two institutional settings are examined where persuasion is not just evident in the communication process but paramount. In the narrow sense—that persuasion "induces change by convincing a person through the merit of the reasons put forward"[4]—advertising and public relations are two prominent organizational systems in which this purpose is fulfilled. They are designed specifically to produce favorable results. Their prime objective is to motivate, to make something happen.

Obviously the persuasive dimension comes to a head in other places also—families persuade each other regarding appropriate lifestyles, teachers convince their students of a scientific theory in the classroom, ministers urge their parishoners to serve the community, and employees ask for better working conditions. All such persuasive contexts and more are routinely studied for greater clarity about the nature of persuasion and to examine the ethical issues involved. But few social arenas are more dramatic and productive for investigation than advertising and public relations.

Persuasion is a time-honored function of the mass media; many of the debates are similar in principle to those facing the news and entertainment functions as well. In a twist on Marcy Darnovsky, the media in all their functions systematically "attempt to win people's hearts and minds"; the concern for ethics are those practices "that warp the heart and cripple the mind."[5]

NOTES

1. James W. Carey, "A Cultural Approach to Communication," in his *Communication as Culture* (Boston: Unwin Hyman, 1988), ch. 1.
2. Jacques Ellul, "Information and Propaganda," *Diogenes: International Review of Philosophy and Humanistic Studies* (June 1957): 61–77; cf. *Propaganda*, trans. Konrad Kellen (New York: Alfred A. Knopf, 1965).
3. Martin Buber, *I and Thou* (New York: Scribner's, 1958).
4. Stanley I. Benn, "Freedom and Persuasion," *Australasian Journal of Philosophy*, 45 (December 1967): 265–66.
5. Marcy Darnovsky, "The Propaganda Environment," *Propaganda Review*, no. 5 (1989): 8.

Advertising

Over the years there have been a great many nasty things said about advertising and its people. For example, after reviewing a number of novels about the advertising business published in the post-World War II period, historian Stephen Fox concluded:

> From these dozen novels came a remarkably consistent picture of the advertising world: false in tone, tense in pace, vacant and self hating, overheated and oversexed.[1]

The picture was no more flattering in the decades before, or since, in spite of such relatively benign treatments in more recent films such as *Nothing in Common* and television shows such as *thirtysomething*.

- In 1976 economist Robert Heilbroner called advertising "the single most value-destroying activity of business civilization." Reviewing his remarks more than 10 years later, he found no reason to recant.[2]
- After an extensive investigation of "all North American authors known to have written on the culture of advertising," advertising historian Richard Pollay concluded:

> They see advertising as reinforcing materialism, cynicism, irrationality, selfishness, anxiety, social competitiveness, powerlessness and/or loss of self respect.[3]

- Or consider this thought by the late Howard Gossage, a member of the Advertising Copywriters Hall of Fame and one of advertising's most penetrating gadflies: "To explain responsibility to advertising people is like trying to convince an eight-year-old that sexual intercourse is more fun than a chocolate ice cream cone,"[4] or the observation of a current practitioner, confiding in correspondence that "The dominant ethic—particularly in times such as these when the business is shrinking—is to keep or get the business at all costs."

■ A mid-1980s Gallup poll of the public on "honesty and ethical standards" listed a category called "Advertisers" third from the bottom of 25 occupations, just below labor union leaders but above insurance salesmen and car salesmen, and a 1989 survey of business executives placed advertising executives number 8 among 16 professions.[5]

THE LARGER ETHICAL CLIMATE

Now, it could be contended with considerable force that advertising (as well as the other areas of interest in this book—journalism, public relations, and the entertainment industry) is hardly alone in the ethics jungle. By way of sample:

■ A seven-page article titled, "A Nation of Liars?" appeared in *U.S. News & World Report* in early 1987.[6]

■ A *Time* cover story asked, "What Ever Happened to Ethics?" later in the same year.[7]

■ In early 1988 Professor David Rankin, editorializing in *Newsweek* under the title "A State of Incivility," offered these thoughts:

We have come to accept as normal broken contracts and broken dates; public display of pornography and profanity and, I fear, even theft.[8]

■ In a column commenting on the host of ethical confrontations during drought-stricken mid-1988, involving politicians, TV evangelists, inside traders, Pentagon officials, defense contractors, and even West Point cadets, columnist Cal Thomas observed, "the water table for ethical behavior is sinking faster than the Mississippi River."[9]

- In relation to the general business climate, a 1987 poll of *Industry Week* readers revealed that 30.6 percent felt business ethics had declined in the preceding two years, while only 23.2 percent saw an improvement.[10]

Thus advertising can be categorized as being in good (or bad) company on the larger societal ethical scale as well as being within the realm of general business practice. This perspective is not, of course, a new one. In 1927, advertising pioneer Bruce Barton observed:

> If advertising persuades some men to live beyond their means, so does matrimony. If advertising speaks to a thousand in order to influence one, so does the church. If advertising is often garrulous and redundant and tiresome, so is the United States Senate.[11]

THE BUSINESS PERCEIVES ITSELF

Rather than taking Barton's we're-no-worse-than-the-other-guy position, the trade organizations that represent the advertising business frequently emphasize what they perceive as advertising's *contributions* to society. Apart from the common litany of serving the sovereign consumers and lubricating the economy, they point to the following:
   "Enforced" social responsibility through:

- Codes of advertisers, media, agencies, and trade organizations.[12]
- A much respected National Advertising Review Board.
- A Federal Trade Commission that is still a presence in spite of its relative inactivity during the Republican 1980s.
- A more combative Food and Drug Administration, which has become increasingly concerned as advertisers are tempted to move toward health claims with assertions about "natural" ingredients, fiber content, and the like.
- A downright feisty group of state attorneys general, who have already attempted to establish national guidelines for airline and rental car advertising, in addition to their often robust activities within individual states.

   "Voluntary" social responsibility through:

- The Advertising Council, generating more than $1 billion on be-
  half of crime prevention, arresting high blood pressure, the United
  Negro College Fund, AIDS education, and hundreds of other
  causes.
- The "Partnership for a Drug Free America," with its $310 million
  in donated space and time since mid-1987 through early 1990.
- The American Association of Advertising Agencies' $25 million
  effort to combat functional illiteracy.
- Virtually daily goodwill efforts on the part of advertisers, agencies,
  and media for a host of state, regional, and local concerns. (The
  Leo Burnett agency reported that in 1987 it devoted 6,639 hours
  to *pro bono* projects for 46 organizations.[13])

THE ETHICAL BATTLEFIELD

It seems clear, then, that in order to understand the dimensions of the
ethics cases in this section, it is first necessary to explore why these
seemingly contradictory visions of advertising thought and practice
exist. Some understanding may be found in the essential elements of
advertising practice. As William Leiss and associates observe in their
provocative work *Social Communication in Advertising*:

> Because it stands at the intersection of industry, commu-
> nications, and group interactions, advertising can come
> under attack from anyone who is upset about any feature of
> these three domains.[14]

Thus advertising is—by its nature—positioned to affect, and be
affected by, "industry" (marketing practices), "communications" (the
mass media), and "group interactions" (stereotyping), all fertile fields
for ethical encounter. Pursuing this perspective, there are at least seven
areas of potential ethical confrontation that are *inherent in advertising
practice* and that need to be understood before we address cases that
emerge from any of them. They form the backcloth against which
many of the major subjects of advertising and its ethical performance
can be seen with greater clarity.

   1. *The advertising business is rationalized predominantly by
classical liberal assumptions.* The basic assumptions of self-interest,

the individual as a competent decision maker, and the virtue of competition leading ultimately to the good of all concerned through a "natural harmony of self interests" are central to the classical liberal idea system, and of the ensuing ideology of the market system within which advertising thrives.

If one *accepts* these positions (as practitioners generally do), there will be a tendency to endorse the concepts of (1) consumer sovereignty and (2) advertising as a mirror, a socially passive force. If, however, one *questions* these positions (as critics generally do), there will generally be a tendency to accept the concepts of (1) the *advertiser* as sovereign, with the consumer open to manipulation and (2) advertising as a shaper/selective reinforcer, a socially influential force.

Advertising practitioner Don Peppers recently caught the confrontational dimensions of these assumptions when observing:

> A free market economy undisciplined by a common set of ethical standards can easily become an economy of greed.[15]

But, it may be argued, under the classical liberal assumptions of the market, self-interest (greed) *does* represent "a common set of ethical standards." The ethical battle lines are, then, quite fundamental indeed.

2. *The advertising message is one-sided communication, with the inherent potential of deception by omission.* In his important work, *The Making of Modern Advertising*, historian Daniel Pope addressed the issue of the bias of the advertising message:

> For advertising to play a large part in market strategy, consumers had to be willing to accept this kind of self interested persuasion as a tolerable substitute or compliment to more objective product information.[16]

Thus advertising is seen as a trade-off, sacrificing value-free information for a form strong on convenience but laced with persuasion. The ethical mine fields in volatile areas such as disclosure of relevant health/nutritional information, the parity of many consumer products, and the essential question of what constitutes adequate "information" seem apparent.

3. *The purpose of all advertising is to cause us to think or act in accordance with the advertiser's intent, whether it be noble or venal.* This factor has certain implications at the societal level.

Legendary advertising practitioner Theoedore MacManus (creator of the much honored "Penalty of Leadership" ad) was an eyewitness to what several historians consider the beginnings of the "culture of consumption" in the 1920s. His 1928 thoughts on advertising's role are insightful.

> The cigarette has become almost a health food—certainly a weight reducer. The humble cake of soap has risen far above its modest mission of cleansing, and confers the precious bloom of beauty upon whomsoever shall faithfully wash. We are all glowing, and sparkling, and snapping, and tingling with health, by way of the toothbrush, and the razor, and the shaving cream, and the face lotion, and the deodorant, and a dozen other brightly packaged gifts of the gods. Advertising has gone amuck in that it has mistaken the surface silliness for the sane solid substance of an averagely decent human nature.[17]

Advertising attempts to set the consumption agenda, and also suggests to us, as Leiss and colleagues observe, interpretations of

> interpersonal and family relations, the sense of happiness and contentment, sex roles and stereotyping, the uses of affluence, the fading of older cultural traditions, influences of younger generations, the role of business in society, personal autonomy and persuasion, and many others.[18]

Thus it seems inevitable that advertising will be accused of unethical practice by those who disagree with (a) the *ends promoted* and/or (b) advertising as the *means*.

4. *Frequently advertising seeks out the individual rather than the individual seeking advertising.* Except for catalogs, classifieds ads, directories, the food ads in the daily newspaper, and the like, we are frequently the sought rather than the seekers. Not surprisingly, this situation raises a host of questions with ethical dimensions in many areas, the most obvious being timing, privacy, and frequency.

It can be contended that some of this potential conflict subsides as market and media fragmentation continues apace. That is, readers of *Golf* magazine are likely to find advertising for golf clubs compatible, and readers of *Modern Maturity* may welcome messages about low cost insurance. Indeed, even television, clearly the lightning rod in this and other areas of advertising/ethical encounters, may find it easier to match viewer interests with appropriate advertising as cable watching becomes even more routine, with appropriate selectivity in program content.

Yet, it is clear to all that advertisers will be seeking us more relentlessly than ever before, through the mass media as well as increasingly untraditional forms. The ethical signal flags are, then, apparent.

5. *Advertising continues to be a controversial third party with the mass media.* From the mid- to late nineteenth century with newspapers, through the early twentieth century with magazines, to shortly after the earliest days of radio, and from the outset of the American television system, advertising has been a third party in the traditional publisher/reader and broadcaster/audience relationship. The ensuing trade-offs are the ongoing stuff of pride (advertising makes the media more available less expensively without dependence on government subsidy) as well as controversy. Following are some of the more common ethical charges.

- 1. *Advertising can change the subject of media coverage itself.* The most obvious example is in television, where the availability of advertising dollars for some kinds of programming in particular time slots has proven a seductive lure. It is common, for example, for college football and basketball teams to reschedule their starting times, almost oblivious to the wishes of the spectators or athletes, to accommodate television time preferences.
- 2. *Advertising can alter the content of the media coverage.* A study by the American Council on Science and Health indicated that cigarette and health issues received relatively poor coverage in magazines with heavy cigarette advertising, such as *Time, Newsweek, Mademoiselle, Ladies Home Journal, MS, Redbook,* and *Cosmopolitan.*[19]
- 3. *Advertising can affect the type of available media.* Media follow markets, so it seems evident that we are more likely to see advertising-supported magazines with titles such as *Self-Indulgent Jogger* and *Young and Possessive* than *Ghetto Life, Migrant Worker, Old and Poor,* or *Street People.*

6. *The advertising agency commission system continues to reward agencies for what they buy (media space and/or time) rather*

than what they produce (ads). Historically, the advertising agency receives a commission (usually 15 percent or less) on the cost of the advertising space or time it buys with the advertiser's money. This venerable system has somewhat declined as a form of compensation in favor of fees and other arrangements, but it still represents a significant force in the process. According to former practitioner Howard Gossage:

> You show me a business where one's income is dependent on the amount of money spent rather than the amount of money that comes in and I will show you a business that is doomed, even with the very best of intentions, to mutual distrust and enormous psychological barriers.[20]

It is difficult, for example, to imagine an agency recommending that an advertiser *cut* his or her advertising budget and devote the savings to some other aspect of marketing activity, such as beefing up the sales force. In addition, some claim that the value of the advertisement itself is diminished, since the best ad and the worst ad have equal (media) value, although, the argument would follow, the "good" ad is more likely to be repeated, and thus benefit the agency.

Ethical concerns related to such a compensation arrangement are apparent, and, judging by agency mega-mergers and subsequent squabbling from advertisers about what constitutes "fair value" for advertising service, they are still quite real.

7. *The underlying uncertainty regarding the outcome of the advertising process leaves it wide open for differing interpretations of the same event*. As long-time advertising observer Edward Buxton noted:

> The advertising business is rife . . . with baffling intangibles. Nobody knows for sure how it works in many cases. The ad-making process itself is highly subjective, opinionated— and largely unprovable as to what is a good ad and what is not. Such pervasive uncertainties are breeding grounds for disquietude.[21]

Contemporary examples abound. Consider the ill-fated IBM PC Jr., the notorious "Herb" campaign from Burger King, the futile attempt of the fashion industry to reintroduce the short skirt, the Coca Cola "classic" fiasco, and on and on. All were heavily advertised and all, to one degree or another, were considered failures, the most advanced expertise of modern advertising notwithstanding.

Of course this ongoing climate of uncertainty provides ample breeding grounds for ethical ferment. Given the ambiguity of the process, critics and supporters will "see" different advertising realities, just as individuals "see" different shapes in the classic ink blot test. For example, suppose a critic and a supporter assess such topics as advertising to children and advertising of cigarettes. In one "reality" these activities can be seen as a highly principled meshing of the self-interests of sellers and buyers in a strictly voluntary relationship, while in another they can be seen as the unprincipled actions of manipulation and exploitation involving crafty communicators and hapless, if not helpless, audiences.

PERSPECTIVES ON THE ETHICAL DIMENSIONS OF ADVERTISING PRACTICE

Some preliminary observations seem in order at this point. First, these seven areas of ethical confrontation are likely to be an ongoing presence for advertising practitioners and critics in the foreseeable future.

Second, some of these areas of concern are simply not high on advertising's ethical agenda. For example, studies by Rotzoll and Christians as well as Hunt and Chonko[22] have revealed that practitioners' primary areas of concern are (1) agency/client/vendor relations and (2) the advertising message. At the very least, these don't touch such sensitive areas as advertising as a third party with the media, and advertising as the seeker rather than the sought.

Third, critics will tend to regard advertising practice as *unprincipled* to the extent that (1) they regard advertising practice in any of these areas as *not* being based on ethical principles and/or (2) the ethical principles that the practitioners *do* choose to invoke to support their decisions are different from those the critics would deem appropriate.

WORKING ADVERTISING ETHICAL SYSTEMS

In the cases that follow, many of the common ethical systems employed by practitioners will be explored. Based on observation and the findings of research, they would seem to be of three types.

The first type of system is based on the *personal criteria* of individuals—advertisers, agency people, media personnel, and others—which frequently involve some standards of *fairness*, often based on variations of the golden rule, the golden mean, and so on, as well as on such *prima facie* (deontological) ideals as "Don't lie." It is obvious that the advertising business does contain many principled people, yet there is no assurance that these highly individualistic criteria will have an impact on the overall ethical standards and performance of the business, or that they have been well thought out by these individuals in terms of application in the real world.

A second type of ethical system is based on some *formal principles* embodied in a host of codes, guidelines, and federal, state, and local regulations. Some examples:

- The American Advertising Federation and its predecessor have offered a set of principles from the early 1900s, with a recent revision in 1984. The American Association of Advertising Agencies has provided similar standards.
- Guidelines and codes have been formulated by dozens of trade associations, ranging from the American Wine Association through the National Swimming Pool Institute.
- The various media maintain gatekeeping activities, including the standards of individual magazines, newspapers, television and radio stations, as well as the now somewhat less vigorous activities of the networks' commercial clearance offices.
- The National Advertising Review Board, without question the business's most serious self-regulatory effort, offers some normative guidelines in regard to, for example, children and women, but it generally operates *post hoc.*

Ethical thinking at this level of formal standards seems largely deonotological, involving the assumption of basic truths that should be applied to all—do this, don't do that—some very general, some quite specific.

Historically, advertising's efforts at self-regulation have been spurred only by the threat of government regulation, which itself tends to wax and wane with the political winds, thus providing an unstable platform for ongoing ethical standards. Currently, for example, there is a relative lull in regulatory activity at the federal level, and the resulting vacuum is being filled in part by vigorous state activity. The NARB represents a serious and now institutionalized effort toward maintaining some ethical standards, but it is limited as an ethical force by its predominately *post hoc* functions as well as by lack of exposure to the general public.

There are several assets of the use of these relatively formal standards for ethical decision making. They do provide touchstones for practice, if utilized. Also, they provide the business with showpieces to promote their good works and to ward off potential regulation. Further, in the development of such principles and codes, there is likely to be some thoughtful discussion of ethical principles and their application to everyday practice.

The limitations, however, are equally apparent. For example, the stipulations of the codes are sometimes too general (e.g., "Advertising shall tell the truth, and shall reveal significant facts, the omission of which would mislead the public"[23]) to be readily transferred to moment-to-moment decision making. In addition, no matter how well intentioned, they may not be part of the mind set of the working practitioner when ethical decisions are made moment-to-moment.

The third type of ethical system is on the level of *inherent business ethics*. This is the "world taken for granted" level that is part of the enculturation process of those in the business. It is learned from watching the actions of others, hearing them explain decisions, and hearing and reading pronouncements from the trade organization.

In advertising, the ethical system is often expressed in terms of "market forces," based on classical liberal thinking, and rationalized in the ethical sphere by the now familiar concept of utilitarianism, "the greatest good for the greatest number," based on some notion of cost/benefit analysis. Basically, it is assumed, the pursuit of self-interest will result in the good of the whole, "as if by an invisible hand," to cite Adam Smith's well-traveled phrase. Thus the system is assumed to be self-corrective: "If they don't like the advertising we do, they won't buy the product and we'll be punished at the cash register." A representative statement is found in the American Association of Advertising Agency's response to a government inquiry regarding whether limits should be imposed on the number of commercials in children's programming.

> The A.A.A.A.'s position is that advertising self-regulation provides adequate safeguards against advertising abuses; that advertising does not harm children and that, therefore, there is no need to protect them from it; and that if a program has "too many" commercials, children will stop watching

it. In sum, market forces will serve the interest of children
by naturally regulating what is broadcast to them.[24]

The classical liberal heritage is clear: market forces will regulate—
naturally.

Thus the primary asset of the use of utilitarianism as the working
ethic for the advertising business is its use to rationalize the entire
market system, of which advertising is a part. It is, of course, a system
that can be quite appropriate as an ethical touchstone when the "greatest good for the greatest number" can be estimated—a situation not
common in the ambiguity of advertising outcomes.

Hence there is potential irony at the heart of advertising practice;
advertising's most frequently utilized ethical system (utilitarianism)
is often incompatible with its primary products (ads) because of the
frequent unpredictability of outcomes.

PREAMBLE TO THE CASES

Many of the basic areas of confrontation we have discussed so far are
more likely to be spotlighted by the advertising of national consumer
goods and services—particularly on television—than, say, business-to-
business or retail. Yet *all* forms of advertising practice will be tested,
to one degree or another, by these inherent dynamics of advertising,
and their ensuing ethical dimensions.

As was previously mentioned, a 1980 survey of advertising practitioners by Rotzoll and Christians, and a more extensive polling of
advertising executives in 1987 by Hunt and Chonko[25] revealed that
the basic areas of ethical concern for advertising practitioners were
agency/client/vendor relationships, and a clutch of issues culminating
in the advertising message. The cases in this section focus primarily
on consequences of the advertising message; to a great extent, agency/
client/vendor problems are typical of those encountered by virtually
any major service industry, but the consequences—and concerns—of
the advertising message are unique to advertising.

The cases are drawn from formal surveys such as those just cited,
informal interactions with practitioners, and ongoing perusal of the
trade and academic literature. The perspective is usually that of the
ordinary practitioner rather than the star, and each case is followed by
a commentary illuminating some of the dimensions appropriate to

disciplined ethical analysis. All cases attempt to build on the social ethics foundation offered in the first section of the book.

Advertising has been, and remains, a highly provocative subject in the American experience. It is hoped the following pages will broaden and deepen your understanding of its ethical dimensions.

NOTES

1. Stephen Fox, *The Mirror Makers* (New York: Vintage Books, 1985), p. 206.
2. Robert L. Heilbroner, "Advertising as Agitprop," *Harpers*, January 1986, p. 71.
3. Richard W. Pollay, "The Distorted Mirror," *Journal of Marketing*, April 1986, p. 18.
4. Howard Luck Gossage, *Is There Any Hope for Advertising* (Champaign; University of Illinois Press, 1987).
5. "Gallup Poll," Champaign-Urbana *News-Gazette*, 15 August 1985, p. 5; and "Ad Execs Stumble in Ethics Poll," *Advertising Age*, 14 August 1989, p. 39.
6. *U.S. News & World Report*, 23 February, 1987.
7. *Time*, 25 May, 1987.
8. David Rankin, "A State of Incivility," *Newsweek*, 8 February 1988, p. 10.
9. Cal Thomas, "Lack of Moral Values 'Trickling Up,'" Champaign-Urbana *News-Gazette*, 23 June 1988, p. A-4.
10. Stanley Modic, "Forget Ethics—And Succeed?" *Industry Week*, 19 October 1987, pp. 17–18.
11. Quoted in Fox, *The Mirror Makers*, p. 108.
12. See, for example, Eric J. Zanot, "Unseen but Effective Advertising Regulation: The Clearance Process," *Journal of Advertising*, no.4 (1985): 44–51; Lawrence B. Chonko, Shelby D. Hunt, and Roy D. Howell, "Ethics and the American Advertising Federation Principles," *International Journal of Advertising*, October 1987, pp. 265–274; and Jean J. Boddewyn, "Advertising Self Regulation: True Purpose and Limits," *Journal of Advertising*, no. 2 (1989): 19–27.
13. "Burnett's *Pro Bono* Work Through the Years," *The Burnettwork*, May/June 1988, p. 5.
14. See William Leiss, Stephen Kline, and Sut Ghally, *Social Communication in Advertising* (New York: Methuen, 1986), chap. 12.
15. Don Peppers, "Make Money—Have Fun—Be Ethical," *New York Times*, 24 July 1988, p. F-3.
16. Daniel Pope, *The Making of Modern Advertising* (New York: Basic Books, 1983).
17. Quoted in Fox, *The Mirror Makers*, p. 117.

18. Leiss et al., *Social Communication*, p. 3.
19. *ACSH News & Views*, May/June 1986, pp. 1, 8–10.
20. Gossage, *Is There Any Hope*.
21. Ed Buxton, "Fear and Loathing on Agency Row," *Adweek*, 5 September 1983, p. 34.
22. Kim B. Rotzoll and Clifford G. Christians, "Advertising Agency Practitioners' Perceptions of Ethical Decisions," *Journalism Quarterly*, August 1980, pp. 425–431; and Shelby D. Hunt and Lawrence B. Chonko, "Ethical Problems of Advertising Agency Executives," *Journal of Advertising* 16; 4 (1987): 16–24.
23. American Advertising Federation, "Advertising Principles of American Business."
24. Patty Siebert, "A.A.A.A. Files Kid-Vid Comments with FCC," *The 4A's Washington Newsletter*, January 1988, p. 2.
25. Rotzoll and Christians, "Advertising Agency Practitioners;" Hunt and Chonko, "Ethical Problems."

CHAPTER 6

Special Audiences

Several of the cases in this chapter are the products of the television era. Although there has been a basic concern about special segments of the population throughout much of American history—child labor laws, women's suffrage, Medicare, for example—television's ascendancy as a pervasive force in American society has heightened preoccupation with advertising's influence on particular population groups. This is so partly because television is the most indiscriminate of our mass media. It reaches the rich and the poor, the well read and the illiterate, the young and the old. In some cases advertisers have isolated particular target markets, such as children. In other situations, the advertising intended for some (the affluent) may also reach and affect others (such as the poor).

Thus advertisers have been called to account for their use of television as well as other media. In some cases their own consciences have prompted them to raise the issues, even though they have not always resolved them. There is, for example, no clear agreement in the advertising business concerning the morality of advertising to children. In other cases, outside special-interest groups have issued calls for change. (For example, in mid-1989 the Supreme Court of Canada upheld a Quebec law prohibiting advertising on programs in which 15 percent or more of the audience comprises children under 15.)

One prominent ethical matter is the question of *who* is morally responsible. Advertising practitioners tend to believe, rightly or wrongly, that the pursuit of their craft is socially beneficial, that for most people, most of the time, advertising performs a useful service. Those carrying the banner of special audiences, on the other hand, contend that the system is simply unfair to their constituencies and hence it must change.

It is appropriate, then, that the advertising section of this book begin with the ethical questions raised by the concept of special audiences. Today this issue remains among the top concerns of advertising's critics.

27. FANTASY FOR SELLING

This was only one of the several groups of kids who had been gathered over the last several weeks. Perhaps it would be the last, if they could finally arrive at a winning combination. So hoped Cynthia Marx, a 35-year-old specialist in market research for one of the country's largest advertising agencies. Her most recent assignment had been taxing in a number of ways.

One of the agency's clients, a nationwide fried chicken chain, had been anxious to develop some edge in its ongoing competition with Colonel Sanders and others in the field. Impressed by the star quality and marketing prowess of Ronald McDonald, someone suggested that a search begin for some memorable fantasy character who might create the same competitive pull. Not surprisingly, the agency had suggested a chicken. That's when Cynthia entered the picture. She had been asked to set up and supervise research to assess the appeal of certain chicken characters to an appropriate audience—the important market segment of children.

For Cynthia this was a new experience. Her previous research work had not involved children as a market. In order to work efficiently with the agency group responsible for the account, and to be properly informed for directing her research, Cynthia examined the existing research in the area. She found, of course, considerable controversy, with outspoken figures such as Peggy Charren of Action for Children's Television contending that "legally and morally, TV advertising is unfair and deceptive" and that advertising not only has harmful effects on the young viewers, but also lowers the quality of the programs themselves.[1]

Marketers, however, are clearly convinced of the virtues (at least pecuniary) of marketing to kids. McDonalds, Sony, Scott Paper, Oral-B, General Foods, K-Mart, Kraft, Hormel, and many others have developed special products and promotions directed to children, and Levi Strauss recently announced the largest campaign—$7 million—ever targeted exclusively to children. For Cynthia, there was one indisputable conclusion: children can be influenced by television advertising (and, it is estimated, they are potentially exposed to more than 350,000 TV spots before graduating from high school) and that influence can be strongly affected by the presenter of the message. As a curb on this influence, self-regulatory practices of the television networks and the advertising business now discourage the star of a children's show from selling products on the program. (Captain Kangaroo, for example, used to promote Schwinn bicycles on his popular program.) But Cynthia found nothing to prohibit the use of imaginary personages or fanciful presentations, as long as they are not part of a clearly deceptive message. So Tony the Tiger becomes an accepted figure in the advertising environment, and children in one study believed that Fred Flintstone and Barney Rubble would like them better if they ate Cocoa Pebbles.

Well, she concluded, the company and the agency seemed on the right marketing track, and nothing in the message itself, or in the use of the chicken figure, would violate any business, media, or government stipulations.

Another group of kids had just arrived to be tested. The research design was sound, the audience appropriate. Over the past several weeks Cynthia had tested different actors in different costumes, different theme songs, and chicken voices from high tenor to basso profundo. She had shown the chicken in a typical restaurant, in kids' homes, in a special chicken coop. The approaches had been varied from clownish to dramatic, including the chicken as an adventure hero. Through it all the researchers kept asking the children, "Which do you like best? Do you like this chicken? Would you like to see him on TV?"

Cynthia had no doubt that she would ultimately discover the most effective character. The device had worked for others; it would work for their client. But *should* it? The strategic manipulation of children's love of fantasy for purely pecuniary advantage? The child, first and foremost, as a *consumer*? Well, the kids certainly seemed to like *that* chicken. . . .

Cynthia is a researcher. She has been trained to gather information in a systematic way in order to help answer some particular question.

In this case the assignment is to get children to develop a preference for the client's product. The heart of Cynthia's undeveloped ethical problem is a feeling that she is using empirical means for morally troubling ends.

How undeveloped is her thinking? First, she recognizes the legality of her actions and of the client's intent. Nothing in the formal stipulations of the advertising business, including the Children's Advertising Review Unit, the television networks, or the Federal Trade Commission, prevents the advertiser from using this particular approach on this particular audience, as long as the message is not deceptive. Cynthia may also have reasoned that the results of a successful promotion using the chicken figure would be generally positive: first, parents will ultimately make the purchase decision in any event, and second, the food is generally wholesome, not the crinkly snacks and sugar-laden products that have so irritated groups such as Action for Children's Television. Cynthia also apparently implicitly accepts many of the assumptions of the market system. Thus far at least, she seems willing to regard children as markets and to think in terms of the need for competitive pull. She observes that fantasy approaches have worked for others, with the implicit understanding that advertisers can legitimately pursue their self-interests in this way.

But now her reasoning begins to muddle. Does the system also work for the *parents*? The *children*? Does it turn kids into little nags on behalf of the advertiser's product, replete with unreal expectations based on their belief in the fantasy figure? Is it proper to use the best tools of market research to "get at" children, some of whom are still too young for school?

To whom does moral duty belong in this case? As the Potter Box emphasizes, choosing our loyalties stands at the heart of the real issues. But Cynthia has not yet thought the issue through clearly enough to address the question. Is she troubled by advertising to children per se, merely by the use of fantasy figures, or only by her involvement at the moment?

If Cynthia concludes that advertising to children is wrong under any circumstances, then she could be assuming that moral duty is owed to the society at large. To be consistent, she should not only refuse to continue with the project, but actively protest the agency's involvement with clients promoting products to children.

If her trouble is merely the device of the fantasy figure, then she could still refuse further participation, or at least attempt to persuade agency strategists to take another approach. Her moral duty is seen to be owed to society in some cases and not in others; thus Cynthia could presumably operate comfortably with other approaches to the same audience.

If she simply wishes to abandon the project for the moment and thereby postpone her ethical confrontation, then Cynthia would be asserting that moral duty is owed to herself, based solely on the quandaries of this particular situation.

(All of these choices do, of course, pose questions concerning the reactions of her *employer* to her requests—not a question to be treated lightly. One of the largest American agencies now routinely asks candidates for employment in their research department if there are *any* of the agency's clients they couldn't work for. If the answer is yes, no job is offered.)

Cynthia follows none of these alternatives. Rather, she continues with the project, somewhat troubled as she moves ahead. The ethical issue is left undefined, with an unfocused allegiance to her job and, indirectly, to her firm and client. Thinking through the ethical dimensions of complex situations requires reflection. If that is lacking, the routine of standard professional expectation frequently prevails as the alternative of least difficulty—in the short run at least.

28. *ANIMATED SALES CATALOGS MASQUERADING AS ENTERTAINMENT*

He-Man. The Care (and *Gummi*) *Bears. Strawberry Shortcake.* The *Transformers* and *GI Joe.* Not to mention the *GoBots*, the *Adventures of Raggedy Ann and Andy*, and *Captain N: The Game Master.* Is there no end to it? Sara wondered. As a parent concerned about the interactions of television and children, she had supported Action for Children's Television (ACT) in its ongoing complaint (going back to at least 1985) against product-themed television programs aimed at children. Now it was almost five years later, and the problem, it seemed, was worse than ever.

Of course, tie-ins between popular entertainment figures and merchandising have a long history. Just think of the Mickey Mouse and Donald Duck items, or Superman, or the coonskin caps inspired by the Davy Crockett television show, or the tons of merchandise spawned by the original *Star Wars*. Those, it seemed to Sara, were inevitable, if occasionally annoying when the kids' nagging reached formidable levels. A popular show or movie caught on and tie-ins followed, all in the spirit of making a buck on a good thing.

But what bothered her, and why she had been inspired to at least minimal activism by the initial ACT complaint, was a new breed of tie-in. According to *Newsweek*: "Instead of deriving the product from the program, toymakers and animation houses now build entire kidvid shows around planned or existing lines of play-things."[2] What we end up with, according to ACT and others, are essentially "program-length commercials."[3]

What's more, there had already been a Care Bears movie, and He-Man and She-Ra did a brisk business in a feature-length film. (The local movie critic found the He-Man film innocuous enough but warned parents that taking their children to the film could cost them more than the price of admission, because the young-sters would want to stock up on all the related merchandise.) Sara had also just read about a rash of cheap (under $5) videotapes containing animated programs based on a company's product (e.g., Dino-Riders action figures) with commercials for other toys included.[4]

The whole thing is out of control, she thought. Kids are being entertained and sold to at the same time, whereas in the past they were taught that there's usually some difference between efforts to entertain and overt attempts to sell. (The advertising business and the media had in fact made efforts to make apparent the distinction between programming and ads by providing breaks in children's television programs such as, "We'll be back to . . . right after this. . . ." But now it seems there are no holds barred.)

And what do the advertisers say? Well, things like this:

> What difference does it make if the toy comes first? Our business is kids. You find out what the kids want.
> Children don't have a broad range of interests. One of the things they're interested in is toys. The net of it is, if it's good entertainment they'll watch it. If it's a good toy they'll probably buy it."[5]

Good entertainment, Sara mused. Good by whose standards? Many of the toys—Transformers, GoBots, Voltron, Masters of the Universe, GI Joe—are nothing less than war toys, promoted in violent programs, and they have many parents and child psy-chologists concerned.[6] They are good for sales, that's certain.

"The marketplace talks," one of the toy company executives had said. Well, ACT and others have talked too, and it would seem the marketplace talks louder.

Where do we go now, she wondered. Is there any chance for Senator Tim Wirth's Children's Television Educational Act of 1989 that would bar some of these program-length commercials?

The battle lines seem clearly drawn. The representative manufacturers see no ethical problem. Children watch the television programs. Children go to the movies. Children buy, or others buy on their behalf, the toys. What's good is what works, and the evidence of the marketplace suggests that toys–programs interaction is working quite well indeed. (Tyco reports that it has sold more than 500,000 copies of its Dino-Riders video and is producing a sequel.)[7]

Sara, ACT, Senator Wirth, and other opponents are apparently arguing for a different standard of accountability than simple stimulus and response. The complaints, calling for an outright ban on product-inspired television programs, appear to rest on the assumption of exploitation. That is, children may be watching the programs and wanting to buy the toys, but only because they are being used. Without the powerful program–toy one-two punch, it may be implied, the child would not feel as compelled to participate in the viewing–buying cycle. The greatest responsibility, then, is not the child as a consumer, but as a developing individual who deserves more than "animated sales catalogs masquerading as entertainment."[8] It may "work," by market standards, critics imply, but it shouldn't.

Sara and her counterparts are fighting an uphill battle. The evidence suggests that the intended audience—the children—are apparently satisfied with the existing symbiosis as, arguably, are many parents. Thus they would be hard pressed to argue that the "greatest good for the greatest number" is not being achieved. Rather, they seem to be resting their case on the assumption of a categorical imperative: it is simply wrong to level this degree of merchandising at a vulnerable audience (and it is this assumption of vulnerability that is critical). There is no call for compromise—such as a display of greater social responsibility on the part of the advertisers—but rather the clear message that the form is wrong and must be eliminated.

The conventional wisdom, however, offers powerful resistance to the reformers. Consider this: A sympathetic *Newsweek* article on the subject closed by referring to children as "TV's least powerful and most vulnerable consumers."[9] Very supportive from Sara's point of view, but note the use of the word "consumers" rather than "viewers" or "individuals." Consumers of what? TV? Toys? Both? To identify an individual in terms of his or her ability to consume is clearly a market-oriented concept. And it may be contended that if a market philosophy is assumed, the existing practice is sanctioned because of its success by market standards. Thus the existing order can be easily defended by persistence in the marketing mode. In regard to the description, "least powerful," the advertisers respond that the children are the sovereign consumers who drive the market. We serve them by providing what interests them, or we fail when they refuse to watch—or buy. "Most vulnerable"? To what? Satisfying entertainment? Enjoyable toys? Where is the exploitation here?

Thus, to a great extent the critical elements of this ongoing issue hinge on whether the rules of the market apply to children in the same way as they do to adults. If it is assumed they do not, the no-compromise position toward "30-minute commercials" becomes more compelling. Lacking that, the dynamics of the market offer a formidable challenge for those desiring to define an arresting ethical issue, no matter how heartfelt.

29. SAYING "NO" TOO OFTEN

Stan Clark had expected a routine evening. As the program director of a network outlet in a middle-sized midwestern city, he always had his ear to the ground for any rumbles of discontent that might become serious during the FCC license renewal cycle. The invitation to speak to a local parent–teacher association (PTA) on the subject "Children and Television" hardly seemed threatening. He anticipated the usual complaints about kids logging more time watching television than studying. He would agree, and would suggest lightly that this was a problem we all faced.

Teachers, and some activists who always seemed to show up at these events, would suggest that the quality of most programming available for children is poor. This complaint Stan could not dismiss so lightly. There was certainly not an overabundance of children's programming that approached the capability of the talented people associated with children's television. The so-called kidvid of Saturday and Sunday mornings was populated by fantasy or television heroes or their clones moving through often violent confrontations by means of production-line animation, or by the currently cynical *Camp Candy, Beetlejuice,* and *Rude Dog.* Virtually nothing original was shown during after-school hours; Stan's own station offered a daily diet of "Hogan's Heroes," "Gilligan's Island," and "The Brady Bunch."

If all else failed, Stan could wring another drop of juice from the economics of television: expensive time subsidized by advertisers at no direct cost to the viewers, and so on. No one except the lunatic fringe seriously wanted to cut back on the total hours of television available. Given that fact, there was always room for negotiation. All things considered, perhaps the current system filled the time frame as well as anyone could hope at the present time.

Stan's speech went according to plan until he opened the floor to questions. What happened then was something for which his administrative position and socioeconomic background had not prepared him—a cry of anguish from the inner city. Perhaps it was the time of the year—early December—but a large part of the audience came alive with the question: "Can't you do anything about the stuff our kids see advertised? The ads drive me nuts!"

Before he could give the usual response about parent–child interaction and the like, another parent sounded off: "That's right. My kids watch TV as much as anybody else's, and they see all these wonderful toys and expensive snacks and they bug us." "Yeah," came another protest, "and when they get to school, they hear their friends talking about the same things. But there's one big difference. Their friends will probably get those toys; our kids won't." From yet another parent: "You know how much some of that stuff costs? Those He-Man and Strawberry Shortcake things? Sorry, friend, but there's no way I can buy that stuff. But that's what the kids want because they saw it all on TV. Do you know how that makes me *feel*?" "Damn right!" yelled another frustrated parent. "I work, and when my little ones get home I want them to stay in the house. So they watch TV. And they get a *big* dose of what the kids on the tube are playing with and eating. Hell, my kids are human. Why shouldn't they want it all? And I'll tell you, brother, I get damned tired playing the heavy."

Stan was getting uncomfortable. Finally he responded. "You

folks are really asking for a way to prevent some advertisers from reaching into your homes. Obviously that's not possible, unless advertisers totally withdraw from children's programming. And if that's what you want, you'll also get a drastic cutback in the time devoted to children's programming and lower production quality of what little might still be offered."

The audience obviously did not like that alternative. With television viewing in low-income households consistently higher than in the affluent (and only 10 percent of American households consisting of a working father, a housewife mother, and children younger than 18), the frustration was deep seated. Stan tried to end on an upbeat note: "I hear what you're saying. The system isn't perfect, but given the way it's paid for, it seems to work out reasonably well most of the time."

"That may be," a woman said as Stan sat down, "but it wears you down saying 'no' so often. And some of us have to say it a lot more than others."

When this case was shown to a senior advertising executive, he commented, "Is there an answer to this question?" His point is well taken. Most observers see something harmful here, but what can be done about it? What is the source of the wrong?

Is it Stan Clark's station? Probably not. It is a network affiliate and carries a high percentage of network programming and advertising. The children's programming provided by the network is at least slick and professional. According to the ratings, the kids seem to like it. As for the late afternoon programs offered, such as "Gomer Pyle," "The Munsters," and the like, children watch them. If Stan's station dropped those shows in favor of more elevated (and potentially less commercial laden) fare, one of his competitors would probably snatch them up and win over the viewers for his advertisers.

Is it the advertisers? As we have observed, most companies operate on the assumptions of the free market system: "I take actions in my own economic self-interest and, by the very nature of the system, end up satisfying the needs of others." This system prompts the advertiser to seek programs that attract the largest audience in the most attractive markets. By advertising on such programs, then, the advertiser is also supporting entertainment demonstrably valued by the children.

Are the parents to blame? Certainly they could forbid children to watch certain kinds of programming, and most parents do. But the problem here is not directly the programming, but the advertising. Short of saying, "Watch the show but not the commercials," many parents are left with the alternative of encouraging their children to watch the public television channel (if the community has one) or the Draconian measure of throwing out the baby with the bath water by ruling out television altogether. Given the importance of television in American life (an average of 70 hours a week for children), particularly as a baby-sitter in homes with working parents, the latter hardly seems a palatable solution.

Where, then, are the villains, the guys in the black hats? The parents are crying out at one result of the television system: the continuing stimulation of their children with messages for products beyond the parents' financial capacity. Apparently even relatively affluent parents—for example, Barbara Kantrowitz, a senior writer for *Newsweek*—find the situation trying: "Of course, it's my job to say 'no' and I do, over and over again. But that job seems to be getting tougher every day as the siren songs on the TV become more and more alluring."[10] Yet at the same time parents register at least implicit support for the programming underwritten by the advertising. They don't want to let the salesperson into the house to tantalize their children, yet this salesperson also entertains, occasionally enlightens, and quite often provides a needed baby-sitting service.

Stan Clark acknowledges that the complaints are legitimate, but he is a card-carrying member of the system. His response ("It seems to work out reasonably well for almost everyone most of the time") is pure utilitarianism—the greatest good for the greatest number—which certainly underlies capitalist economics and the system of commercial television in this country.

Can an equitable solution be found within this system? One remote possibility, following the perspective of John Rawls, is to reconceive the greatest number to better account for minority rights through the public airwaves. In relation to children, this could mean conceiving of the child as something more than a potential consumer. A few ad-free programs could be offered (perhaps subsidized by higher rates for the other shows) or some measure of consumer education could be implemented as an act of social responsibility. The idea of helping children become judicious consumers could be an attractive compromise, with the reasoning that since they are exposed to the tantalizing promises of advertising, they can at least learn to be more cautious of advertising, as well as more informed about the costs involved in some of the advertised products and services. (For example, *Consumer Reports* is now offering a television version of its popular publication for 9- to 14-year-olds, *Penny Power*, which provides such an alternative view.) Most advertisers would not see such an effort as a threat, and many parents could be greatful.

A more radical approach was suggested by Action for Children's Television. The networks, they suggested, ought to conceive of children's programming as part of their public service requirements, part of the reasonable price to pay for access to the people's airwaves. Children's programming should carry no commercials. The same thinking, of course, could apply to local stations as well.

As Stan Clark drove home that night, he reflected that the commercial system presumes a duty to advertisers. To change that—to alter the priorities so that the preeminent obligation is to an extremely variegated public—would severely wrench the rules that currently govern the game. And it is, Stan reminded himself, a game that most enjoy. Perhaps another system, such as cable television, would provide a solution. Of course, how many low-income families could afford cable? In the meantime, he saw the utilitarian rationale as workable and enduring. Or is it, perhaps, inevitably flawed, as Mill warned, by the "tyranny of the majority"?

30. *"BLACK PEOPLE DRINK TOO MUCH"*

"Black People Drink Too Much" was the headline of the ad from the Black Newspaper Network, a company representing black newspapers to advertisers. "Too much, that is, for you to ignore the reaching power of black newspapers," the first paragraph of the body copy teased. The ad, directed at advertisers of alcoholic beverages, continued with an excited recital of black boozing habits: "720 million dollars worth of gin, 540 million dollars of scotch, 122 million dollars worth of rum."[11]

Maynard Brown sighed. As head of a midwestern organization attempting to help alleviate what it perceived as the pain and misery stemming from rampant chemical dependency among blacks, he often felt discouraged. Alcoholism has been called the number one social problem in the black community, and having black newspapers offer their readers up to the "booze merchants" (as a recent book was titled) as prodigious consumers of beer, wine, and liquor was disheartening indeed.

There's enough to deal with already without the advertisers of alcoholic beverages targeting the black population with a particularly seductive combination of appeals, he thought. Maynard looked over the clippings on his desk from *Ebony, Essence,* and *Black Enterprise* and thought about some of the TV spots:

- The use of darker models, with less emphasis on Eurocentric settings.
- The use of Kool and the Gang and the SOS Band in televised beer commercials appealing to black youth.
- The use of the singing legend Joe Williams, and even Louis Armstrong and Nat King Cole, to tie in with the black culture's jazz and blues heritage.
- Special ads run during Black History Month featuring paintings of famous African kings and, of course, selling booze.
- The usual pervasive appeals to upward mobility aimed at "Buppies"—black urban professionals.

These are very powerful appeals to black citizens, Maynard admitted, and the companies certainly aren't likely to abandon them. But, at the very least, shouldn't they incorporate messages of moderation in their ads? Is that too much to ask?

Maynard's organization is calling for advertisers of alcoholic beverages to rise above the imperatives of the marketplace and assume a posture of social responsibility toward black citizens, a presumably vulnerable population segment. What is the advertiser's perspective? Two responses may be typical:

Beer marketing is brand competition within an established market. The desire for the product already exists. One person may want a Hershey's chocolate bar and another a Clark Bar. Beer marketing is based on the same principle.

What advertising can accomplish is quite limited. Advertisers don't even try to reach nondrinkers.[12]

A dissenting voice from within the advertising business is offered by Barbara Proctor, president and creative director of one of the most successful black-owned advertising firms in the country:

> I take the advertising responsibility very seriously. A lot of people in this business say we only provide options for the public. I think that's burying your head in the sand. What we really do is generate need. The nature of advertising is to persuade—to create insecurities in the consumer that only the advertised product can fulfill. Therefore, I'm very careful how I use that power. I will not hype products that I believe are detrimental, such as cigarettes or alcohol.[13]

Let's examine the positions. First, Maynard and his organization are concerned about chemical dependency in the black community, and they see the advertising of alcoholic beverages directed at blacks as instrumental in that crisis. They see advertisers' targeting this presumably vulnerable population as a serious ethical issue, particularly since advertisers are using significant symbols of black culture, such as musicians and depictions of African heritage. Yet, they call only for advertisers to include "messages of moderation" in their ads, assuming that such messages will somehow blunt the presumably powerful associations in the rest of the ad. Second, the advertisers, predictably, generally stick to the ethos of the market; that is, they are attempting to sell legally available products to adults. They are not, they contend, attempting to encourage people to drink, but merely to choose their brand rather than those of their competitors. Finally, Barbara Proctor, representing her agency, states that advertising does indeed stimulate demand in general, not simply for brands. Therefore, in her judgment, it is irresponsible to promote alcohol (and cigarettes).

Proctor is operating from a position of absolutism—that is, it is simply wrong to advertise these products. The advertisers are, as usual, assuming the utilitarianism of the market, with the assumption that its natural mechanisms will correct any abuses. Maynard and his organization seem to be attempting a golden mean somewhere between the promotion of an outright ban on this type of advertising and the current *laissez-faire* practice.

Perhaps it could be argued that Maynard's case is underdeveloped. Is he assuming that blacks are more vulnerable than others to this type of advertising? If so, is his perception shared by the black community at large? Who, in other words, is Maynard's constituency? Is he concerned that this type of advertising will encourage individuals to start drinking, or that it will stimulate them to drink to excess? If the former, then a mere message for moderation would not seem destined for success. If the latter, is it assumed that the message of moderation will overcome all of the other carefully crafted symbolism urging consumption? Given the history of the cigarette warning labels and their problematic effects on smoking behavior, there seems little reason for optimism, even if messages of moderation were included by alcohol advertisers in a spirit of social responsibility.

Unless one wishes to encompass all of alcoholic beverage advertising, as does Barbara Proctor's agency, the pivotal issue would seem to be whether members of the black community are particularly vulnerable. Given the degree of concern expressed by Maynard's organization, and given advertisers' assumptions of the basically ethical nature of the market, the call for messages of moderation seems an ethically underformulated proposal.

31. CIGARETTE SMOKING IN AMERICA IS BECOMING A CLASS ACT

"Look at this," Charlie Abbott gestured toward Knight-Ridder's newspaper article headed, "Tobacco's Hot Pitch to the Poor."[14] "It says that about 40 million Americans have stopped smoking and that those who haven't are overwhelmingly minorities— blue-collar workers, the poor, and the ill educated, with all the expected overlap in those categories. And of course it confirms what we already know—talk to someone from the Tobacco Institute, and they'll tell you straight out that that's where a lot of the advertising and promotion money goes. And why shouldn't it, from their standpoint? If that's where a large percentage of their market is, it makes good marketing sense to spend a high proportion of their ad dollars there.

"Here, look at these examples from Philly's inner city. Here's a good-looking black woman on a billboard telling all about the 'Salem Spirit,' and a black Yuppie telling everybody to 'Come Up to Kool.' The reporter says that if you look in the *Philadelphia Tribune* you could well see an ad with a 'Kool Achiever,' a minority role model honored by the tobacco company. Did you know about these 8-sheets, the eye-level billboards? They weren't around ten years ago, but there are plenty in the inner cities now. Hell, the tobacco companies know what they're doing. Did you

know they put millions in the National Urban League, the United
Negro College Fund, and the NAACP, not to mention a bunch
of community activities?

"The reporter did his job. Here, look at these figures:

- Lung cancer rates among blacks were half the white rate in
  the 1930s, and today the black rate is 63 percent *higher!*
- smoking-related illness now accounts for 55 percent of all
  minority deaths.

"Now, this is one sticky wicket, because, as this black minister
was quoted as saying, smoking has a high symbolic value for some
people who don't have much going for them. Kids need to grow
up fast there and 'be cool,' and cigarettes are a way of showing
some status, because everybody knows the image that a particular
brand projects. And if we here in government get too preachy
about these things, well, as he says:

> You can talk to them about smoking until your tongue
> hangs out, but until they can see pictures of a lung turning
> black, like they can see a crack house on the block, it
> won't be a real problem to them.[15]

"So, in my government office we have an annual budget for
antismoking activities of about $3.5 million. Well the tobacco
companies spend about $2.4 billion on advertising and promotion
each year. Some contest, huh? Anyway, I still think we need to
inundate the inner cities with 'Stop Smoking' messages to the
best of our ability. And we have got to find some way to get
through."

Earlier in the text we learned that "Ethics . . . appraises voluntary
human conduct insofar as it can be judged right or wrong in reference
to determinative principles." What, then, are the ethical dimensions
(if any) of smoking in America becoming increasingly a "class act"?

Clearly Charlie Abbott considers the activities of the cigarette
companies targeting those in the inner cities to be unethical, presumably on the basis of the "principle" that it's wrong to exploit a vulnerable population—that is, the strong should not victimize the weak.

This is certainly a commonly accepted position, at least "in principle." Because of their disadvantaged status, Charlie might argue, these people are hungry for easy avenues of self-expression, even if those avenues involve clear and present health risks.

Do the tobacco companies recognize their practices as unprincipled? As a spokesperson observed:

> Emotionally, it sounds good for these health fascists to say that the powerful industry is preying on people who don't know any better. But it's elitist and offensive to imply that a lower-class person doesn't have the good sense or judgment to make his or her own decision.[16]

Thus, the companies could argue, they are operating under the well-established principle that individuals should be able to make decisions concerning their own welfare. Certainly, they could argue, there is a government warning message along with every enticing advertisement, thus providing an adequate opportunity for individuals to make informed choices.

With the proposal that the inner cities be inundated with anti-smoking messages, Charlie Abbott seems to be endorsing the same principle of informed choice, with the additional assumption that, because of the massive and seductive advertising efforts, the presumed "informed choice" is unevenly weighted, and that more anti-smoking messages are needed to offset the symbol-laden seductiveness of the cigarette brands.

Clearly, if Rawls were invoked, Charlie would feel that the decisions made behind Rawls's veil of ignorance would somehow favor the dwellers of the inner city more than the present situation allows. But who would be the participants behind the veil? The cigarette advertisers apparently do not define the situation in a manner that would suggest that they are engaged in an unethical practice. The smokers of the inner city may in some cases regret their habit but find the pleasure, addiction or the symbolic weight too compelling to jettison.

It could thus be contended that Charlie's argument is, at heart, a categorical imperative—that regardless of consequences, it's simply wrong to advertise a potentially dangerous product to a population one defines as ripe for exploitation. (This position, of course, raises the interesting question as to what criteria he applies to define exploitable.)

The cigarette companies rest comfortably on the greatest good for the greatest number—that is, for the smokers, at least in the short run—and the smokers champion their rights to choose.

So Charlie proposes using government (public) money to confront an entrenched ethical system (it works for me) with another (it's wrong for you even though you may not know it), with the major perpetrator watching from the sidelines. No golden mean—and no satisfactory resolution—seem likely.

The president of a major black-owned advertising agency recently put the core conflict plainly:

> Marketers could and should advertise products to blacks, and that includes cigarettes and alcohol as well as bread and candy.[17]

Clearly, as we have seen in this and the preceding case, there are those who disagree.

32. THE MARKET ILLITERATE

Speakers hostile to advertising have regularly appeared on the program of the American Association of Advertising Agencies (AAAA). Indeed, throughout the years the advertising business has been remarkably open to the views of those critical of its activities. Various public-interest and government speakers have had their hour at the forum, not to mention critics from within, such as the late Howard Gossage, an iconoclast of the first order. The business's principal trade paper, *Advertising Age*, has consistently editorialized with candor and opened its pages to dissenting positions. The following address by a congressman from Michigan, however, was unusually sweeping and poignant, getting to the very heart of advertising as a communication form. The highlights:

> Advertising has a special obligation to the hundreds of thousands of Americans who are unrepresented by any special-interest group. Call them the "market illiterate," if you will. They are generally low in income, low in education, and consequently limited in their abilities to maximize the use of their resources in the market. As a result, they may be far more trustful than others of the most

accessible form of market communication—advertising—yet they have a lower tolerance for shopping error
because of marginal or submarginal incomes.
   Consider this:

- Those with lower incomes are more likely to buy
  the national brands you commonly promote—which
  are almost always more expensive.
- Alternative forms of information such as *Consumer
  Reports* are overwhelmingly used by those
  who *least need them*—the market sophis-
  ticates.
- Working market knowledge, such as of the parity of
  many soaps, beers, detergents, shampoos, paper products, and the like, is extremely limited among low-
  income shoppers.
- The potential for abuse is rampant in the "medicine
  show" of off-the-shelf drugs and other health-related
  products, because of this population's tendency toward self-medication.
- The nutritional habits of this segment are generally
  poor. Lacking even elementary nutritional knowledge in many cases, these consumers, even if motivated, have no dependable way of learning the sugar
  and salt content of heavily advertised products.
- The U.S. Department of Education now states that
  27 million Americans—*one in five adults*—are
  functionally illiterate! Thus the types of market
  information they are limited to are predominately word-of-mouth and television and radio
  advertising, arguably the least informative of the
  breed.

   You are all well aware of this. Yet some of you react
like the employee of an agency known to all of you. He
said, "I can appeal to uneducated consumers with possibly
unnecessary product appeals. Uneducated, lower-income
consumers, for example, are 'easy sales' for laxatives and
the like."
   Your advertising business is not wholly insensitive. It

has opened its meetings to voices such as mine, and individuals in the business have donated their talents as
well as media space and time to countless meritorious
causes. Yet who would deny that the dominant ethic of
the business is one not of social responsibility, but rather
a pecuniary philosophy? What praise is there in alerting
Americans to the dangers of high blood pressure when
few but the most market wise will be able to learn the
sodium content of the foods portrayed in your alluring
ads? What are the consequences to these market illiter-
ates of the normal practice of excluding potentially negative (but arguably relevant) information?

Minutes later the speech concluded. The audience of account
executives, copy writers, art directors, television producers,
media buyers, and researchers was left to ponder the parting challenge:

What is *your* obligation to the "market illiterate"? What
decisions, what actions, can you take every day to ensure
the elevation of this significant group from exploited markets to meaningful participants in the system you cher-
ish? The need is real. The obligation—at least is part—
is yours.

Since the first organized outcries against abuse early in this century,
the advertising business has attempted, with various degrees of success, to consider social responsibility as part of its milieu. On the more
formalistic level, the result has been a host of codes, advisory papers,
and the like. On the workaday level there may simply be a pulling of
the punches, particularly in the creation of advertising messages.
Whether or not this loose patchwork of formal and informal safeguards
has been adequate depends on where you look, who you ask, and what
is defined as the central problem.
    In the case raised by the speaker, the problem is a fundamental
one indeed—fundamental in the sense that the speaker is striking at
the very heart of the advertising process—the nature of biased communication. Consider his charge that some out there, lacking formal
and functional education, are ill equipped to participate intelligently

in the market. When lack of knowledge is coupled with low buying power, the possibility of painful purchasing mistakes becomes quite high. And advertising can be the seducer.

What is advertising's responsibility compared with that of other relevant institutions such as schools or community organizations, which could also provide some form of market education? What action is the speaker recommending? Does he want the AAAA to take a stand on the matter? If so, what? Or is the problem a matter of individual responsibility? If so, are conscientious individuals adequate for the dimensions of the problem?

The speaker failed to deal with these and other relevant issues and may have done the cause a disservice. (He could, for example, have proposed that advertisers subsidize targeted consumer education programs as acts of social responsibility.) The audience, left with an uneasy and unfocused sense of guilt, and lacking a structured call to the barricades, could shrug off the issue as something somebody ought to deal with—that is, it is simply too pervasive for one individual's actions to make a difference.

Advertising, in keeping with the ethos of the market system, is self-interested communication. Given the assumptions of self-interest, the presumed rationality of individuals, and a sufficient number of buyers and sellers so that market power is diffused, it is philosophically consistent for sellers to offer persuasive communications in their own behalf. Thus, puffery, the use of fanciful themes, and selective presentation of factual material are considered justifiable. And all of the cases in this chapter have challenged that set of assumptions in relation to particular market segments.

If we assume that one-sided communications will collide in a marketplace of ideas and that deliberate and calculating humans will make the wisest decision among alternatives, well and good. Lacking that, it must be assumed that individuals are not getting enough information to make intelligent choices, or simply are not capable of sorting through the conflicting claims, no matter how completely presented, to make a wise decision.

The latter case builds an argument for government intervention, but in the area of insufficient information, advertising comes most directly into play. To alleviate the problems outlined by the speaker, advertisers would need to supply more information *in* their own advertising than they are now doing. For example, would it be realistic for Anacin to reveal that its extra ingredient is caffeine? Should the producers of compact cars note the danger of injury in the event of a crash? Should shampoos disclose that their primary ingredient is water? If this information is not now coming out through the natural flow of market forces, and if it is relevant to wise purchasing decisions, then it presumably should be made available in some manner. But is it asking too much of an advertiser's working ethics to disclose potentially negative information about his or her product or service for some hazy ideal of serving some undefined segment of a generally complacent consuming public?

Most advertisers assume that it is right to attempt to persuade. Furthermore, they assume that successful persuasion will be financially rewarding, and they take favorable consumer response as a vote of confidence. In short, successful persuasion is seen as socially beneficial.

But what of those whom the speaker claims are victimized by this presumably symbiotic relationship? Lacking a clear call for action from the member of Congress, the practitioners in the audience could be excused for assuming that the problem is best handled by institutions—such as churches, schools, or community groups—whose ethical concerns identify specifically with the disenfranchised.

Advertising, by its nature, is biased communication. To alter its form to serve the minority better would likely dilute its effectiveness both to the self-seeking seller and to the materialistic majority who are willingly seduced by the promises and perils of consumer abundance. So speaks the utilitarian. But what of those who find themselves between the cracks of the greatest good for the greatest number? Whose constituency are they?

NOTES

Author's Note: There is, at the time of this writing, considerable controversy about Whittle Communications' proposed "Channel One" service to secondary schools. Whittle offers participating schools $50,000 worth of video equipment, including a satellite dish, central recording and transmitting equipment, and about 40 video monitors. In return, the school agrees to air a daily news program, 12 minutes in length, *but including 2 minutes of commercials*. (Initial participants in test schools were Procter and Gamble, Ford, Warner-Lambert, Nike, Levis, Wrigley, Maybelline, Gillete, Heinz, Columbia Pictures, and M&M/Mars.) Whittle plans a national roll-out of the program in 1990, in spite of rejection from California and New York, various educational groups, and the competition from a number of other educational ventures including Ted Turner's commercial-free service—all without the equipment. This project, of course, raises a thicket of ethical questions centering on the idea of the "captive audience" of students. Because of some doubt about the viability of the Whittle program, we have not included it as a case, but, should it succeed, it should provide an attractive subject for class discussion.

1. John P. Murray, "Quebec Law Leads the Way Out of 'Kidvid' Wasteland," *Toronto Star*, 19 June 1989, p. A-15.
2. "Toying with Kids' TV," *Newsweek*, 13 May 1985, p. 85.
3. Ibid.
4. Kate Fitzgerald, "Toy Ads Find Homes in Cheap Videos," *Advertising Age*, 20 March 1989, p. 10.
5. "War Toys on the March," *Newsweek*, 1 July 1985, p. 54
6. "Toying with Kids' TV."
7. Fitzgerald, "Toy Ads Find Homes."
8. "Toying with Kids' TV."
9. Ibid.
10. Barbara Kantrowitz, "Saturday Morning Classroom: 15- and 30-Second Lessons," *Adweek's Marketing Week*, 30 November 1987, p. 58. See also "Watch What Kids Watch," *Newsweek*, 8 January 1990, pp. 50–52.
11. "Alcohol Advertising: A Black Problem," MIBCA (Minnesota Institute on Black Chemical Abuse), Spring/Summer 1984.
12. "Alcohol Advertisers Need Not Apply," MIBCA, Spring/Summer 1984.
13. Ibid.
14. Dick Polman, "Tobacco's Hot Pitch to the Poor," Knight-Ridder syndication, reprinted in *Chicago Tribune*.
15. Quoted in ibid.
16. Ibid.
17. Judann Dagnoli, "RJR's 'Uptown' Targets Blacks," *Advertising Age*, 18 December 1989, p. 4.

CHAPTER 7

What to Advertise

As a way to approach the cases in this chapter on content, consider three premises:

1. Because we as a people are often skeptical about the "deliberate and calculating" nature of individual decision making, the subjects of advertisements are matters of concern. That is, if we all believed that people can, in fact, make up their own minds about the products and services they want, we would not be concerned about their being "targets" of advertising's persuasive appeals.
2. Given the nature of advertising as a potentially powerful form of mass persuasion, individuals, groups, and organizations will desire to use it on behalf of their products, services, and ideas.
3. The real dilemmas in this area arise because of the alleged effect of advertising content on the thinking and/or behavior of individuals. But, because of the complex stimulus field in which advertising operates, there is often no clear-cut proof of either the presence or the absence of these effects.

Our approach to case studies in this chapter requires also that we recognize certain regulatory structures already in place. In addition to consumer choice, the following serve to a greater or lesser degree as gatekeepers.

1. *Government.* Federal, state, and local governments regulate the advertising of some types of products and services. For example, certain regulations deal with the advertising of liquor and par-

ticular types of drugs and firearms, in addition to the well-known
ban on cigarette advertising in the broadcast media.

2. *Media.* Regulation by the media occurs on two levels. The first
    is represented by media-wide codes such as those of the American
    Business Press, the Direct Mail/Marketing Association, and the
    Outdoor Advertising Association of America. The second level
    consists of particular media vehicles such as the acceptance cri-
    teria of CBS, the *New Yorker*, and the *Los Angeles Times*. It can
    be contended that this is the key pressure area concerning what
    is advertised. Simply stated, if a media vehicle assents or demurs,
    advertising opportunities are affected accordingly.

3. *Individual Enterprises.* Particular advertisers and agencies take
    stands regarding the appropriate forums for their advertising or
    regarding what should be advertised. For example, Kraft, Procter
    & Gamble, and several other large advertisers have adopted guide-
    lines concerning the types of television programming in which
    their advertising will appear. Generally these companies will ad-
    vertise their products on shows designated as "family fare" rather
    than excessively violent or sexually oriented programs. (Pressure
    groups such as Christian Leaders for Responsible Television have
    been very active in this area; see case 49) Also, some advertising
    agencies refuse to accept certain types of accounts, most com-
    monly politicians and cigarettes, although the majority are not
    so discriminating.

Against this backdrop, there is ample opportunity for complex
ethical confrontation. In some cases the issue concerns the advertising
of a subject per se, in others whether a particular medium or vehicle
provides an appropriate forum. In the absence of clear cause-and-effect
data, heat is often generated by the fires of passionate conviction, col-
liding with equally intense economic interests and, as we shall see,
different assumptions about nothing less fundamental than human
nature.

33. A MAGAZINE AND ITS AUDIENCE

Sue Chord had recently accepted the position of assistant advertising manager with one of the country's leading magazines for
the "modern" woman. She was justifiably proud. She thought her

new employer was several cuts above the *Cosmopolitan* vision of the woman as a sexually obsessed, narcissistic, clothes and recreation zealot. *Women*, in contrast, prided itself on sensitivity to the triumphs and tragedies of American women through thoughtful editorial content, ranging from case histories to provocative interviews, serious features, and a smattering of well-balanced self-help articles. It was, in short, a magazine worthy of the name, and Sue was happy to be on board.

Women, she knew, was also extremely popular with a wide range of advertisers interested in reaching the magazine's generally well-educated audience—the people called "opinion leaders" by media buyers. She had not, however, realized how much advertising was carried in a particular product category—cigarettes.

The pages were festooned with colorful ads extolling the virtues of brands aimed directly at the modern woman. All were screened by the magazine's standing ban against sexist ads (their current horrible example in other magazines was Camel's four-page "Tips on How to Become a Smooth Character," which included advice for beach bums to "run into the water, grab someone, and drag her back to shore . . . the more she kicks and screams, the better"[1]) but there were plenty nonetheless, with women and their cigarettes embracing provocative lifestyles.

Now beginning to identify with the publication's editorial mission, Sue found the presence of these ads troubling. She was a nonsmoker but recognized the rights of others to choose for themselves. What bothered her was the seeming incongruity between the careful and respectful treatment of women in the editorial pages and the seeming disregard for their well-being in the advertising material. She recognized that there are differences in tastes, as well as in the kinds of products and services individuals prefer. However, in her judgment there was no longer any reasonable doubt about the hazards of smoking in general, and for women in particular. Consider:

- Advertisers are increasingly singling out women as a distinct market.
- Women have now achieved virtual equality in a formerly male-dominated area—lung cancer.
- In addition to its linkage with gastric ulcers, chronic bron-

chitis, emphysema, and heart disease, it is now known that
smoking may cause hazards for unborn children.
- The Dean of Harvard's School of Public Health has called
  cigarettes, "the only legally available product that is harmful
  when used as intended."[2]

To be blunt, *this is a harmful product!* Cigarettes, Sue felt,
should perhaps not be advertised at all, but certainly not in
Women. To do so was simply inconsistent. If the magazine staff
chooses editorial material with the goal of helping modern
women live more fulfilling lives, should they advertise products—particularly when using them involves clear-cut danger—
that work contrary to the best interests of these same women?

It was not a matter of not trusting the readers—as if the ads
might lure them into smoking—but rather of bringing the caring
attitude from the editorial pages over to the advertising. Sue's
approach was, if readers want to smoke, okay, but this magazine
should not promote habits that have been proven harmful. Such
a policy seemed reasonable enough to her. Was she the only one
who thought so?

Sue approached the advertising manager with her observations.
She was told that cigarette advertising constituted a significant
part of *Women's* advertising revenue, which in turn helped finance the vigorous editorial side she found so attractive, that
cigarettes are still legally sold in this country and can be legally
advertised in the print media, and that *Women's* readers are wise
enough to make their own decisions.

During the next six months Sue's dilemma became more and
more discomforting. Cigarette advertising directed solely at
women was increasingly plentiful and *Women* was a marvelously
efficient, even prestigious, vehicle. Meanwhile the press—though
not necessarily *Women*—carried new studies on the health-
threatening effects of cigarettes. Eventually, she resigned.

On the surface, Sue's ethical dilemma may seem relatively straightforward: an act of personal defiance against what she perceived as an
unconscionable practice. However, the issues here may be more subtle.
What is her basic objection? She apparently is not against the

advertising of cigarettes per se. Rather, she claims that it is the apparent incongruity between the editorial dimensions of the magazine, which seem to demonstrate a care and responsibility for its readers, and what she sees as the callous indifference to that responsibility when a harmful product is advertised. Sue presumably recognizes the rights of intelligent individuals to decide about smoking, but if she really has faith in the readers to make their own choices, why is she upset about the potential effect of the advertising material?

There is no disagreement between Sue and the advertising manager about the facts of the case. First, the presence of large amounts of cigarette advertising is acknowledged, as is its profitability. Second, the manager does not debate the potential dangers of smoking. Therefore this is a genuine ethical conflict, not merely a disagreement about the interpretation of facts.

One way of focusing the issue is to see it as a disagreement about consequences. Sue, despite her disclaimer, does seem concerned about the types of choices the readers will presumably make as a result of exposure to the cigarette advertising. She assumes they will be harmful. The magazine staff, by contrast, seems indifferent to the direct effects of the cigarette advertising, but rather sees it as the means to the ends of financial support for the editorial dimension and, ultimately, profits.

To Sue, the greatest good to the greatest number is served by eliminating cigarette advertising from the magazine. Implicit in this assumption seems to be a lack of faith in the decision-making power of the readers. For the magazine staff, the greatest good for the greatest number is achieved through accepting the advertising of legal products and using the revenue to produce a high-quality editorial product. Implicit in this assumption seems to be a belief that individual decision making should not be guided, at least in relation to advertising content.

Sue may find it difficult to justify her position on utilitarian (consequentialist) grounds, given (1) the indifference of the magazine staff to her concern, and (2) the apparent lack of protest from the readers. Ultimately her resignation can be seen as an act of personal relativism; that is, I am protesting a practice that is wrong because I say it is wrong.

The magazine, on the other hand, is apparently operating in a split-level ethical house. On the editorial level there is concern for what is best for its readers, with certain normative values implicit. Yet on the advertising level, guidance is left entirely to the individual readers.

Sue forced an ethical dilemma for herself by noting that the concept of what was right in her area of concern, advertising, was incongruous with the concept of "right" on the editorial side. However, confronted by the rationale that if advertising abuses existed they would be brought to the fore by troubled readers, she could find little ethical support other than her personal belief in the wrongness of the system. Given the apparent strength of that belief, she acted consistently.

Meanwhile, the publication continues to function with coexisting credos of (1) responsibility (editorial), and (2) *laissez-faire* (advertising). The magazine presumes this dichotomy to be sufficient justification for the promotion of a controversial product. This split-level ethic is not uncommon in the media. Neither, then, are the ethical questions that ensue.

34. DR. KOOP'S VALEDICTORY

"Well," Jake Smith thought, "I suppose it could have been worse." The representative from the American Advertising Association had just finished listening to retiring U.S. Surgeon General C. Everett Koop's remarks on the marketing of alcoholic beverages before the Senate Governmental Affairs Committee. Of Dr. Koop's ten key recommendations, several involved advertising and marketing:

1.   A call for the matching of alcoholic-beverage ads with an equal number of pro-health and pro-safety messages.
2.   The restriction of certain types of advertising and marketing practices, especially those that reach people under the legal drinking age.
3.   The elimination of tax deductions for alcohol advertising that focuses on lifestyle rather than price or product.[3]

"The good news," Jake thought, "is that appeals for government regulation are less extensive than usual.

"And consider where the most recent battles started. . . ." During its 1988 session, Congress asked the Surgeon General to declare drunk driving a national crisis. Among the claims presented:

- That alcohol is America's number 1 drug problem among youth.
- That about 10,000 people between 16 and 24 are killed yearly in alcohol-related accidents.[4]
- That "drinking is endemic among American youths, and alcoholic beverages remain easily accessible to those under 21."
- That "peer pressure encourages young people to drink and leads many adolescents to consider alcohol a necessary accompaniment to social events."
- That "advertising normalizes alcohol consumption and makes it more difficult to raise concerns about alcohol abuse."[5]

Then came the Surgeon General's Workshop on Drunk Driving in December 1988, "without," Jake remembered vividly, "a single representative from alcoholic-beverage advertisers, the advertising agency business, or the broadcast networks." Among the panel's 200 or so recommendations:

- Eliminating the tax deductibility for most alcoholic-beverage advertising.
- Prohibiting alcoholic-beverage marketers from sponsoring sports events.
- Banning the use of celebrity endorsers or spokesmen who appeal to youth in alcoholic-beverage advertising.
- Requiring counteradvertising "with equivalent exposure" to current alcoholic-beverage advertising.
- Eliminating alcoholic-beverage advertising and promotion on college campuses.
- Eliminating alcoholic-beverage sponsorship of concerts and other public events where a majority of the audience might be minors.
- Requiring warning labels on all alcoholic-beverage advertising.
- Considering shifting regulation of the alcoholic-beverage industry to the U.S. Food and Drug Administration.[6]

Not surprisingly, the major advertising trade associations, including Jake's, objected vigorously to these recommendations, arguing (1) that many of them are unconstitutional in that they violate advertisers' First Amendment rights, and (2) that there is no research showing any link between alcohol advertising and alcohol abuse, let alone drunk driving.[7]

"So," Jake thought, "considering that a recent public opinion poll indicated that 39 percent of the public favored an ban on beer advertising, and that 34 percent felt beer advertising was targeted to minors,[8] and given the biased group on the panel and their sweeping recommendations, then the Surgeon General's centering on only a relative few, and his calling for them to be implemented primarily through cooperation rather than regulation, isn't bad.

"But," Jake wondered, "how much cooperation is possible? And, if it's not seen as enough, what then?"

Let's examine some of the issues. First, that alcoholic-beverage ads should be matched with an equal number of pro-health and pro-safety messages. Obviously there can be different interpretations here. For example, the American Association of Advertising Agencies recently estimated that the media, through the Advertising Council, the AAAA, and the Department of Transportation, have donated close to $112 million for a campaign designed to increase public awareness of the drunk-driving problem.[9] There are also the efforts of Anheuser-Busch ($30 million behind "Know when to say when"), Coors ($5 million), and the probable revival of Miller's moderation campaign.[10] Is the Surgeon General arguing that these are not sufficient? Apparently so, possibly alluding to the annual advertising budget of alcoholic beverages, well in excess of $1 *billion* a year. And who, short of the government, would pay for these new "counter" ads? The brewers, thus effectively cutting their television advertising budget in half? The networks and local stations?

Certainly the beer industry and a number of individual brewers would claim that they are acting ethically by attempting to depict beer consumption as an adult activity, and also by providing explicit support for messages of moderation as well as various educational efforts in schools and other institutions. They might confidently contend that they have already retreated behind Rawls's curtain and have felt comfortable with the outcome, a balance between concerns of brewers and those of reformers. They would, predictably, find the one-for-one proposal excessive, and, given the choice between that extreme and no counteradvertising at all, would feel comfortable with the middle ground they already see themselves occupying.

Koop obviously does not regard the existing situation as acceptable. He could be seen as relying on a modified absolutism—for example, "Advertising of alcoholic beverages on television is acceptable *only* when there are an equal number of opposing messages, and when the messages that do exist do not in any way suggest the association of beer consumption with desirable lifestyles."

In the process of suggesting a broadening of the "marketplace of ideas" rather than a ban, Koop seems to be endorsing at least the basic mechanisms of the market system (including the "deliberate and calculating" individual) once the market is rigged with anti as well as pro messages.

Yet the proposals for restricting the types of advertisements that can be tax deductible (i.e., only those emphasizing product or price) as well as for discouraging practices such as "college promotions, celebrity endorsers, musical- and sporting-event sponsorships, and alcohol ads fashioned around race car driving or other activities that are dangerous with alcohol"[11] seem to suggest that if the beer/event associations continue, "the wrong messages about alcohol consumption "will be sent to the wrong audiences,"[12] thus implying a lack of faith in the good judgment of the individual.

Are the beer advertisers currently operating ethically—that is, in harmony with determinative principles? They would certainly contend that they are not simply relying on the "natural" mechanisms of the market to provide them with assumed utilitarianism signals but are currently acting with social responsibility as well. Koop clearly would contend that they are *not* operating ethically currently and that they need to implement his proposals to raise their level of performance.

We seem to be dealing, then, not with completely opposing positions, but rather with degrees of compromise. Given the advertising business's standard defenses—first, that it's unconstitutional (which simply dismisses the objections), and second, that there's no cause-and-effect between beer advertising and alcohol abuse (which denies the need for change)—it seems unlikely that the brewing industry will move a great deal more than it already has, and which it considers notable.

V. J. Adduci, chairman of the National Commission Against Drunken Driving, recently urged advertisers to "take a look at your advertising . . . act like a parent."[13] Where, on the ethical landscape, does that leave the advertising of these popular—and troublesome— beverages?

35. *THE 30-SECOND CANDIDATE?*

The selling of political candidates via some type of advertising has been around for the better part of this country's political life. However, it was really with the successful use of television spots by Dwight Eisenhower in the 1952 campaign that the modern dimensions of the political sell began to take form. (It is said that during the filming of these short and simplistic messages Eisenhower was overheard to murmur, "To think an old soldier should come to this.") Now the use of television and radio spots (usually 30 or 60 seconds long) is a commonplace in today's political campaigns at the federal, state, and local levels and, indeed, discussions on advertising's role in politics almost inevitably focus on television advertising.

That's what bothered Jason Bradley. At 32, a successful copywriter with a large East Coast advertising agency, Jason had been asked if he wished to join the ad hoc agency team that would play a major role in the advertising efforts of a presidential aspirant. The primaries were only a few months away, and it seemed likely that the candidate could make it at least to the party convention. Indeed, there was a possibility he could become the party's candidate in the fall elections.

The candidate was well qualified, personable, and with the kind of liberal voting record and inclinations that Jason found attractive. Perhaps most important, he was financially well heeled. The combination seemed to make him close to the ideal type to make effective use of advertising—particularly broadcast advertising— as a political vehicle. Finally, the candidate's past and present media exposure had been solid. He was thus reasonably well-known and exquisitely marketable on the national level.

So why not join the group and get on with it? There were certainly no company constraints on Jason. The agency had always been careful to avoid pressuring any of its employees to participate in the promotion of causes (and to a lesser extent, products and services) in which they personally did not believe. He would, of course, have a more frantic work schedule than he normally experienced in the already high-charged realms of big-time advertising. Time pressures would be severe, changes in the copy approaches would be frequent because of the thrust and counterthrust of opponents, and, worse, there would be a multilayer approval process involving various strategists, technicians, advisors, and hangers-on. Still, it was heady stuff. He would be participating in a major way in the quest for political power, and for a candidate he honestly believed would serve the country well.

He was also aware that the advertising business took political advertising seriously, and not simply in terms of ad hoc revenue. Late in 1983, for example, the American Association of Advertising Agencies had presented an invitation-only program on "Responsibility in American Advertising in 1984."[14] Among other material presented in this much-acclaimed session in the Senate Caucus Room was the "4A's Code of Ethics" concerning political advertising:

1. The advertising agency should not represent any candidate who has not signed or who does not observe the Code of Fair Campaign Practices of the Fair Campaign Practices Committee, endorsed by the AAAA.
2. The agency should not knowingly misrepresent the views or stated record of any candidates nor quote them out of proper context.
3. The agency should not prepare any material which unfairly or prejudicially exploits the race, creed, or national origin of any candidate.
4. The agency should take care to avoid unsubstantiated charges and accusations, especially those deliberately made too late in the campaign for opposing candidates to answer.
5. The agency should stand as an independent judge of fair campaign practices, rather than automatically yielding to the wishes of the candidate or his authorized representative.
6. The agency should not indulge in any practices which might be deceptive or misleading in word, photograph, film, or sound.[15]

It was not, then, a subject that had escaped ethical scrutiny by professionals such as himself. The bottom line for him, though, was still what he felt to be the unholy alliance between broadcast advertising and the quest for political office. During his career he had helped scores of clients promote hundreds of products and services on television. Many had succeeded. Some, for a variety of reasons, had not. Yet the very nature of the advertising dimensions of the medium imposed the same discipline upon all. In 30 or 60 seconds the message had to be simple rather than complex. It needed to strive for high memorability with the aid of striking visual images and/or musical themes. Basically, it had to leave an impression favorable to the advertiser.

People watching television are usually in a passive state. They are not actively seeking information and, as a result, are not likely to put forth the mental effort to acquire a great deal unless the subject is particularly meaningful to them personally.[16] And, even here, the discipline of time imposes itself. (Stations will not usually sell television time in segments of more than one minute; longer segments interfere with other programming.)

Now all of these characteristics of the medium may not seriously interfere with the successful promotion of a beer, cosmetic, soft drink, soap, automobile tire, or bra. But a serious candidate for political office? At the very best the message could concentrate on some aspects of his record—in either the candidate's own words or those spoken by an appropriate high-credibility announcer. And what then of all that is *not* said? The nuances? The complexities of real-world issues, programs, events, compromises?

Many of the accepted forms are beneath contempt. Consider the "man in the street." Or the candidate as a man of the people. Or carefully edited campaign appearances with a lot of crowd reaction. Or, God forbid, the candidate and his family. Perhaps worst of all are the negative spots that can quickly achieve saturation levels and then disappear, leaving the opponent pondering whether or not to clarify—or counterattack—all with the enormous pressure of time slipping away.[17] The impressions may linger, but the substance of intelligent evaluation is almost inevitably eliminated by the form itself.

Of course the candidate would go on without Jason. Of course his opponents would use television, and their use might be more skillful and contribute in some way to his candidate's voice being stilled in the national arena, at least for that year. Jason knew these things, and he regretted them. But someone somewhere must put his or her reservations into some form of action, ineffectual though it may seem at the time. Television advertising time of 60 seconds or less, Jason asserted, is simply not a proper forum for political discourse. The stakes are too high, the medium too restricted, and the influence on an often passive public too potentially compelling.

Let it be one small act of protest, he concluded—not against the candidates, but against the promotional system upon which so much of their political success has come to rely.

The decision not to join the agency team is based on a generalization about the relationship of broadcast advertising to politics. Jason could have resolved the question by checking the specific situation. Undoubtedly several others in the task force may also have worried about the increasing trends toward political ads of 60 seconds or less but then reasoned that each situation must be evaluated on its own terms. The question for them may not have been the selling of politicians using television spots as a broad problem, but whether a campaign could be designed with integrity for a particular politician.

Jason, however, decided on the basis of principle. This candidate, in fact, pleased him. This issue centered on his perceived complicity in weakening the democratic process, and he therefore declined to participate. But does he now have a responsibility to do more? Jason's complaints were apparently serious, and he presumably believed them deeply. In that light the simple act of not joining the team seems incongruous and even meaningless. A vital aspect of social life is being threatened, he declares, and yet he reacts in a way that costs him little.

At a minimum, should he not protest his own agency's involvement? Several advertising firms in the United States refuse all political accounts. For some, this policy is one of self-protection, arising from the poor credit risk that most campaign accounts represent. But a few object on grounds similar to Jason's. The question he ought to face is whether he has a responsibility to pursue every means possible until his agency adopts such a policy, or at least more enlightened guidelines. Some television stations have chosen to refuse to allow anything less than five minutes for paid political broadcasts. Jason's agency could enact a similar policy for the political campaigns it creates. Perhaps one can even argue that he should resign if all attempts fail to influence his firm.

The public policy arena is an important one also. Laws regarding campaign expenditures are constantly discussed and frequently rewritten. The 1974 Campaign Reform Act placed a ceiling on the total amount that presidential candidates could spend on their campaigns, but in recent years the spending of Political Action Committees (PACs) has resulted in more intense use of broadcast advertising than ever. Stronger regulatory alternatives are possible. Great Britain has had a long-standing policy preventing anyone from buying commercial time for election campaigns. The major parties are allocated an equal amount, and television stations are required to broadcast the programs free. All other exposure occurs in news coverage, over which politicians have no control. Regardless of the options proposed, should not such possibilities of reform be on the forefront of Jason's agenda?

In the absence of Jason's making any effort to take his own conclusion seriously, an observer could be suspicious that he is only using rhetoric to make himself appear righteous. Underneath the expression of concern might really lie the factors of the extra work hours and the possibility of failure. In other words, he may be choosing not to join because he is not sure this project will prove useful to his own career as an adman. He does not excuse his own responsibility for making a decision; he does not argue that political commercials are only a fraction of the material available to voters and they must seek out more details before voting. It is not obvious that he declined to participate for any reasons other than highly personal ones.

There is a possibility that the moral dimension needs sharpening before more radical action becomes compelling. Precisely what is Jason's ethical objection to political advertising? In working through the problem, he thinks largely in sociopolitical terms about the need for enlightened citizens. He warns against slick and simplistic ads in a complex world. Clearly these concerns represent strong political values, but the ethical issue could be focused better. Has he concluded that political commercials of 30 and 60 seconds are inherently deceptive? Even if no outright lies are permitted, he could contend that short spots inevitably and fundamentally distort both the style and content of the candidate.

A form of deception seems to be the moral issue here, and if Jason defined the question in those terms he might be motivated not simply to decline participation in the task force, but to demand changes in his company, and in public policy as well.

36. FEMININE HYGIENE IN THE LIVING ROOM

"Most people are aware," former advertising practitioner Jerry Mander wrote nearly a decade ago, "that advertising is an invasion of privacy; this is not a new revelation. But the fact that we can be aware of it and not be furious about it, and do nothing about stopping it, is not so much a sign that it's an unimportant issue as it is a sign of the level of our submission."[18]

"Well," Dr. Josh Farleigh asked his class in media ethics, "was Mander right?"

The first response hit a common theme: "We have a choice. We don't have to pay attention to ads, or any other media content that we don't like."

"That may be," Josh responded, enjoying his role as devil's advocate, "but doesn't most advertising seek us out rather than the other way around? And we really don't have all that much choice about whether we want to encounter some ads, particularly on television or over the radio, not to mention billboards."

"Well, the ads are there because they help pay for the media, and beside that, we all get used to shutting out ads we don't want to see, particularly with the broadcast commercials."

"But," Josh probed, "why should you have to have to work at avoiding things? If you had a friend that constantly tried to 'get at' you, whether you were interested or not, you wouldn't tolerate him or her very long would you? Then why should you tolerate unwelcome advertisers, particularly in the privacy of your home?"

"Okay, but if you're going to choose to have a television set, and watch commercial television, you know you're going to see ads. It's a compromise we all understand, so I don't see it as an ethical issue. It's simply a matter of choice."

"Well, then, let's get specific. Here's an article from *Advertising Age* last year. Look at the headline: 'Feminine Hygiene Ads Are Rated Most Hated.'[19] It's based on a nationwide survey of 1,000 adults who were asked to name TV commercials they find really objectionable. The article says the research 'turned up a clear winner: the whole feminine hygiene product category. For men and women alike, these commercials made them squirm with discomfort.'[20] Listen to that—'squirm with discomfort.' Why should we have to do that, in our own homes, because of a commercial form we can't anticipate and find it very difficult to avoid when it does intrude. Listen to Mander again about the general issue of advertising's supposed invasion of privacy: *Why do we tolerate this? What right do advertisers have to treat us that way? When did I sell the right for them to run pictures in my mind? Why is it possible for people who are selling things to feel perfectly free to speak to me, over public airwaves, without my permission, all day long?*[21]

"Well, what do you think now?"

Is there an ethical problem here? Mander, whom Josh quotes, is obviously operating at a very basic, absolutist, level. In his view it is simply wrong, apparently under any circumstances, for advertisers to "invade our privacy." That statement, of course, is directed at the very essence of the advertising form in its modern arrangements with the media—that is, it seeks us out rather than the other way around—and it's abundantly clear that the media frequently think of themselves as the means to the end of gathering potential customers together for advertisers.

If Mander did choose to operate at the consequentialist level, he might find it difficult to muster support for "the greatest number." For example, it could be argued that:

■ *Advertisers* feel that the present arrangement offers them a chance to put their messages before potentially interested individuals.

■ The *media* would argue that individuals do have choices and that the presence of advertising—sometimes welcome, particularly with more specialized media—is simply a trade-off that most readers, viewers, and listeners seem ready to accept.

■ Even the *viewers, listeners, or readers* themselves would probably contend that the presence of advertising is occasionally illuminating, sometimes entertaining, and generally a reasonable subsidy for some of the nonadvertising content.

So Mander remains—properly, it can be contended—in Kantian territory, asserting that to the extent that advertising seeks us out so relentlessly through the media it is inherently flawed.

Perhaps the issue becomes less close-ended if we narrow the

scope. First, there is no clear evidence that many find ads in most of the print media objectionable, so the argument is primarily about television, the most intrusive of the forms. Second, it seems likely that certain kinds of television advertising, regardless of execution, are more likely to promote disquietude than others. Obviously, feminine hygiene products are the prototype, as, to a lesser extent, are broadcast advertisements in such sensitive areas as condoms; a member of the Catholic clergy recently stated with exasperation, "America is bound and determined to make sex as casual and unsupportive as shaking hands."[22]

So the issue is narrowed to the advertising of certain product categories *on television* being seen as objectionable by some segments of the population—and apparently a substantial segment in the case of feminine hygiene products.

Advertisers can still argue on the basis of the greatest good for the greatest number, although they apparently could find it difficult to make that case for the advertising of feminine hygiene products on television. Still, they could fall back on the comfort of the "natural" signals from the market—that is, if they really objected to us they wouldn't buy our products and we would do something different.

The media are, of course, the gatekeepers, but they seem increasingly inclined to open the doors wider—for example, by accepting ads for condoms and allowing bra commercials with live models. Why? Condoms are justified as products of disease prevention, and television is one of the few media that guarantee sure access to appropriate population segments—frequently the poor and lower educated; and the presence of bra-wearing models is justified on the basis of the growing liberality of the audience. And there is always money. These advertisers buy time. It would be difficult for network television to make a "public need" case for information on feminine hygiene products in order to justify lifting their self-imposed ban on that product category a number of years ago. And given the response to the *Advertising Age* poll, as well as simple grass roots sampling, it must be evident that viewers dislike this form of advertising more than virtually any other. Therefore, simple economic self-interest looms large.

Perhaps there are Rawlsian dimensions of fairness here that could be explored, such as restricting the feminine hygiene product advertising to late prime time or daytime shows, when the adult female audience is likely to dominate, potentially an audience more appreciative of the ad's content. The medium's income would be maintained, and at least some of the irritation level might be diminished.

Is there an ethical problem here? Having a significant portion of a television audience "squirm with discomfort" because of an intrusive advertising form dealing with a sensitive subject area would certainly suggest so.

NOTES

1. Judann Dagnoli, "Groups Smoking Over Camel Ad," *Advertising Age*, 17 July 1989, p. 49.
2. "Harvard Public Health Dean Asks Bar on Cigarette Ads," Champaign-Urbana *News Gazette*, 13 May 1985, p. 85.
3. Steven W. Colford, "Koop Seeks Voluntary Curbs," *Advertising Age*, 5 June 1989, p. 6. See also, "Advertising Abuse—The Surgeon General's Recommendations," *AAAA Washington Newsletter*, July/August 1989, pp. 1–3.
4. "Facts Which Are Not Trivial," in *S.E.A. Briefs*, McKinley Health Center, Urbana, Ill. November 1988. (Figures from National Council on Alcoholism.)
5. Associated Press, "Limits Urged on Ads That Glorify Drinking," Champaign-Urbana *News-Gazette*, 8 December 1988, p. D-3.
6. Steven W. Colford, "Ad Industry Is On Guard," *Advertising Age*, 29 May 1989, p. 45.
7. "Surgeon General Holds Drunk Driving Workshop," *AAAA Washington Newsletter*, February/March 1989, p. 1.
8. Steven W. Colford, "Survey Shows 39% Favor Beer Ad Ban," *Advertising Age*, 5 June 1989, p. 6. See also Steven W. Colford, "Cabinet Execs Back Limits on Alcohol Ads," *Advertising Age*, 18 December 1989, p. 2.
9. Hal Shoup, "Editorial," *AAAA Washington Newsletter* July/August 1989, p. 3.
10. Ira Teinowitz, "Coors Pours $5 Million Into Moderation Pitch," *Advertising Age*, 29 May 1989, p. 45.
11. Colford, "Koop Seeks Voluntary Curbs."
12. Ibid.
13. Associated Press, "Limits Urged."
14. *Responsibility in Political Advertising in 1984*, presentation by the American Association of Advertising Agencies in the Senate Caucus Room, 9 December 1983.
15. Ibid, pp. 22–23
16. One of the most influential arguments about the television mode is to be found in Herbert Krugman, "The Impact of TV Advertising: Learning Without Involvement," *Public Opinion Quarterly* 29 (Fall 1965).
17. For a particularly illuminating perspective on the Bush–Dukakis campaign, see "The Campaign You Never Saw," *New York*, 12 December 1988.
18. Jerry Mander, "Four Arguments for the Elimination of Advertising," in

Kim Rotzoll, ed., *Advertising and the Public*. Urbana, Ill.: Department of Advertising, 1980, pps. 14–21.

19. Scott Hume, "Most Hated Ads: Feminine Hygiene," *Advertising Age*, 18 July 1988, p. 3.
20. Ibid.
21. Mander, "Four Arguments," p. 21.
22. "Ads That Shatter an Old Taboo," *Time*, 2 February 1987, p. 63.

CHAPTER 8

How to Say It

In some of the research conducted for this book, advertising practitioners were asked to cite the ethical confrontations most common to their day-to-day activities. The nature of the advertising message led the pack.

Advertising is, by its nature, communication with a purpose. It seeks to alter the thinking and/or behavior of those receiving the message in a manner beneficial to the advertiser. In the previous chapter we examined some of the ethical controversies centered on the subject of that message. Here we consider the decisions about execution, the host of verbal and nonverbal symbols that can be arranged in virtually infinite combinations to attempt to achieve advertisers' ends.

Whether this potential is considered a problem or not depends to a great extent on what assumptions are made about human nature (about whether or not an individual is deliberate and calculating, for example) as well as on the ultimate fairness of the market system within which advertising flourishes.

The cases in this chapter were chosen to represent some of the more persistent and bedeviling situations confronting practitioners in the practice of their craft:

- Exaggerated differences
- Sins of omission
- Matters of effectiveness versus taste
- Puffery

Keep in mind that advertising's actual effects are often quite difficult to determine, even when there is agreement as to what "effect"

means (for example, does it mean awareness? attitude change? an increase in sales?).

37. A MINUSCULE (AND TASTELESS) DIFFERENCE

Cynthia Brace was the advertising manager for a large regional
soft drink company, one of many in a highly competitive market.
The line leader for the company was its strawberry soda, and that
was the current bone of contention.

The advertising agency had recently finished a comprehensive
study of the company, its competitors, and the soft drink market
in general. Its basic conclusion was complimentary: Brandco offered a product of consistent quality. Indeed, production control
was such that its product could be properly identified as high
quality. The problem was that this particular selling point had
little impact on potential consumers. Quality was, at best, an
elusive concept, perhaps better associated with cars or television
sets than an essentially taste-dominated product such as a soft
drink. So the agency had been searching for another way of asserting a competitive edge. In essence, it sought a proxy for high
quality.

It thought it had found it with a "natural" theme, expressed in
the slogan, "A little bit of natural flavor in every drop." After an
initial screening, the legal department, extremely sensitive to natural themes because of concerns of the Food and Drug Administration, asked, "Can you prove it?" The agency turned to
Cynthia for the anticipated verification that Brandco's strawberry
soda did indeed contain natural flavoring.

It did not, she told them, for the simple reason that natural
strawberry juice simply tastes terrible. All of its other flavors do
contain varying degrees of natural flavoring, but not strawberry,
its best seller.

The agency was adamant. The natural theme would not only
imply Brandco's justifiable high quality, but also nicely catch the
country's move toward healthier lifestyles. "Natural" had certain
highly positive symbolic connotations at the present time, and a
competitive edge could be gained through using it.

Cynthia was subsequently asked if Brandco could add some
natural strawberry flavoring to verify the claim. She pointed out
that any amount that could be tasted would result in a negative

change for the popular soda. What, then, they asked, of a min-uscule amount, just enough to support the slogan, "A little bit of natural flavor in every drop," but not enough to affect the taste?

The president would have to decide that, Cynthia knew. After all, it would represent the first change in the formula in the 70-year history of the brand. (Shades of "Classic" Coke, she thought cynically.) But should *she* support it?

Ultimately, she did, on the basis of the attraction of the prom-ised competitive edge, as well as her assessment that no real harm would be done to anyone. The media could honestly clear the advertisement. The agency could stand behind the slogan. The customer could continue to enjoy the taste of a soft drink that had become a best seller on the basis of its flavor. And, finally, the company could continue to offer high-quality soft drinks in an extremely competitive market.

As standards in the soft drink industry go, Brandco apparently has a good-quality product. The initial problem here is to discover some way to get across the idea of quality without stating that theme explicitly, since it apparently has little motivating power for consumers. There-fore "natural" was seen as the best proxy. It was necessary to add only enough natural strawberry juice to verify the claim, but not enough to change the taste.

Cynthia's decision to support the addition seems to be based on her feeling that no real harm would be done to anyone. That assump-tion needs close examination. As we have seen, businesses frequently rely on basically utilitarian assumptions interwoven with a belief in the basic fairness of the market mechanism. But where is the greatest good for the greatest number here? Presumably Cynthia's company will benefit from increased sales. But there is apparently no enhanced good to existing customers, and possibly negative effects for new cus-tomers to the extent that their reasons for brand choice are based on misleading impressions. In short, Cynthia's action, under closer scru-tiny, seems narrowly self-interested in the corporate sense.

She could have relied upon the categorical imperative of truth-telling. Operating from this premise, she could have concluded that it is simply wrong to misinform, whether by what is included in the message or by what is omitted. Even utilitarianism, carried through to such conclusions as those discussed, could have challenged her decision.

Basically it would seem that Cynthia acted without any overriding sense of what is right, short of what is best for the company. Certainly this position is expedient for an employee in terms of her or his business career. In a larger context, however, it assumes that the company good is to be equated with the public good. In this case, at least, that seems a dubious assumption.

Lacking any apparent set of working premises that does not begin with the company, Cynthia seems destined to confront each issue anew with increasingly predictable conclusions. As her longevity with the company grows, past decisions may well solidify into an operative set of company-servicing rules that shortcut thoughtful ethical considerations in all future situations.

Making an ethical decision requires reflection. On the basis of this case, and Cynthia's apparent decision-making criteria, she seems destined to avoid its trials as well as its triumphs.

38. SINS OF OMISSION: PARITY PRODUCTS

Harry Feldner was a 46-year-old creative supervisor with more than 23 years' experience in the agency business. He paused over the question on the form before him. A group of faculty were trying to find out something about the ethics of the advertising business. Talk about old wine in new bottles! The question read, "Do you feel that you encounter ethical decisions in the practice of your job?" Harry immediately wrote, "Not really. All our work is carefully scrutinized by lawyers internally, as well as the client and the networks." He stopped, thought a bit, and then added, "I have not yet decided whether 'puffery' is unethical. Yet I do feel that if an advertiser has to tell the whole truth he may as well not advertise—there would be no competitive advantage since most products are parity, with only minor shades of difference."

Parity products, Harry reflected. Advertising's bane and triumph.[1] Face it, a very large number of the mass-advertised mass-consumption brands are substitutable for one another without any noticeable difference in performance. Hadn't the BBDO Worldwide study revealed that two-thirds of the consumers in 28 countries considered brands in 13 major product categories to be *virtually identical*? Hell, Harry thought, parity products are all

over the home-medication shelves in the drug store, not to mention deodorants, margarines, VCRs, "natural" and synthetic vi-
tamins, household cleaning aids, as well as a great number of the
army of laundry products. And what of the beers and cigarettes?
Test after test had demonstrated that even the most brand loyal
could not consistently pick out their brand from other, unidentified samples. What was it *Consumer Reports* wrote recently?
"As far as we can tell, relatively inexpensive shampoos contain
perfectly adequate cleaning and conditioning ingredients. If you
want to spend money on an expensive shampoo, do it knowing
that you're indulging your psyche, not your hair."[2] And, on another subject, "When it comes to ordinary cleaning, all soap is
created equal. . . . One real difference is price. The most expensive
of the bars we tested sells for nearly 45 times the price of the
cheapest."[3]

In some cases the products are identical, because of government
requirements (for example, regarding some drugs), or because producers commonly sell some of their output to retailers for marketing under their brand name(s). Simply, parity products are a
fact of the contemporary marketplace. And to think, he reflected,
a shaker and roller like Marion Harper, Jr., could have predicted
that "by the 1980s few parity products . . . will be advertised extensively."[4] Tell that to Kellogg's Corn Flakes and Post Toasties,
or many detergents, or canned vegetables, or bottled waters, or
dungarees, or ketchups, or peanut butters, or dishwashing liquids,
or. . . .

The intriguing thing about parity products, he thought, is their
curse and their challenge. The curse is best summed up by that
memorable quotation from the old master of the hard sell Rosser
Reeves: "Our problem is—a client comes into my office and
throws two newly minted half-dollars onto my desk and says,
'Mine is the one on the left. You prove it's better.'"[5] The challenge, of course, comes precisely from the lack of physical or
functional difference. It enables the copywriter and art director
to move with considerable ease into the realm of the consumer's
emotions—to manipulate symbols, to create moods and distinc-
tive product identities:

- A green giant? A doughboy? A talking rabbit? A rugged cowboy? A "modern" woman? Attach them successfully to
  chemical or paper or plastic things and to real or artificial

substances and, behold, there is more projected than the
functional performance of the item.

- Or have recognizable personalities speak for the product and
  let their charisma wash over. (Just think of the "celebrity
  wars" waged by Pepsi and Coke!)
- Or sing. Yes indeed, sing about that thing made of bubbles
  and syrups and water. Sing about the beer, about toilet paper,
  about the joys of carpet.[6]

The challenge is, then, to suggest a difference where none in
fact exists in any real sense. A former colleague, the late Howard
Gossage, used to make much of the distinction between image
and identity. "An image," he often said, "is how you want others
to see you. An identity, on the other hand, is what you really
are."[7] Obviously, Gossage felt one is on much firmer ethical
ground dealing with identities. But, Harry added, the essence of
a great deal of advertising lies with images. And, until the government tells us we cannot sell differences where none exists, I
will lend my talents to the cause.

In a review of several books by practitioners of advertising, the *New
York Times*'s Roger Draper put the ethical issue succinctly. Much consumer goods advertising, he asserted, attempts "to suppress an important fact: the similarity among competing brands. If 'some of the
truth' in this sense is an acceptable alternative to all of it, the value
of truth itself becomes puzzling."[8]

Harry was responding to the first question on a form the authors
of this book sent to advertising practitioners. His initial response
tended to equate right with what is considered legal. In other words,
if the lawyers at the agency, the client, and the network consider it
acceptable, then it is. But Harry knew there was more. His response
about puffery seems to address the more fundamental question in this
case: Regardless of specific consequences, is it wrong to imply differences where, functionally, there are none?

This question strikes at the heart of parity products, as Harry
knew. His wanderings in difficult ethical territory were short-lived,
however. He was soon reflecting on the curse and challenge of parity

products—but his reflections were focused on the *advertising practitioner*, not on the public. Parity products, Harry seems to be saying, are a curse in the sense that it is hard to provide a successful difference where none exists, but they are also a challenge in that the advertiser has to create a difference that establishes brand loyalty.

Harry seems to shrug aside concern over the effects of this type of advertising with "We all do it, don't we?" We are, he seems to be suggesting, all creatures of symbolic meaning and are therefore not ill served by communications of high symbolic content. Indeed, we may feel more comfortable with one virtually identical brand over the other—such as Bayer versus generic aspirin—because of the symbolic content that makes the difference for us. (After explaining how consumers could save $2,500 a year at the supermarket buying store brands rather than national brands, *Consumer Reports* noted that a poll revealed most of *its readers* "opt for buying name-brand products despite the cost."[9]) Harry seems to imply that the greatest good for the greatest number is served by making parity products different because people want them different, either consciously or unconsciously.

But is this in fact so? Would it make a difference if people knew that certain brands were identical in performance? Would they say, "I don't care if my brand *is* the same as another, I want to buy it anyway"? Perhaps. But if knowledge of the parity nature of some brands *would* make a difference in purchasing decisions, then the greatest good for the greatest number is not being served by concealing it, and the utilitarian justification is weakened if not eliminated. Harry does not even address that question.

What ethical justification would he have left if he had? Basically the conviction that moral duty is owed specifically to the advertiser ("I need to establish a difference for his product because it's my job"), or, more generally, to advertising as a communication form ("That's the essence of a great deal of advertising" or "That's the way the game is played"). If utilitarianism fails, his loyalty to his client or business would, it seems, be the only ground left.

Harry's experiences as a practitioner could have led him to confront two troubling premises: (1) What is good is what is legal. (2) What is legal is not necessarily what is good for the public. Wishing to believe his work ethical, Harry has refused to address the second premise. Venturing into that area beyond his currently uncritical thinking could force him to ask questions that he would apparently not wish to have answered.

39. SINS OF OMISSION: WHAT SHALL WE LEAVE OUT?

Blair Richards hung up the phone with a sense of satisfaction. His West Coast agency had inherited a brand of hair conditioner with its basic claim, "Helps Stop Oily Hair." The formula was, in fact, oil free. The problem, it turned out, was that it was a wax-based rather than a water-based formula, and when the product interacted with naturally oily hair, it actually led to an oily buildup. Now *that* presented some interesting choices!

- Recommend to the advertiser that it drop the claim or the brand? (A great way to greet a new client!)
- Do nothing and assume that women will deliver their own verdict with declining sales?

As a research director, his solution seemed particularly apt. He recommended to the client that the agency undertake a research project testing the reaction to the product by women of various hair types—oily, normal, dry, and so on. When the results were in, as was expected, the women with oily hair had the greatest trial rate, *but also the lowest retention rate.* He had passed on this information to the client and, in the phone call he had just received, the advertiser had decided to drop the misleading line.

Deception by omission, Blair thought, was one of the ongoing, and perhaps most vexing problems of advertising practice. This time the problem was resolved because the agency was able to demonstrate that it was not in the best economic interest of the advertiser to continue the potentially deceptive claim. This time. But would the win/win strategy work the next time, or the time after that, or. . . .

Blair apparently had inherent faith in the greatest good for the greatest number being achieved by the market system. Eventually, he seemed to be implying, the brand would have suffered, as more women with oily hair—those targeted by the claim—tried it and found it wanting. His particular ethical standards led him to shortcut the process with a test that made it clear to the client that the offending claim was not practical. Certainly, here the greatest good for the greatest number was served. However, the client was left without a truly distinguishing claim.

Advertising is, by its nature, one-sided communication, and as long as one assumes (1) that people are active (and reflective) information seekers, and (2) that there are enough competing sources of information to enable them to make wise decisions, the "marketplace of ideas" can be seen as a stimulating and satisfying environment. But *do* people act this way and, if not, what responsibility, if any, do advertisers have to compensate? Consider:

■ Plax mouthwash claimed it "removes 300 percent more plaque than brushing alone." An inquiry by a self-regulatory body of the advertising business revealed that one of the key studies used to support the claim had panelists limit their brushing to 15 seconds—and didn't let them use toothpaste.[10]

■ *Adweek's Marketing Week's* annual "Pinocchio Awards" included the following:

Gasoline companies pushing premium gasolines with claims such as "the highest octane unleaded gas ever . . . No other gas can make your car perform better," while it is estimated that only 10 percent of the cars in America can benefit from higher octane.[11]

Sun tan lotions promoting products with sun protection factors as high as 33 when "an SPF higher than 15 is overkill for the average pasty face taking the sun on the beach or out at a ball game."[12]

Potentially misleading use of health buzz words such as "low sodium," "high fiber," "lowers cholesterol," "low fat," "fat free," "guards against cancer and heart attacks," "calcium enriched," and, of course, "light." For example, "a tablespoon of Bertolli Extra Light 100 percent Pure Olive Oil has exactly the same number of calories as a tablespoon of Bertolli Extra Virgin Olive Oil."[13]

■ In their "Clues to Bad Advertisements," the American Newspaper Publisher's Association cautions, "If it sounds too good to be true, it probably is," and warns customers to be wary of promises such as "free gifts," "guaranteed trade-in allowance," "breakthrough," "secret," "medically approved," "no risk," "erase bad credit," "free vacations," and "guaranteed results."[14]

■ Discussing food claims, John Corwin of the New York Attorney General's office has said:

> The issue in food is that it's a big-ticket item in people's budgets, so the people who sell food have an interest in making health claims for their products. If you have a claim for a product that says the product is good for you because it contains X, and you don't disclose that it also contains Y, which is more harmful than the benefit that X gives, I don't think you're telling the truth about the product.[15]

Note that with all these examples the statements made in the ads are usually literally true but the impressions received by the potential consumer may be misleading. These are murky waters indeed. *Advertising Age* recently defended the advertising for Kellogg's new "Heartwise" cereal as containing a "health *statement*," not "health *claims*."[16] Yet, it could be claimed that, *in the context of the ad or the package*, the "statement" becomes associated in the potential consumer's mind with the brand, hence taking on the properties of a claim.

Advertisers will commonly justify the withholding of potentially useful information on the assumptions of self-interest and the essential fairness of the marketplace: "I say this, but they say that, and the consumer can figure it out on the basis of other forms of competing information, their own experience and intelligence, and so on." They would argue that it is, after all, a persuasive form of communication, recognized as such by the potential consumer.

Practitioner Win Roll recently admonished his colleagues, "If the copy stretches the truth even by a hair, or can be misinterpreted by anyone exposed to it, find another way."[17] Most advertisers, it may be argued, will have little trouble with the first requirement—what is in the ad must be truthful—but the second requirement seems to be the heart of the matter. Is it the responsibility of the advertiser to ensure that no misinterpretation occurs?

Advertisers certainly have the resources to ensure so if they choose. Small research efforts among typical consumers would quickly reveal whether the impression potential consumers receive from the ad is misleading. If advertisers or their agencies choose not to pursue this course, then it could be argued that (1) they trust the market with its inherent assumptions of utilitarianism, or (2) they intend to thwart the market for their own good. The latter scenario is, of course, far easier to condemn ethically than the first. In any event, the issue is common, complex, and ethically exotic.

40. Sins of Omission: Teaching about Advertising

Kevin Rothschild had never satisfactorily resolved his personal dilemma about the material. Although he had now been teaching advertising at the university level for more than five years, he still confronted the issue anew before every semester.

It centered on the Survey of Advertising course that Kevin taught twice a year at a large midwestern university. Over the academic year the course attracted between 500 and 1,000 students, a healthy percentage of whom later declared themselves to be advertising majors. More majors meant more student credit hours, more interdepartmental budget clout, more faculty, healthier salaries, and more research funds.

It was a fascinating area for many students. They enjoyed hearing about the strategies behind familiar advertising campaigns, jousting—albeit briefly—with issues such as the morality of advertising to children, and were generally left with most of their stereotypes of the glamorous world of advertising relatively secure. Here, Kevin knew, was the crux of the dilemma. There was another side to advertising to which he could expose them far more readily than he did now, a side that pondered whether advertising was, in fact, a desirable institution.

Should he give more class and reading time to assertions such as the following:

> National advertising serves primarily to artificially differentiate parity products and to inhibit existing and potential competition, making possible pricing discretion and discriminating and manufacturer domination of markets, with consequent misallocation of resources and monopoly transfers. All these functions are incompatible with both classical and neo-liberal values; and we have said nothing of advertising's harmful effects on the mass media and its questionable (at best) effects on other aspects of our lives.[18]

Or this sweeping statement from UNESCO's widely discussed MacBride Report:

> Regarded as a form of communication, it [advertising] has been criticized for playing on emotions, simplifying real

human situations into stereotypes, exploiting anxieties, and employing techniques of intensive persuasion that amount to manipulation. Many social critics have stated that advertising is essentially concerned with exalting the materialistic virtues of consumption by exploiting achievement drives and emulative anxieties, employing tactics of hidden manipulation, playing on emotions, maximizing appeal and minimizing information, trivializing, eliminating objective considerations, contriving illogical situations, and generally reducing men, women and children to the role of irrational consumer. Criticism expressed in such a way may be overstated but it cannot be entirely brushed aside.[19]

In this area of advertising's presumed social impact, should he expose them to at least the major findings from scholar Richard Pollay's sweeping review of "all North American authors known to have written on the cultural character of advertising"?[20] After compiling the observations of prominent psychologists, sociologists, anthropologists, historians, educators, communications specialists, linguists, philosophers, theologians, and political scientists, Pollay commented, "What may be shocking . . . is the veritable absence of perceived positive influence."[21]

Then of course there is the not inconsiderable body of commentary from some advertising practitioners with less than charitable views of the working conditions of the business. One of the classics is from agency principal Jerry Della Femina:

> When you think of advertising, don't think of Rock Hudson manipulating Doris Day. Think of H. R. Haldeman trying to screw up some tapes, because that's closest to what large-agency advertising men are like.[22]

Nicholas Samstag, late director of promotion for *Time*, said, "The half-truth is the essence of advertising." He continued:

> But what impact has this on the advertising man? The need to deal only with truths which further his purpose cannot help carrying over into his life outside his work. As he proceeds along the path of his career, he is likely

to become less and less real, more and more lop-sided ("half-assed" is a good word for it).

What he is *really* paid for is a quality that we might term "eclectic amnesia," the ability to select the weaknesses in his product and bury them in his forgettery, so that he can concentrate on what's left for his advertising campaign. The better he does this the more he prospers. If he cannot do it, he is fired. He alone ... must, in a sense, blind himself to earn a livelihood.[23]

Anthropologist Jules Henry came to the same conclusion:

Advertising men do not contradict themselves or lie to one another *in terms of their own culture*. The central issue is that they have lived so long where double-talk is the *only* talk, and where *contradiction* is *affirmation*, that they do not perceive in what they say what we of the more traditional culture perceive.[24]

And what will Kevin's students' peers think of them should they decide to become advertising majors? Well, it's an extremely popular major, but they're going to have to live with a lot of flack too. What was it that the "Teen Scan" of Backer Spielvogel Bates, Inc. just revealed?

Only 30% of teens give advertising an "enjoyable" rating, versus 45% for adults. 73% believe advertising makes people buy what they don't need. 45% of female Proto-Adults [teens] believe advertising depicts women in a degrading way. And two-thirds of the Proto-Adults think advertising doesn't show teenagers as they really are.[25]

Not exactly an overwhelming vote of confidence.

Kevin could, of course, include all of this bad news of the business's alleged effects on society and on the individuals in advertising, but then offset it with strongly supportive information and opinion, of which there was plenty—a fair balance, in other words. If he did that, however, the amount of time consumed would require him to eliminate a lot of other material, including some of the most popular stuff. The tone of the course would become considerably more somber, analytic rather than simply descriptive. Kevin could predict the results: a possible decline in class enrollment, and certainly a drop in the percentage of students who would then elect to pursue advertising as a major.

But didn't Kevin owe the students as penetrating a look at the business as he was capable of offering? After all, many of them would be making decisions about the direction of their careers. Would he serve them well if they decided to commit themselves to a future on the basis of an incomplete picture? Indeed, couldn't it be argued that the greater the potential hazards in a business—to the society and to its employees—the greater the ethical necessity to examine them?

Still, there was the enrollment, and the subsequent well-being of his colleagues. Of course, his department head would surely view declining enrollments with alarm, and he might be shifted to a teaching assignment of a less critical nature. In any event, advertising majors are required to take a number of professionally oriented courses before their graduation. They would, he reasoned, certainly get enough of a balanced picture in those courses to determine whether they had made a wise choice.

So, better not fool with a successful course, at least this time around. Kevin will, however, try to include a bit more controversial material in his lectures. If only he can find time to fit it in. . . .

Here is a clear conflict between belief and behavior. But before focusing on that, it is useful to examine the various ethical rationales Kevin might have employed in deciding to endorse his class's status quo. He could have decided on the basis of personal relativism: My act (or rather lack of it) is right because I say it is right. Using utilitarian thinking, he could have argued that the greatest short-run good to the greatest number (his students) was served by keeping the course light, keeping enthusiasm high, and soft-pedaling the negative material. Certainly his teaching colleagues and members of the advertising business would be served by his decision as well. But what of the long-run good? Here his decision can be questioned. Is it serving the greatest number to leave students with an incomplete understanding of the business they seek to understand? Shouldn't they be exposed to the critics as well as the cheerleaders? And what of those who decide to become advertising majors? Is it serving their best interests to encourage them to become part of the business when they may be subsequently disillusioned?

The same type of thinking pervades questions of where moral duty is owed. Student short run? Student long run? Colleagues? Himself? It could be contended that, apart from the long-run interests of the students, Kevin's decision would seem to be supported.

If only short-run consequences are considered, the ethical answer is a resounding "Don't change!" Consideration of long-run consequences, however, is much more difficult because of the degree of conjecture involved. How will his present decision affect students in their advertising careers several years in the future? Obviously that question is more difficult to answer than the question of how the department head would respond to declining enrollment.

Now we return to the matter of principle. Kevin would appear to be ethically inconsistent. He knows that the negative material is there and is important, and therefore that its absence from the course gives students an incomplete picture of the range of opinions about advertising practice. In short, he appears to believe in the ideal of the rational mind and the notion that conflicting ideas in the classroom enhance education, yet he has chosen to act in a manner that makes that process impossible.

Thus considered, Kevin's decision is unconscionable. From a Kantian perspective there is only one right course, and it is not affected by perceived consequences. Kevin did not choose that course; rather, he compromised the key element in this dilemma—his moral integrity as a teacher rather than as an advocate.

41. Gun for Hire?

The 27-year-old copywriter had been in this business long enough to experience the evolution of a great deal of broadcast advertising, and once again she was ready to make a judgment. Before her was a blank sheet of paper in a typewriter. Shortly (and it better be shortly!) the paper would be full of words and suggestions for visual elements in regard to a well-known packaged good—in this case a product for relief of cold symptoms. The commercial would eventually be aired during the heart of what she had come to know as the flu and cold season, the high-water mark for the client's annual sales.

She had written dozens of commercials for this client before.

Perhaps that was one of the problems, she thought. You get locked into certain formulas, certain predictable ways of dealing with the challenge of promoting the client's product, and you crank out the next entry. The central problem was that she hated a lot of advertisements, sometimes including her own.

She was reminded of the words of another copywriter from the early years of television:

> My children know I'm in advertising, but it doesn't interest them much. They don't ask me about it. The other day, though, we were all sitting watching television, and one of these cartoon commercials came on. It showed two big wrestlers coming into a ring, one with the label PAIN on his robe, and the other with the label ORDINARY PAINKILLER. Something like that. Anyway, PAIN threw ORDINARY PAINKILLER right out of the ring, and stomped around afterward. Then another wrestler came on, with the brand name stenciled on his robe, and he threw PAIN out of the ring, knocked him out completely, you see.
>
> I didn't think much of it, one way or the other, but my younger boy called me aside, out of the room. He said, "Dad, am I to understand that a bunch of grown men sat around and thought up that thing? And another bunch of grown men sat around and said it was a good idea? And another bunch of men went to all the work to make a movie of it?"
>
> What could I say? I told him that was just what had happened. He walked away, shaking his head.[26]

Well, thought the copywriter, my advertising does not include cartoons, unless you can regard the characters I create as cartoons. But what of the simplistic and repetitive dialogue I put in their mouths, or their relentless concern with suffering, and their shining gratitude at the relief provided by the client's nostrum?

All advertising is not pap, she mused. A great deal of magazine advertising reflects the interests and tastes of its audience. A lot of newspaper advertising is a good friend—informative and helpful. Industrial and business advertising has to be straightforward most of the time. And some broadcast advertising is certainly memorable, in the best sense. It's just the combination of television and certain products that seems to provide the most fertile climate for this tripe.

The bottom line is that it appears to work. Look at the classic success of "Ring Around the Collar," R-O-L-A-I-D-S, Mr. Whipple, the doublemint gum gang, Madge the beautician, and those awful ads for deodorants and women's hygiene products. Her own agency's research had indicated that brand name recognition and recall of major sales points was higher with the simplistic approach she had been using for this client than with a more civilized (she thought) technique she had been allowed to test in rough cut form. So what does that say about the television audience, she wondered. Break through their passivity with the blunt instruments of repetition and stereotypical characters? So it would seem. After all, whose money is being spent anyway? The client produces an honest product and deserves the most productive advertising we can give him. Awards would be nice, but the advertiser expects *sales*.

And if it happens that I am reluctant to claim authorship? If I am ashamed to admit a grown woman created that? Maybe it's enough to know that the client can laugh all the way to the bank.

Rather than the information content of the advertisement, or the lack of it, this case focuses on the dilemma of a "creative" person producing a product, in this case an ad, that does not fit her own tastes even though it may serve the best interests of the advertiser. The copywriter has apparently dealt with this problem sufficiently to indulge in at least some preliminary reflection. She has concluded that the problem is not one of advertising per se. She recognizes that there are other combinations of media and product classes that result in advertising messages that reflect the interests and tastes of those in the audience.

Yet this thought suggests that she has not pushed her thinking as far as it could productively go. Her concepts of "audience," in particular, seem muddled. Basically, she helps produce advertising that she personally finds offensive, mind dulling, repetitious, and simplistic. The unasked question seems to be whether the audience shares this assessment. She has apparently not followed this idea through very carefully. She could make the following conjectures to the question, "Does my advertising do harm to the public?" *Yes*, in the sense that it is vapid, superficial, and ultimately downright irritating. It fails to treat them as intelligent human beings and, in the process, demeans them. *No*, in the sense that this type of advertising seems to work. The "work," of course, refers to the best interests of the advertiser. But, since she is promoting an honest product, and people seem to be buying it, at least in part as a result of the advertising, is this not a mutually satisfactory arrangement?

If she accepts the first argument, she seems to be saying that the audience's tastes agree with her own and something should be done. But what of the fact that the advertising seems to work? Perhaps the product succeeds in spite of the advertising?

If she accepts the second argument, she is admitting that her tastes are different from those of her audience, that she, not the advertising, is not synchronized with the system, and that the audience may see the ads, properly, as means to the end of buying a potentially useful product. She would thus seem to be disillusioned with the people whom she is attempting to sell.

It is a quandary of personal standards then, and it is not easy to know the depth of her concern. This could be a relatively insignificant thought at a random moment, or it could represent a recurring theme that is increasingly important to her self-concept. In either event, some steps could sharpen the issue.

She should reflect more about her concept of the audience of her messages. Does she really believe they are being harmed? If so, then she must test her commitment to their well-being over her own.

She states that her more civilized approach did not test well, according to recall criteria. However, it is possible that it would test well at the behavior (sales) level, which is the ultimate criterion for most advertising success. Since recall is sometimes a poor proxy for sales, she could encourage more testing (albeit expensive and complex) at a level closer to actual sales behavior. If those tests proved reassuring, her approach might yet win the day. She could ask for a transfer to an account where the message and medium combination would allow her to produce advertising that is closer to her own taste and still "works." This option assumes a considerable depth of commitment on her part. She would, after all, be leaving a relatively easy job for one less certain, and, in the process, rock the boat by requesting a transfer.

Or she could attempt to make herself content as a "gun for hire" and take pride in the execution of her art form for the best interests of her client, not herself—a question, ultimately, of where loyalties lie.

Given the need for advertising communicators to develop symbol packages that are arresting and persuasive with a relatively disinterested audience, conflicts between communicator tastes and effectiveness seem inevitable. Perhaps the key factors in resolving these questions are some reflection on the communicator's concept of audience, as well as the depth of personal commitment to the issue. What works, be it in advertising, painting, films, novels, or plays, may not always be what the communicator likes. Thus, inevitable conflicts between creator and audience will present themselves. The ethical options are suitably complex, and, as always, require sometimes painful reflection, and perhaps even more painful action.

42. Larger Than Life

One of the accounts of a large New York agency is a major regional potato chip company. The agency is preparing to launch a new campaign for the chips and has sent commercial scripts to the production department. Mike Skillings, television production coordinator, reviewed the scripts and made preparations for taping. The script called for a party scene in which an attractive woman opens a bag of chips and pours them into a bowl. Mike made the necessary arrangements for the needed properties and talent, setting the taping for one week later.

Two days before the taping, Mike received a phone call from Marsha Young, the account executive, who wanted to know how the commercial was coming along. Mike assured her that all was arranged and that she would have the commercial on time. Marsha was pleased and explained that the new campaign was critical to the continued success of the chips in an increasingly competitive snack food market.

At the taping the actors and actresses were briefed and rehearsed the scene. When the actress opened and poured the bag of chips, some were broken and discolored. At the end of the scene, Marsha called Mike aside and suggested that they open several bags of chips, collecting the light, unbroken chips to make one perfect bag. She argued that consumers expect some chips to be dark or broken, so that no harm would be done by this simple exaggeration. After all, she noted, puffery is an acceptable element of advertising expression, even today.

She's right there, Mike thought. A certain amount of puffery is regarded as part of the advertising process, even by the FTC. Leaf through any magazine:

- "Incredible Art Value!"
- "The Ultimate Weapon in the War on Grass and Weeds"
- "Sophisticated"
- "The Symbol of Imported Luxury"
- "A New Standard of Value in Sports Sedans"

This is true in a visual sense as well, he knew. Not much attention had been paid to puffery through nonverbal symbols, but it was all around—exaggeration, a symbolic boast, a bit of presumably acceptable wishful thinking on the part of the advertiser. Consider the following:

- *The models chosen.* Memorable. Frequently handsome, beautiful, articulate, cute.
- *The settings.* Awful or splendid as the selling argument calls for. Quite often simply fanciful. Consider a car dancing on a moonlit beach to the haunting "Do You Want to Dance?" Rain-slickened streets reflecting the night life of young urbanites.
- *The colors.* Show the girl with drab hair in somber colors, the one with revitalized no-fuss in brights.
- *The mood.* Upbeat/exciting or dull/flat—at least until an application of the sponsor's product.
- *The graphics.* Absolutely brilliant photography or cinematography. Crisp editing. Deft retouching. Careful matching of type of music with the mood desired (the colas were masters here).

These are common and acceptable practices. Sure they exaggerate. Advertising is almost always larger than life, is it not? Perhaps because people want it to be. What was it that Pierre Martineau, the researcher, had said?

The consumer doesn't feel that he is being victimized or cheated by the retailer and the producer. On the contrary, he loves his stores and the mechanical triumphs of his age—the colorful automobiles, the pink washing machines, the garage doors with electric eyes. He is far, far more interested in the people who make Polaroid cameras and power tools, color TV sets and low-cost air conditioners than he is in what the intellectuals and politicians have to offer. This is what he works for; this is what he wants from life—not the frustrated pouting of some university hermit.[27]

Okay, Mike reflected, puffery may not be real life, but it doesn't seem to victimize either. So let the commercial's potato chips be a little better than they would normally be. The consumer's previous experience with chips, and the general expectations about advertising, should provide enough safeguards against deception.

Scholar Ivan Preston has noted that puffery in advertising receives forgiving legal treatment because it is assumed to have no effect, but it is used by advertisers because it does.[28] A puffing of claims about a product or service is generally to be expected in advertising, the courts have decided. It is presumed as unlikely to have any detrimental effect on even a relatively naive consumer. In short, when an advertiser says his product is the greatest, no one *really* believes him.

This stand has been arrived at largely through assumptions rather than facts, although this situation may be changing. Several research studies have cast doubt on puffery's presumed noneffect[29] and have demonstrated that the common form of puffery called "implied superiority claims" (e.g., "Nobody does it better") can have potentially misleading effects.[30] But, as this case suggests, there is still ample room for interpretation.

It is doubtful that the potato chip advertisement would result in any legal challenge, unless a competitor raised objections. This is, after all, a visual (rather than verbal) puff, and potato chips are not a product closely linked with health or safety concerns, such as, for example, a cereal extolling its contributions to lower cholesterol. No, most likely Mike would be able to offer the public a commercial with perfect chips without any legal ripples.

The ethics of the situation are another matter. In deciding in essence that everybody does it, Mike is embracing misrepresentation as part of the nature of that self-interested form of communication called advertising. In the process, he is apparently making certain unreflective assumptions about the audience, their capabilities, and their priorities. Specifically: (1) People *are* deliberate and calculating. They have had previous experience with potato chips and will carry that experience over to this commercial. They realize that advertising is paid propaganda, and they will weigh their own experience against the advertising in favor of experience. (2) People are *not* deliberate and calculating. They live in worlds of symbols where colors, moods, design, and psychological and sociological suggestions are very real parts of their lives. Hence they frequently confront exaggeration in many facets of their lives and may, in fact, like it. For example, scholar Theodore Levitt has suggested that advertising serves the function of "alleviating imagery" for many consumers and thus should not be relegated to transmitting mere product information.[31]

Buttressed with these all-encompassing assumptions, it is not surprising that Mike could conclude that puffery is not likely to victimize the individual. In the first case an individual is constantly on guard against advertising's exaggerations, and this defensive posture is usually adequate. In the second case, the individual apparently *welcomes* the blandishments of the advertisements, a willing seduction. Here the encounter is between not adversaries, but friends.

From an ethical perspective it could be contended that in the first case Mike is shifting the burden of what is right to potential consumers. Let them be on guard. Let them filter advertisements through their own experiences and make appropriate judgments. This position is very close to the idea of humankind as deliberate and calculating, as envisioned under classical liberal philosophy, finding its market manifestation in the concept of *caveat emptor*, let the buyer beware. But should Mike endorse the second set of assumptions, the responsibility would seem to shift back to the advertiser, for he is dealing presumably with a vulnerable public, one open to the spinning of symbolic meanings and the manipulation of priorities. Here, Mike might find more difficulty in justifying his decision.

In any case he has refused to examine his assumptions in light of the conditions of the situation. He could, for example, ask that a rough cut of the commercial be tested with both a perfect and a normal bag. If individuals are left with the impression that these chips are more likely to be lighter and unbroken than those of competitors, then it is clear that normal chips must be used if the public is to be served. If there is no difference reported in the test, however, then no practical harm (or good) would seem likely to occur. There would, however, still remain the more fundamental question of whether, *regardless of the consequences*, it is right to misrepresent the experience that an ordinary consumer is likely to have with this or any product.

From the perspective of Preston's observation that puffery is not extensively regulated because it is assumed that it *doesn't* work, and it is used by advertisers because it *does* work, it could be contended that Mike made his decision about puffery in an extremely casual manner. Further thought might have led him to the conclusions that (1) if it *does* make a difference, then it is at least wrong on ethical grounds and probably on legal as well, and (2) if it does *not* make a difference, why indulge in the exaggeration anyway, particularly when its effect in the long run may be a devaluation of advertising as a credible medium of market information.

Simply, the chips do *not* look perfect under normal circumstances. Mike concluded that it was permissible to suggest they do. In the process he apparently assumed both a guarded and an open model of potential consumers, yet he also assumed that the responsibility should rest with the consumer in both cases. However supported, expediency triumphed over reflection.

NOTES

1. See E. John Kottman, "The Parity Product—Advertising's Achilles Heel," *Journal of Advertising* 6 (Winter 1977): 34–39.
2. "Shampoos," *Consumer Reports*, September 1984, p. 192.
3. "Hand and Bath Soaps," *Consumer Reports*, January 1985, pp. 52–55.
4. Marion Harper, Jr., "The Agency Business in 1980," *Advertising Age* 44 (19 November 1973): 15.
5. Quoted in Martin Mayer, *Madison Avenue, U.S.A.* (New York: Harper & Brothers, 1958), p. 3.
6. See Harry Wayne McMahan, "How to Sell a Product Without an 'Advantage,'" *Advertising Age* 44 (31 December 1973): 15.
7. Howard Luck Gossage, *Is There Any Hope for Advertising?* (Urbana: University of Illinois Press, 1986), p. 61.
8. Roger Draper, "The Faithless Shepherd," *New York Review*, 26 June 1986, p. 18.
9. "How to Save $2500 a Year at the Supermarket," *Consumer Reports* March 1988, p. 163.
10. "The Facts on Plax," *Consumer Reports*, August 1989, p. 507.
11. "The Pinocchio Awards," *Adweek's Marketing Week*, 31 October 1988, p. 20.
12. Ibid, pp. 20–21.

13. Ibid., pp. 21–22.
14. Michael deCourcy Hinds, "The Battle Against Fraudulent Ads," *New York Times Consumer's World*, 30 January 1988.
15. "N.Y. Attorney General's Aide Defends Guidelines," *The 4A's Washington Newsletter*, March 1988, p. 5.
16. "Sensible Start for Heartwise," *Advertising Age*, 11 September 1989, p. 54. See also "Battle of the Food Blurbs," *Time*, 11 September 1989, p. 66.
17. Win Roll, "A Valuable Lesson in Integrity," *Advertising Age*, 25 May 1987, p. 18.
18. Vincent Norris, "An Ethical Problem for Advertising Teachers." Unpublished manuscript, School of Journalism, Pennsylvania State University, 1980.
19. Sean MacBride, *Many Voices, One World* (New York: UNESCO 1980), p. 154.
20. Richard W. Pollay, "The Distorted Mirror: Reflections on the Unintended Consequences of Advertising," *Journal of Marketing*, April 1986, p. 19.
21. Ibid.
22. Speaking on Public Television, January 1975. Further discussion appears in Della Femina's *From Those Wonderful Folks Who Gave You Pearl Harbor* (New York: Simon & Schuster, 1970).
23. Nicholas Samstag, *How Business Is Bamboozled by the Ad Boys* (New York: James Heineman, 1969), pp. 98–100. Italics in the original.
24. Jules Henry, *Culture Against Man* (New York: Random House, 1963), pp. 92–93. Italics in the original.
25. *Teens Are Dead. Long Live the Proto-Adults* (New York: Backer Spielvogel Bates, Inc. 1989), p. 7.
26. Martin Mayer, *Madison Avenue*, pp. 119–120.
27 Pierre Martineau, *Motivation in Advertising* (New York: McGraw-Hill, 1957), p. 192.
28. Ivan Preston, *The Great American Blow Up* (Madison: University of Wisconsin Press, 1975).
29. See Herbert Rotfeld and Ivan Preston, "The Potential Impact of Research on Advertising Law: The Case of Puffery," *Journal of Advertising Research* 21 (April 1981): 9–17.
30. See Robert G. Wyckham, "Implied Superiority Claims," *Journal of Advertising Research*, February/March, 1987, pp. 54–63.
31. Theodore Levitt, "The Morality (?) of Advertising," *Harvard Business Review* 48:30 (July/August 1970): 84–92.

CHAPTER 9

Media Considerations

For most of this century U.S. newspapers and magazines have relied heavily on advertising revenue as a major source of income. Virtually from their inception, radio and television networks and stations as well sought their funds for operation and profit from advertising subsidy. In this arrangement, the media exist in part as conduits of advertising messages to particular audiences. The larger consequences of this accommodation will be discussed in the next chapter. Here we will concern ourselves with the ethical confrontations faced by some media staff in their unique and sensitive positions between advertiser and audience.

The very nature of these positions is central to many of the problems raised in this chapter.

- Which advertisers will be granted access to the pages or to time in order to expose their message to a particular audience?
- What are the ethical considerations when the interests of the media channel and those of the advertiser conflict?
- How should media personnel use confidential information gleaned from their normal exposure to advertisers who are often competing for the same business?
- Which media are appropriate for advertising purposes?

The situations described in these cases are scarcely of cosmic consequence, but they are very real to individuals involved in this intriguing dimension of the advertising process.

43. GATEKEEPERS I: NONE OF 'THOSE ADS' IN THIS PAPER.

Some days, Andy Scott thought, being an advertising manager for a newspaper is a lot more painful than it seems. Today was one of those days. Andy was responsible for the advertising content of the *Telegraph*, a monopoly newspaper in a northeastern city with a population of 100,000. The matter causing him anxiety at the moment was a relatively innocuous ad for a local group of gays. It was a straightforward announcement of the availability of a "Gay Switchboard" in the community. He was now ready to reject the ad, but not without some second guessing.

The issue had some history. Several years earlier a similar ad had been brought to the paper. A representative from the advertising department had deemed it controversial and had taken it to the owner of the paper. The owner declared he wanted none of "those ads" in his paper. Subsequently, the board of directors supported the position, although there was not, nor was there now, a written policy manual. The gay organization took its case to court—and lost. This outcome was hardly surprising, since the courts have generally interpreted freedom of the press to mean freedom to publish or broadcast, not freedom of access to the pages of a newspaper, even the "rented" advertising space.

Now the group was trying again. Its arguments were basically the following:

- The *Telegraph* provides the only print medium to reach virtually all of the community with any degree of efficiency.
- The information in the ad is proper. It offers a telephone number to facilitate counseling and other support activities.
- The paper has run ads from the organization before—both in display space and in the classified section—although they were not as prominent as this particular message. The paper also runs news stories about gay groups when such are warranted.

Andy had even agreed to meet with a local Presbyterian minister, who was speaking on behalf of the group's request to send what it considered to be a reasonable message—the availability of the telephone number—to the community at large. There was certainly no attempt to recruit, merely to inform. Andy had explained that policy was policy and that any previous appearance of an ad was due to lapses in the gatekeeping system—for example, new employees accepting ads or the owner being out of town—rather than to inconsistent policy.

There is, Andy knew, the argument that the "rented" space of a newspaper should be open to all to ensure that the "marketplace of ideas," held dear by libertarians, could function properly. After all, they argue, the newspaper controls the editorial content, so shouldn't the advertising spaces be available to anyone with something legitimate to say? Indeed, if the paper trusts people to make up their minds when faced with divergent positions on the editorial page, should it then assume that these same individuals can't cope with some diversity in the advertising content? Still, this seems to be a vexing issue for everyone. Where were those ideals, he thought, when the liberal campus newspaper recently pulled an informative ad from the White Aryan Resistance after "adverse reactions"?

Well, the law is certainly on our side, Andy thought. There's no doubt about that. And we do reject ads with some regularity, such as some potentially libelous political ads, those that smack of solicitation, scams, and so on. Still, this is a classification that's rejected without concern for content.

Well, the policy and the law are clear. Might as well get on with the rejection. . . .

It can be contended that this is easily one of this book's least ambiguous cases on an ethical plane.

There is no question of the *Telegraph*'s legal right to control both the editorial and advertising content of the newspaper—but there is absolutely no evidence of critical ethical thinking. The existing policy lies solely on an assertion of ethical relativism: it is right to reject these ads because the owner says it's right. (The board of directors was brought into the picture only after the fact.)

There is no evidence that the absolutism of this decision is carried over to other potentially sensitive product or service categories, such as cigarettes or liquor. Apparently all of the other advertising submitted is accepted or rejected solely on content.

Nor is utilitarianism a useful defense. There was no explicit mention of the newspaper's audience in the decision to reject the advertising of the gay organization. Even if this was implied, is there any assurance that the newspaper readership would, in fact, find the advertisement objectionable? If this issue was put to its proper test, the ad would be run and the "market" would speak, in terms of indifference, protests, cancelled subscriptions, and so forth. Also, there is apparently no audience-oriented thinking in the existing practice of accepting ads for other products and services which some may find objectionable.

Clearly there was no attempt to establish a middle ground through compromise or accommodation. Doing this might have involved evaluating each advertisement on the basis of its own merits, perhaps rejecting those that were perceived as provocative but accepting those with strong informational content in a relatively neutral mode.

Apparently, then, the marketplace of ideas, at least in advertising content, is *relatively* sanctioned in all areas save one—gays are denied access granted to virtually all others. The *Telegraph* rests on legal precedent and moral idiosyncracy. It exists as a monopoly newspaper whose advertising policy, in the absence of any evidence of ethical reflection, can justifiably be called arrogant.

44. GATEKEEPERS II: I'M STILL TRYING TO BE FAIR.

Well, Alice Jeffers thought, they told me there would be days like this. She had just completed a telephone call (more a monologue than a conversation) with a listener of her central Ohio radio station, which served a market of about 50,000.

"How dare you," the caller had begun, "run those horrible right-to-life commercials!" By this time, Alice knew the commercials well:

- One noted that there were more than 1.5 million babies killed by abortion annually, and a total of some 18 million since 1973—"More than all the American solders killed in all our wars." "The most dangerous place in America today," the announcement concluded, "is inside a mother's womb."
- Another played an eight-week-old fetal heartbeat, followed by a period of silence; one stated that a beating heart, brain waves, organs, and so on are all functioning shortly after conception; and still another asserted that when a 7-pound,

2-ounce baby was born it wasn't the first day of her life—
"just the first time we get to *see* her."

As Alice expected, she had gotten some feedback (negative, predictably)—about half a dozen calls, including this one. They
should have heard the ad that the local group wanted to air but
that she had rejected as "too strong":

"Gee Mom, did you notice that I have fingers now, and
gee. . . . And can you feel me kicking? And Mom, I can
hear what's going on. Could you tell me, when you were
talking to the doctor, what 'abortion' means?"

She had explained her position to each caller: She found the
ads honest but realized they were clearly on a controversial subject and, lacking a Federal Communications Commission "Fairness Doctrine," she still tried to be fair. Therefore she had contacted pro-choice groups to see if they would be interested in
running responses, but they were not, even though she knew that
the National Organization for Women probably had prepared
pro-choice ads for local groups, just as these spots being used by
the local pro-life group had been prepared by National Right to
Life.

Well, she knew the same right-to-life ads had run in the local
newspaper (which, of course, didn't have even a legacy of anything
resembling a fairness doctrine) but she knew that the radio versions would spark a response. Still, it was an election year, this
was a controversial and topical subject, and she had tried to be
fair. Certainly not as easy as accepting Pepsi's money, is it?

What were Alice's options in this situation?

1. To refuse to accept the right-to-life spots because of their con-
    troversial topic, or their execution.
2. To accept all the spots.
3. To accept some of the spots but eliminate those considered most
    likely to offend.

4.   To accept some of the spots and also seek out opposing points of
      view.

In accepting the fourth option, Alice was apparently seeking a
middle ground by, first, refusing to air at least one of the spots, thus
presumably protecting her audience, and second, alerting the pro-
choice groups that these ads would be running and inquiring whether
they wished to use advertising of their own. (Of course, it could be
contended that she was simply interested in increasing the station's
revenues, since these were advertisements in paid time, but it seems
unlikely, because both pro-life and pro-choice groups tend to operate
on extremely limited budgets.)

Rather, she seemed to be striving for the "marketplace of ideas"
ideal assumed under the now defunct Fairness Doctrine by (1) permitting a partisan position on a controversial (but arguably important)
subject to be aired, and (2) making an effort to air the other contending point of view as well. She knew that these spots would generate
protest, yet she aired them anyway, perhaps with the assumption that
the greatest good for the greatest number is served when important
subjects of national interest are given salience, albeit through biased
voices.

Her actions provide a sharp practical and philosophical contrast
to those of the *Telegraph* in the preceding case, particularly given the
intrusive nature of the commercial time on radio versus the relatively
passive presence of print forms.

45. ADVICE FROM A BIASED SOURCE?

The advertising manager for retail accounts had just issued the
marching orders. Given the tight economic times, increasing
pressure from the free-subscription shopper, and the new aggres-
siveness of television salespeople, the newspaper was beginning
to see a decline in its retail linage. The message was clear: we
need to be more aggressive in promoting the use of our newspaper's advertising space by the community's retailers. Sell them
on the idea of:

- The newspaper as a preferred advertising medium
- This newspaper as the best of that breed

- Frequent advertising versus infrequent
- Big space versus small space

That, Dick Lutz thought, is the nature of the business, at least in his ten years in retail sales. Newspapers are convinced that they need substantial advertising subsidies in order to function. As economic times grow uncertain and competition becomes tighter, that income source is threatened, and then comes the call to the barricades. Sell harder. Be more creative. Become indispensable to your accounts.

There, Dick reflected, may be the heart of the dilemma that virtually all media salespeople face. Advertising, by its very nature, is an uncertain process. Most people, most of the time, cannot determine with any accuracy just what they are getting for their advertising dollars. And although retailers are closer to the actual sales transaction than a manufacturer like Procter & Gamble, the problem is no less real. Maybe the ad was fine but the timing was lousy. The timing may have been fine but the ad was not. Both may have been great but competitors were more active. In addition, few retailers are able to use the expertise of advertising agencies, and so they often handle advertising in their free moments or delegate it to some idle employee. Sometimes this practice works to their great advantage; frequently it does not.

And here, Dick knew, is where people such as himself enter the picture. He can offer at least the appearance of expertise to retailers struggling with the question of advertising—and at no cost. The actual preparation of a newspaper ad—the writing of the copy and the physical layout—is provided by the paper's staff, without charge. Within this set of expectations—a desirable service offered in an ambiguous area—it was hardly surprising that Dick and his colleagues would be consulted for answers to more fundamental questions such as: When should I advertise? How big should my ad be? The answer to these questions from the paper's point of view was simple: Advertise as much as you possibly can. (Dick also knew that it would be desirable to encourage advertising in the paper's light editions, Monday and Saturday, rather than the popular Wednesday and Friday editions.)

Of course his own financial future was linked to the paper's prosperity, both directly (commissions) and indirectly (the paper's overall financial health). Ideally, as retailers prosper through increased advertising, so will the paper. But those reasons rarely allowed Dick the opportunity to suggest:

- "You don't need to advertise as much as you're doing now."
- "You can get by with smaller space than you're using."
- "I honestly think you'd be better off in radio."
- Or (horror of horrors), "Jack, I really think you'd be better off not advertising at all and putting the money into hiring better salespeople."

   In the land of the blind, Dick mused, the one-eyed man is king. He may not have all the answers about advertising's effectiveness, but his experience can certainly be helpful to uncertain retailers. But should his advice be followed when his motives are so clearly directed by self-interest? What kind of person can rise above self-interest when it conflicts with the well-being of another? Perhaps a salesperson who is thereafter unemployed?

The ethical dilemma Dick Lutz faces is common for media personnel dealing with unsophisticated advertisers. Under the best of circumstances and intentions, advertising is an uncertain process. Because of the host of other variables that can confound a simple cause-and-effect assumption, even giant advertisers with state-of-the-art research are often unsure exactly what they should be saying, to whom, and with what size and frequency. And for every advertising colossus there are thousands of small producers and retailers whose advertising savvy is extremely limited. They represent a potentially vulnerable population.
   It is often difficult to get some retailers to advertise at all ("I tried it once and nothing happened") or to switch from one medium to another ("I've had good luck with radio; why should I use television?"). Once an account has been established, however, and a salesperson becomes a regular partner in the advertising efforts of the store, the door is open for him or her to become something more than simply an order taker.
   Dick can satisfy himself with the knowledge that the services he and his paper provide, particularly the actual preparation of the ads, are valuable to many retailers and may well increase their advertising efficiency. Indeed, the advice and services that he offers often approach

the ideal of enlightened self-interest for all parties. That is, "We help you because you're advertising with us, and if you succeed you'll advertise more with us, and. . . ."

But Dick knows full well that the formula—big ads + high frequency = success—does not work for all retailers all the time. What are his options then? His first choice is to seek the self-interest of the newspaper in all situations. Often that will result in sound advice for the advertiser as well. If not, the decision to advertise still belongs to the retailer, who is certainly aware that an ad salesperson is a biased advisor. Therefore, moral duty is owed first to the paper, and second to the retailer, assuming the harmony of self-interests.

Dick's second alternative is to serve the best interests of the retailer in all situations. As the retailer perceives Dick operating against the newspaper's short-term interests, respect may grow. The result could be more business in the long run, either from that retailer or from others who respect Dick's advice. Then when Dick does recommend a major campaign, his suggestion may be taken more seriously. Here Dick honors his notions of fairness to the retailer. The *potential* market payoff can be seen to be long term rather than short term.

Dick's dilemma is intensified by the reality of the marketplace. His media competitors—salespeople for the weekly newspapers, radio and television stations, and others—are likely attempting to persuade the same retailers from their own narrowly defined self-interests. Thus, if Dick pursues the retailer-sensitive option, the newspaper may suffer losses, at least in the short run. Since the advertising manager's call to the barricades was stimulated by short-run losses, how receptive will he be to Dick's argument that unbiased advice will benefit the paper in the long run? "If they want unbiased advice, let them hire a consultant," may well be the manager's reply.

Depending on the depth of his moral convictions, that may be another option Dick could pursue. By quitting his job and becoming a hired consultant to retailers, he could use his knowledge of the local advertising scene to benefit all of his clients, and in a far more objective manner. But that is a difficult and uncertain way to earn a living.

46. INSIDE INFORMATION—I

As a food advertising specialist for a northeastern city's dominant newspaper, Kristine Larrimore called on the supermarkets and specialized food stores of the area. Depending on their needs, she would simply take their prepared advertising and arrange for scheduling, or get information for an ad to be turned over to the paper's copy department for layout and production. Given the monopoly position of her paper, little hard selling was necessary. Rather, she simply pointed out opportunities in upcoming food supplements and the like, and she downplayed the growing number of free shopper papers that some advertisers were beginning to find attractive.

In the course of her job, Kristine acquired a great deal of inside information concerning promotional plans and general advertising philosophies of her regular advertisers. One morning a few weeks before Thanksgiving, a manager in one of the city's largest supermarket chain stores told her just how much that information was worth.

First, Joe Gibbons reminded her of the cutthroat nature of food retailing, particularly during uncertain economic times. Second, he pointed out that the ultimate beneficiary of all this competition was the consumer, and if the customer does enough business with a store offering low prices, everybody benefits. Then came the clincher. Joe offered Kristine $500 for one small piece of information: Saveco's Thanksgiving turkey prices. "Frankly," Joe pointed out, "we don't want to go any lower than necessary. But if we knew Saveco's price, we could at least match it, if not undercut it. The customer wins, and you'll be $500 richer for helping."

In that awkward moment, Kris refused. (She wondered later if she would have done the same thing if her paper had not been in a near monopoly position and Joe had someplace else to go.) First, she told Joe that the paper explicitly forbids the leaking of confidential information to interested parties. (She knew, of course, that there were breaches of that ideal.) But, perhaps of greater importance, she contended that if she shared such information with Joe there was no guarantee she would not share his prices when it was in her interest to do so. To work efficiently for both of us, she said, we have to trust one another.

Joe was embarrassed and angry. Without the information he wanted so badly, he set his turkey prices and found them two cents a pound higher than those of Saveco. Joe's chain suffered relatively heavy sales losses in the holiday rush.

Kristine's subsequent dealings with Joe could be best characterized as strained, but, over time, they regained much of their previous rapport.

This case provides an opportunity to use relatively structured ethical criteria for examining four fundamental questions for ethical analysis:[1]

1.   *What makes a right act right?* In this situation, Joe Gibbons relies on the standards of personal relativism. It is right to offer a bribe to Kristine because it is in his best interests to do so. His allusions to a public benefit are a point to be examined later. Kristine initially equates right with her paper's policy. Her employer explicitly forbids it, therefore she cannot. Her second argument, however, transcends that limited standard. The criterion that violating the trust of advertisers is simply wrong, regardless of the consequences or the guidelines imposed by others, depends on such universal principles as justice and fairness. Does it say anything about her own standards to note the order of argument?

2.   *To whom is moral duty owed?* Joe feels that moral duty is owed to himself. By serving himself, he argues, he will ultimately be serving others, namely his customers. Kristine first suggests that her duty is to her employer. Secondarily, she asserts that an obligation is owed to her clients, those advertisers she contacts on behalf of the paper.

3.   *What kinds of act are right?* The contrast here is particularly instructive. Joe is concerned with the consequences of the situation. His self-interest is evident, but he also contends that the public will benefit; in other words, the greatest good for the greatest number. The strength of this conviction weakens, however, with his admission that he has no desire to price his turkeys any lower than necessary. His profit margin is still the important factor. There is the unspoken concern that, lacking Kristine's information, he might price his turkeys too low—for him, not the public. Kristine, by contrast, is arguing on a relatively more formal level. Regardless of the consequences, the bribe is wrong, specifically because her paper forbids it, and generally because it would represent a breach of faith. Obviously, the second rationale is more fundamental than the first.

4. *How do rules apply to specific situations?* Joe is stressing the
    importance of this particular set of circumstances. Kristine, in
    the first instance, is equally concerned with this particular sit-
    uation since it is covered in her employer's rules. Her fairness
    argument, however, touches on basic standards of human conduct
    that transcend specific conditions.

Both parties felt guilty: Joe, because he recognized that his action
transgressed accepted norms and was held to account on their behalf;
Kristine, because her client had been compromised and, perhaps, because she was uncertain how much of her decision was due to leverage
created by her paper's monopoly position.

Kristine's initial reliance on the situation-specific criteria to
make her decision suggests that her ethical standards could be compromised in the future. How will she decide when the company's rules
do not cover a particular situation? Are her more universal standards
of fairness and justice strong enough to stand the pressure of a moment
without the support of her employer's rule book?

Ethical thinking requires reflection and analysis. Lacking that,
an individual may assume a mantle of righteousness when one is, in
fact, a prisoner of events.

47. INSIDE INFORMATION—II

The classified advertising section of any reputable daily newspaper comes as close to the ideal of pure market information as
any advertising is likely to provide. Sellers and buyers find it a
constantly renewing forum of exchange, generally free from the
verbal and graphic hyperbole of the more pervasive display advertising. As such, its information is frequently prized.

Martha Louwens, a 28-year-old mother of two, had recently
reentered the work force as a classified advertising salesperson
for the town's only paper. Actually "salesperson" was misleading.
Basically she was an order taker. Individuals would call when they
had decided to place a classified ad. Martha and her colleagues
would then tell them the rates, take down the exact wording for
the ad or, rarely, help the customer compose the ad over the
phone.

In this role Martha acquired a great deal of timely information. She learned of the pending sale of items prized by herself and her friends: "Big Wheels" for the kids, room air conditioning units, used children's clothing, home furnishings in good condition, and so on. Then there were the job openings. Frequently employers listed a telephone number and placed priority on a first-come first-served basis for qualified applicants.

Since Martha had this information a day, or at least several hours, before the paper's next edition, she got into the habit of sharing the news with friends who she felt might be interested. (On some occasions she would follow up herself.) As a general rule she asked her friends to wait until just about the time the paper hit the streets. That way no suspicion could be cast on her or her department. Such caution had caused her friends to lose a few good opportunities to sharp-eyed early readers, but usually not. When someone can plan an action in advance, she or he can usually operate with considerable advantage.

Martha's caution indicated the presence of an ethical, if not administrative, question. Though there were no specific prohibitions, she knew that the information in the classifieds was intended for the newspaper readership in toto, not for a select few and their friends. Indeed, some people out there could possibly use the items or jobs a great deal more than Martha or her friends. The classifieds as an open forum were less open when she handed out information in advance. She knew that.

Still, Martha was not troubled enough to stop. First, it happened with only a small fraction of all the material she handled. Also, was not the purpose of a classified to sell the item, fill the job, or whatever? She was certainly facilitating that. Finally, she had to admit, there was the special feeling of being an insider who could offer her friends favored treatment. She might not be able to give them inside information on Wall Street, or tips on a "hot" restaurant, but at least this was something.

Martha is scarcely a shaker and mover in the advertising business. Yet, even in an ordinary job dealing with matters of little economic significance, she confronts ethical decisions.

Apparently she feels vaguely guilty. Why? It is not clear whether her coworkers offer similar favors to their friends, but the basic cause for her unease may be that she knows full well she is violating the spirit if not the letter of the newspaper's policies. Would she have acted in the same way if the ethical dimensions had been made explicit? Perhaps her desire to feel important in her first venture into the workplace since her children were born may have proven too strong even then. In any case, the absence of a specific rule has allowed her the latitude to act on her own.

Who is served by her actions? Without doubt the seller, who is usually not concerned with who buys, merely that someone does, and as rapidly as possible. Her friends benefit, of course. Given the bite of inflation, an inside track on bargains or a desirable job is extremely valuable. And, at the heart of the matter, Martha benefits by being important to others in a job whose objective dimensions are not likely to impress.

Martha has apparently constructed her rationale so that her decision making has become routine. She will provide information to friends unless it is of no use to them. Her rule of serving the relatively small universe of self, friends, and seller supersedes the spirit of fairness.

Suppose Martha encountered Rawls's veil of ignorance, and was unsure whether she would emerge as the ad taker with inside information or as a member of the public at large, interested in good buys and good jobs. Would she choose the course she now follows, or assure access to the marketplace by *all* the newspaper's readers?

Others handle this type of information too—her coworkers in classifieds, those in the composing room, and the printers. Each kind of worker is in a position to short circuit the normal function of classified ads.

Given that the purpose of the ad is to sell, never mind to whom, and the relatively elusive notion of fairness, it may be that responsibility lies with the newspaper's administration to develop an ethical code that explicitly protects the interests of the readers.

In the meantime, Martha will probably remain a functionary at her newspaper. Yet her custom-made ethical code raises questions, not only about her own moral integrity, but about the effects of her actions on others. Jules Feiffer called his book about the day-to-day tribulations of living in New York City, *Little Murders.* Similarly, it is the little compromises of people such as Martha that establish and maintain a working environment where short-run advantage triumphs over long-term integrity, personal gain over fairness.

48. THE CAPTIVE AUDIENCE

Susan Lomax put down the phone. As an executive for the world's largest motion picture chain, she and her company were under virtually constant pressure to accept cinema advertising (screen commercials or advertiser-related music videos featuring popular music performers to be shown before features).[2]

It wasn't as if they hadn't given it a try, she thought. Over the years they had experimented with advertising supplied by Screenvision, the major source of cinema advertising for national and regional advertisers in the United States, in addition to local merchant advertising during the Christmas season, and even audio spots, advertising messages played over the theater sound systems behind a blank screen.

Screenvision was particularly bullish:

■ An affiliation with the supplier assures virtually "found money," with the theater owners receiving about a third of the income paid by national advertisers such as the U.S. Marine Corps, California Raisin Advisory Board, Toyota, Puma, Oldsmobile, and so on, with the business growing about 20 percent a year.

■ The theater owner will receive a "flight" of as many as three commercials each month, and can refuse certain categories—for example, cigarettes or alcoholic beverages.

■ The Screenvision network now involves about 35 percent of the U.S.'s 17,500 first-run movie screens, with "several million dollars" going to theaters faced with rising overhead and expense costs.

■ Some survey data indicate that theatergoers respond favorably to big budget ads made specifically for cinema presentation with Screenvision claiming that although two-thirds of those polled object to the idea going into the theater, two-thirds say they liked the spots after they've seen them.

■   The very nature of the cinema advertising experience promotes extremely high advertising recall for advertisers.

As one observer noted:

> In cinema advertising, the advertiser has "captive" view-
> ers, with little or no "noise" in the channel. As can be
> seen by its very construction, a theater is suited for pre-
> sentation of information. The finest acoustical studies are
> used by cinema architects to insure a quality presenta-
> tion. Bolted chairs direct the viewers' attention. . . .[3]

All true, reflected Susan, but since January 1984 we have set
down a company policy against *any* commercial advertising on
our screens except those promoting other films. This corporate
decision, she knew, was based, at least in large part, on a perception that advertising was simply not a part of the motion picture experience.
Susan liked that.

This case gives us the opportunity to examine the situation from the
viewpoints of the interested parties.

The Advertisers

The "captive" nature of the audience in the viewing situation can
certainly result in much greater attention being paid to an advertisement than in the often distraction-laden environment of television
viewing. There is also ample evidence that cinema advertisements are
generally remembered longer and in more detail than the typical television commercial. Costs are a bit of a concern. The production costs
for an advertisement that will do justice to the cinema setting are high.
This may, however, be offset to some extent by cutting out shorter
versions of the ad for television, thus stretching the production dollar.
In a relative sense, buying exposure on screens for cinema advertising
is about 25 percent more expensive than buying television time, but
the virtually assured impact of the message may more than compensate. And what of possible theatergoer backlash? Well, there is certainly concern about adverse reaction, but it can be rationalized by the
creation of "special," more entertaining commercials.[4]

The Theater Owners

The foremost advantage is obvious—a source of income without direct expense. Yet only about one-third of the screens in this country carry cinema advertising. (And Disney has recently refused to allow ads before their films.) Theater owners are undoubtedly pressured by rising costs and uncertain revenues from ticket sales and concessions, as well as often demanding arrangements from major distributors—for example, agreements to run the feature at least so many weeks, etc. Thus an additional source of income—particularly one of virtually "pure profit"—could be compelling. Yet more than two thirds of theater owners have chosen not to participate, at least at the moment.

The Audience

Cinema advertising would seem to have two distinguishing characteristics for the movie-going audience:

1. Cinema movies are probably the only major mass medium that they have been accustomed to experiencing *without* advertising. Cinema advertising has now altered that expectation.
2. It is, arguably, the only prominent form of advertising that does not in some way require the assent of the potential receiver, and provide some reasonable possibility of choice concerning exposure to the message. With magazines, newspapers, radio, and television, individuals are aware that they will be exposed to advertising. They can, if they wish, choose to avoid it in one manner or another. With cinema advertising the individual is neither forewarned, nor able to choose not to participate without extraordinary action—for example, leaving the theater or closing one's eyes and plugging one's ears. There have been reports that "hoots and howls are common when commercials flash onto screens in New York City."[5]

Susan's company's decision to decline the obvious financial benefit of cinema advertising was presumably based on concern for the audience. Given that many polls about public reaction to cinema ads are based on the *absence of hostile reaction*—for example, 65 percent "don't mind them" or two thirds are opposed going in but tolerant of what they've been forced to see going out—it is difficult to argue that the theater-going public is well served by this advertising form as part of a previously commercial-free environment. To decide to accept cinema advertising ethically, then, would seem to require a relatively narrow conception of who is benefitted—the advertiser, the theater owner, and Screenvision or other suppliers—rather than the far larger constituency of the "captive audience."

49. NEVER HAVE SO FEW SCARED SO MANY

Well here's another one, mused Roland Willard, media editor of the advertising trade publication *National Advertiser*. The full-page ad was headlined "An Open Letter to Advertisers." In it, Dr. John C. Wilke, president of the National Right to Life Committee, chastised advertisers and NBC for the television movie, *Roe v. Wade*, dealing with the Supreme Court decision allowing abortions. He concluded, "On behalf of the members of NRLC as well as millions of other Americans who hold human life sacred, I urge you to seriously consider the shows you sponsor in the future."

This is a tough time for television advertisers, Roland thought. Networks have been pressured by individuals and groups who have objected to this or that program, this or that portrayal, from the beginning of the television era, but things have gotten especially sticky lately, particularly for the advertisers.

Five years or so earlier it was the National Parent-Teachers Association raising alarm about violence on much prime-time television fare. And lately it's been a combination of individuals and special-interest groups that are now regarded by some as championing a "new puritanism."[6] He thought about some of the recent flurry of events:

■ Terry Rakolta, a suburban Michigan housewife, watched Fox Broadcasting Company's top-rated show "Married . . . With Children" with her children, found it offensive, and wrote to 45 companies that had advertised on that and other episodes, criticizing the "blatant exploitation of women, sex, and anti-family attitudes." Within a short time, Procter & Gamble, McDonald's, Tambrands, and Kimberly-Clark instructed their agencies not to buy any more time on the program, and Mrs. Rakolta received a personal letter of apol-

ogy from the president of Coca-Cola USA. Several other advertisers promised they would review their participation in
the program.

■   Ralston-Purina and General Mills both agreed to pull their
    advertising from "Saturday Night Live" after the American
    Family Association objected to sexually explicit skits.

■   Chrysler Corp. and Sears pulled spots from NBC's "Nightingales" after the American Nursing Association mounted
    a massive letter-writing campaign. The program was not renewed.[7]

■   Commenting on the networks' programs for the 1989–90
    season, an agency media director noted, "You cannot look
    at their schedules and do anything but conclude that they
    have taken a major step back in terms of risqué material."

And then, Roland thought, there is the matter of the moment.
The Reverend Donald Wildmon's newest group, Christian Leaders for Responsible Television, had recently announced a boycott
of two companies considered by CLeaR-TV to have been associated with prime-time programs containing high levels of sex,
violence, or profanity.

Now the free speech advocates were calling for ad agencies,
advertisers, and the media to form a united front to resist this
and other examples of what one advertising spokesperson called
"sort of a new McCarthyism." The voices formed an angry chorus:

> This boycott is nothing more than a scheme of a few zeal
> ots to override the will of the general public.[8]

> Each individual corporation has to make its own decision
> about appropriate [programming] standards based on its
> own corporate values. It's not a decision advertising agen
> cies can or should make, and there's nothing the ad com
> munity as a whole can or should do about it.[9]

> This boycott is nothing more or less than a form of cen
> sorship. It's asking for advertisers to control the content
> of the communications medium, which they have no
> right doing. I'd rather put up with a rotten program any

day than risk doing away with a program that serves a social purpose, just because somebody finds it unacceptable.

I hope the major consumer goods marketers will join in support [of the targeted companies] and say publicly, "We'll promote our products in the best way we know how, but we will not kowtow to the Reverend Wildmon."

Roland sighed. It was time for him to write his publication's editorial stand on the matter, knowing full well that it would carry some weight. What were his options?

1. Endorse an advertiser–agency–media stand on the issue.
2. Disapprove of the boycotters but argue that this is a matter for the individual companies involved.
3. Position the boycotters as a legitimate form of protest and let the chips fall where they may.

Is there a useful ethical perspective here?

One perspective that might be applied is that of collectivism versus pluralism. The protestors claim to be representing substantial numbers, but the targets of their concerns are some of the most popular shows on television, including "Married . . . With Children," "Saturday Night Live," "thirtysomething," "L.A. Law," "Night Court," "Cheers," and "Golden Girls." If these are truly objectionable programs, why are they so popular? Specific advertisers are singled out, yet the multiple sponsorship so common to current television practice makes it exceedingly difficult for the average viewer to remember the advertisers on any particular program. Thus the protests are most likely to originate with an extremely interested party who takes the trouble to catalog the names of the advertisers and distribute the information to presumably sympathetic individuals and groups in order for them to take action, such as writing to the networks or advertisers and not buying their products.

It would, then, seem difficult to support the critics' position with utilitarian arguments. If one were to argue that individuals are free to choose which if any television programs to watch, then the sheer popularity of many of these offerings would seem to contend that the "greatest good for the greatest number" is currently being served and that forcing advertisers to withdraw, thus jeopardizing the future of the program, could be seen to represent the usurpation of priorities by those not choosing to watch over those who do.

The protestors seem unwilling to let individuals, through the television rating system, determine by their individual viewing choices whether or not the programs are offensive; rather, they feel a need to collectivize any protest effort. In a similar manner, the so-called free speech advocates are calling for collective actions by advertisers, agencies, and media, rather than relying on the actions of individual entities.

The advertisers could contend that they have already attempted a middle-ground position by requiring more rigorous prescreening of the programs, ultimately leading to "a major step back in risqué material" noted by the industry analyst. Their arguments that they were suddenly "up in arms"[10] over the content of some of the programming on which their advertising had appeared rings hollow, since many used market-based reasoning and chose the programs that would provide the most efficient conduit for their messages toward a particular audience. It could be argued that they were well aware of the programming but that its potentially offensive nature simply wasn't an issue until it was promoted as one. Then, wishing to avoid any hint of "negative impact," they backed out, letting the priorities of the vocal protestors supercede those of silent viewers.

"Let's not mince words," an advertising columnist asserted, "the agency and advertiser executives who do not stand up to the Reverend Wildmon's minions are gutless."[11] Yet, as another advertising practitioner observed:

> Do networks have the right to choose what programming to broadcast? Yes. Do companies have the right to choose whether or not to sponsor programming some may object to? Of course. Do groups have the right to object to programming or call for product boycotts? Absolutely![12]

The protestors have chosen to use group action, and the advertising community may attempt to raise a collective voice on behalf of individual action—that is, to let viewers decide by their attention, or lack of it, which programs are attractive to advertisers and hence which remain on the air and which fail.

Utilitarianism seems to be on the side of the advertisers. The question that seems to be vexing them, as well as Roland Willard, is to what degree (if any) the self-interests of the advertisers need to be adjusted to accommodate other sincere interests, albeit those representing a vocal minority who may or may not command a wider following.

Roland finally wrote a column calling for a conference of interested parties, sponsored by his publication, which would enable a presumably reasoned discourse, apt compromise, and possible development of policies or guidelines. Thus in this case the Rawls "veil" would need to be encountered by, it is hoped, contending, but reasonable parties to arrive at the desired outcome of fairness. A taxing issue, he thought, and one that he hoped would be resolved fairly, particularly if yet another party is represented behind the veil of ignorance—the viewers of the offending programs.

NOTES

1. Summarized from Robert Veatch, *Case Studies in Medical Ethics* (Cambridge, Mass.: Harvard University Press, 1977).
2. Information for this case was taken from Kim B. Rotzoll, "The Captive Audience," *Current Research in Film*, vol. 3 (Norwood, N.J. Ablex, 1987), pp. 72–87.
3. Keith F. Johnson, "Cinema Advertising," *Journal of Advertising*, (Fall 1981): 11–19.
4. Marcy Magiera, "Advertisers Crowd Onto Big Screen," *Advertising Age*, September 18, 1989.
5. "Hoots and Howls at Ads," *Time*, September 18, 1989, p. 70. See also "Advertising in the Dark," *Newsweek*, April 9, 1990, pp. 44–45.
6. See "Advertisers 'Up in Arms,'" *Advertising Age*, 27 March, 1989, p. 1.
7. See "One Woman Campaign Prompts Advertisers to Examine TV Policies," *Wall Street Journal*, 5 March, 1989, p. F1.
8. Judith Graham, "'New Puritanism' Colors TV Lineup," *Advertising Age*, 29 May, 1989, p. 46.
9. All from Judith Graham, "Ad Industry Rears Up at Boycott," *Advertising Age*, 24 July, 1989, p. 16.
10. "Advertisers 'Up in Arms,'" *op cit.*
11. Craig Reiss, "Ad Execs Duck Wrongs of Right," *Advertising Age*, 14 July, 1986, p. 52.
12. Kim A. Koppelman, "Free Speech for Boycotters," *Advertising Age*, 25 September, 1989, pp. 64–65.

CHAPTER 10

Macro Issues

In this final chapter of our inquiry into the ethical dimensions of advertising, we present not case histories, but issues. These issues, it can be contended, are inherent in the practices of advertising. That is, all advertising must face questions of setting priorities; all advertising must face questions of privacy; all advertising in using the mass media must encounter questions of the effects of that usage; and all advertising is related to resource allocation.

So merely by entering the field the individual becomes a part of the rules by which the institution performs and is perpetuated. There is a great deal to grapple with here. As we shall see, whether advertising is considered saint or sinner is strongly affected by the assumptions made by individuals about such fundamental concepts as human nature, the proper role of the individual and the state, and so on. They are not issues with starkly clear resolutions. It is hoped that the analysis will illuminate some of the dimensions of ethical decision making that are evident for all those wishing to see.

50. *The Alteration of Priorities*

Advertising, by its nature, is self-interested communication. The advertiser is paying for this form of communication because it is hoped that its use will provide a financial return in excess of his investment. The advertiser seeks to reduce the risk of financial loss, or sustain existing financial gain, by attempting to rivet the consciousness of the intended or existing patrons of the product or service.

This is endemic to virtually all forms of advertising. Thus advertisements attempt to elevate the choice of one brand of beer over another to significant social proportions. They associate personalities with inanimate objects (witness the Marlboro man, the Chanel woman, Charlie the tuna, the Keebler elves, etc.) in an attempt to associate the "good life" with the acquisition of relevant products and services rather than with the enduring qualities that may be associated with the internal dynamics of character. In general ads say, "Pay attention to this! This is important!" And "this" is for sale.

Obviously all advertisers do not succeed. Some are simply inept. Others offer little of perceived worth. Many cannot achieve their wishes because of lack of funds. Virtually all, however, would like dearly to try, and therein lies a systemic element of advertising, fraught with ethical dimensions. Consider:

- Christopher Lasch comments that advertising "manufactures a product of its own: the consumer, perpetually unsatisfied, restless, anxious, and bored. Advertising serves not so much to advertise products as to promote consumption as a way of life.[1]

- Sociologist Michael Schudson observes in his 1984 work, *Advertising, the Uneasy Persuasion:*

   An egregious instance [of advertising promoting bad values] in the past year is the advertising for home computers which, on negligible evidence of the importance of computers in children's educational development, encourages parents to believe they will be ruining their children's lives if they do not shell out a few thousand bucks now for a computer. This advertising, and too much other advertising, takes advantages of people's anxieties or fondly held hopes in order to make money. Whether it works or not, it is indecent.[2]

- In their evaluation of so-called "fade creams," *Consumer Reports* states that, "Radio and television ads for *Porcelana*, the most heavily advertised fade cream, try to make middle-aged white women feel like spotted pariahs."[3]

- In what has been called a true milestone in television, the producers and performers of the day-long rock concert *Live-*

Aid apparently raised more than $70 million in donations for East African relief. To put that in the context of advertising weight, this enormous sum represents about 4 percent of the annual advertising budget of a *single* advertiser—Phillip Morris Cos. with their myriad products—and far less than the advertising budget of a single cigarette brand—Marlboros.

- And in the context of the presumed advertising clout of the most currently controversial product, cigarettes, a newspaper editor comments:

> For the young boy who thinks, perhaps, that smoking will make him a man, Camel offers ads and billboards with anthropomorphic Old Joe, a stud camel in flashy bow tie surrounded at the beach, near the pool table and at the gambling casino by curvaceous young women.
>
> For girls, an ad for Newport Stripes shows a beach scene with a gaggle of giggling, healthy, swimsuit-clad young women who look no older than my 16-year-old daughter. An ad for Virginia Slims still associates smoking with female independence: a modishly dressed young woman, cigarette in hand, complements the headline—"You've come a long way, baby."[4]

Individually and collectively, then, advertisers are basically attempting to alter priorities. To get their product, their brand, their idea, their suggested life-style, to the top of our mental priority lists. To get us to think: "I *must* see that movie. I *must* try that brand. *That* is a great way to live. I never thought of *that* before."

None, of course, have the power to compel, no matter how vast their promotional efforts. They do, however, have the power to *prevail*—prevail in our magazines and newspapers; prevail in our radio and television programs; prevail on the shelves, and in the store windows; ultimately, perhaps, prevail in our priorities.

Virtually all advertisers wish to do this. It is, again, part of the system. And so, then, are the ensuing ethical consequences.

As we have noted many times, advertising tends to thrive in a market system of resource allocation. It is hardly surprising that advertising practitioners frequently use the ideology of the market to defend and promote their craft. Thus, advertising is defended because it promotes competition among self-seeking advertisers who are always held in check by the inherent rationality of consumers and the relentless forces of competition. The mechanism of this constant interchange of self-interest is thought to be the "invisible hand," leading self-interests in directions which will ultimately serve the best interests of all.

To the charge that advertising by its nature attempts to direct human consciousness to serve the advertiser's self-interest, the practitioners respond "Guilty!" But, it would be added quickly, what works well for the successful advertiser also works well for customers. We rely upon the basic assumptions of the classical liberal market with its strong utilitarian rationale (greatest good for the greatest number), they say.

Consider by way of example the shifts in product planning/marketing/advertising strategy brought on by a single factor—the move toward lighter diets. Fast food outlets now feature offerings such as salad bars and baked potatoes, while entire new chains are starting to feature nothing but "healthful" choices. Low-calorie products now appear in regular supermarket displays rather than being relegated to "dietary foods" ghettos. *Advertising Age*, predicting product successes for the 1990s, spotlights:

> Milk in new forms—carbonated, flavored, aseptic, even high-fat.
> "Fresh" prepared dinners; fresh packaged salads, Olestra and Simplesse, shelf-stable foods, chemical-free produce, branded fresh meats, kids' foods, rice bran, healthy frozen meals, premoistened cleaning wipes.[5]

Public tastes, not the whims of the advertisers, presumably set this "healthy" agenda.

Why then the ethical concern? Because two of the key assumptions underlying the harmony of interests of the classical liberal market can be strongly contested, and, with them, the inherent fairness of the system.

There is the matter of human beings' rationality. It has been well documented that most people, most of the time, are not careful shoppers, and do not have extensive knowledge about alternatives, including the advantages of not buying at all. The continued success of Bayer aspirin in the face of countless lower-priced and functionally comparable competitors serves as a case in point. Heavily advertised movies frequently are rewarded by strong initial patronage, regardless of the quality of the film. So, if consumers are not always driven by the internal drummer of a deliberate and calculating nature, the argument for humankind's inherent good sense weakens, and the contention of manipulation is strengthened.

And what of the safeguard of competition? The ideologues of the classical liberal market assumed a large number of competitors offering virtually identical products, all competing on the basis of price, with no one big enough to influence the outcome. Contrast that with the prepared cereal industry, where three companies dominate, the cigarette industry, soft drinks with the giant Pepsi and Coke power blocs, and so on. Concentration, rather than diffusion of market power, continues to be the fact of the marketplace. It is instructive to note that the ten biggest mergers in U.S. history have taken place *since 1981*. Enjoying market power, the firms commonly choose to avoid price competition and compete on the level of brand, with a rich supporting cast of symbolic dimensions contributed through packaging, advertising, and merchandising.[6]

If one takes the erosion of these two assumptions of the market's supporting ideology seriously, then advertising emerges with the potential for exploitation. The biggest advertiser, not necessarily the producer of the most efficient or satisfying product or service, is able to attract patronage due in large part to the pervasiveness of the symbol packages we call advertising.

Defenders renounce this thinking. Advertising, they assert, cannot compel. The self-interest of the advertiser requires that the product or service be interpreted in terms of the self-interest of potential consumers. So constituted, advertisements serve complex individuals as handy guides for buying—sometimes based on "objective" criteria, frequently value-laden, mirroring the ambiguity of the human condition.

As historian Stephen Fox concludes in his recent history of American advertising, "The people who have created modern advertising are not hidden persuaders pushing our buttons in the service of some malevolent purpose. They are just producing an especially visible manifestation, good and bad, of the American way of life."[7] If the buyer is not interested, the effort fails, and the producer is left to ponder new advertising or, perhaps, a new product.

Frame the issue in terms of moral responsibility. By asserting belief in the rationality of consumers (consumer sovereignty) and the basic fairness of the market, the advertisers are in essence pressing responsibility onto the consumers themselves. They are the final judges. *They* can best make the decisions between competing stimuli. *They* know what they can afford, what satisfies them.

Those who raise ethical dimensions, on the other hand, are arguing that moral responsibility is not served by simple reliance on the impersonal forces of the market. The advertisers, government, or some combination need to assume the task of ensuring that the best interests of individuals are served. The system, they contend, is not working for the good of all concerned. People are more driven than they need to be and are spending their money less wisely than they could be. It is unethical to assume that responsibility rests with individuals alone.[8]

Where, then, should responsibility lie? The answer chosen has enormous implications for advertising.

51. THE INVASION OF PRIVACY

Regardless of the content of the messages, advertisers simply are trying to get at us. This is inherent to the system, and the advantages are strongly on the side of the advertiser. Critic Jerry Mander asserts, "All advertising is an attempt by one party to dominate another."[9] The first party is presumably the advertiser, and the second, the potential customers.

With the exception of predictable market information forums like the *Yellow Pages*, classifieds, and weekly supermarket ads, advertising seeks us out; we do not seek it. Against the backdrop of that relentless seeking, ethical dimensions must necessarily emerge.

As Mander sees it, the essence of the advertising process is that the advertiser talks and we listen. We have very little opportunity to alter the monologue or even avoid it. If a friend constantly talked at us, we could tell him to change the subject, request his silence so we could respond, or walk away. Advertisers, however, monopolize the subject in whatever manner, frequency, and volume they choose; seek us out in virtually every facet of our lives; make it extremely difficult for us to avoid them; and provide us with no opportunity to respond except at the point of purchase. The result is a system destined to intrude.

The term "behavioral interdiction" in advertising circles refers to putting an advertisement in front of someone who is going about his or her daily affairs—to interdict the person's behavior.

Thus, as advertising practitioner Rod Miller recently observed, we now have:

■   Ads in toilet stalls, both on the ground and in flight.

■   Ads on parking meters and garbage cans on city streets.

■   Ads on grocery store shopping carts (including tiny video screens and safety belts), ads on shopping bags, even television monitors playing commercials at checkstands and in the aisles.

■   Commercials on movie screens, on rented videocassettes (even little billboards on the box they come in), on giant screens at sporting events, and on television monitors at airport baggage claim areas.

■   Advertisements sent to fax machines.

■   Telephone sales calls to people at home (usually during dinner, it seems), from other people or—heaven forbid—computers.

■   Commercials on the telephone while you're on hold.

■   A wealth of specialty items from T-shirts to sunshades for windshields to fortune cookies.

■   The much-publicized Channel One, in which school systems force-feed students commercials in exchange for a few television sets and VCRs.

And that's not to mention increasing clutter in traditional media: 15-second TV spots, more commercials on cable TV, more and more free-standing inserts falling out of newspapers, magazines stuffed with bound-in and blown-in response cards, mailboxes overflowing with unsolicited advertising, and so on.[10]

The result of all this special pleading, Mander would contend, is that we develop a defensive posture; we shut ourselves off in order to retain our privacy. But at what cost? And why should we have to? In Mander's words: "Why do we tolerate this? What right do advertisers have to treat us this way? When did I sell the rights for them to run pictures in my mind? Why is it possible for people who are selling things to feel perfectly free to speak to me . . . without my permission, all day long?"[11]

From the perspective of our system of business, these are crackpot complaints; the right to persuade is assumed. From the perspective of ethical reasoning, the question of privacy is harder to dismiss.

Privacy has been an essential element of civil liberty from the founding of this republic. Chapter 5 deals with some of the ethical issues faced by journalists when considering where the individual's privacy ends and the public's right to know begins. Here, however, the issue is raised in relation to a form of communication that is both pervasive and generally tolerated: advertising. Why is privacy an ethical issue here? Simply because of the advertising process itself, whereby the advertiser talks and we either listen, try to ignore it, or hide.

The best defense of advertising practice is found in the classical liberal ideology of self-interest ultimately serving the public good. In practice, however, this ideology faces three staunch challenges: (1) The mass media that carry advertising messages in this country are often indiscriminate for advertising purposes. Those watching a given television program, for example, are likely to span virtually every demographic category. Thus it is likely that a sizable number in any television audience will not be interested in the advertising carried on that program. (2) The messages must inevitably tend toward the common denominator in order to make the appeal as wide as possible. As a result, even those interested in a toilet bowl cleaner may not be attracted by the particular appeal in a specific message. (3) Finally, there is the simple reality that advertisers control both the content and the frequency of the messages. That is, rather than having the messages appear at our convenience with a message content that reflects our needs, the advertiser decides what is in his or her best interest to say (and not to say) and how often and where to say it. Sometimes (as the classical liberal ideology would suggest) this system works well for all parties. Sometimes it does not, leading to frustrations from inappropriate timing and irritating repetition, or exasperation from mindless content.

It can be contended that the ethics of civilized communication require a polite and attentive interchange of ideas between two consenting parties; thus an individual has a perfect right to attempt to persuade another as long as (1) the targeted party initially accepts the attempt to persuade and (2) after making the best possible attempt at persuasion, the initiating party accepts the judgment of the other and ceases his or her efforts.[12]

Can advertising meet either or both of these criteria? Perhaps it can deal with the first in the sense that any astute individual in this culture who picks up a magazine or newspaper or tunes in a radio or television station is aware that a sizable portion of the content will be persuasive appeals. It is easier to avoid this element in print than in the broadcast media, but in any case, forewarned is forearmed. (As we have contended, however, such is *not* the case with some other forms, including cinema advertising, airplane banners, T-shirts, advertising in videotapes, and others).

In the second instance, however, it is difficult to see how the current state of the art offers much hope. No advertiser, no matter how zealous, wishes to waste money attempting to persuade someone who will not be budged. Rather the problems here rest with the indiscriminate reach of the media and the complexity of consumer behavior.

If advertisers could neatly reach *only* those interested in their offerings, they would surely do so. Regrettably, the media frequently do not gather audiences with that kind of precision. Even with highly specialized publications, such as, say, *Jogger's World*, some readers will not be interested in the content of a given message. Thus a lot of advertising reaches people who are simply disinterested, and there is no apparent benefit to the advertiser from subsequent exposures.

And consumers can be fickle. An old advertising axiom is, "Your customers are a parade, not a mass meeting." Thus advertisers may feel reasonably justified attempting to reach the unpersuadable with the expectation that, perhaps one day soon. . . .

In spite of its obvious successes, advertising can be seen as a potentially wasteful form of communication for both advertiser and receiver. The advertiser frequently pays to reach disinterested individuals and is unsure how often to advertise to achieve the desired ends. The consumer does not always find advertising when he or she is interested, and, when it is accessible, it may not be in a form that serves his or her particular needs. Perhaps, in order to address this sensitive area concerning the balance of advertiser and individual interests, we need to pose a simple question and consider it inherent in any attempt to persuade, particularly through indiscriminate channels: Am I welcome here?

Certainly advertisers can be, or can alter their message or media strategies to increase their chances. Given the rising clamor of adver-

tising in both traditional and unconventional forums, the discrete advertiser may reap unexpected benefits from an embattled public.[13]

52. THE MEDIA SUBSIDY

If one were asked to select adjectives to describe the mass media
of the United States, one of the first phrases offered would be
"privately owned." Close behind would be "advertiser supported."

The two have not always been so closely linked. For the better
part of the eighteenth and nineteenth centuries in this country,
publishers were essentially producing low-cost convenience
goods. Their efforts were supported largely by reader subsidy; that
is, the reader paid the entire cost of the newspaper or magazine.
By the early twentieth century, however, the pattern had been
altered. Rather than continue to raise the price of their com-
modity to reflect increases in production costs, most publishers
chose to keep the cost low and use the contented readership to
attract more advertisers. Thus the advertising subsidy increased
as that of the reader diminished. The consequence was inevitable:
publishers became "brokers in blocs of consumers" as advertiser
support became proportionally greater than that of readers.

Today the vast majority of the media vehicles in this country
owe their financial livelihood to advertisers first and readers/
viewers/listeners second, although Norris offers compelling evidence that, at least in the case of magazines, the advertising "subsidy" may be more myth than substance.[14] Today, presumably,
one constituency could not be satisfied without the other, for if
the readers/viewers/listeners are not attracted, advertisers will
not be attracted.

Yet it is undeniably clear that the needs of the three central
parties—publishers/broadcasters, advertisers, and listeners/view-
ers/readers—do not always harmonize.

PUBLISHERS/BROADCASTERS

How far does the publisher/broadcaster go to accommodate the
advertiser? It is, for example, ethical to do any of the following:

- Attempt to accommodate more advertisers either by adding

more advertising pages or by (as in broadcasting) reducing
the length of a standard commercial so that more may be
aired?

- Create new units (for example, home-buying sections, network news breaks) largely for the purpose of selling more
  advertising?

- Arrange the magazine, newspaper, or radio or television programming largely for the benefit of the advertiser—for example, spread editorial material throughout the magazine so
  overall advertising readership may be higher, break into televised movies at points of advertiser rather than viewer convenience, stop televised football games at predetermined
  times, and so forth?

- Attempt publishing and/or broadcasting ventures only in
  terms of market-dominated criteria? "Are there enough advertisers willing to pay to have me gather these people into
  an audience?" It could be argued that there is a need for a
  mass-media vehicle dealing with the concerns of the urban
  poor, but can you imagine an advertiser-supported vehicle
  called *Ghetto Life*?

- Stop publication entirely of a newspaper or magazine because of weakened advertising without even questioning the
  readers as to whether or not they would be willing to shoulder more of the fare to keep their publication in business?

- Purposely blur the division between advertising and nonadvertising material by accepting "editorial" style advertising in print or "infomercials" in cable TV programming?[15]

ADVERTISERS

What are the ethical dimensions of advertisers' doing the following:

- Withholding support from magazines or newspapers whose
  editorial treatment of company-sensitive issues is not supportive?

- Regarding the audience as individuals who were gathered to
  read/view/listen to nonadvertising material and are there-

fore due no particular respect? And thus feeling free to repeat, shout, badger, seduce, or frighten as their needs dictate?

- Selecting media vehicles predominantly on the basis of impersonal readership/viewership/listenership criteria rather
than making an attempt to determine the degree of commitment that exists between the vehicle and its audience?
- Knowing that withdrawal of advertising support for a particular vehicle may be partially responsible for depriving
thousands or millions of individuals of that vehicle?

LISTENERS/VIEWERS/READERS

Audiences are consigned to a passive role if advertisers seek them
out rather than the other way around. The audience must realize
that their patronage of particular media vehicles sends messages
back through the system. If they respond positively (or at least
passively) to particular television/radio/newspaper/magazine
content, they are likely to get more of the same. If they watch
"whatever is on," they are clearly responsible for perpetuating
the television forms so favored. If they find it less demanding to
read *People* than *The Atlantic*, the consequences are predictable.
If they silently tolerate advertising abuses in terms of volume,
content, taste, or sheer leverage, they encourage these abuses to
continue.

Other ethical dimensions to all of these aspects should readily
suggest themselves to the perceptive reader. We are talking here
of ethical quandaries inherent in our system of media. Merely by
participating in advertiser-subsidized mass media, the individual
confronts potentially troubling issues. Given the nature of these
elements so related, there is no way around it. The issues are
there.

If one assumes that the sole purpose of media vehicles in this country
is to make money, then the ethical issues are simplified considerably.
The publisher or broadcaster simply produces an editorial or entertainment package that attracts the largest possible audience of interest
to advertisers. Advertisers and their agencies, in turn, select those ve-

hicles with the lowest cost per thousand or those that yield the most efficient demographic segments. Both can rationalize their single-mindedness by assuming that they are supporting media vehicles that offer the public what they want. And the attraction of listeners, viewers, and readers completes the circle.

If, however, one raises questions of whether reliance on advertising revenue leads to a vigorous and satisfying mass media for the society, then other questions emerge. For example, how might advertising support be related to the quantity of media vehicles in this country as well as the quality of their content? Some interpretations suggest themselves.

Quantity

The media landscape in the United States is abundantly populated. Daily and weekly suburban papers have flourished even as the number of urban dailies declines. Magazines appeal to every vocation and avocation and a great many are supported by advertisers grateful to reach a homogeneous audience of professional wrestling addicts, antique buffs, or science fiction enthusiasts. Specialized programming abounds on both AM and FM radio, and even television, still the most indiscriminate of the mass media, continues to fragment through ad hoc networks, cable, pay cable, and other accommodations to the laws of competition for advertiser money and viewer tastes.

As media vehicles serve advertisers, their missions change accordingly. They become brokers in blocs of consumers; they seek out not simply interest blocs, but markets. Since markets are associated with the kind of disposable income needed to buy the baubles of our consumer society, it follows that the media will follow markets. Thus the young, affluent, and well educated will likely be overindulged with media attention while the impoverished will be ignored.

Quality

Regardless of the quantity, is the content of these media vehicles strongly affected by advertising? If so, for good or ill? Here the critic and supporter fail to reach even tentative agreement.

CRITIC: Mass media in the United States are, regrettably, in the business of gathering audiences for advertisers. As a result, they try to attract as many from a desirable market as they possibly can. This is typically accomplished with lowest-common-denominator content that emphasizes the titillating and sensational rather than the substantive and thoughtful. In short, the media "attract the eye without engaging the mind" while offering a degrading diet of truncated news, violence, sex, and simplistic comedy and drama.

SUPPORTER: The media in the United States are diverse and vigorous, their content ranging from the profound to the profane. The variation in content is a reflection of the interests and tastes of the American people. The media, after all, are surviving in a market. If they do not serve the needs of an audience, they will falter and disappear. The reader, listener, or viewer has the ultimate veto authority. Finally, support from a variety of advertisers is far more likely to produce a press free to criticize the government than would be the case if government supported the media, as it does in many other countries.

With the situation thus perceived, only an extremely narrow, profit-only conception of the media would free advertising practitioners from ethical questions regarding the interplay of commercial messages and media programming. Given the stakes, the issues must be raised and confronted.

53. RESOURCE ALLOCATION

Any planet, any continent, any society, any city, home, or individual, faces the problems of resource allocation. There is only so much time, so many raw materials, so much money. Decisions must be made and resources allocated appropriately. Advertising has been both criticized and championed as playing a significant role in this allocation process, either through reinforcing existing values or, far more ominously, through altering the old and shaping the new. This is a matter laden with ethical questions.

A favorite classroom gambit is to suggest to students that the instructor will be visiting them in their hometowns and wishes to be taken for a ride around the city. The only stipulation is that "somewhere along the line we travel past the homes of the most successful people in town." Asked where their tour would go, students almost inevitably offer descriptions of well-manicured lawns, large and impressive houses, ample driveways, and so on. And then the sting: "I didn't tell you to include the homes of the *richest* people in town, only the most *successful*." What, they are asked, of the school janitor in his inconspicuous home. He has worked hard all his life to support a family and make their lives better than his. He gives his time and money (such as it is) to others and, after 35 years of thick and thin, is still devoted to the same woman. Why is he not "successful"?

One answer would be that those are not the values that our market system has come to honor. Advertising, critics assert, is very influential in this market enterprise, since its overall effect is to equate achievement with things, and fulfillment with the consumption of goods and services. If the market has no goal except to meet consumers' demand, advertising can be said to help direct that demand toward a warped system of values that sees more spent on the advertising of pet foods than on many social programs.

By contrast, assume for a moment that advertising is merely a reflection of consumer sovereignty. Here, if we have too many cars and not enough beautiful drives, it is the consumers' will that it be so, and advertising is only following the market directives. But if advertising does lead, if it shapes and directs demand, then the tens of billions spent for it may well lead us to equate cars with social status, cigarettes with the assertion of gender, and pills with relief from the strains of everyday living.

At the time of this writing, many secondary and elementary schools are in deep financial trouble. Library acquisitions are being cut, educational programs curtailed. Suppose that for a period of one year the amount now spent for advertising and promoting cigarettes (well over $2 billion) was spent (with similar expertise) on advertising school bond issues. Would we have better schools?

The matter becomes more troubling when one's perspective is widened. A church publication offered this picture from the mid-1980s:

> If the world were a global village of 100 people, 53 of them would be unable to read, 1 would have a college education, 67 would be poor, 35 would be suffering from malnutrition, and 50 would live in what we call sub-standard housing.
>
> If the world were a global village of 100 residents, 6 of them would be Americans. These six would have one-third of the village's entire income, and the other 94 would exist on the remainder.[16]

An authoritative scenario for the year 2000 depicts a widening gap between the haves and have-nots. Does advertising accelerate the situation? Can advertising improve it? Or is it merely a passive element totally dependent upon other, more fundamental forces such as political systems? Should those who work in advertising be concerned with these matters? By way of extreme example, should ethical questions be raised about the promotion of a throw-away ethic when the planet is threatened by enormous problems of pollution and refuse disposal?

These questions, and the difficulties inherent in any answers, are not likely to disappear.

Well over a decade ago, Carl Ally, one of advertising's more outspoken figures, proposed that advertising should take upon itself the task of helping to solve the world's economic ills. He noted that the condition of 20 percent of the world's population consuming more than 80 percent of the world's products cannot long endure, particularly with the rising aspirations of many Third World countries. Advertising, Ally suggested, can help by leading the more affluent countries to accept a new ethos featuring curtailed consumption, assuming that the resources thus conserved could be more equitably distributed.[17]

Many of us may remember, as youngsters, being admonished by our parents to finish the food on our plates because of the starving children somewhere else on earth. It was never made clear how eating our remaining food, which was to be thrown in the garbage if we did not oblige, would fill the stomachs of children half a world away. Yet the idea was right: waste less and have more to share.

Many would nod in agreement with the sentiments suggested in Ally's message. Yet to implement them would involve enormous change. As we have seen throughout this book, if one endorses the motivating force of self-interest inherent in the market system and also assumes that the safeguards of a rational humankind and atomistic competition are in place, then good will be the ultimate result. Thus the producer of a cheese-flavored dog food can believe he is behaving ethically by seeking his self-interest, which will in turn affect the well-being of his employees, contribute to the viability of the domestic economy, and keep the country in an economic position that will enable it to respond to the less fortunate of the world.

Basically, it is contended, the market follows the currents of demand from the multitude below rather than the edicts of planning from above. If advertising merely reflects that demand, it is a relatively passive force and, at best, may reinforce values already held.

On the other hand, if advertising, fueled by self-interest, helps shape that demand and direct the market, then two conclusions follow: (1) To the extent that advertising encourages private consumption, particularly of products and services high in social costs such as pollution potential, it can be held to account for a shameful misallocation of resources to the few at the cost of depriving the many. (2) If advertising is, in fact, powerful enough to direct this allocation of resources, it could also be used to *redirect* it to more socially beneficial ends (for example, using the ad budget of cigarette companies to advertise the needs of schools, as was suggested earlier). And, indeed, there are examples, both large and small, of such efforts. A brief sampling:

- The efforts of the Advertising Council on behalf of such noteworthy causes as aid to black colleges.
- The advertising of the foster children programs and the various relief organizations.
- The numerous charitable promotions for hospitals and research on crippling diseases.
- The enormous advertising and promotional endeavors associated with the *We Are the World* and *Live-Aid* fund-raising efforts.
- The daily examples of advertising in support of "good causes."

To the argument that these and other efforts are woefully underfinanced, there are two answers. The first answer is yes, but even a little of the right advertising can make a difference. For example, a *single* ad in each of the following cases played a major role in:

- The reintroduction and subsequent passage of a rat extermination bill for the city of New York.
- Killing of a bill that would have led to the damming of the Grand Canyon in order to provide hydroelectric power for the peak-hour needs of Phoenix.
- Asserting the independence of the tiny Caribbean island of Anguilla in the face of a pending landing by the Royal Marines to establish British sovereignty.

The second answer is yes, it is a drop in the bucket and the only real solution is to introduce a more authoritarian political and economic system than we now have. In essence, government should then take control of the market to direct it in ways deemed desirable by those in power.

For advertising practitioners, three possible courses of action suggest themselves: (1) To endorse the values of the market system and assume that the good for all will ultimately prevail because of the motivating force of private interest and the basically fair allocations produced by the "invisible hand." (2) To find (or encourage) work in companies, agencies, or special-interest groups that promote socially helpful causes. (3) To agitate for change in the political and economic system to replace the market as a resource allocation device with a more authoritarian system, expecting that the subsequent direction of resources will be more just.

Innocent bystander or dynamic agent of change? Channel of charity or selfishness? Advertising and resource allocation is an appropriate cosmic issue with which to signal the end of this discussion of the ethical dimensions of advertising, and, we hope, the commencement of your ongoing study into the ethics of this complex, pervasive, and controversial element of our culture.

NOTES

1. Christopher Lasch, *The Culture of Narcissism* (New York: W. W. Norton, 1978), p. 72.
2. Michael Schudson, *Advertising, the Uneasy Persuasion* (New York: Basic Books, 1984), p. 240.
3. "Fade Creams," *Consumer Reports*, January 1985, p. 12.
4. Loren Ghiglione, "Stop Running Cigarette Ads," *Advertising Age*, 13 November 1989, p. 48
5. "Parting Shot: Goodbye '80s: Hello Health," *Advertising Age*, 13 November 1989, 5–16.
6. For a far-reaching discussion of this milieu, see Vincent Norris, "Advertising History According to the Textbooks," *Journal of Advertising* 9 (Summer 1980): 3–11.
7. Stephen Fox, *The Mirror Makers* (New York: William Morrow and Company, 1984), p. 381.
8. For a provocative statement of many of the issues in this chapter see Jerry Mander, "Four Arguments for the Elimination of Advertising," in *Advertising and the Public*, ed. Kim Rotzoll (Urbana: University of Illinois, Department of Advertising), pp. 17–28.
9. Ibid., p. 19.
10. Rod Miller, "No Escaping Ads," *Advertising Age*, 11 December 1989, p. 34.

11. Mander, "Four Arguments," p. 21.
12. Paul Keller and Charles T. Brown, "An Interpersonal Ethic of Communication," in *Messages*, ed. Jean Civikly (New York: Random House, 1974), pp. 41–50.
13. For a discussion of the advertiser's concept of "audience," see Kim Rotzoll, "Gossage Revisited," *Journal of Advertising* 9 (Fall 1980): 6–14.
14. Although advertising revenue is still the Holy Grail of virtually all magazine publishers, there is evidence that the so-called advertising "subsidy" may not, in fact, be the financial bedrock that some advertising trade organizations suggest. See Vincent P. Norris, "Consumer Magazine Prices and the Mythical Advertising Subsidy," *Journalism Quarterly* 59 (Summer 1982): 205–211.
15. See Rader Hayes and Herbert Rotfeld, "Infomercials and Cable Network Programming," *Advancing the Consumer Interest*, 1:2 (1989): 17–22. See also, Michael Hoyt, "When the Walls Come Tumbling Down," *Columbia Journalism* Review, March/April 1990, pp. 35–41.
16. *That All May Have Life*, Flyer for One Great Hour of Sharing, United Church of Christ, 1985.
17. "Advertising Must Help Solve World Economic Woes: Ally," *Advertising Age*, 29 July 1974, p. 1.

AFTERWORD

On March 2, 1984, the Board of Directors of the American Advertising Federation adopted the following *Advertising Principles of American Business*.

Truth

Advertising shall tell the truth and shall reveal significant facts the omission of which would mislead the public.

Substantiation

Advertising claims shall be substantiated by evidence in possession of the advertiser and advertising agency prior to making such claims.

Comparisons

Advertising shall refrain from making false, misleading, or unsubstantiated statements or claims about a competitor or his products or services.

Bait Advertising

Advertising shall not offer products or services for sale unless such offer constitutes a bona fide effort to sell the advertised products or services and is not a device to switch consumers to other goods or services, usually higher priced.

Guarantees and Warranties

Advertising of guarantees and warranties shall be explicit, with sufficient information to apprise consumers of their principal terms and limitations or, when space or time restrictions preclude such disclosures, the advertisement should clearly reveal where the full text of the guarantee or warranty can be examined before purchase.

Price Claims

Advertising shall avoid price claims which are false or misleading, or savings claims which do not offer provable savings.

Testimonials

Advertising containing testimonials shall be limited to those of competent witnesses who are reflecting a real and honest opinion or experience.

Taste and Decency

Advertising shall be free of statements, illustrations, or implications which are offensive to good taste or public decency.

Thus stated, these principles serve as a touchstone of present concerns by a major advertising trade organization. Combined with other self-regulatory efforts such as the National Advertising Review Board mechanism and the clearance departments of the media, they can be seen to represent the current priorities of American advertising in relation to the ethical dimensions of its practice.

Public Relations

The ancient sages would not be surprised by our modern interest in public relations. A citizen of Athens was by nature an advocate, salesperson, purveyor of ideas. Perhaps their only surprise would be the professionalization of this common human enterprise. Even at that, however, the sophists might be expected to regard this development as merely an extension of an old, if not honorable, calling.

Surely public relations is now ubiquitous and omnipresent. The need for advocacy and information extends from PTA councils to councils of war. Dwight Eisenhower recalls in his memoirs of the D-Day invasion that soon after his arrival in London in the summer of 1942, he recognized that the Allied plan to break into Germany through France would impose immense hardship on British families and farms as American sailors and soldiers massed in preparation. His solution was to establish early "an effective Public Relations Section of the headquarters."[1] While the general went on to describe battle plans, readers were left to wonder what role public relations played in the success of the Allied cause and hence in the continuation of pluralist democracy in the West. We suspect that this part of the untold story is complicated and considerable.

Histories of modern public relations usually follow the contours of communications technology and progressive capitalism. The need to fill columns of newspapers generated press agents paid to supply words which would serve purposes similar to the words in adjacent advertisements. But the genius of press agents was to shield their advocacy in the paper's news functions. Ivy Lee and Edward Bernays and perhaps P. T. Barnum expanded agentry to encompass the creation of cultural archetypes to explain the ways and means of their mostly corporate clients. Big business needed this crucial help, especially as Congress moved to curtail capitalism's excesses and the muckrakers rushed to expose them. Nowadays, along with farming and health care, public relations seems like the profession we could least imagine living without.

Are public relations professionals advocates or information specialists? The debate rages. Journalists have jealously regarded their own role as informational, whereas public relations engages the task of persuasion. Advertising professionals clearly define themselves as pacesetters in the advocacy function—people who know attitude change and consumer behavior and apply that knowledge in campaigns to promote special interests of clients. Does this leave P.R. professionals somewhere in the middle?

The work of this important profession is clearly informational and decidedly persuasive. But why not both? Truth is never neutral, so why should the telling of truth be any less the professional mandate of someone paid to communicate a particular perspective? In one important sense, this is a more honest mode of media work, since one's biases as a communicator in a P.R. setting are usually transparent. Shedding pretenses is normally the first lesson in public relations training.

The two chapters in this new section cannot claim to be encyclopedic. We have selected cases representative of the dilemmas encountered in corporate public relations and its counterpart in public agency-charity-nonprofit work. We suspect that the contours of media ethics scholarship will be shaped more and more by the needs, pressures, contradictions, and promises of this expanding, influential profession.

NOTE

1. Dwight D. Eisenhower, *Crusade in Europe* (New York: Doubleday, 1948), p. 58.

CHAPTER 11

Corporate Public Relations

Perhaps the fastest growing field in communications today is public relations. Ambitious writers and producers are attracted by its multitiered challenge, its chance to be where corporate decisions are made, and its frequently generous salaries. An enormous amount of news appearing in each day's paper comes from the pens of public relations writers.

Yet the field of public relations is full of ambivalence. A recent cartoon in *Punch* shows a couple seated in an exquisite restaurant being instructed by a waiter who explains: "Chicken nouvelle cuisine is the same as roast chicken, but we get a graphic designer to lay out the veg." Is public relations the specialty of putting old information into new form? Newspaper journalists often consider P.R. writers as "hired guns" yet depend on their releases for leads and even stories. Public relations professionals claim they are in the information business pure and simple—not neutral information surely, but information that clarifies and educates the public on the role and mission of the client firm. Both reporters and P.R. specialists are persuaders and providers of news, advocates with a professional's sense of obligation to truth and fairness. By their numbers and their expertise, P.R. professionals are some of the most powerful information sources in the world.

It is no longer responsible to dismiss such an important field as "all flacks and liars" as did one recent speaker.[1] Public relations professionals have made noteworthy efforts to provide fellow workers with a code of ethics (introduced already in 1950) and with agencies to monitor that code. The dilemmas inherent in the dual role of advocate and information source make a professional's training in applied ethics all the more important to the long-range health of the firm, the client, and the culture.

The cases in this chapter echo dilemmas found in news and advertising. "Lambert Voss" looks at the serendipitous nature of information gathering and considers how much one can use such surprises to one's own advantage. "Regal Holding" worries over the encroachment of P.R. duties onto the inviolate news function. "MCB Corporation" raises concerns about the internal processing of information. Are there silent walls between the P.R. office and the sales office next door? Under what conditions is marketing information put to the advantage of the firm that gathered it? "Acme Parts" puts the public relations professional in her most humane role—as mediator and conciliator. Since when do P.R. people need a college degree in counseling? Finally, "SCM Computers" raises old ghosts from Dante's level reserved for freebie-takers. This time a P.R. professional makes the offer and tries to do it right.

54. LAMBERT, VOSS, AND BROADBENT, INC.

Alan Broadbent was a principal and account executive for the public relations agency Lambert, Voss, and Broadbent in Seattle. Broadbent had recently been sent an invitation by Airtran, a large aircraft manufacturer in the area, to make a presentation for the company's account. If Alan's agency could get this account, he estimated, it would double the agency's billings.

Airtran had sent him a document outlining its strategic communications objectives for the upcoming fiscal year as well as a host of documentation about the company itself. He was invited to spend a day at the company in order to meet the key corporate communication personnel and tour the corporate offices and plant site. Broadbent had heard through the grapevine that his firm and one from Washington, D.C., were the main competitors for the account. He was worried because he felt that the Washington agency, which served several international accounts, could be at a competitive advantage.

The day arrived for Broadbent and several of his colleagues to visit corporate headquarters. He hoped that this visit would provide important political and strategic insights for making the all-important presentation.

After a tour of the plant and several meetings with corporate management, Broadbent was asked to take a seat in the senior corporate communication manager's office while the manager attended to a small emergency. Several minutes passed in the office, and Broadbent was getting nervous. He began to pace about. His eyes scanned the office, the credenza by the window, the certificates and photographs on the wall, then the manager's desk. What! He thought he saw there the formal written proposal of his Washington competitor. His eyes quickly moved away from the document toward the office door. All was quiet. Most of the employees had left for home.

"Should I just take a quick look at it?" he thought to himself. "It's not as though I would be going through any files or desk drawers. And I really need to get this account." Nervously, Alan scanned the document and made mental notes. He found several intriguing strategies. He quickly placed the document back on the desk, just as he found it. Only a minute of speed reading, but what a difference a minute can make. Soon after, the corporate communications manager returned and the two men summarized the day's events.

Broadbent did not tell anyone what had happened. When Lambert, Voss, and Broadbent, Inc., completed its proposal, it clearly contained some of the insights that Broadbent had seen in the Washington agency document.

The formal proposal to Airtran went well, and the agency was awarded the account. Alan Broadbent was the hero of the day. At the end of the first year of the relationship between LVB and Airtran, the agency's contract was renewed with great enthusiasm.

Alan Broadbent was not a newcomer to public relations war games. His name was on the firm's letterhead, and he was the company's choice to represent it at the most important new client visit of the year. Broadbent was a home-run hitter on a Triple-A franchise, but he was up against a barnstorming bunch of major leaguers from the East Coast. A little nervousness is understandable.

Broadbent needed something to give him a competitive edge. He had made some of his biggest deals with old Seattle friends. On some clients he could work his native gift of schmooze. The graphs, charts, and diagrams—data generated by his firm—could bedazzle hard-core numbers-or-nix types, usually recent graduates from marketing schools. But that afternoon at Airtran the competitive edge required "intelligence"—not the common-sense type, more the kind associated with collars-up trenchcoat snoops.

And there he was, temporarily sidetracked while his corporate host attended to a late afternoon emergency. Alan had not pilfered the files or photocopied anything. He had just looked, that's all, as he would have done with the magazines outside the office door had his host been less collegial. The intelligence he gathered that afternoon could have come to him in other ways, too. In fact, some of the ideas in that file had filtered out in tidbits of conversation he had had during the day. He was not raiding the Watergate; this was just competitive information-gathering that Alan subsequently used to win the account and build it into one of LVB's prize winners.

Alan had every right to feel proud of his work at the one-year anniversary of the account. Serious questions about purloining information—stealth or stealing—were part of the past. Of course, someday he wanted to tell his story to his new Airtran friends, just to get their reaction. He wondered if they would slap his shoulder in admiration of his spy skills, or laugh it off as part of the craziness of the P.R. business, or perhaps, though not likely, show some irritation at what could be interpreted as invasion of corporate documents.

Alan also wondered at times whether that emergency and the strange willingness of a corporate manager to let him occupy an office alone for all that time, and the coincidental desk-top availability of that important file, were all a set-up, a kind of test of his and LVB's integrity under fire. What a twist, he dreamed. Had Airtran concocted a fake file and purposely left it in the open just to see how much of it would get reproduced in Alan's LVB proposal? Nah, Alan mumbled, that's too sophisticated for these busy corporate types; things like that happen in Paul Newman films, but not in Seattle. Nonetheless, Alan admitted that he would have felt like the world's biggest chump had his claim to an original creative proposal been challenged by the very people he was trying so hard to impress. Thank heavens Airtran is not a devious type of company, Alan surmised, or he would not have gotten away with his ploy. He wouldn't care to work for such people anyway.

55. REGAL HOLDING COMPANY

Over the years Saul Harper had been a very successful businessperson in this southwestern city. From his family he had acquired a bank which had grown to be the largest in the community. He also had acquired the town's most popular television station (KBNK), popular at least in terms of local news programming. Its 12 noon, 6 P.M. and 10 P.M. news ratings were three times higher than those of the competition. Both the bank and TV station were operated under the Regal Holding Company.

Vinita Compton was the public relations professional for Regal and was responsible for all public relations activities for both the bank and the television station. Compton and the television news staff had met over the years to discuss what she thought the relationship should be between the news department and the bank. She always stressed that the news department should act in a completely independent manner even when it came to news concerning the bank.

In January 1990 a competing television station was about to air an investigative report on local bank policies, accusing the three leading banks in town, including Harper's, of engaging in discriminatory lending practices toward minority groups. It was alleged that these banks engaged in red lining—not offering mortgages or business loans to specific geographic areas of the community, the areas that contained mostly minority individuals and businesses.

As soon as the story broke on the competing station's 6 P.M. news, Compton called the KBNK's news department and asked them not to air a report on the story until the bank's officers could prepare a reply. That might mean missing the 10 P.M. news, but a reply would be ready early the next day.

When the news director protested, Compton said: "All we are asking for is a small delay so that the bank can put together some important numbers to repudiate the charges. A bank's reputation is all it has. To have that reputation damaged by irresponsible reporting is unacceptable. We'll respond to this sensationalistic muckraking as quickly as we can."

"But 10 P.M. gives you four hours. That's time enough," the news director insisted.

Compton replied, "Mr. Harper is not at a phone just now. We're trying to find him. Hold the story until I get back to you."

Vinita Compton knows she is stepping where every textbook tells her to fear to tread. She is trying to muscle into the news operation of the company's station, in the interests of her boss and his reputation in the community. Despite the advice of textbooks—and she read plenty of them in journalism school—Regal is not a university and Mr. Harper is not a professor. Her grade in this stretch of life is her paycheck, and the world on this side of the classroom is generally called "real" for good reason. Now she has interests to protect and a negative media campaign to mitigate. And she needs all the help she can get.

Vinita is careful not to demand cooperation. She knows the newsroom/public relations tension too well to try a frontal power play. But she hopes her not-too-subtle suggestions will carry the weight of Mr. Harper's own words. If KBNK news thinks she is speaking for the owner, they will at least think twice before rushing on camera.

Vinita is also careful not to avoid the story. She is engaged in damage control, not censorship. There is no way Saul Harper can simply take a pass on this story; he will have to respond. Her job is to design the best possible response: sincere, to the point, aggressive, nothing said that would have to be retracted later, nothing mentioned to give ammunition to the muckrakers for a counterpoint. The story is coming, she assures KBNK, so let it come right from the top.

Vinita is also careful to cover herself, and this may be her greatest professional triumph here. If KBNK goes on the air with the story at 10, at least the story airs over her protest. Mr. Harper cannot blame her for not caring about his image and business reputation. If he sullies himself by firing employees in a rage over the negative coverage, he will have little reason to fire her . . . unless, of course, he is provoked that his chief P.R. specialist did not know beforehand what the media were working on.

Vinita knows she has "brought time" at KBNK. At least, her urgent requests will cause some confusion in the newsroom, and perhaps by 10 o'clock she will be able to find Mr. Harper and put together a bona fide reply. That would make her a kind of mini-hero, except of course to the muckrakers, and perhaps to the minorities whose concerns this news story is supposed to promote. There will be time enough for that. She will recommend that Saul Harper head up a city-wide commission to address minority banking problems. "Hey," she realizes, "that's just what the KBNK 10 o'clock news needs! An announcement! A call to action! Now . . . where does that old man spend his evenings?"

56. MCB CORPORATION

Jason Smith was head of the public relations department of a large multinational corporation located in Boston. The company's products ranged from those sold to individuals through retail outlets to those sold to other businesses. One of his main tasks was to gauge how these different publics felt about MCB, its corporate image, the reliability of its product design, its market support system, its advertising, and its sales program.

It had been several years since MCB had done any survey work to measure attitudes of purchasing agents toward MCB. Since MCB was considering a major sales campaign in the business-to-business area, it made sense to conduct the survey not only for public relations purposes but also to help the sales force in the new campaign. After a suggestion to management, Smith received approval to proceed.

Although his department was primarily responsible for developing the questionnaire, it was necessary to present a rough draft at a meeting of corporate management and sales force representatives. The primary purposes for the meeting were to ensure that nothing in the questionnaire could be considered offensive to the critical target of purchasing agents as well as to gather insights for additional questions.

The meeting did not go as smoothly as Smith expected. Although all felt the project was necessary, they insisted, first, that the questionnaire be disguised (that is, respondents would think they were in a phone conversation only) and second, that corporation people be allowed to see the answers along with the names and phone numbers of the respondents. Management did not want the intention or the sponsor of the project to be revealed to the purchasing agent respondents. They argued that to identify MCB would bias the results and alert competitors that MCB might be "up to something."

Smith argued that disguising the questionnaire and sponsor of the project was unethical. He stated: "By calling someone at his or her office and attempting to gather information from them under false pretenses, we are invading their privacy. We are eavesdropping on their thoughts." He also argued that a sales representative should not be allowed to see any questionnaires that identified a respondent. He said: "The only purpose of the project is to gather research data. Its intent is not to develop leads or provide information about the private thoughts of a particular customer. Sales representatives would be more than welcome to see the completed research report, which of course would not identify any specific customers."

How confidential is the information in your attaché case, or notebook, or head? The question is pervasive. News reporters usually know more than they tell. Ad sales people know things about competitors which could turn some firms into eagles, others into gnats. In almost every case, how a professional media person uses information depends on how it was obtained, whom its dissemination would hurt, and what the repercussions would be should the "leak" be revealed.

For example, information obtained under conditions of strict confidentiality is often not disclosed directly. Newspeople do not run to police departments with every tip. Sports writers do not rush to print with every inside detail of trades and contracts. True, the ultimate goal is to print and broadcast news, but successful news reporting in the long range requires careful handling of information—ethical judgments on what's ready for public viewing, and how it should be framed. Raw information can be explosive, and while truth heals and helps, information can also hurt and destroy.

Jason Smith stands in a solid tradition when he insists that trade information gathered by his office is not necessarily company property for indiscriminate use by salespeople and management. He rightly argues that company credibility depends on careful control of his survey results. It is one thing to ask buyers about their attitudes toward MCB, but the sales force is short-sighted if they think buyers would naively surrender specific details of their purchasing plans to an "anonymous" survey only to welcome a sales call from MCB which pinpoints their plans with almost psychic precision. The mind of the sales force is muddled by visions of short-range profit.

While some of Jason's results will hardly be hot news (the general image of MCB), some findings could make trade sector headlines. Therefore Jason would do well to search for an appropriate middle ground in his response to the MCB sales force. He is not a lone ranger in MCB, and his company benefits from his work only if sales increase. If Jason wants to gather information for its own sake, he should become a librarian. Aristotle would remind him that information on market trends, appropriately collected with subsequent usage reasonably clear to all respondents, could be put to strategic use by MCB without his sacrificing the ethical high ground.

For example, Jason could restructure his approach so that respondents know they are talking directly to a corporation which will claim "first use" privileges to the specific product information its survey uncovers. He could wrap the promise of a cordial sales visit into his first approach to a respondent, clarifying up front any conceptions that his salespeople will receive only summaries and not specific questionnaires. He could promise to release his survey results at a trade convention, as a service to that corporate sector, but a month after MCB sales leaders have had their own briefing. He could offer to distribute survey results simultaneously to all respondents and to other corporate clients willing to purchase his findings. He could call a press conference.

Jason's worries over gathering information "under false pretenses" need not be an insurmountable barrier. He should make his pretenses public and truthful and avoid the moralistic posturing that claims his project is "only to gather research data." If that is really his purpose, he should take that university teaching job he has always dreamed of and leave the tumult of corporate competition to the sly and the wary.

57. ACME PARTS, INC.

The history of Acme Parts, Inc., reads like the history of a number of privately held U.S. companies in the 1980s. Established in 1932 by the Johnson family to produce drive shafts, clutches, and other transmission components to the off-and-on highway markets, it prospered and showed steady growth during its first 50 years of existence. It grew from one to three plants, all located in the Midwest.

In the early 1980s the Johnson family decided to sell the company to a large American firm, ANOVA, which was also in the off-and-on highway business. The transition was a difficult one for employees, who were used to the Johnsons' rather *laissez-faire* management style.

Within a year of its purchase by ANOVA, the employees decided, in a very close vote, to join the United Auto Workers. As one employee said: "You need some protection around here. The new bosses are only concerned with production quotas and expenses. It just ain't the same without the Johnsons." After three years of ownership by ANOVA, a bitter strike ensued over wages, fringe benefits, and working conditions. The six-month strike ended with a compromise settlement that left negative feelings between management and the employees.

Shortly after the strike settlement, it was suddenly announced that ANOVA was selling Acme Parts, Inc., to a West German firm. Within six months, most of ANOVA's management teams had been replaced, by both American and West German managers. New production techniques and management styles were rapidly introduced without employee or union consultation. Grievances, anger, and confusion became the watchwords during this transition period.

After a few years, conditions seemed to be returning to "normal" at the plants when it was announced on July 2, 1990, that some elements of the existing management team—the American managers plus several outside investors—were going to attempt a leveraged buyout of Acme Parts, Inc. The deal was completed in October 1990. New managers were again brought in to the company along with a new public relations person. The public relations function was established at the insistence of a major outside investor, who had been involved in a public relations firm; it was the first time such a function existed at Acme.

Among management's first acts was to change the company name to Brighton Parts, Inc. Another was to hire a team of production consultants from Boston to evaluate existing production techniques and pay schedules at the three plants. Management considered all options to be open, from closing and consolidating plants to a major reorganization of production procedures. Employees were not to be informed of the consulting group's existence, however, since it was felt that it could cause great uncertainty and anxiety.

The first assignment for the new public relations person was to deal with the employees. Sandra Eble initiated an employee survey with the input and consent of the union. The results were devastating. Over 80 percent of those surveyed had a negative perception of their job and the company. Comments included: "Here we go again." "The only way I know who I work for is by the name on my check." "I seem to have a new boss every few months. Everyone wants to do things differently. No one ever asks me, and I have been here 25 years." "I am afraid and worried about my future here." "They will probably want some wage concessions, given all the money they borrowed." "It is just insane around here—no one ever tells you anything; everything is a secret."

The public relations person's objectives, as given by management, were (1) to inform employees about the changing conditions, (2) to build employee morale and develop a sense of belonging, and (3) to prepare the employees for some difficult times ahead.

On the one hand, Acme was long overdue for a public relations office. It had already had 58 years of corporate life with only the owners and managers, apparently, to represent the company to the community and to articulate corporate concerns to employees. On the other hand, the emergence of public relations professionals as part of a new management team could create the impression that the company was taking a turn toward appearances over substance, toward snow jobs instead of clutch jobs. Much of the P.R. staff's image, both inside and outside the reorganized company, would depend on their integrity and openness in explaining and clarifying changes already underway. That's what made Sandra's survey so important.

From her first week on the job, Sandra could already see that she would have to choose between limited-objective utilitarianism or a Kantian first duty frosted by Judeo-Christian others-as-self icing. Under the utilitarian option she could adopt a role as part of a new management team with a mandate to achieve the long-range goals of Brighton Parts's owners, even if those goals were not harmonized with the style to which workers were accustomed. The needs and desires of some senior workers would have to be sacrificed to the greater good of the new company. While some people might feel exploited or ignored, new workers would come in to advance the new agenda. On the other hand, Sandra could choose a prior duty of establishing the communication channels that would alleviate worker anxiety and enhance the mutuality of each part of the Brighton team. Transmissions are not made by managers, she reasoned, but the skilled machinery operators need direction to stay viable and competitive. In other words, an interdependent company needs a modicum of trust and mutual goodwill to the benefit of all, and she could be the universal joint, so to speak, that keeps the drive shafts turning.

Sandra decided on the latter course, partly because of concern about her own future. If management wanted to conduct its campaigns and reach its decisions in isolation, there could well come a day when she too would be part of the isolated crowd. In fact, maybe she already was like a pawn and didn't know it. In an environment where a few determine the course for all, everyone is vulnerable. Just as Sandra

hoped her own advice would get a fair and professional hearing, so she
reasoned that other workers could and should have input, too.

Her survey was a first step, but much work remained, both above
her and below on the corporate ladder. She could proceed with stated
objectives 1 and 2 only if management granted an ear and a voice to
workers who would be first to feel the difficult times forewarned in
objective 3. She would also insist that management not mislead or
seek advantage over workers. Sandra knew that surveys could signal
a new attitude of openness, or a subterfuge for sudden announcements
and pink-slip notices. Her top priority would be a corporate communication environment in which workers could gradually shed their
sense of isolation, and managers their sense of bottom-line profits
wrenched from the company at all human costs. It would not be an
easy task, since each group was suspicious of the other's real interests,
but she felt that if she kept before her the ideal of caring for others as
if she herself shared their status (and their problems), Brighton Parts
could become, if not a family again, at least a company where people
could say, "I was treated like a human being, not a drill press."

58. SCM COMPUTERS

Adam Reschke, a recent public relations graduate, had been assigned the task of coordinating the public relations area with the
marketing function to help introduce a new desktop computer
model for SCM. This new model had been in development for
three years, and the future viability of SCM would depend upon
a successful introduction.

Since SCM's communication budget was very small relative to
that of its key competitors—IBM, Apple, and Compact—management understood that public relations efforts would be a key
in obtaining positive editorials and evaluations of the new model
in key trade computer magazines and newsletters.

Adam's strategy was to obtain these positive editorials and evaluations through a two-day press event. He proposed to invite the
top computer magazine and newsletter editors and reporters to
New York City. All expenses would be paid by SCM and would
include (1) airfare to and from New York, (2) a two-night stay at
a prestigious New York hotel, (3) all meals, (4) entertainment
expenses, and (5) taxi costs. The editors and reporters would be
asked to attend a half-day "press conference" where the model

would be introduced and demonstrated. Hands-on demonstration would be encouraged. A major banquet would be given that evening with top SCM management and sales force representatives, and appropriate entertainment would be provided.

Adam hoped that these editors and reporters would be favorably enough impressed with the new model to give it glowing reviews in their publications; these writeups would be worth more than all the advertising SCM could muster on its limited budget. The outline of the public relations program was positively received by management, and Adam was told to proceed as quickly as possible.

After top management's praise for his efforts had subsided, Adam began to think about some of the ethical dimensions of his plan. He remembered from school that according to the Society of Professional Journalists guidelines, journalists should refuse free trips when those trips could involve a conflict of interest. He reasoned, however, that many other industries had used these press events to introduce new products and services. He further mused that "Whatever I do for these people, they always have the right to refuse the offer. My job is to get as much exposure as possible for this new model, and anything I can do to achieve that exposure is okay."

Adam is not the first person to try to win friends and influence people with freebies and junkets and a general good time. All businesses work this territory, and Adam happens to be in the product promotion business. Adam is bright enough to know that, apart from special incentives, his information will probably join the great pile of disheveled papers on and around the desks of technology editors worldwide. Such piles are quickly forgotten.

Adam's plan actually has much to commend it. First, he wants to bring reporters together with engineers, designers, and SCM big bananas to talk. That's a giant stride ahead of merely sending press releases with studio photographs. In New York the people and the product will come face to interface with media writers themselves—the best possible combination for accuracy and thoroughness. There is ethical value in that kind of reporting.

Second, Adam is creating an important event and establishing voluntary means of participation. He rightly observes that no editor is forced to accept a free anything. Adam merely makes the meeting accessible without cost. He knows that the *Washington Post* did not attend Disney World's fifteenth anniversary extravaganza at Disney expense, and that thousands of writers and broadcasters from smaller units did. He also knows that outright freebies (every reporter gets an SCM computer for home use) would far exceed a journalist's standards and create a lot of skepticism about SCM intentions. The only free things Adam offers have to do with getting to and from the banquet and eating while there. These are basic life needs: when you travel, you have to eat!

Third, he creates no conditions on the coverage of the event or the new computer product. No meal or airline ticket is contingent on column inches. The judgment on how and how much to write is the journalist's alone. Adam does not ask for prior approval on copy before he entertains the writers. He does not threaten a news blackout from SCM for columnists critical of the new PC. Adam thus disconnects his alleged freebies from the stories potential customers will read. Any press kit from SCM can be dumped into the nearest trash bin; dinner is still served and SCM is still the gracious host.

The Society of Professional Journalists' code that gave Adam momentary second thoughts is intended to do just what Adam has already determined to do: seek no editorial advantage by playing to a journalist's natural human acquisitiveness or love of a good time. Adam can orchestrate the event, but the timing and enthusiasm of subsequent coverage is the sole business of his guests. Adam is confident enough of his company's product to believe that the clips will be upbeat.

"So," Adam concludes, "it's not as though I'm manipulating naive peasants who do not understand my interest in showing off the SCM-PC. The people I invite to the Big Apple bring their critical intelligence with them. Their columns cannot be so easily bought as journalism professors and other purists imagine. My job is publicity, their job is reportage, and nothing is so helpful—and fair—to get that process rolling as a pleasant meeting of the minds in a setting of elegant conviviality." What readers of the resulting stories would say, behind the Rawlsian veil, that their concerns were forgotten and their intellects deceived? What is written (by the writers) is written.

NOTE

1. Quoted in Donald K. Wright, "Individual Ethics Determine Public Relations Practice," *Public Relations Journal* (April 1985): 38.

CHAPTER 12

Public Relations Beyond Corporate Walls

At a Department of Energy experiment station in northern Illinois, high-energy physicists are discovering the behavior and make-up of nature's building blocks. This is science of the first order, and the teams assembled are international in scope. Most of the action occurs underground, in the particle accelerator, and in above-ground quonset huts packed with computing gear and neutrino-sensing devices. To most of us, it is a netherworld of research, vital but distant, probing the *Urstuff* issues but arcane and esoteric. We need help to take even a first step toward understanding.

Fortunately for nonphysicists, Fermilab is an open facility. Guard gates greet visitors off the Batavia Road entrance, but the guard is rarely on duty, and when she is, it is mostly to provide directions. Once on the grounds, visitors can roam nearly at will, and the miles of paths on this former farmland are used often by joggers and cyclists seeking reprieve from accelerators on suburban highways.

Serious visitors at this multi-billion-dollar operation, however, are hard-pressed to find guidance. If the guard is not in, good luck in finding the one public relations professional who writes the press notices, conducts the tours, organizes briefings, develops brochures, produces videos, edits the in-house publication, etc. She is a busy P.R. specialist, whirling around this sedate preserve like an electron around the nucleus. When fire is reported at Fermilab, it is usually because someone has mistaken this one-person P.R. staff for a small atomic explosion. She is an accelerated particle the cyclotron cannot contain.

What a oddity: so much investment in physics, so little in explaining it to the public.

What a commonplace: charities, hospitals, social service agencies, churches, and private schools with tight budgets, lean staffs, and little left over for public relations. In these settings, the P.R. professional discovers that versatility and resourcefulness are prerequisites which the textbooks could not teach.

Public relations in the non-corporate world ranges from the dingy hallway where political hopefuls first assemble their leaflets to the Washington restaurants where lobbyists shape public policy, from the police spokesman explaining a drug bust to the monsignor urging support for an inner-city school.

Habitat for Humanity enjoys a national reputation because former president Jimmy Carter helps with its carpentry—but would we know it apart from the work of a public relations professional? The Jewish Guild for the Blind has been rated the most cost-effective social service charity of the nation's 100 largest, but who's to know apart from public relations?

Cases in this chapter explore the difficult P.R. challenge of the many non-corporate agencies which sprout like wildflowers, reach for the sun, and either find a constituency or wither for lack of support. Case 59 asks whether the gripping appeals that tug at heartstrings have a role in meeting a community's needs. Case 60, the St. Luke Hospital case, approaches fundraising from a different angle—how much of the truth needs to be told. "Fudging," Case 61, is a common problem in the competition to find students still willing to pay to learn history and literature. Case 62, "Spin Doctors," takes up the tough calls of a political campaign under pressure. Chemical and nutritional issues are increasingly complex; in "Pesticide Panic" (Case 63) the media's competence in covering them is the central question.

This is only a beginning, not a comprehensive set of cases to settle all the issues of our variegated volunteer culture. The wildflowers of non-corporate P. R. will never be a formal garden, but neither should we assume a trillium only to pick a stinging nettle. Public relations is at the center of decisions by donors to give money, by volunteers to give time, by neighbors to give support to worthy causes; the cases in this chapter help us make the important commitments.

59. THE EMPTY CHEST

The Empty Chest is a charitable organization run by Barb and Stan Adams. They collect clothing, canned goods, and money from individuals and businesses in the community to assist low-income individuals and the elderly. They organize tutorial programs for underachieving youngsters and provide a job placement file for single parents of preschoolers. The organization has three employees handling clerical and service chores; Stan and Barb run the organization. The Adamses are advised by a board composed of prominent citizens, clergy, a school principal, and two elected county officials.

With recent changes in the income tax laws and a skittish securities market, gifts had fallen by over 35 percent in the previous two years, making it very difficult for Empty Chest to maintain its normal level of service, much less take on the care of those additional needy who had felt the secondary effects of the market slowdown. At a board meeting in June, a member suggested that Empty Chest attempt to seek a "public relations type" to assist in fund-raising efforts. The board quickly agreed to the suggestion, saying that Empty Chest could no longer rely solely upon its reputation, no matter how good that reputation was. The Adamses were skeptical but agreed that the matter should be pursued.

At the July board meeting, Sue Lyons, an executive vice-president of a local public relations agency, indicated she would be willing to assist. The board was delighted and gave her the charge of developing a fund-raising campaign that would increase donations by 25 percent for each of the next four years.

Sue spent considerable time developing the campaign, drawing upon her experience with the United Way and the American Red Cross. She felt that the Adamses were possibly in "over their heads," that is, their eleemosynary work had grown past their capacity to maintain it. But she also knew that on average, more pennies of a dollar given to Empty Chest found their way to the poor than was the case in many similar organizations. The Adamses, it seemed, were genuinely caring people.

At the next board meeting Sue made her presentation. Although it was warmly received, some board members and especially the Adamses felt that Sue's campaign proposal painted a rather bleak picture of Empty Chest, bleaker than it really was. The Adamses said it focused too much on what the Empty Chest had not been able to do rather than on its many positive accomplishments. The campaign was based on an extremely pessimistic forecast of donations for the coming year. Certainly, if present trends continued some services would have to be curtailed, but not so severely as the campaign implied.

Sue defended her plan: "You sometimes have to stretch things just a little to get the public involved in a particular charity. Sometimes you have to get a little emotional. You have to focus on unmet needs. You have to touch people's hearts."

The Adamses know that there is a thin line between "stretching things" and telling a lie. They insisted: "This community has trusted us for almost ten years to do the right thing with their contributions. That's why they have been so generous to us."

Sue replied: "To broaden the constituency, and to get them to dig deeper into their pockets, we can't treat Empty Chest like an old family pet. We have to show need, concern, and potential—but especially need. We need to make some people cry, some others cringe."

The board agreed with Sue and gave permission to move ahead with the campaign. The Adamses reluctantly gave in and told Sue they would offer whatever support she needed.

There was a time, perhaps, when goodwill and a good reputation were all it took to be successful in the charitable field. Churches seemed to be particularly trustworthy then, and private citizens who wanted to help their neighborhoods could often do so without a lot of people raising eyebrows, suspicious of whose pocket was being filled.

Not so now. Ministers are in jail for major league pilfering. Charities are as likely to be asked for a copy of their annual audit as for their list of needs. Board members of most charities carry omission and errors liability insurance to protect themselves from charges of malfeasance. Many contributors to worthy charities feel fortunate if half of their dollar gets to needy recipients. The goodwill industry is facing a much more complicated and cautious market than it did a decade ago.

The Adamses have felt the pinch. There is never enough really to go around, but now their receipts are declining while calls for their services are increasing. Who, if not Empty Chest, is to fill the interstices of our culture where disadvantaged people, for reasons often summarized in the peculiar phrase "hard luck," do not have adequate housing, food, shelter, or medical care? Government programs are one avenue of solution, surely; but organizations such as Empty Chest show another face: local agencies doing good, often thankless, work within a square-mile radius, or a city ethnic settlement, or a rural county. Sue Lyons has every reason to do her best work for Empty Chest.

And perhaps she has. Each charity ought to have a personality, she can rightly argue. People expect faceless agencies and foreboding bureaucracies from government social services, but a private charity should have a distinguishable personality. If Sue designs a fund-raising campaign around the cluster of people and projects (current and potential) that make up the Empty Chest family, she has done so because that kind of campaign tells the Empty Chest story as truthfully as stories can be told. Exaggerations are acceptable within that story, as long as a potential donor could call the Empty Chest office some sunny July afternoon and conceivably meet the type of needy person Sue Lyons will highlight. Just as social science researchers use "maximized comparisons" to develop types of social interactions which press away from the statistical middle ground, so public relations specialists may responsibly use "extreme need cases" which are legitimately within an organization's orbit of concern.

Even pessimistic forecasts are acceptable, if a potential donor who cares to ask can be shown how those projections were developed, without losing credibility.

Sue needs to listen to Stan and Barb more empathetically, however. They are not beggars and never have been. They do not want to hang their heads like a skid-row hobo. Sue needs to provide a campaign that the Adamses, their staff, and their volunteers can be proud of. Sue's gift to the Adamses, above and beyond the four-year goals of the campaign, is to give them the tools to look a new donor squarely in the eyes, set out the needs, ask for a contribution, accept it gratefully, and know that an honest transaction has been accomplished that serves everyone's interests.

Stan and Barb may need Sue's pushiness to bring them into the 1990s' eleemosynary world. Sue may need the Adamses' conscience, honed against the poverty they have seen firsthand and tempered by the dignity of the poor they have served. False humility and pseudo-righteousness won't get the job done; a campaign that extrapolates from the present into the future, and that seeks to make that future better, is Sue's specialty. If a tear is shed along the way by someone who comes to understand poverty as an unnecessary condition of people of great dignity and honest ambition, there is no moral fault in that.

60. ST. LUKE HOSPITAL

St. Luke Hospital, located in the southern part of Chicago, had existed for over 80 years. It had seen its patient base change over the years from a community of Eastern European immigrants to one of poor Hispanics and Afro-Americans. Its mission was to serve all who came to its door for help. A major part of its service to the community was through its emergency and trauma units.

Chief financial officer Frank Bailen had always felt that reimbursements from Medicare and Medicaid for emergency room and trauma treatment were inadequate; he made a suggestion, or what really seemed like a demand, that St. Luke no longer provide these services. At a board meeting, he presented objective financial evidence that the emergency room and trauma services were literally driving the hospital out of business. Since two other hospitals in the area had recently been forced to close their doors, Bailen's statement had added impact. Bailen stated that it would be better to provide a more limited array of services than to provide none at all. "Our mission is to service this community, and we are the only hospital left in this area. We should not close our doors because we were trying to do too much. Why can't we educate people to use our outpatient clinic rather than going to the emergency room for every little thing? Anyhow we can't even begin to serve all these people in the emergency room given that we will get the spillover from the two hospitals that have closed."

A spirited debate ensued at the board meeting about this conflict between serving the community and remaining in good financial health. A compromise decision was reached to keep the emergency rooms and trauma unit open but allowing the hospital to go on pass-by when needed. Pass-by is an alert condition, lasting a few hours or even a few days, in which the hospital will not accept emergency patients arriving by car or ambulance. Pass-by would be instituted when there was severe overcrowding or the possibility of exceeding a daily quota of emergency room patients. The daily quota concept was a compromise between Bailen and the board to reduce the emergency room's negative cash flow.

Mary Jones, the public relations officer, was to help institute the program. She was to set up a system that would let the community know when a pass-by condition existed at the hospital. She was also to explain these new policies to the press. Although the board felt that the overcrowding dimension of the pass-by system was legitimate, they were worried about the quota dimension. They told Mary to not devote a lot of time on it with either the press or the community. One board member told her: "Smooth over the quota side of the problem. Not everyone will understand. It is either this or no emergency room services at all. We're trying to do our best to serve this community."

Public relations specialists are constantly called upon to present information to various groups, and occasionally to *not* present information to various groups. Should P.R. professionals become part of a conspiracy to hide valuable information?

Generally, no. A society that treasures justice also requires that information be widely shared and readily available. Tyrannies enjoy monopolies on information. Sometimes yes, however. Some information is hard to come by, and rightly so. Checking account numbers and salary figures are not so accessible, and with good reason. Mary Jones must decide whether the quota system devised by the hospital board is information vital to public justice, or merely in-house financial maneuvering that every business and service enterprise uses to keep the doors open and the bills paid.

The test devised by Sissela Bok for judging cases of deception might be helpful to Mary. Professor Bok insists that truthtelling is mandatory unless a jury of disinterested peers can agree that the lie is justified. (The proposed lie must also reckon with the conscience of the teller and that of the teller's trusted associates.)

Mary could accept the hospital board's judgment and keep the quota system out of the newspaper if she could reasonably anticipate that most readers would misunderstand and misconstrue the system. Such a judgment is fraught with potential for abuse, but if community interest is foremost (and hospitals, like hardware stores, must show black on the bottom line), the possibilities for abuse can be minimized.

One way to minimize the abuse of keeping secrets is to find an appropriate jury of peers and lay out the hospital's case before them, quota system and all. Mary should insist that St. Luke Hospital present its innovative and questionable system at a convention of hospital administrators. Typically such conventions do not receive thorough press coverage, and there her peers could critique the plan, judging its merits on the basis of their own expertise.

What if such an informal jury were to assail the quota system as

inhumane and contrary to the hospital's pledge of providing medical
services unilaterally? Mary could then effectively promote the development of alternative strategies for keeping the hospital afloat, such
as cutbacks in peripheral but not traumatic services. A sensible board
would have to listen.

What if such a jury were to applaud the plan as present-day realism in health care delivery? Mary could prevail upon the chair of
such a group to join her in a press conference explaining the plan to
reporters and interested community constituencies. Outside help
might not settle the case for the quota system, but Mary could at least
rest on the claim that she and St. Luke Hospital had not jumped off
their own private gangplank, impervious to the judgment of professional colleagues.

The jury system is not a final answer to all questions of secrecy,
of course. Juries can be virulently self-interested and callously self-
protective.

There will be occasions when a duty to tell all the truth must
prevail over outside expert advice. Such duty will likely arise from
claims of nonnegotiable human rights, or from compelling, theologi-
cally based moral responsibilities. Kant's imperative may come to bear
on a secrecy question. Also a vision of the world based on the love–
justice continuum of Jewish and Christian (and other religious) morality may compel publicity of certain sensitive information, in order
to prevent injustice and human suffering caused by greed and power.

Mary's problem is not that acute, however. She has not been told
to lie, only to guard the facts. A morally sensitive guardian in this case
would release and rehearse the facts before responsible groups who can
render an appraisal in the interests of the whole community. If such
a jury were not available, or if Mary's board prohibited her from locating one, she would have every reason to worry that a cover-up was
the actual agenda here. Let Mary propose her convention presentation
to the St. Luke board without delay. They should be as eager for Mary's
professional skills at that meeting as they are for her services at the
upcoming press conference.

61. FUDGING ON THE FUTURE

Just as magazines and ad agencies have discovered that special-
ization is the key to the future, so some of the best public relations
firms have begun to narrow their range of clientele, or to hire
"experts" to serve specialized clients.

Thus Jeri Sanders had forged her path into the industry. Her doctorate was in geography, and she had taught in the field at a branch of the state university. But her real love was promotion. So when she decided to leave academe for public relations, naturally she presented herself as just the sort of account representative who could serve the interests of smaller colleges struggling to locate and recruit students.

The personnel officer at Buxter-Heide knew an asset when he saw one. Jeri was hired and soon thereafter began to work on the "Better Person" campaign, a brainchild of the new president of Maple College, Kenneth Hermann.

Jeri's role was to advise Hermann and the board of trustees at Maple on how best to expedite their plan to draw students toward a traditional liberal arts college at a time when most students were keenly interested in learning job skills. Maple College had a proud 75-year tradition of liberal arts education, and its leadership was committed to the idea that the most capable worker in any field is broadly trained in science and the humanities, though now that included learning computer software too. The "Better Person" idea had come to Hermann as a way of distinguishing Maple's approach to higher education from that of vocational schools and community colleges.

The week after Jeri's first meeting with Hermann, she began to do the kind of research that she sensed Maple's board had neglected. Would the "Better Person" idea work? Would employers buy it? As she inquired among her friends in the business world, she began to have misgivings. "History is fine and dandy," one contact told her, "but we're not fighting the French Revolution, we're selling apple sauce!" Another contact who did employee interviewing emphasized that his company had the highest regard for "theories and stuff, but if the youngster doesn't know numbers, we can't look at him."

By the time of her next meeting with Hermann, Jeri was well prepared to argue her case: Whatever appeal the "Better Person" campaign might project, its bottom line must be the preparation of trained workers with saleable skills—that is, if Maple College really wanted to tap today's student pool.

Despite Jeri's thorough homework, she could not convince President Hermann to modify the direction of his campaign. He was determined, in the face of her impressive research, to insist that Maple could produce a "Better Person," and he wanted Jeri to develop the idea to the hilt.

Well, it was her first assignment with Buxter-Heide, and who could do a better pitch for higher education than someone like herself with firsthand experience in the field? Jeri accepted the president's directive and set to work on the campaign.

Jeri knew that she was no longer a professor in a classroom, able to say and do pretty much what she wanted without outside interference. She had entered the business world, and in that larger classroom the client is king, or queen. Jeri had done her duty by presenting research to President Hermann, research that suggested his plan needed serious revision if Maple were to realize its recruitment goals. But Jeri was not obliged to surrender the account if Hermann's plan was slightly misconceived. Or was she?

Jeri continued with Maple's campaign under the assumption that in a free marketplace, her highest goal was to generate business and to do it honestly. "Let the buyer beware," was modified in her case to "let the buyer decide," and she had done her part to influence the client's decision. With that duty to honesty accomplished, she could now spend Maple's P.R. budget on a campaign she believed was almost certain to fail.

But Jeri had lost something in the transaction. As a professor she had taught her courses well, knowing that her students needed the basics of geography before they could fully understand issues such as overpopulation, urbanization, and ecology. As a public relations professional, however, she had allowed the student to write the syllabus. Her pursuit of the business had clouded her sense of professional responsibility.

As a consumer, Jeri deplored shoddy products put out by manufacturers intent on quick sales. As an active member of her community, she had protested when the community cable franchise wanted to double its rates for subscribers, knowing that lower-income families would be that much further removed from important information sources. But with Maple College, Jeri had agreed to pursue a costly plan that her own research had indicated was out of touch with the future. The obligations that she unhesitatingly applied to other products and services were forgotten in her own profession. She had become a "hired gun," churning out material she did not believe in, generating excitement over the objections of her own studied beliefs. Jeri had forfeited the benefits of her own liberal arts training, a living example that the "Better Person" campaign might be more fluff than substance.

62. Spin Doctors

The 1988 Democratic race for the presidency began with a menagerie of hopefuls, all eager to displace a Republican machine which had been one of the most popular, but arguably among the least effective, administrations to occupy the White House in this century. Among the contenders was the senator from Delaware, Joseph Biden.

Not a dream candidate in every sense, Joe Biden had assets which gave him early momentum. He was articulate, known for biting one-liners and populist rhetoric, a quality public speaker. His team of political consultants (the black belts of political public relations) were talented veterans. And Biden had an intuitive sense for the blue-collar, farmer, laborer, voter—a "Heartbeat of the American people" candidate, direct, honest, and classy.

But Joe Biden ran into trouble with the press—the big Eastern press first, all others quickly thereafter—which proved to be terminal for his campaign. The problem was plagiarism.

"I kinda thought I could just do it off the top of my head," Biden explained on the *Today Show* in response to reporters' charges that he had used a speech by British labor leader Neil Kinnock in his own presentation at the crucial Iowa Forum. Biden had been looking for a dramatic close, but his choice was on the wrong side of "borrow," a hairbreadth away from "copy."

Kinnock	*Biden*
Why am I the first Kinnock in a thousand generations to be able to get to university? Why is Gladys the first woman in her family, in a thousand generations, to be able to get to university? Was it because all our predecessors were thick?	I started thinking when I was coming over here. Why is it that Joe Biden is the first in his family to ever go to a university?
Did they lack talent? Those	Why is it that my wife, who is sitting over there in the audience, is the first in her family to ever go to college? Is it because our fathers and

people who could sing and play and recite and write poetry.

Those people who could dream dreams—see visions.
But why didn't they get it? Was it because they were weak?

Those people who could work eight hours and play football weak?

Those women who could survive eleven child bearings— were they weak?

Does anybody really think that they didn't get what we had because they didn't have the talent or the strength or the endurance or the commitment? Of course not. It was because there was no platform on which they could stand.[1]

mothers were not bright? Is it because I'm the first Biden in a thousand generations to get a college and graduate degree that I was smarter than the rest? Those same people who read and wrote poetry and taught me how to sing verse.

Is it because they didn't work hard?
My ancestors who worked in the coal mines in Northeast Pennsylvania and who would come up after twelve hours and play football for four hours.

No, it is not because they weren't as smart. It is not because they didn't work as hard.

It's because they didn't have a platform on which to stand. That's what my party's always been about. We provide people a platform upon which to stand. That's what government is for.[2]

Long before the Iowa debate, Biden had been using the Kinnock close, each time with attribution. But at the crucial moment in Iowa, he dropped the attribution. And on subsequent occasions, too, the senator seemed so accustomed to these words that he in fact made them his own.

Borrowing words and appropriating ideas is fair political strategy, but in this case, strangely miscalculated. The Kinnock material was from a 10-minute video distributed to all the Democratic candidates— so it took no monumental feat of investigative reporting for the *New York Times* to headline its coverage: "Biden's Debate Finale: An Echo from Abroad." A follow-up story documented other Biden "lifts" from Robert Kennedy and Hubert Humphrey. The Kennedy material was the result of speechwriter Pat Caddell's hasty work, Biden claimed. Not a real problem—just campaign clumsiness.

Then the law school matter surfaced. While a student, Biden had used five pages of a law article in a paper of his own without attribution. He received an F for the course, took it again, and passed with a B. Together with the campaign speeches, this new revelation began to make plagiarism look like a character trait, which hurt the proud politician deeply.

As the allegations mounted, and further instances of inaccurate self-puffery were reported, Joe Biden sought the advice of his ace staffers. All but one knew his candidacy was over. Pat Caddell, alone, urged that Biden take the offensive with an anti-press campaign. Beat them off with charges of bias, he urged. Salvage a run for the presidency by going on the attack—and by watching his words with great care the rest of the way.[3]

Public relations can make or break a political campaign. Candidates for most every office beyond county coroner depend for image, speeches, and press contacts on professionals who follow in the illustrious footsteps of Ivy Lee and Edward Bernays, founders of the idea that realities beg to be constructed and reconstructed by people trained to build modern Babels out of symbol and icon. Bernays went so far as to claim that P.R. professionals constitute a braintrust behind and above government—the apparatus of democracy a gameboard for players who hold the magic keys to mass persuasion.[4]

Nowadays, after every debate, forum, or speech, P.R. pros gear up to "explain" the candidate's words to an eager press corps. With an intuition for hermeneutics that some might call fanciful, the "spin doctor" interprets the meaning of the speech, correcting its minor flaws, underscoring its prescient themes. It is heady territory for a new class of communication experts, yet their task is justified by the vengence of reporters looking for a candidate's flaw, scrutinizing for a flinch that becomes a damaging angle in tomorrow's headlines. The public may forget the ephemeral TV appearance, the doctors advise, but they will not forget the press's retelling of it. In reports about the debate a candidacy is made strong, or undermined.

In this complicated interplay of story and image, first impression and afterglow, the key to moral action is the golden mean called integrity. It stands as the virtue between manipulation and rigid stenography.

Does a spin doctor have the right to remake a candidate, to revise the meaning of the office seeker's message, to add meanings not present in the candidate's personal appearances, to create a mirage candidate based on possibility and potential but disconnected nonetheless from Mr. Mayor himself?

No. Reporting based on such a massage of the candidate invariably deceives; it is tantamount to seeing a different face while looking in a mirror. Citizens of the city have a right to know the candidate herself, not a mannequin image of her. Virtue demands that a public relations specialist interpret her subject in terms consistent with her subject, so that the real person, not a shadow image, achieves clarity and distinction in the public mind.

Is a spin doctor then obliged to merely rehearse and repeat a candidate's own words for the sake of accuracy? No, no more than a reporter is obliged to insert in quotation marks all the uhs, ohs, and profanities that might find utterance in the course of an on-the-record conversation. Stenographic exactitude is not a news story's glory. Public relations specialists may rightly enhance, expand, and occasionally clean up their candidate's rhetoric—provided the real candidate comes through. Integrity requires that the report the public depends on to make informed voting possible is a truthful account of the person named on the ballot. Spin doctors act with moral resolve when their efforts at interpretation serve to sharpen the distinctions that make their candidate unique.

Did Biden's P.R. staff have reason to believe that the senator—whose success was their own ticket to Washington power—had carelessly appropriated the words and life experiences of other people as his own? Should they have counselled a counterattack with the press as viper? Biden's advisers, all but one, had apparently come to realize that national exposure had accentuated a flaw the public would not condone. They counselled retreat with integrity, a morally virtuous and personally painful path. All the citizens who comprise the *polis* we call American democracy owe that P.R. team a small debt for an honest day's work.

63. Pesticide Panic

In February 1989 the television show "60 Minutes" aired a story that apples treated with the chemical Alar were dangerous to small children. It was initiated by a report from the Natural Resources Defense Council, a nonprofit environmental group, stating that Alar could raise the levels of daminozide dangerously high in children.

Since 1968 Alar had been important to the apple industry for making apples redder and to slow ripening. "Without Alar," explains one of the growers, "we must get in and pick four to six days sooner, before the apples drop." Without Alar some of the varieties go to market green and lacking visual appeal.[5] But when scientists reported in 1985 that Alar and one of its breakdown products could cause cancer in animals, many growers stopped using it. Now the NRDC was extending the possible danger to small children.

Actress Meryl Streep immediately picked up the cause as part of her ongoing crusade against pesticides. She was quickly booked on "Donahue" and other major talk shows and invited to testify at an emergency hearing on Capitol Hill.[6]

An apple scare followed. School cafeterias in Los Angeles, Chicago, and New York City ordered apples removed from the menus and store rooms. An official of the International Apple Institute received a call from a panicky consumer asking whether their apple juice could be poured down the drain or had to be taken to a toxic waste dump. Signs were posted above bins stating that the apples therein were Alar free. Washington State, which grows 50 percent of the nation's apples, faced crippling economic losses.

Said one school official, "It was overreaction and silliness carried to the point of stupidity." Kenneth W. Kizer, director of the California department of health services, said the panic created a "toxic bogeyman." And, in fact, at the height of the apple furor the U.S. embassy in Santiago, Chile, received a phone call that a grape shipment on the cargo ship *Almeria Star* headed for Philadelphia had been laced with cyanide. Having been chided for inaction with Alar, the Food and Drug Administration impounded 2 million crates of fruit at U.S. airports and docks and advised consumers to avoid all Chilean fruit—and that included most of the peaches, melons, green apples, pears, plums, blackberries, and

blueberries on the market in early spring of that year. Japan and
Canada followed suit. Fruit worth $15 million piled up on Chilean
docks with no buyers anywhere. Twenty-thousand Chilean food
workers were laid off and another 200,000 placed on temporary
assignments. FDA Commissioner Frank Young, accused by Chi-
leans of overreacting, insisted he would rather be safe than sorry.
Given the apple frenzy the week before, the public fruit phobia
was a foregone conclusion. Dramatic government intervention in
that climate was the only alternative.

David McDonald, head of the National Food Processors Association, condemned the Natural Resources Defense Council for
seeking visibility rather than seriously facing the scientific evidence. Scientists had not produced convincing conclusions as to
whether Alar was poisonous for humans, but rather than presenting its findings to experts for debate and evaluation, the
NRDC through its public relations counsel, negotiated an "exclusive coverage" arrangement with "60 Minutes." The news
people, in McDonald's view, did not make clear that only 5 percent of all apples grown are still sprayed with Alar. It also staged
the story as a confrontation between a money-hungry commercial
industry and inept government agencies. In addition, critics consider the news media part of the problem, because they are not
adept at covering complicated issues in science and economics.
Saying a chemical is toxic without clarifying the meaning of that
phrase, for example, leads the public into thinking that by eating
an apple you get cancer.[7]

In order to keep modern society from becoming terrified and immobile,
one body of opinion insists that strong government surveillance and
more detailed consumer information in the supermarket should carry
the responsibility. On this view, the press should not consider itself
the guarantor of public health but should play an adjunct role to those
social units that can treat issues in a more discriminating way—in
this case, the local retailer—without creating a social crisis. At the
other extreme, some media advocates insist that media warnings about
potential dangers are essential in a fast-paced and complex age, even
though they often lead to societal dysfunction. From this perspective,
if the media give too much deference to economic and legal interests,

the public will be lulled into a self-destructive complacency. The "watchdog function" is never so important as when powerful industries stand to save millions of dollars by equivocating on the safety of their product.

John E. Cox, president of the Foundation for American Communications in Los Angeles, has proposed a set of guidelines based on Aristotle's golden mean which he believes place risk reporting in an appropriate context.[8]

1. Journalists should delay the presentation of a story until all the facts are in. As McDonald complained, "We have in our laboratories the largest database available on pesticide residue; we offered the information to '60 Minutes' and they wouldn't listen to us."

2. Journalists must put risk in perspective, not by simply reporting two points of view but through presenting careful analysis. Figures from the National Safety Council, for example, show that less than one dozen people per year die in the United States directly from food poisoning—though approximately 1,500 perish annually from diseases connected to food contamination. With 46,000 dying each year in motor vehicle accidents, 12,000 in falls, 5,000 in fire, 5,000 in drowning, and so forth, the public needs a broader picture of risk and safety, not one centered predominantly on warring regulatory agencies or confrontational politics.

3. Reporters must have the training and education to deal with complex data and ask tough questions, particularly in such areas as toxicology, chemistry, and medicine.

4. Journalists must develop neutral sources of information other than industry and public interest groups. Their concern should be seeing the viability and competence of such neutral agencies over the long term, rather than periodically traumatizing the citizenry. At least to some observers, if the news media had shown adequate sophistication, the issues regarding Alar could have been focused on the Environmental Protection Agency, giving EPA an opportunity to act. As a matter of fact, EPA has now banned Alar as a potentially dangerous pesticide, though available scientific evidence is not conclusive. Accepting any data blindly is irresponsible, but the public is entitled to know of tests systemically gathered in a non-industry laboratory.

NOTES

1. Statement by Neil Kinnock, British Labor Candidate, ten minute video commercial (video transcript).
2. Statement by Joseph Biden, *NBC Today Show*, 17 January 1989 (audio transcript).
3. The authors are indebted to a comprehensive treatment of this case by Professor L. Patrick Devlin, "The Biden Presidential Campaign: A Study in the Ethics of Plagiarism and Puffery," International Communications Association Convention, Dublin, Ireland, June 1990. Write the author at the University of Rhode Island, Kingston, Rhode Island 02881-0812.
4. Cf. Marvin Olasky, "Bringing Order Out of Chaos: The Public Relations Theory of Edward Bernays," in his *Corporate Public Relations* (Hillsdale, N.J.: Erlbaum, 1987), ch. 8, pp. 79–88.
5. "Apples without Alar," *Newsweek*, 30 October 1989, p. 86.
6. Details of this event and the quotations that follow are from Margaret Carlson, "Do You Dare to Eat a Peach?" *Time*, 27 March 1989, pp. 24–30; cf. also "Alar as a Media Event," *Columbia Journalism Review* 28 (March/April 1990): 44–45.
7. "Inquiry: Reporting on Risks," *USA Today*, 15 May 1989, p. 9A.
8. Ibid.

ENTERTAINMENT

When the question whether to worry about motion pictures came up before the Hutchins Commission on Freedom of the Press, the first reaction of several of those august scholars was "rubbish." The movies are diversionary, escapist, and silly. What claim can they make to be counted part of the modern press?

Fortunately, a more farsighted view prevailed. However unsophisticated, movies were part of the culture and needed to be looked at carefully. The commission invited Will Hays (chief of the Motion Picture Producers and Distributors of America) to present the case for industrial self-regulation, and eventually the Hollywood model of codes and intra-industry regulations was adopted by the commission as the best way of expressing social responsibility in a democratic society.

On both counts the commission displayed wisdom. While news and consumer information are the vital stuff of media programming, clearly entertainment occupies most of the broadcast spectrum, the cinema screen, and a healthy share of the printed page as well. From these media we receive symbols of who we are, what we should believe, and how we should act. Entertainment, for all its recreative value, does much to educate and socialize its patrons, who are all of us.

Should entertainment programs be subject to ethical reasoning? Robert Redfield, distinguished anthropologist and one of the Hutchins' commissioners, urged that the direction of all our social productivity be toward a "new integrity" of idea and institution, a creative order wherein symbols and practices make "coherent sense when we state them and when we comply with them," leading to a "model society that will command the confidence of other free peoples everywhere."[1] Redfield, no dreamy chauvinist, was arguing the interdependency of social institutions (like the media) and social beliefs (like the sanctity of life). Yes, he would argue, the entertainment media must be put to the test of ethical reasoning.

Redfield's intuitions were a preface to ethical theorizing in the 1980s, when narrative discourse and narrative communities became important concepts in the work of Duke University ethicist Stanley Hauerwas. Hauerwas argued that culture is built around stories that distinguish good from evil, hero from villain, success from failure. Because of the importance of story, a community that wants to live responsibly among other communities is obliged to set its compass on truthful narratives, without which a social ethic becomes detached intellectualism.

> The ways the issues of social ethics are identified—the relation of personal and social ethics, the meaning and status of the individual in relation to the community, freedom versus equality, the interrelation of love and justice . . . are crucial categories for the analysis of a community's social ethics. The form and substance of a community is narrative dependent and therefore what counts as "social ethics" is a correlative of the content of that narrative. . . . Good and just societies require a narrative . . . which helps them know the truth about existence and fight the constant temptation to self-deception.[2]

Hauerwas begins his appeal for narrative ethics with a long analysis of the novel *Watership Down*, a rabbit story with a profound political message, a fictional narrative that helps us construct our own. Constructing journalistic narratives, P.R. messages, advertisements, and entertainment programs involves process, hierarchy, imagination, constraint, profits, and power. Our aim is to examine the moral dimension and press toward justified solutions.

George Gerbner underscored the importance of this examination in his lecture at the fortieth anniversary of one of the country's premiere communications research faculties: "I think of communications as the great story-telling process that guides our relationships to each other and the world." Later he warned that "children are born into a home in which a handful of distant corporations tell most of the stories to most of the people and their families most of the time."[3] His point was to urge a more careful study of the field, entertainment primarily, and its cultural and moral foundations.

The following chapters raise only a few of the questions and suggest some ways of approaching answers. Violence is a pressing concern; its threat to social order is immediate and dramatic. Nearly 500 U.S. citizens die every week from gunshot wounds, many self-inflicted or tragically accidental. Many are the result of a momentary act of passion among friends and relatives. Media violence, some argue, is the same threat one step removed and a hundred times more potent. TV violence sets the stage for social maladjustment, argues Purdue University researcher Glenn Sparks, especially among children. While "media effects" researchers debate the audience impact, ethicists ask how much media violence is tolerable, even though only one person be affected, or none.

And what about problems generated by big media's huge financial stake, with fortunes and careers riding on fractions of rating points, and with pervasive doubt that ethical reasoning has any word to speak at all—money alone counts.[4]

Other problems in entertainment programs are less overt than violence or greed: the stereotyping and typecasting of racial groups, age groups, geographic groups, and communities of faith; or the bias expressed by the omission of substantive narratives about our society's smaller cultures; or the offense created by our no-punches-pulled video explorations of sexual experience, scatological language, profanity, and glorified criminality. It becomes clearer, as we proceed, that every level of the entertainment industry—producer, actor, writer, and viewer— is involved in close encounters with decisions of an ethical kind.

NOTES

1. Robert Redfield, "Race and Human Nature," *Half a Century—Onward* (New York: Foreign Missions Conference of North America, 1944), p. 186.
2. Stanley Hauerwas, *A Community of Character* (Notre Dame, Ind.: University of Notre Dame Press, 1981), pp. 9–10.
3. George Gerbner, "Telling Stories: The State, Problems, and Tasks of the Art," 40th Anniversary Program Highlights, Institute of Communications Research, University of Illinois at Urbana-Champaign, n.d.
4. See Clifford Christians and Kim B. Rotzoll, "Ethical Issues in the Film Industry," in *Current Research in Film: Audiences, Economics, and Law*, vol. 2, ed. Bruce A. Austin (Norwood, N.J.: Ablex, 1986), pp. 225–237.

CHAPTER 13

Violence

Few issues have commanded as much attention from media reformers as violence on television and in film. Some violence, of course, is inevitable in any drama, or even in comedy, as when Fred Flintstone bangs his nose into a doorjamb. But the irrepressible climb in real violent crime, much of it perpetrated by juveniles, has been often linked to the rough and tumble lives of Dirty Harry, Kung Fu, John Rambo, and the ever-growing circus of animated Superheroes. What a juvenile sees, it is argued, too easily becomes what a juvenile does. Since society cannot endure the anarchy of criminal rule, it must move to eliminate the causes.

Against the censors of violence are combat-hardened libertarians who want all speech protected. Violent programming may or may not breed violent behavior, they contend, but curtailment of speech surely heralds a retreat from democracy into feudalism, a return to the medieval monastery where utterances are controlled and political choices programmed. Such a fate, they claim, is worse than all others, and avoiding it is worth the risk of giving too much latitude.

Much of the current debate over violence in entertainment takes up the arguments of the controversial Meese Commission and its outspoken opponents. Established in May 1985 by Attorney General Edwin Meese, the commission was charged to "determine the nature, extent, and impact on society of pornography in the United States" and to recommend to the attorney general how pornography "can be contained, consistent with constitutional guarantees."[1] The commission's research included content analysis, participant observation, case studies, interviewing, and experimental studies. Its findings supported the cultivation hypothesis advanced by George Gerbner and others and at points suggested an even more direct link between pornography and the acting-out of sex crimes in certain persons. The commission's 92 recommendations were nearly all in support of tougher enforcement of existing obscenity laws, with even stricter measures against child pornography. The rationale for control and enforcement was a widely shared conclusion that viewing and reading sexually violent material create an incentive for sex crimes and develop a socially destructive linkage of sex and violence in the minds of persons who may or may not immediately act out their new attitudes.

From the first commission hearing, opponents issued charges of comstockery (a pejorative term recalling Anthony Comstock's anti-obscenity crusades). The ACLU published a "Summary and Critique" of the commission; entertainment professionals organized to protest the commission's implied call to curtail cinematic art; journalists trailed the commission and reported on the bizarre nature of some of its testimony; and columnists pointed to "dark lunacy" and "potential danger" underlying the commission's report. Much of the opposition can be summarized around four claims:

1. Artistic freedom and esthetic integrity demand a *laissez-faire* approach. Government has no business policing writers and directors.
2. No direct effects can be documented or proven. Indirect effects are the consequence of living one's life in a world of mediated messages and cannot be made the basis of criminal prosecutions.
3. Violence is a social and historical problem, not the result of violent TV or film. To think otherwise is like blaming John Wayne for the Vietnam War.
4. Much of the worry about media violence is really our fear of changing social institutions. To suppress TV and film is to forcibly maintain traditional notions of family, friendship, and marriage in an era when these social arrangements are undergoing radical change.

The cases in this chapter raise these questions and struggle with these rejoinders. The first case, "Hear It, Feel It, Do It," brings up the effects argument: hear violent lyrics, do violent deeds; show a violent program, reap a violent crime. One of the standard industry replies to the effects argument is the rating system, which alerts responsible adults to potentially harmful programs. Who is responsible when ratings seem to fail? That is the problem in *"Papillon,"* the second case presented. If violence is tragic, a lot of violence is tragic for a long time. Such is our feeling about the Jewish Holocaust, now five decades past. Do we prosecute an injustice to those who suffered if we fail to communicate the depth of the tragedy? Case 66 probes that possibility.

Are media practitioners oblivious to the violence they contribute to the culture? Hardly. "The Storyteller" explores the problem from inside the industry. In the last case, "Comic Capers," we look at the persistent issue of violence in children's media.

64. Hear It, Feel It, Do It

Friday evening in October. John McCollum, 19 years old, is alone in the house. An Ozzy Osbourne fan, he cranks up the family stereo—loud, intense, reverberating. Side one: "Blizzaard of Oz." The first song, "I Don't Know," celebrates in the manner of heavy metal the chaos and confusion of human life. The second song, "Crazy Train," points to insanity as the inevitable result of our inability to explain life's contradictions. The third, "Goodbye to Romance," advocates cutting ties to the past as the only way to personal freedom. The last song is "Suicide Solution":

Wine is fine but whiskey's quicker
Suicide is slow with liquor
Take a bottle drown your sorrows
Then it floods away tomorrows
Evil thoughts and evil doings
Cold, alone you hand in ruins
Thought that you'd escape the reaper
You can't escape the Master Keeper
'Cause you feel life's unreal
And you're living a lie
Such a shame who's to blame
And you're wondering why
Then you ask from your cask
Is there life after birth
What you sow can mean Hell on this earth
Now you live inside a bottle
The reaper's traveling at full throttle
It's catching you but you don't see

The reaper is you and the reaper is me
Breaking law, knocking doors
But there's no one at home
Made your bed rest your head
But you lie there and moan
Where to hide
Suicide is the only way out
Don't you know what it's really about.

Masked in a 28-second instrumental break, and heard at one and a half the normal rate of speech, are the lyrics:

Ah know people
You really know where it's at
You got it
Why try, why try
Get the gun and try it
Shoot, shoot, shoot (repeated)

John McCollum turns off the family stereo, walks to his bedroom, puts another Osbourne album, "Speak of the Devil," on his personal stereo. Volume up, headphones on, he lies on the bed. Nearby, a handgun, .22 caliber. Music. The cool small muzzle against his right temple. Volume up. A muffled pop.

John's body was discovered the next morning. He was still wearing headphones and the stereo's needle was riding around and around the center of the album. John had had problems with alcohol abuse which complicated other serious emotional problems, but in their suit against Osbourne and CBS Records, the McCollum family claimed that these lyrics had a cumulative impact on a suspectible listener, that the impact was antisocial in its emphasis on despair, Satan worship, and suicide, and that the record company had sought to cultivate Osbourne's "mad man" image in press releases and sales promotions and to profit from it. The music was a proximate cause in John's death, the suit alleged, because CBS negligently disseminated Osbourne's albums to the public and thereby "aided, advised or encouraged John to commit suicide." The beat and the words had created in John "an uncontrollable impulse" to kill himself, a consequence entirely foreseeable and therefore intentional, the suit contended. John's death was brought on by pressures and forces hidden in the grooves and ridges of a plastic disk, made and sold by an industry that does not care.[2]

Can media inspire violent crimes, even self-destruction? The argument that linked repeated rock album listenings to John McCollum's suicide is similar to the argument in the celebrated "Born Innocent" case that occurred a decade earlier. In September 1974, NBC sent to its affiliates a program starring Linda Blair as a girl whose innocence is shattered through her experience in a girls' reformatory. Because the drama would include violent scenes possibly objectionable to some viewers, NBC ran a warning at the start of the program: " 'Born Innocent' deals in a realistic and forthright manner with the confinement of juvenile offenders and its effects on their lives and personalities. We suggest you consider whether the program should be viewed by young people or others in your family who might be disturbed by it." As a portent of the show's later troubles, fifteen sponsors withdrew shortly before the broadcast.

"Born Innocent" did, in fact, raise objections from viewers. Hundreds of calls and letters were received by NBC affiliates across the nation, 700 in New York alone. (Only a few callers, notably social workers familiar with reformatories, applauded the network for its realistic portrayal of a pervasive problem.) Particularly troublesome was one scene in which Blair was raped by four female inmates using a plumber's helper for penetration. The victim was shown naked from the waist up.

The program and its forthright realism would have been largely academic but for a real-life rape three days later. On Baker Beach near San Francisco, 9-year-old Olivia Niemi was attacked by three girls and a boy, ages 9, 12, 13 and 15, who "raped" her with a beer bottle in a fashion similar to the attack on television. Olivia's mother filed suit for $11 million against NBC and the owners of KRON-TV, charging that NBC was guilty of negligence in broadcasting the program during family viewing hours (8 P.M. on the West Coast). One of the assailants had in fact referred to the television show when she was arrested. The link between dramatic and real violence might not be strictly causal, but the network had not taken adequate precaution against the program's potential effects on young viewers. The case was strengthened by the absence of any similar type of rape on the casebooks of juvenile authorities. If Olivia's attackers had perpetrated a first-of-its-kind rape, their teacher and proximate cause was the television network which had prestaged the event.

NBC declined to argue the facts. Instead, defense attorney Floyd Abrams contended that the First Amendment protected his client from damages from alleged effects of a media program. California Superior Court Judge John Ertola agreed. In September 1976 he ruled in favor of NBC without calling a jury, claiming, "The State of California is not about to begin using negligence as a vehicle to freeze the creative arts."

But the California Court of Appeals overturned the ruling. Niemi had a right to a jury trial on questions of fact, the appellate panel contended.

Before the case was argued, NBC urged the U.S. Supreme Court to quash the trial. At stake, the network claimed, were basic constitutional rights. On behalf of NBC, the American Library Association filed an amicus brief suggesting that the Appeals Court ruling might lead to libraries being sued by victims of crimes suggested in books. The Writers Guild of America wrote of the "chilling effect" on popular drama that a trial on the facts could have. For Niemi, the California Medical Association filed a friend-of-the-court brief. The Supreme Court declined to intervene.

Each side geared for the coming courtroom battle. NBC would argue that a warning had been given before the drama, that the four attackers had previous juvenile records, and that some testimony suggested none of them had seen the televised rape. Causal explanations for the crime other than the television show rested on stronger psychological evidence. One of the attackers, for example, had been molested by her father. In theory, NBC insisted, the plaintiff's case would shift accountability for criminal acts away from the persons responsible and toward the producers of televised drama.[3]

Niemi's attorney would argue that the rape scene in "Born Innocent" ignored NBC's own production code and the NAB Code that at that time proscribed graphic depictions of violence. The rape scene, in fact, had been abridged in telecasts after the first one. No one should be absolved of civil liability because of the First Amendment, the plaintiff said.

Commercial television networks would be hard pressed to justify graphic violence based on Kant's imperative. No reasonable person could will that such portrayals become standard TV fare, since reasonable people do not, by definition, seek to promote gratuitous suffering. There should be little argument here. People who delight in

causing or feeling pain are pathologically disturbed or criminally insane. Reasonable people may not choose to avoid all suffering (for example, running into a fire to rescue a child), but suffering without
purpose (merely running into a fire, or pushing someone else in) is
irrational by any common definition. Likewise a constant media diet
of violence and pain is irrational on its face.

Notice how close are Kant (the doer of duty) and Bentham (the
calculator of pleasure) on this issue. Bentham, the father of modern
utilitarianism, wrote: "Nature has placed mankind under the gover-
nance of two sovereign masters, pain and pleasure. It is for them alone
to point out what we ought to do, as well as to determine what we
shall do."[4] Kant's appeal to rational duty would have little prescriptive
value if people were unclear about whether to seek pleasure or pain.
Let us assume that the history of human civilization is not remiss
here: The avoidance of gratuitous violence *is* the normal response of
a rational person.

But "Suicide Solution" is only one song, and "Born Innocent" is
only one program, and the shower-room rape only one sequence in that
one program. This is hardly a trend. Certainly not an unrelieved diet
of mayhem and bloodletting.

Yet to describe the problem in this way is to miss the point of
even the utilitarian response. Hans Jonas, a modern utilitarian, has
argued that the consequences of a nuclear holocaust are so incalculable
that we must set our goals specifically at eliminating even its possibility.[5] (Notice an underlying Kantian-style commitment to the rea-
sonableness of human survival.) A similar argument warrants eliminating graphic violence on television: If the possibility of increased
real violence or loss of sensitivity to violence exists, and the means to
avoid the possibility are available and not onerous, then reasonable
people will take them. And ought to, violence being hurtful.

What means are available for avoiding graphic violence on TV?
Certainly viewers can choose not to watch, which is the preferred
solution of the networks since it imposes no direct obligations on
them. Let the buyer beware!

On the other hand, the state could impose limits on TV violence
in the same way it regulates cigarette and liquor commercials. (Is there
any objection to banning the advertising of unsafe medicines?)

Or again, the television industry—in this case NBC—could set
its own limits based on steady evidence that TV violence at least creates a culture of suspicion and fear,[6] and on fidelity to the belief that
violence is never inherently justified.

There are some important distinctions between the McCollum case and the "Born Innocent" incident. First, John did not take his handgun onto the street to apply the "solution" to any passersby. Grievous as were its consequences to his family, the harm done was self-inflicted. Second, the message blamed for inspiring McCollum's violence was in an easily repeatable format, unlike the 1974 television show. Whereas Olivia's attackers could have been influenced by a single viewing, McCollum had occasion for a total environment of Osbourne's music, as loud and as often as he chose to listen. Third, the Osbourne persona created by marketers and P.R. writers—with his cooperation—corresponds to his music's destructive themes. Neither Linda Blair nor NBC suffer under reputations aligned with shower-room violence. Finally, NBC issued a warning as part of its message; CBS Records did not.

Is moral blame less heavy if no one other than the self is directly harmed in a violent act? In quantitative terms, yes. Given the choice of a terrorist blowing up an airliner in the sky or that same person blowing up herself on the ground, we would reasonably opt for the latter. But the McCollum case involves the suicide of a young man who had a history of emotional and behavioral troubles. For these individuals we bear obligations to offer aid, not a gun. Self-destruction is no solution to life's turmoils, and promoting self-destruction in music, film, or word is perpetrating a lie. Osbourne did not hand the gun to John McCollum, but his music is distributed in a format that carries no alternative point of view. No voice is heard after "Suicide Solution" arguing that self-destruction is morally wrong. McCollum heard only the most errant element of a many-sided ethical issue.

Is artistic integrity in jeopardy if we attach moral blame to a mere message? Roxanne Bradshaw of the National Education Association, commenting on violence in media, said: "We're not interested in censorship. We're interested in reeducating ourselves and our children about electronic media."[7] No moral theory would excuse media managers and artists from helping in the task Bradshaw describes. The more vulnerable the viewer/listener, the greater the obligation to talk, to help interpret, and to channel responses toward beneficent ends.

California courts excused both CBS and NBC from liability in these two court proceedings; the First Amendment would not tolerate damages sought by aggrieved plaintiffs. But our mutual human responsibility to seek each other's best interests, and to help each other avoid meaningless hurt and harm, knows no constitutional boundaries. CBS Records has no moral right to make profit through the genius of an artist who would be foolish and wrong to practice what he preaches. If the corporation chooses nonetheless to exercise legal rights to such expression, fair warnings—if not outright disclaimers—would put record buyers on notice. People directly in line to help troubled, vulnerable users of such media could then make more informed choices. In the present case, our objective is to prevent the lie of Osbourne's music from becoming John McCollum's final word.

65. Papillon and Prescreening

Chicago attorney Paul Bernstein heard the radio ads plugging a family adventure film and noted the PG rating awarded to *Papillon* by the Motion Picture Association of America (MPAA). Satisfied, Bernstein chose the drama of a seamy French prison camp and its victims for a family evening with his three daughters, aged 7, 11, and 14.[8]

Following the show, however, it was Bernstein who felt like a victim: Misleading ratings had not conveyed a true warning of the movie's violence. He filed suit in Cook County Circuit Court for seven dollars in compensatory damages (the cost of the theater tickets) and $250,000 in punitive damages. It was the first consumer action against the six-year-old MPAA rating system. Named as defendents were Allied Artists, the producers; General Cinema Corporation, the distributors of the movie and owners of the Highland Park theater where the Bernsteins had viewed the film; and the MPAA. The suit charged that *Papillon* showed "in explicit detail" a decapitation, a homosexual assault, and various gruesome killings and beatings.

Federal Judge Richard B. Austin, in dismissing the suit, stated, "Plaintiff was accurately put on notice that he should exercise caution in letting children view this movie and he failed to do so." The MPAA attorney claimed that PG carries the warning that some material in a film might be unsuitable for preteenage viewers and that the rating system contains no warranty—it is merely an expression of opinion by the MPAA.

Only on rare occasions does the viewing public raise a significant voice in this industry-controlled procedure. One recent example was the fuss over Steven Spielberg's *Indiana Jones and the Temple of Doom* and *Gremlins*. Rated PG, the films frightened enough youngsters and angered enough parents that in 1984 the Classification and Rating Administration (CARA) of the MPAA adopted PG-13 ("Parents are strongly advised to give special guidance to children under 13. Some material may be inappropriate for young children"). This was the first change in the rating system in sixteen years. But this change only modified the established system; it was not a wholesale renovation.

In the case of *Papillon*, if it could be established that the assigned rating was patently deceptive, we could summarily condemn the MPAA as ethically abhorrent under each of the five criteria described in the Introduction to this book. Such condemnation, however, would be too simple a solution, and not entirely deserved.

What happened in this case is an example of doing the least to satisfy a moral requirement. Movie producers (represented by the MPAA) do not wish to discourage box office patrons, and neither do theater owners, so ratings are issued in the most inoffensive manner possible: a single letter or two letters with a terse explanation of their meaning, and there are only five categories. It is the least noxious deterrent for a paying customer.

What if producers and theater owners were to treat customers as reasonable creatures responsible for the moral tenor of their viewing experiences? Synopses of plots, descriptions of the kinds of scenes in a film, even a more sophisticated set of rating symbols would show good faith toward the viewing public.

In this case, however, we cannot fault the movie industry entirely. With little investigation beyond noting the film's rating, Bernstein took his children to see it. Was parental guidance a sufficiently active element in his decision? Probably not. The PG rating should have prompted him to ask questions of friends, read reviews, and perhaps even call the theater manager.

Proponents for greater liberty in television programming typically emphasize the viewer's right to turn off the set. The wider liberty of the magazine and book publishing industry also presumes that parents will monitor their children's reading material and prevent their exposure to inappropriate material. Surely the same supervisory responsibility must apply to children's selection of motion pictures.

At each point from movie producer to consumer, application of the persons-as-ends principle would help. The movie audience surely needs more reliable, less laundered information on which to base viewing choices. Yet parents and other adults are responsible also. The chair of CARA has observed, "Our main objective is to provide an early-warning signal to parents, who may then exercise their own responsibility to expose their youngsters to more mature film content only as they individually mature."[9] The military analog embedded in this caveat tells an important tale. Parents still control the last, vital link in the movie market system. Exchanging money for tickets is the free act of a consenting buyer who, even in the course of collecting on his purchase, can decide to get up from his seat, go home, and read a book.

66. "Holocaust" and Television's Limits as a Medium

A generation plus has passed since the terror of Hitler's New Order was unveiled, and survivors of the Holocaust are concerned: When the last of them pass away, will anyone be able to tell the story in its full tragedy, passion, and horror? Perhaps the task will fall to the media, but that prospect is less than comforting to those most interested in preserving the memory and meaning of their suffering.

On 16–19 April 1978, NBC aired a nine-and-a-half-hour docudrama called "Holocaust," the story of two German families from 1935 to 1945.[10] The Weiss family is Jewish. Josef and Berta are the parents of a typically close-knit clan which fails to interpret the first signs of Nazi persecution. Their oldest son, Karl, and his Roman Catholic wife, Inge, are sent to Buchenwald and Theresienstadt. Their daughter, Anna, is brutally raped, then killed in a "hospital" for the mentally ill. The middle son, Rudi, escapes the German net and after much hardship takes up arms against the Nazis.

The Dorfs, Erik and Marta, live in Berlin. He is an unemployed lawyer, she an ambitious wife who convinces Erik to join the German SS. He becomes an aide to "blond beast" Reinhard Heydrich and in that capacity travels the breadth of Europe engineering schemes for ridding the Reich of the Jewish "menace." To add realism to the drama, writer Gerald Green included portrayals of such personages as Adolf Eichmann, Heinrich Himmler, and Heydrich.

NBC worked hard to generate an audience for the financially risky miniseries. The network invited prominent leaders from the three major faiths to preview the series, and it encouraged the preparation of study guides for school and church discussion on the meaning of the Holocaust and the ways of avoiding another one. Rabbi Irving Greenberg of New York wrote the introduction to the interfaith guide.

Such careful preparation—plus a lot of advertising—worked well. An estimated 120 million Americans saw some part of the four-night series. The first installment drew a 43 share; the third evening drew a 49 (59 in New York City). Ratings were higher in many of the 40 countries which played "Holocaust" in the year following. In the Netherlands, 54 percent watched at least one episode; in Austria, 61 percent.

Reviewers across the country applauded. The *Washington Post* called it "the most powerful drama ever seen on television." Rev. William L. Weiler, executive director of the Office of Christian-Jewish Relations of the National Council of Churches, called the program a "very effective, engaging drama." Rabbi Marc Tannenbaum, director of national interreligious affairs for the American Jewish Committee, who served as a consultant for NBC, remarked: "I have seen it three times and found myself crying each time. The impact of the series is greater than anything I have witnessed since the end of World War II."

Only in one corner of the country was a dissenting opinion raised, but that corner happened to be the most important one—New York City. Two days before the miniseries began, *Times* critic John J. O'Connor concluded that the production staff of "Holocaust" had faced "a massive problem and were unable to find satisfactory solutions." The plot was contrived, the actors sterile, and the effect superficial. Perhaps commercial television was simply not the medium capable of telling the terrible story, he mused. To throw Jews and Nazis, fictional or historical, into a

> second-rate dramatization that will be seen with inter-ruptions for inane commercials is to enter automatically a process of diminishment. Incredible horror is reduced to "effective" on-location settings in Austria and West Berlin. Unprecedented pain is mixed up with the choosing of 'correct' costumes. . . . The very barbarity of Nazism is whittled down to an image not dissimilar from the fad for a touch of sadism in lingerie ads. No matter the good

intentions of the production staff, the inevitable trivial-
ization is fatal.[11]

Also writing in the *Times*, Boston University historian Elie
Wiesel lashed out at the stereotyped characters, historical errors,
the obsessive theme of Jewish resignation, and errors in the portrayal of Jewish life and liturgy. He called the series "untrue,
offensive, cheap: as a TV production, the film is an insult to those
who perished and to those who survived. . . . It transforms an
ontological event into soap opera. Whatever the intentions, the
result is shocking." Wiesel wrote with the passion of one who
had seen and survived the Nazi terror:

> We see naked women and children entering the gas cham-
> bers; we see their faces, we hear their moans as the doors
> are being shut, then—well, enough: why continue? To
> use special effects and gimmicks to describe the indes-
> cribable is to me morally objectionable. Worse: it is in-
> decent. The last moments of the forgotten victims belong
> to themselves.[12]

On the day after the series concluded, O'Connor followed up
his earlier review with a scathing attack on the "shocking insensitivity" of a network's exploiting such serious material for commercial gain. "A monstrous historical fact has been put through
the peculiar process that is called commercial television. In its
more extreme moments, that processing proved to be almost as
obscene as the Holocaust itself."[13]

Letters from viewers poured in. Many were outraged at the commercial interruptions; others were resigned to them. Some
abhorred what they perceived as trivialized history; others were
gratified that, whatever its shortcomings, the series had raised
the consciousness of millions toward the evils of anti-Semitism.

In the course of the debate, the network lost one of its most
important allies: Rabbi Greenberg. For him the series "lacked the
insight and touch of survivors," especially on the question of Jewish resignation. "Holocaust" had portrayed as heroes those Jews
who took up arms, as they did in the Warsaw Ghetto. The drama

was critical, especially through the character of Inge, of the many who grimly walked in front of the machine guns or into the deadly showers. Why did so many submit? Here was a problem that defied the quick cuts and surface storyline which television requires. Greenberg pointed to the "overwhelming force and cruelty that made death inescapable and often a relief; the collective responsibility and the way family and children tied the hands of those who would have fought. . . . [Real survivors] realize that just living as a human being, refusing to abandon family or religion or dignity was the true, incredible everyday heroism of millions who died and the few who survived. The absence of this insight may be the gravest flaw of 'Holocaust.'"[14]

Television, by its physical dimensions alone, is a limited medium. It cannot convey the grandeur of vast tracts of landscape; it cannot hope to show finely detailed art.

Is the medium limited, also, in the drama its format can adequately portray? Plots that need only stereotyped characters and move along to predictable conclusions are obviously television's strongest trump. Intricate plots and extended character development are much more hazardous, especially where continuity must be sacrificed for sponsors' announcements.

A television producer exploring the idea of a miniseries on the Holocaust would have to consider the potential audience, but satisfying the business criterion ought not determine his decision. Does he have writers, actors, and other support personnel to do justice to the script? Presuming these resources would be available, the decision to produce is still not certain.

Once the technical and financial means are in hand, the producer must ask: Is this a story I really want to do? He may be drawn to the story (or repelled from it) by hopes for recognition and advancement in the field. He may have a native interest in the story: The plot or theme may strike a creative nerve and compel him to do it because of the inner resonance the story provokes. Typically a producer's decision process ends at this point. If the program idea is marketable, if staff and equipment are available, and if he personally wants to produce (for whatever reason), then why not—let's do it!

Has an important criterion been overlooked? Are there ethically sensible reasons why a producer of a miniseries on the Holocaust might choose, in the final analysis, to respect the limitations of his medium, preserving the dignity of those who endured the bitter grief?

This is another form of the question, To whom is moral duty owed? In the case of "Holocaust," network producers were admirably sensitive to duties toward their audience. Providing study aids and enlisting the help of concerned agencies could be seen as a public relations ploy, but on the surface it must be applauded as above and beyond the normal concern given a docudrama.

But Rabbi Greenberg, Elie Wiesel, and John O'Connor were raising the matter of duty owed the subject of the drama itself: the victims of the actual Holocaust. Were their concerns given sufficient attention? Perhaps this is a question only victims themselves can answer. At a minimum, Holocaust victims viewing the docudrama must not feel exploited, simplified, or divinized. They must not feel compromised by the inherent limitations of the television medium. Most important, network producers must not be open to the charge that they used the setting of the Holocaust to create just another human-interest stock drama, imposing familiar plot devices onto the Jewish story.

Assistance from survivors at every stage of the process might have produced a more realistic "Holocaust." Turning the project over to creative talent in Jewish heritage agencies might have given a more realistic, less stereotyped rendering. More sensitive allocation of commercials would have shown greater respect to the victims.

Moral duty in this case is also owned the German people. Few Germans today are not repulsed at the heinous human-rights violations of Hitler's Reich. Modern attempts to dramatize the gigantic moral lapse of their fathers and grandfathers must do justice to the economic and political context which made that nation so vulnerable to Hitler's rhetoric. Simple portrayals of 1930s–1940s' Germany as brutish and barbaric do injustice to the moral agony of the perpetrators and contribute nothing to the healing of intervening years.

If such moral considerations—based soundly on the persons-as-ends principle—are too costly, too time consuming, or too idiosyncratic, then the network should have faced up to the boundaries of its own universe. Perhaps commercial television, with its time constraints and institutional demands, cannot recreate in dramatic form the intense human feelings and tragedy that after more than a generation still stretch the limits of credibility.

67. *"THE STORYTELLER"*

In primitive oral cultures, "storyteller" might connote the village historian or tribal sage, the person responsible for interpreting the outside world to kindred with lesser vision, the personal repository of a culture's myth and wisdom. With perhaps the same idea in mind, script writers Richard Levinson and William Link, creators of the police drama "Columbo," gave the title "The Storyteller" to their introspective drama about the crisis of conscience faced by a television scriptwriter whose work, aired one evening on network television, portrayed several acts of arson. In the story, the show is seen by a youth who immediately after viewing leaves his home to try to burn down his school. The youth dies of smoke inhalation in the fire.[15]

Levinson and Link broke into television writing just as the industry came face to face with questions of the influence of televised violence on the real world. The many studies, essays, and investigations following the Kennedy assassinations, however inconclusive, at least established the intuition that television can be a factor in why real people do some things and not other things. Not that violence was new to popular drama. Levinson and Link grew up on Dashiell Hammett, Zane Grey, the squeaky door of Dr. Frankenstein's laboratory, and "survived not only intact but also enriched." But the next decades brought a new fascination with the "actual moment of slaughter," slow-motion carnage, and the chilling spectacle of audiences cheering the cinematic bloodlust. Whose was the moral burden?

The purpose of "The Storyteller" was, in Levinson and Link's words, to "analyze our own feelings and attitudes, not only about the violence issue, but also about the responsibilities, if any, of those of us who enter so many homes and minds each night of the week." To the consternation of some viewers, the drama did not follow predictable television denouement. Instead of taking a point of view and suggesting answers to their dilemma, Levinson and Link were satisfied to "explore the problem . . . to present the audience with the incredible tangle of pros and cons involved." Yet their sense of moral accountability comes through when the mother of the dead boy asks the writer, "You come into people's homes, the homes of people you don't even know. Do you think about that every time you sit down at your typewriter?" The primitive village sage never faced a question like that.

This kind of self-reflection is a big step toward responsible media; it stretches the mind and draws out the issues, even if it reaches no conclusions.

Perhaps it falls to agencies such as the Screen Actors Guild (SAG) to coalesce opinion and reach positions on these matters. Its members and board formally passed an antiviolence resolution in 1974 (updated in 1977) that reads, in part:

> While various studies do not lead to absolute conclusions, there is reasonable cause to believe that imitation of violent acts seen on television is a potential danger and examples of this phenomenon are well documented. There is reasonable cause to believe that the excessive violence viewed on television can also increase aggressive behavior patterns and that repetitive viewing of violence leads to greater acceptance of violence as a norm of societal mores. . . . What is disturbing in television programming is the emphasis on violence and the degree of violence portrayed. . . . The extent and degree of violence in television programming is excessive. . . . Degrees of violence can be lowered in entertainment just as we hope to reduce such excess in our society. . . . We challenge those who are responsible for the programs aired to make the effort—and for the sake of all— the sooner the better.[16]

Someone might object to these sentiments, of course. The statement assumes that a reasonable cause connects media violence with real behavior. This, someone might argue, is the same kind of speculative hearsay that makes up the rhetoric of media watchdog groups.

And another objection: The SAG statement purports to recommend change "for the sake of all," a clear appeal to the utilitarian principle of the greatest good for the greatest number. But that principle can never demonstrate the difference between too much and appropriate violence. Would the SAG statement suggest that violence is appropriate if and only if no one in real life is physically harmed in any way? Unlikely. Everything from eating bacon to brewing moonshine has some inherent risk. And such a prescription would be too late to help the victims anyhow. Would the SAG statement preclude violence that harms a significant number in a significant way? Impossible. Who could calculate such an application? Ergo, the SAG statement and all others like it are mere rhetorical flourishes and soap-box oratory. The only workable principle is to give writers and producers a free hand in the scripts they develop. True art is achieved only in the context of free expression. Artificial or arbitrary constraints will keep television drama forever immature. Even the SAG recognized the whimsy of their statement; since Kathleen Nolan's retirement from leadership, the SAG has not voiced an opinion on violence in drama.

True it may be that art is achieved only in the context of free expression. The question for media ethicists is to what extent art is accountable to moral principle. Is art good because it is free, or is it good when it captures in poignant and resonant ways a slice of the human search for meaning. The latter principle avoids the facile pairing of art and freedom that excuses so much tripe, and it brings art squarely into the moral domain. Art and ethics are not mutually exclusive categories. It should be possible, then, to conceive a policy for the portrayal of television violence that will remain true to the aspirations of creative talent without violating the genuine moral claims of actors, viewers, and others drawn into the process after major decisions have already been made.

Does the golden mean provide a basis for responsible violence? Appropriate violence must steer away from portraying humans as mere beasts, or as unrealistically angelic. Can specific policies be drawn from such an appeal to principle? While such policy statements often turn into dead letters uniformly ignored, on occasion intelligent manifestoes, conscientiously promoted, have aroused attention and changed opinions.

68. COMIC CAPERS

From the greatest of the old-time crime chasers (Superman) to the most bizarre of change agents (Incredible Hulk), the comic heroes press on from chase to mace in their pursuit of daring and virtue. Often the denouement involves overpowering some dastardly character, defusing some devastating explosive, or derailing a hunk of heavy machinery—all in the name of protecting the innocent and winning the war against cruelty (see Fig. 13.1).

But what of the cruelty required of the heroes themselves? Is it possible that the comics' depiction of cruel means to virtuous ends confuses young minds by suggesting that anything is okay if some good is served in the end?

Concern about violence in the media menu of young children has focused largely on television programming and most recently on music videos, but for the purposes of ethical reasoning, the issue is significant in any medium.

Violence is a dominant theme in the comics. In 1974 John DiFazio analyzed the comic book treatment of fourteen American values and found that "peaceful resolution of conflict" was one of the values least often portrayed.[17] Our own quick review of a grocery store comic rack revealed plot resolutions involving a woman blowing herself up with a shotgun while trying to save an infant from a monster, the crashing of a boulder on the cranium of a muscle-bound cyclops, and the blinding of a Rebel soldier by a "blue belly" bullet. One can almost hear Frederick Wertham, author of the classic 1954 attack on crime comics, *Seduction of the Innocent*, uttering "I told you so" to the numerous critics who disparaged his work.

Such unrestrained violence was not always the rule in children's literature. Note, for example, the ethic of restraint that characterized the popular Nancy Drew detective series:

> There was an abundance of violence in the Nancy Drew series, but it was controlled violence. Clubbings, wrecks, assault and battery were common. Attacks fell indiscriminately on many types of characters with Nancy often the target. Despite this violence no one was murdered. Criminals who assaulted their victims did not go beyond beatings. In a decade [the 1930s] when sensational real life kidnappings stirred the population, these fictionalized kidnappings ended happily and no victim of abduction was killed. Guns were used but were either fired as warnings, and not directly at persons, or used as clubs.[18]

Recent commentary on the comic book industry is as troubling as Wertham's case studies. Writes Joe Queenan in the *New York Times Magazine*:

> Over the last decade, comics have forsaken campy repartee and outlandishly byzantine plots for a steady diet of remorseless violence. "Green Arrow" depicts a woman whose eyes have been plucked out by vultures. In "Spider-Man," seven men are ripped to pieces by a wolf. The back pages of "Wolverine" shows the hero puffing on a cigarette as blood

Figure 13.1 *Everything the cover promises. . . . the inside pages deliver: skull-crushing monsters, prehistoric battles, beatings, and the savagery of war. Copyright © 1982 Marvel Comics Group, a division of Cadence Industries Corporation. All rights reserved.*

Figure 13.1 (Continued)

drips from his lips. . . . "Black Orchid" begins with a woman
being tied up and set on fire, then moves on to child abuse,
a mutant fed live rats, and a jailed hybrid—half woman, half
plant—who avoids rape only because her jailers find her too
repulsive.[19]

The comic industry grosses $300 million a year, with DC Comics
and Marvel in the distant lead, followed by Archie Comic Publications
and then about 200 minor-league hopefuls. Explained one industry distributor: "Our readers are teenaged boys . . . lots of repressed anger . . .
going through puberty . . . like to see characters act out their aggres-
sions."
    One concern that ethicists cannot avoid is the question of the
effects of the violence on impressionable consumers. And here, as
media researchers are well aware, the evidence is both solid and gas-
eous; advocates line up on both sides. A recent report from the Group
for the Advancement of Psychiatry, concerned about televised violence, found unequivocal negative effects; but the American Academy
of Pediatrics could claim with as much gusto that TV can teach beneficial social values. Researchers at Texas Tech in 1980 found no support for the hypothesis that reading violent comics leads to greater
aggression among children, but they admitted "it is possible that the
effects of comic book reading may be long-term and cumulative."[20]
    The ethicist is faced with puzzling questions: Who is hurt by
reading or viewing fictional violence? Would the harm attributed (by
some) to media programming come about anyhow, in which case violence in media becomes an insignificant part of the equation? Who
should assume moral responsibility for children's media menu: publishers, writers, television directors, sponsors and advertisers, parents?
    A reasonable argument could be made that children would read
comics and watch cartoons regardless of the style of the conflict and
the means of its resolution. Children do not demand violence in media;
they are entertained with or without clubs, knives, and pistols. Producers, then, cannot argue that they must provide violence to secure
an audience. "Mister Rogers" and "Sesame Street" give muscle to the
argument that low-level violence or none at all do not diminish a
child's loyalty to the program. Producers might well be confronted with
the Potter Box technique and faced with the question about their ultimate loyalties. Certainly they cannot reasonably choose concern for
their own pocketbooks over service to their juvenile audience. In any

case, it seems apparent that production people could move toward more humane conflict resolution without jeopardizing their enterprise.

Ultimate moral duty must fall to those who are most directly involved in the guidance and growth of children. While not absolving producers and writers, moral reasoning assumes that the parent/guardian–child relationship is primary for the teaching of values. In Western democracies the public marketplace is kept relatively free, while each family exercises the closer selection of what will become part of their perceptual experience.

At the level of family, the ethic of persons as ends is given most prominent play. Here moral duty is to the child first and foremost, not to the marketplace; each child is the most valued part of the sender-channel-receiver process. Here the concerns of the individual rise to prominence as the values of free and unimpeded media programming recede. Resolving the issue of violence in children's media is chiefly a matter of recovering the notion of family as a moral institution. Only on this intimate level can the ethic of persons as ends truly flourish.

Notes

1. *Attorney General's Commission on Pornography Final Report*, July 1986, p. 1957.
2. *McCollum* v. *CBS*, 15 Med L Rptr 2001.
3. Material on "Born Innocent" was drawn from "TV Wins a Crucial Case," *Time*, 21 August 1978, p. 85; T. Schwartz and others, "TV on Trial Again," *Newsweek*, 14 August 1978, pp. 41–42; "NBC's First Amendment Rape Case," *Esquire*, 23 May 1978, pp. 12–13; "Back to Court for 'Born Innocent,'" *Broadcasting*, 1 May 1978, pp. 37–38; "Judge Restricts 'Born Innocent' Case to First Amendment Issue," *Broadcasting*, 7 August 1978, pp. 31–32; Karl E. Meyer, "Television's Trying Times," *Saturday Review*, 16 September 1978, pp. 19–20; *New York Times*, 18 September 1978; *Wall Street Journal*, 25 April 1978.
4. Jeremy Bentham, *An Introduction to the Principles of Morals and Legislation*, ed. J. H. Burns and H. L. A. Hart (London: Athlone Press, 1970), p. 11.
5. Hans Jonas, *The Imperative of Responsibility* (Chicago: University of Chicago Press, 1984).
6. The many writings of George Gerbner and Larry Gross are the tip of an iceberg supporting this contention.
7. *Media and Values*, Fall 1985, p. 9.
8. This case follows a true story described in the *Wall Street Journal*, 1 June, 6 and 12 December 1974.

9. Richard D. Heffner, "What G, PG, R, and X Really Mean," *TV Guide*, 4 October 1980, p. 39.
10. "Holocaust" was analyzed in the *New York Times*, 14–30 April, 4–7 May, 24 June 1978.
11. John J. O'Connor, "TV Weekend," *New York Times*, 14 April 1978, p. C26.
12. Elie Wiesel, "Trivializing the Holocaust: Semi-Fact and Semi-Fiction," *New York Times*, 16 April 1978, sec. 2, p. 1.
13. John J. O'Connor, "TV: NBC 'Holocaust,' Art Versus Mammon," *New York Times*, 20 April 1978, p. C22.
14. Irving Greenberg, Letter to Editor, *New York Times*, 30 April 1978, sec. 2, p. 30
15. Richard Levinson and William Link, "A Crisis of Conscience," *TV Guide*, 3 December 1977, p. 6.
16. "SAG Position Re Excessive Violence on TV." Minutes of the Special Meeting of the Executive Committee of the Screen Actors Guild, 29 November 1976, p. 9919.
17. DiFazio's study is cited in Alexis S. Tan and Kermit Joseph Scruggs, "Does Exposure to Comic Book Violence Lead to Aggression in Children?" *Journalism Quarterly* 57 (Winter 1980): 579–583.
18. James P. Lones, "Nancy Drew, WASP SuperGirl of the 1930s," *Journal of Popular Culture* 6 (Spring 1973): 712.
19. Joe Queenan, "Drawing on the Dark Side," *New York Times Magazine*, 30 April 1989.
20. Alexis Tan and Kermit Joseph Scruggs, "Does Exposure to Comic Book Violence Lead to Aggression in Children?" *Journalism Quarterly* 57 (Winter 1980): 583.

CHAPTER 14

Profits, Wealth, and Public Trust

Entertainment media in America are 90 percent business and 10 percent public service. Or are these figures too lopsided toward public service? Only the most unrepentant idealist would argue that public service or social responsibility is a major consideration in most entertainment media decisions. If such social benefits show up in the product, all well and good. But woe the producer, director, editor, or recording executive whose product shows a financial loss, whatever may be the social gain. The profit motive is the most compelling concern in entertainment industry decisions; some observers would insist it is the only concern.

As Parts I and II in this volume indicate, the bottom line of profit and loss affects media of all types; but the entertainment media feel the impact most directly. A recent major survey of executives in the motion picture industry confirmed the intuition that here was a media system operating on essentially amoral criteria. A vice-president of a major production and distribution company commented: "There are no ethical decisions in the movie business. In a word, the profit motive renders ethics irrelevant. The only counterbalance is that certain individuals—and precious few at that—live their personal and professional lives according to some reasonably high standard."

The first case, "Corporate Takeover," rehearses a scenario more and more common as big media profits attract big investment opportunities. What are the trade-offs between business efficiency and creative independence? "The Book that Squeaked" examines the market for confidential personal information. "The Purpose Is Profit" poses the question, is the business ethos ever sufficient for a creative media person, however necessary it may be to keep royalty checks coming?

"Deep Trouble for Harry" looks at profits in the pornographic movie industry, with all of its First Amendment complications. Finally, "Super Strip" points to an example of fairness that may carry a seed of hope for justice apart from legal constraint.

69. CORPORATE TAKEOVERS OF MEDIA COMPANIES

The irony was remarkable. The feature story in *Business Week* claimed that American Express "seems determined to acquire a big company soon." Little did the editors realize that American Express had ambitions toward *BW*'s own parent company, McGraw-Hill.

The acquisition of one company by another is hardly uncommon any more. Media companies frequently come under conglomerate ownership, or themselves become conglomerates through the acquisition of nonmedia companies. Occasionally the transfer is miniature warfare—a hostile takeover in which a conglomerate buys large blocks of a company's stock until it holds controlling interest.

American Express did not plot a secret hostile takeover of McGraw-Hill. An offer was made in January to pay $34 per share ($830 million) for McGraw-Hill stock, which was then selling for $26. The offer represented an acceptable profit to shareholders, under most corporate circumstances.

But not to the family-controlled board of McGraw-Hill. Chairman Harold McGraw, Jr., had no interest in selling the four television stations, sixty trade magazines and newsletters, Standard and Poors rating service, *Business Week*, and the nation's second largest book publishing company—all of which comprised McGraw-Hill. There would be no takeover without a fight, assured Harold McGraw. The board "strongly believes in the preservation of the independence of the communication media as well as the independence of securities' ratings activities," he said.[1]

One part of the effort to block the takeover was an appeal to the Federal Communications Commission. McGraw-Hill's four television stations could not change hands without FCC approval, a bureaucratic formality that could buy valuable time for the threatened company. American Express countered. It would set up a trust such that the broadcast operations would have their own independent management and board of directors. Furthermore, American Express promised that the independence of McGraw-Hill's media divisions would not be compromised. "Editorial and media integrity are as respected by and as important to us as I know they are to you," wrote the American Express board chair to Harold McGraw.

Despite the assurances, the McGraw-Hill board turned down the offer. Five days later one of the board, Roger H. Morley, resigned. Morley was also president of American Express and had been instrumental in conceiving the deal.

Angry over the appearance of corporate spying, Harold McGraw ran a two-page ad in the *New York Times* reproducing his letter to the American Express board:

> The background and manner of your proposal demonstrates that American Express lacks the integrity, corporate morality, and sensitivity to professional responsibility essential to the McGraw-Hill publishing, broadcasting, and credit rating services relied upon by so many people. . . . The obvious conflict of interest created by your secret plan to pursue acquisition of McGraw-Hill while Mr. Morley remained a director is an unprecedented breach of trust.[2]

American Express countered again, this time with a suit accusing McGraw-Hill of "libelous, false, and misleading statements" designed to deprive stockholders of a "fair opportunity to evaluate" the American Express offer. McGraw-Hill's petition to the FCC was called a "diversionary, shotgun tactic" with the same purpose in mind. Many McGraw-Hill stockholders (including some McGraw family members not on the board) were, in fact, eager to realize the profits of such a sale, and some brought suit against the McGraw-Hill board.

Two weeks later American Express raised its bid to $40 per share. Again the McGraw-Hill board unanimously rejected the offer, claiming that to sell would compromise the editorial integrity and independence of its properties. A month later the American Express offer expired. The battle was over. McGraw-Hill stock, which had climbed to $32 in anticipation of the merger, plummeted to $24. Millions of dollars in potential profit to stockholders was wiped out.

American Express felt that its offer had been generous and its guarantees secure. McGraw-Hill viewed the takeover as a devious, illegal maneuver in which one of its own board had "violated fiduciary duties" to the company and had "misappropriated" confidential company information.

In the midst of the takeover bid, media critics voiced concern. The president of the Authors Guild wrote: "There is no kind of corporate move that the Authors Guild opposes more strongly than the takeover of book publishers by companies with no previous interest in books."[3] Columbia professor emeritus Fred Friendly wondered "whether four centuries of press struggles to break the licensing bonds of censorial governments could end with a new variety of restraints, where the gatekeepers of information are a handful of super conglomerates not steeped in the ethos of the news business."[4] He did admit that many media operate independent of the interests of their conglomerate parents. NBC and CBS had both covered the Vietnam War without interference from the corporate hierarchy, he noted, despite the fact that each parent conglomerate had been awarded large Department of Defense contracts. One question he did not address was whether the networks had covered the war better (or whether, by application, publishers could offer even more diversified cultural fare) because of the enormous resources available to them as part of a complex, profitable conglomerate enterprise.

Two principles were in conflict. Harold McGraw and the Authors Guild were operating on a principle flavored by Kant's categorical imperative: Independence is essential to the purpose of a media company. The pro-merger faction probably had something like the principle of utility in mind: More people (shareholders) are directly served (in terms of appreciated stock value) by the planned merger.

Founded in 1909 by James H. McGraw (grandfather of Harold Jr.), the company is still regarded as "one of the great family dynasties in corporate America," even though the McGraws control less than 20 percent of corporate stock and the company's five major lines of business do not meet national averages for profitability. Its book company, for example, the nation's largest textbook publisher, yields an 8 percent margin compared with an industry average of 10 to 15 percent; its broadcast division has a 29 percent margin compared with a 40 percent national average; and its magazine division profit margin hit four percentage points below the national average of 17. Yet the company's potential, when it "hits on all cylinders" in the same year, could boost stock values into the mid-60s. And that makes McGraw-Hill an attractive takeover target, which will soon be Harold McGraw III's (known as Terry) job to forestall. The great-grandson of the company's founder still holds to the idea that the purpose of the company is service, and service requires independence from the kinds of commitments a corporate merger would demand. The McGraws might view the privilege of shareholding as an opportunity to participate in the purpose of the company as well as in the profits. Whether shareholders would agree does not alter the ethical weight of the McGraws' appeal.

Is such a position hopelessly idealistic? Is profit an end in itself? If McGraw-Hill set as its goal the establishment of a reputable publishing house, financial ratings service, and television division—all of which contribute to the stock of ideas in our culture—then profit would be pointless unless it furthered that end. The final decision whether to submit to a takeover cannot turn on the greatest profit for the greatest number, but on the corporate structure best suited to meet the company's stated goals.

70. THE BOOK THAT SQUEAKED

Marcia Chellis and Joan Kennedy had much in common. Both were raised in well-to-do families, both married wealthy and successful men, both were alcoholics. They became acquainted at a meeting of apartment tenants following Chellis's divorce and Kennedy's separation, and they became friends. When Joan joined husband Ted in his bid for the Democratic presidential nomination in 1979, she hired Marcia as an aide and secretary. For three years the two women were virtually inseparable.

By 1982 the Kennedy star had dimmed. Indeed, Democrats around the country were hushed by Ronald Reagan's stunning victory over incumbent Jimmy Carter. The time had come for Marcia Chellis to find other employment.

Chellis terminated her position with Joan Kennedy, and notes taken while she was inside that near-mythic family went with her: notes on Ted's whereabouts, notes on the family's hardships, notes on Kennedy property and their lifestyle, and notes of conversations with her friend and employer, Joan.

Three years later those notes became the substance of *Living with the Kennedys: The Joan Kennedy Story*, published by Simon and Schuster. The book enjoyed brisk sales, then trailed off, but not before some heated words from the Kennedy family. When the *Chicago Tribune* printed excerpts of the book in its Tempo section, Eunice Shriver (Joan's sister-in-law) wrote to the editor (in part):

> What is the significance of a book that makes a mockery of trust, loyalty, and friendship? What are your readers to gain from the work of a woman who posed as a friend only to make money by peddling gossip and striking at the very foundation of friendship? . . . The values of friendship and trust have been perverted [in this book] and you have played a part in abetting this betrayal."[5]

But author Marcia Chellis saw the problem differently. To *People* magazine she said, "Joan will still see my loyalty in what I chose *not* to include in the book."[6]

At first glance, this case looks as much like an invasion-of-privacy or a reporters-and-sources case as any other dilemma described in this book. But invasion cases nearly always involve outsiders trying to get in (such as photographer Ronald Galella hounding Jacqueline Onassis, before the courts intervened); and Chellis was no reporter, not even a book writer, during her travels with the Kennedys. She was simply a confidante.

Perhaps that puts Chellis in the same dilemma as Victor Marchetti or Frank Snepp, who sought to report, entertain, and profit from reminiscences of life inside the CIA.[7] But again the differences are crucial. The former federal agents had agreed, as part of their employment contract, not to divulge information gained on the job. Chellis had apparently made no formal agreements, and her writing posed no arguable compromise to national security interests.

Chellis's *Living with the Kennedys* speaks with clarity to public figures whose stories command a market: Let the famous beware! During her three years of service, Chellis evidently was faithful to her employer, but when official employment ended, the obligations of a confidante also terminated. Now the stories could enter the marketplace, contribute to the Kennedy legend (or detract from it), and almost certainly add a moment of notoriety to a life otherwise on the fringes of fame.

This case requires a close look at the fourth quadrant of the Potter Box, for here questions of a professional's primary loyalties must be confronted. Should the book have been written? Should a responsible publisher release it? Crucial to any moral resolution is the question: To whom is duty owed?

Marcia Chellis was hired to perform duties that relatively few people need or can afford. She was to be a paid professional friend, companion, coordinator, assistant, sister, spokesperson, secretary, but not a slave. Chellis would take up the cause of the Kennedy campaign, especially Joan's part of it, but not surrender her mind or even ultimately her vote, the ballot box still being secret. From all indications, Chellis performed her duties well. Like most professionals, she invested personal energy and emotion into the job as she became more intimately part of the private Kennedy circle. When the job ended, she left on good terms, soon to become a different kind of professional— a reporter-author.

A careful look at the duties and loyalties attached to each of these professional roles should have given Chellis pause over the book. In the first role, Chellis stood as a guardian against encroachments by reporters into the Kennedy's private sphere. In the second role, she sought the very information she had been hired to protect, and her search needed go no further than her own diaries and memory. She bore no legal responsibility to remain silent, she had easy access to unique data, and she had a commitment to write, probably encouraged by an attractive publishing contract. But Chellis allowed her advantage in the first role to give her prestige in the second without drawing the distinctions that the fourth Potter quadrant requires.

Surely Joan Kennedy would not have hired Marcia Chellis as a reporter and author. Chellis cannot reasonably argue that she would have been part of the family's inner circle had Joan foreseen that Kennedy privacy would be sold in bookstores or discussed on promotional tours. With respect to the private data that aides have and reporters seek, Chellis should have started her writing career like any other reporter—by hard investigative work—and locked her Kennedy memories in a vault.

Chellis did have a book to write. On the Kennedys, her book could have examined the public policy and platform issues that she understood as well as anyone. Former aides need not remain silent about issues that engage positions taken by a former employer. Loyalty does not mean slavery. The mind is free to debate always, and Chellis in her second role was now free to debate publicly. But her "kiss and tell" approach betrayed the loyalty she had pledged. Let her pry into other private lives if she will: the Kennedys should have been a closed book.

Yet another question emerges from the Potter Box, one that should trouble professional journalists. Should the excerpts have run in the newspaper? The *Tribune*'s Tempo section is entertainment, pure and simple—usually good entertainment, sometimes helpful in readers' decision making, informative, and, by any measure of community standards, decent. In the case of *Living with the Kennedys*, editors had the chance to exhibit moral insight for Illinois readers and toward a family on the East Coast as well. They missed their chance. A review of the book, even a point-counterpoint interview with Chellis and a spokesperson for the Kennedys, would have served all parties well. Instead they hyped the excerpts in a front-page box, then titled the series "Joan Kennedy: A Confidant's Story" to heighten excitement over "what lies behind the glamour of being a Kennedy wife." The *Tribune* turned a morally objectionable book into a newspaper soap opera. Eunice Shriver's letter, published two weeks after the series concluded, deserves a response from the editors of the (once proclaimed) "World's Greatest Newspaper."

71. THE PURPOSE IS PROFIT

Larry Dowd (fictitious name) was in his mid-twenties and already had three million books in print. He held a two-year contract with Argo Publishers (fictitious name) which called for eight more books and several cross-country promotional tours.[8]

Dowd's themes came from the news (political scandals, Hollywood affairs) salted with a shrewd instinct for the offbeat twist. One reviewer called his work "very soft-core porn—sex viewed from the soap-suds angle." His books, all mass market paperbacks, were written in a single draft while the author listened to country music or watched television. Dowd told one interviewer, "Yea for TV. I belong to the church of television watchers of America." His editor at Argo said. "Some doctor ought to look at his thyroid to see where he gets all that energy."

Dowd is pleased that his books sell fast even if they die young. "I write stuff I'd like to read, and if it isn't timely any more, I'm really not interested in reading it. I have the attention span of a puppy. Besides, my books are entertainment. They're meant to be read, then exchanged for the next one. Or even thrown away. I'm a very impatient person. I like my books to come out fast. I take a filmic approach to a book. Writing's only part of it; marketing's an important part, too."

Dowd's first novel enjoyed a hefty initial printing of 600,000. He had six other books under the belt by that time, two of which had sold over a million copies. "I like to work," Dowd told a reporter. "It pays me to work hard. Hardcover reviews would be nice, but meanwhile I like my royalty checks. I look on my career as a business. . . . All I want is to be free and comfortable and not bored."

At one point, his first novel held prospects of a motion picture contract, a possibility that prompted the comment, "I'm going to be in the movies! In pictures! Yea for me!"

The writing and publishing of books has traditionally enjoyed a degree of respectability that places its people and products a notch above most others in the creative arts field, perhaps because books and writing have a long and dignified history, because great books live from generation to generation, and because the manufacture of books is a relatively drawn-out process with several checkpoints. Moreover, the enduring nature of a book makes it all the more subject to reflective criticism. An author or publisher guilty of a non sequitur, for example, would likely endure more prolonged embarrassment than a popular singer whose voice quivers during a live performance.

Authors of books, along with symphonic musicians and composers, painters, and sculptors have been considered less commercially motivated, less transient and ephemeral than, for instance, writers of pulp magazine tales and illustrators of advertising material. But these stereotypes have shifted with the coming of high-speed offset printing and inexpensive paperback binding. Yet, to find a book writer who is thoroughly given to mass-market commercialism still provokes a sense of dissonance, as though a sacrosanct profession has been invaded by a crass profiteer. Perhaps competition for the pop-culture dollar makes commercialism in all media inevitable. But wholesale commercialism? It sounds demeaning, exploitative. On the other hand, a writer oblivious to the audience may starve for lack of sales. Clearly, the business element cannot be ignored.

This line of reasoning is based on the assumption that a creative professional, in addition to owing something to the public, also owes a debt to his profession, to his colleagues, and to the professional tradition from which he profits. A creative talent who turns art into the science of marketing—whose short-term gain is his only measure of success—is unfairly trading on a tradition that he is doing nothing to uphold; rather, his actions, as a Kantian would notice, if copied by enough of his colleagues, would subvert the art side of his business completely.

Dowd cannot will that his own standards become the accepted norm. If they were, writers would be public jesters, fools deserving a scornful laugh, but nothing more. Dowd might find his own market significantly smaller. Conceivably, universal application of his standards would do a slow self-destruct to all serious cultural expression. Dowd needs a more mature, more responsible ethic than he currently has. He needs to read a good book before he tries to write one.

72. DEEP TROUBLE FOR HARRY

By most any definition of the horrible P-word, *Deep Throat* is a pornographic film. Released in 1972 at the crest of the sexual revolution, the film tells the story of a frustrated young woman (Linda Lovelace) who cannot "hear bells" during orgasm, no matter who the partner. She consults a psychiatrist (Harry Reems) who diagnoses her problem as a freak of nature: a clitoris in the throat. The promiscuous doctor then joins a long line of other bellringers who gratify themselves on, according to the *New York Times*, "virtuoso talent for fellatio."[9]

Neither Reems nor Lovelace were great acting talents and neither found fortune in this film. Reems had done bit parts in the National Shakespeare Company and other theater when director Gerard Damiano (or Jerry Gerard, Damiano's legal name) invited him to join the production crew of this new "white coater," a porn genre specializing in portraying flaky doctors. Later court testimony revealed that Reems won the lead in *Deep Throat* when the frustrated Damiano asked for volunteers to work the sex scenes. Reems was paid $100 for two scenes, then waived all editing, marketing, and distribution rights to the movie. Two years later Reems was indicted as part of an alleged nationwide conspiracy to profit from the interstate commerce of an obscene movie. He became the first performer to be prosecuted on federal charges for artistic work—a dubious honor. Reems was convicted in Memphis, but on appeal the government declined to retry the case (following the Supreme Court's 1974 *Miller* decision).

Deep Throat made Lovelace a sex queen. Her starring role helped produce the most successful porn film ever made. The same film typecast her and essentially ended her career, but not before silicone injections enlarged her breasts and tainted blood gave her hepatitis and not before the beatings, rapes, and gunpoint perversions of her first husband, who also got her work in the movies. Wrote Lovelace (now remarried): "I was a robot who did what I had to do to survive." Her first husband earned $1,250 for Linda's role in *Deep Throat*; she never saw a penny. Now living on Long Island, she helps at her children's elementary school and gives lectures on the effects of pornography. She also wears a beeper waiting for a liver donor—the result of the silicone that helped entertain 8 million box office patrons of *Deep Throat*.

Civil libertarians point out that 23 states banned this movie at some point in the ten years following its release. In one important legal battle in Texas, a nuisance abatement strategy was turned back by the federal appeals and U.S. Supreme Court as a dangerous movement toward prior restraint.

Whether the film deserved suppression at all is both a legal and moral problem. In a customs case in Massachusetts concerning the confiscation of a film print, the court heard an expert witness say that *Deep Throat* "puts forth an idea of greater liberation with regard to human sexuality and to the expression of it" which would help "many women" overcome particular sexual fears. Yet to argue that *Deep Throat's* blatant appeal to lasciviousness has redeeming social benefits which warrant First Amendment protection is really to nullify common definitions of obscenity. Only the First Amendment absolutist can effectively maintain that this film should be freely allowed to find its audience. Only the true believer in *laissez-faire* popular culture would want marketeers of this film to be let loose on the populace at large.

In its much maligned Final Report, the Attorney General's Commission on Pornography created five broad categories of material around which to organize its 92 recommendations. The first two categories—sexually violent material and nonviolent materials depicting degradation, domination, subordination, or humiliation—were deemed harmful by most of the commission. Class IV, Nudity, was an innocuous category that included classical art and toddlers bounding around in naked innocence. Class V ("the special horror of child pornography") was so blatantly exploitative that commissioners urged strongest measures to disrupt and prosecute this market. But the third category (nonviolent and nondegrading materials) was the most controversial.[10] It included portrayals of "consensual and equal vaginal intercourse . . . oral-genital activity" or "two couples simultaneously engaging in the same activity." The Commission could not cite any film titles which fit this category, so presumably *Deep Throat* was, in their minds, an example of Class II. Yet many people would claim that *Deep Throat* and other nonviolent pornographic films are mere entertainments which hurt no one (in a demonstrably causal fashion) and attract no one other than interested, paying customers. As long as children are not permitted to rent the video, the market logic goes, let adults choose *Deep Throat* if they wish. And obviously many wish.

But the free-market argument will pass no muster with Linda Lovelace Marchiano. She was the exploited star of the show who now faces medical procedures which will keep her in debt for years, if in fact she survives at all. She is the Agent Orange victim of pornographic profiteering, her body devastated by the chemicals which made her sexy.

And the free-market argument must also face the fact that this movie was a financial boon for organized crime. On a $25,000 investment, the Colombo crime family made well over $50 million on *Deep Throat*, with some of the profits being directed to Caribbean drug-smuggling operations.[11]

A principled market cannot exploit (in this case, it was a form of slavery) and abuse its artisans, and it cannot tolerate siphoning wealth into criminal empire building. The porn film business, with *Deep Throat* a shaded example, is too regularly guilty of each count to warrant our waving a free-market flag in its defense. Freedom, Kant argued, is in the pursuit of right reason. Freedom, Niebuhr and his compatriots would urge, is in overcoming greed and prurience through a movement of love guarded by justice. Exploring sexuality in film is inherently a good goal, but this porn film was a heist on humanity. No market potency can justify destroying a life.

A real white coater who sat on the Attorney General's commission, Park Elliott Dietz of the University of Virginia, stated, as the work concluded:

As a government body, we studiously avoided making judgments on behalf of the government about the morality of particular sexual acts between consenting adults or their depiction in pornography. This avoidance, however, should not be mistaken for the absence of moral sentiment among the Commissioners. I for one, have no hesitation in condemning nearly every specimen of pornography that we have examined in the course of our deliberations as tasteless, offensive, lewd, and indecent. . . . It has been nearly two centuries since Phillipe Pinel struck the chains from the mentally ill and more than a century since Abraham Lincoln struck the chains from America's black slaves. With this statement I ask you, America, to strike the chains from America's women and children, to free them from the bond of pornography, to free them from the bonds of sexual abuse, to free them from the bonds of inner torment that entrap the second-class citizen in an otherwise free nation.[12]

73. SUPER STRIP

Jerry Siegel and Joe Shuster were high school teenagers in Cleveland, Ohio, when they came upon the idea of a cartoon figure who, born in a distant galaxy, would escape to earth as a baby, grow up in an orphanage, and, as an adult, impervious to gravity and mightier than a locomotive, would aid the forces of justice in their battle against evil.

Siegel actually conceived the idea. His buddy Joe Shuster liked to draw, so the two fledgling cartoonists set out to sell their story. Five years of pounding on doors finally won them a contract with Detective Comics, and the first "Superman" strip appeared in 1938. Siegel and Shuster were paid $10 a page for their work, about $15 dollars a week per man.[13]

The contract favored the company. The more popular Superman became, the clearer was Siegel and Shuster's loss. Finally they brought suit against Detective and were awarded some money, but still they had no rights to their hero. When the legal dust settled, Detective fired Siegel and Shuster, and the two creators were left to watch others get rich and famous off their idea. More lawsuits proved futile. Late in 1975, with legal routes exhausted, the men defied the advice of their attorneys and went public with their story.

Their tale was one of sadness and struggle. Neither man had received any money from Superman since 1948, though profits from the Man of Steel were in the multimillions. Shuster now was legally blind, living in Queens with a brother who supported him. Siegel was ill and lived with his wife in a tiny apartment in Los Angeles, where he worked as a government clerk typist for $7,000 a year. The men appealed to Superman's current copyright owner "out of a sense of moral obligation," said Shuster. The National Cartoonists Society and Cartoonists Guild lent their full backing to Siegel and Shuster's moral claim.

The appeal brought results. Warner Communications, which owned movie rights to Superman, claimed "no legal obligation," but "there is a moral obligation on our part." Two days before Christmas, Siegel and Shuster signed a contract with Warner: They would each receive $20,000 yearly for life, and their heirs would also be helped. The creators' names would appear on all Superman productions. At the signing, a Warner executive commended the two cartoonists. The contract, he said, was "in recognition of their past services and out of concern for their present circumstances."

The money awarded Siegel and Shuster presented no threat to the profits of Warner Communications. The sum of $40,000 a year may be less than the company spends in processing receipts from Superman sales. But as a gesture neither required by law nor essential to public relations, it represents an application of the Judeo-Christian ethic of othermindedness.

Consider the dynamics of the award. Siegel and Shuster had sold their idea under the duress of the Depression and at a time in their youth when neither could be expected to negotiate a contract with business savvy. Events had changed dramatically since then. One was now handicapped, and the other ill; both were living on a bare-bones income. Exhausted by fruitless legal efforts, they claimed a moral right to some relief.

Warner could have called their appeal a nuisance. Business is business, after all. Investors who cash in stock certificates, for example, never qualify for post-facto profits. Farmers who sell a corn crop in

November may not appeal for extra payment when the bushel price rises in January. Buyers and sellers each assume part of the risk, and each understands that one could emerge from the deal a clear winner. Because the terms are understood, the bargain is fair.

But contracts are not independent from the economic milieu in which they are made. Were they selling a cartoon character today instead of in 1938, Siegel and Shuster might negotiate for a compensation clause should their idea become a bonanza. The economic climate of the late 1930s was not ripe for such risk-reducing appendixes.

So the recognition awarded Siegel and Shuster was for the cartoonists a humanitarian gesture of life-sustaining aid, while to Warner it represented no loss to shareholders and no risk to corporate solvency. Perhaps a thorough application of "others as ourselves" or Rawls's ethic of undifferentiated negotiators would have resulted in larger awards, or royalties for Siegel and Shuster, or a cost-of-living adjustment in their $20,000 annual amount, or life insurance policies to establish an estate for each man. Maybe so. It may be argued that Warner hemmed and hawed until it was expedient for them to make a gesture, quite apart from what was fair for the two penniless cartoonists. But the award, such as it was, points to a residual sense of group solidarity and caring, a dissonant but hopeful interlude in the normally amoral entertainment business.

NOTES

1. Quoted in Robert C. Cole, "$830 Million in Cash Bid for McGraw-Hill by American Express," *New York Times*, 10 January 1979, p. D16.
2. *New York Times*, 17 January 1979, p. 12.
3. John Brooks, as quoted in Herbert Mitgang, "McGraw-Hill Bid Stirs Editorial Fears," *New York Times*, 14 January 1979, p. 51.
4. Fred Friendly, "McGraw-Hill and a Free Press," *Wall Street Journal*, 26 January 1979, p. 14.
5. *Chicago Tribune*, 5 November 1985, sec. 1, p. 12.
6. *People Weekly*, 23 September 1985, p. 35.
7. Victor Marchetti and Frank Snepp wrote *The CIA and the Cult of Intelligence* and *Decent Interval*, respectively. Both were subjected to national security proceedings.
8. This case is based on J. Howard, "Yea for Me!" *New Times*, 2 November 1973, pp. 46–47.
9. Quotation and background material from Edward de Grazia and Roger K. Newman, *Banned Films; Movies, Censors, and the First Amendment* (New York: R.R. Bowker, 1982).

10. The full report is summarized in Michael J. McManus, Introduction to *Final Report of the Attorney General's Commission on Pornography* (Nashville: Rutledge Hill Press, 1986), pp. xix–xxi.
11. Ibid., p. 295.
12. Ibid., pp. 491–492.
13. Material in this case is from the *New York Times*, 22 November, 10 and 24 December 1975.

CHAPTER 15

Media Scope and Depth

For every medium there is a scale; we may call it an esthetic scale. On one end are the serious artists and producers, careful about the integrity of their craft and insistent that their labors give audiences a better insight into meaningful human life. On the other end are writers and producers who want to provide the most popular product possible. They care little if lofty artistic visions are part of their work; theirs is the task of attracting the largest possible share of the audience, because if they do not, the competition will. Success is measured by the best-seller lists and the top ten Nielsen rankings.

The pull of the media's commercial base may inevitably lead to television programs, movies, and books that trivialize human dilemmas or escape entirely from them. Perhaps the forces resisting such trends are too weak to mount much of a counterthrust. Yet only the cynic will claim that money is really all that matters in popular culture, and only the most cloudy idealist will assert that money does not matter at all.

Between the demands of art and the marketplace are a host of moral questions that media practitioners face every day: Must art be compromised when it passes from one medium to another? Are stereotyped characters fair to real people? How far should commercial concerns dictate cultural products? What is a fair portrayal of an ethnic character on television?

These cases focus on ethnic diversity and dramatized history—in one sense, two views of the same moral reality. All history turns on community values, since no human life is a social vacuum. Can mediated visions of historical experience, frosted for entertainment purposes with drama and romance, convey the suffering and spirit of people who have resisted the melting-pot metaphor in favor of promoting their linkage to generations past? Are media stereotypes still as troublesome as in the cowboys and Indians era of the 1950s? Given the profound demographic changes now underway in North America, ethnic diversity and ethnically viable history are more vital than ever. In another sense, a minority of one would warrant the same moral care as a minority of 49 percent. The recent explosion in ethnic presence only makes more apparent the need for a louder voice in the public chorus.

In the first case, an episode from the civil rights movement serves as story line for a dramatic film on race and police power. But the small victories for justice won both in 1967 and in the 1989 film were accomplished by vastly different means. Has fiction become fact for a generation of viewers born after the last lynching? The second case takes a different look at ethnicity and community values. Who besides film critics and cinema esthetes cares whether the resolution of film drama is contrived or realistic? If a film is set in ethnic territory, should that environment—with its people, folkways, and institutions—become a moral concern? The third case ponders whether a television show's gambling incentive is also a glamorization of one culture at the expense of others.

Is moral imagination served by the no-punches-pulled sparring of ethnic warriors in public debate? "Bigotry as Debate" explores that dilemma.

Surely one of our most pernicious habits is entertainment at the expense of someone else's self-respect, and especially so through the trivializing of someone's ethnic or peer-group identity. Can the media avoid it? To compress dramatic action into a thirty-minute television show or a two-hour movie demands some degree of stereotyping, but how much is too much, and is any amount right at all? Stereotyping of the elderly is the subject of case 78.

The last case examines media cross-over—a piece of literature finding its way into television. Can the nuances of the author's characters survive? Or does TV so radically change the creative context that stories written in a book are unrecognizable on the screen?

American entertainment has come a long way from the Jack Armstrong radio dramas in which stealthy orientals threatened the welfare of right-living Anglo-Saxons, or since Sitting Bull was portrayed as a public menace and George Custer a national hero. However, problems of stereotyping and historical storytelling are still part of the media's difficult moral agenda.[1]

Long before television, Justice Louis Brandeis wrote: "Triviality destroys at once robustness of thought and delicacy of feeling. No enthusiasm can flourish, no generous impulse can survive under its blighting influence."[2] Ought we to wink at mass mediated entertainment—its coquettish romance and addlebrained simplicity—or is the beast really more fearsome than mad Dr. Frankenstein imagined? These cases raise the question and spotlight the moral issues.

74. History Burning

Two days after the U.S. Senate passed the Civil Rights Bill of 1964, three civil rights workers heard jail doors close behind them in Philadelphia, Mississippi. The charge was reckless driving, a discretionary offense, like disturbing the peace, that can mean whatever a law officer wishes on any given day. That year in the rural South, discretionary judgments did not favor Northern whites and activist blacks. Yet this charge seemed to be just a nuisance. Goodman, Chaney, and Schwerner were back in their car just after nightfall, on to the next town, the next rally, the next voter registration. . . .

The federal investigation into their disappearance and deaths took three years, an alleged $30,000 payoff to an informer, and considerable FBI perseverance against local police who were themselves part of the crime. Murder indictments were never brought, though seven of nineteen defendants were convicted of violating federal civil rights statutes. The crime and its aftermath became one tragic chapter in the sad story of resistance to racial justice throughout the 1960s. Against the stories of other martyrs, notably Medgar Evers and Martin Luther King and four children in a Birmingham church, the Neshoba County murders were heinous but not otherwise memorable, unfortunate but not monumental.

Until the motion picture. Titled *Mississippi Burning* and released by Orion Pictures in 1989, the film starred Gene Hackman and Willem Dafoe as FBI agents who cracked the case with dogged zeal and backroom muscle. The odds against them, these warriors from Washington (who frequently warred among themselves) turn Klan-like tactics against the Klan and retrieve for burned-out blacks a moment of righteous vengeance, a small political portion of the deliverance sung about in the black spirituals that introduce and end director Alan Parker's movie.

Not everyone, however, saw restitution and virtue in this factually based drama. Black columnist Vernon Jarrett complained: "The film treats some of the most heroic people in black history as mere props in a morality play." David Halberstam, who covered the South in 1964 for the *New York Times*, said: "Parker has taken a terribly moving and haunting story and . . . betrayed it . . . into a slapstick between two cops." Julian Bond appeared on the TV program "Nightline" to complain that blacks were not as passive and forlorn as *Burning* suggested, nor were Hoover's agents so inventive. Indeed, everyone admits that the use of a covert agent in *Burning* was pure make believe and that the characters of the sheriff and his deputy were radically changed to meet dramatic requirements. Critics contended, and filmmakers never denied, that the script "underplays the Klan's impressive organization" and "presents little of the context, much less the content, of the civil rights movement. . . . Nor does the film give much sense of the national dimension of the case," wrote William Swislow.[3]

Nonetheless, the National Board of Review gave *Burning* its Best Picture award, and the Academy of Motion Picture Arts and Sciences nominated it for seven "oscars", including Best Picture. About historicity, the film itself concluded with this statement, after the long roll of credits: "This film is inspired by actual events which took place in the South during the 1960s. The characters, however, are fictitious and do not depict real people either living or dead."

If documentary film uses footage of actual events to tell a historical story, and dramatic film recreates a period to provide context for fiction, docudrama roughly combines both. But does it do justice to either?

Los Angeles *Times* media critic David Shaw remarks that one of the worst examples of the dangers of docudrama was the CBS production of "The Atlanta Child Murders," the story of convicted child killer Wayne Williams (implicated in 23 homocides, convicted of 2 in 1982). The obvious slant of "Child Murders" portrayed Williams as the victim of circumstantial evidence. CBS did precede the two-part show with an advisory that the program "is not a documentary but a drama based on certain facts. . . . Some of the events and characters are fictionalized for dramatic purposes." Viewers were left to their own knowledge of the case to sort out the factual from the fictionalized scenes. Shaw called this kind of television the "bastardization and confusion of fact and fiction."[4]

Professor Gregory Payne was a consultant to NBC during the making of "Kent State," a docudrama of the 4 May 1970 National Guard shootings of four university students. While a proponent of the docudrama genre, Payne has meticulously described the fictionalized interactions of guardsmen and students in "Kent State." For example, the burning of the ROTC building at Kent State on May 2 has never been definitively explained, and only last-minute insistence by consultants and actors kept those ambiguities intact. Payne observes that whatever were NBC's exaggerations (such as building much of the drama around Allison Krause's romance), they were nothing compared with the distortions of James Michener's book, *Kent State: What Happened and Why*.

At a conference in Boston, actor Rick Allen, who played Guardsman Wesley, noted that his portrayal of being overcome with tear gas and retreating from the line of march just moments before the Guard fired was pure fiction intended to humanize the "bad guys" and, in addition, to win a couple of seconds of additional on-camera time—a valuable asset for a young actor. Allen was troubled that history was being written for thousands of viewers on the basis of a director's urging his people to ad-lib.

In 1988 the plight of surrogate mother Mary Beth Whitehead put a spotlight on the womb-for-hire business and its legality. Whose child was Baby M—her natural mother's or William and Elizabeth Stern's, who held the contract? (William was the natural father through artificial insemination.) ABC would help the nation decide with a four-hour, $6 million docudrama. Since neither the Whiteheads nor the Sterns would cooperate, ABC used court transcripts, published accounts, and psychiatric evaluations made public with court records. Of course, the obligatory disclaimer preceding the telecast notes that "certain scenes and dialogue are interpretive of this material."[5]

In 1644 John Milton was confident that truth would emerge in a free marketplace of ideas, though falsehood might grapple for a while; human rationality would eventually make the distinctions, since the universe could not end on a lie. In 1985 psychiatrist M. Scott Peck began to forge a new vocabulary based on clinical observations that in some people, deception that was never overcome leads to the grim realities that destroy their lives.[6] Perhaps human rationality was not as powerful as the great liberal democrats believed. And if not, is truthtelling all the more a moral imperative, fragile of understanding as we are?

Is the docudrama genre a powerful vehicle for reviving our culture's important stories, or a cheap distortion based on television's insatiable need for new material?

In favor of docudrama: How many students in the 1990s would know or care about Kent State's Allison, Jeff, Sandy, and Bill were it not for the efforts of NBC, albeit profit-tinged, to give new life to that fateful spring weekend in northeast Ohio? How many dry eyes and stoic hearts walked out of theaters after *Burning*, unmoved by the suffering and careless about the future of racial justice? Journalist Bill Minor covered the Freedom Summer of 1964 and won the Elijah Lovejoy award for most courageous weekly editor in the nation following his exposure of Klan activity in Mississippi. He defended *Burning* as "a powerful portrayal." For viewers who depend on film for stories not experienced firsthand, the movie "got the spirit right."[7]

If a film recreates the ethos of an event such that participants and principles can affirm the veracity of context and struggle, is that not sufficient? History is more than mere facts, and no story corresponds exactly to events. Perhaps the docudrama is our best vehicle for keeping at bay those who claim the Holocaust, in whatever version, never occurred.

The crucial variable is the judgment of the subject. If a docudrama wins the approval of those closest to the real-life drama, viewers are assured that a truthful perspective on events survives the dramatic process. If the subject cannot recognize his or her struggle for all the romantic clichés and garbled characterizations, we rightly worry that rampant revisionism threatens to obscure and distort the meaning of the past. Morally sensitive producers of docudrama will incorporate fictional elements without padding history or violating the pain of those whose stories they tell.

75. ARE FAKE, UNHAPPY ENDINGS ANY BETTER THAN FAKE, HAPPY ONES?

The motion picture *Chinatown* has little to do with the Los Angeles ethnic quarter but much to do with political and moral corruption. The city is in a drought, and a powerful city boss, Noah Cross, is buying parched Los Angeles County farmland while at the same time arranging for the dumping of reservoir water into the ocean to force farmers to sell cheaply.

Private detective J.J. (Jake) Gittes has been hired by Evelyn Mulwray. Her husband, Hollis Mulwray, chief water engineer for the county, has been murdered after discovering the land/drought scandal. Evelyn wants to find the killer.

Gittes does his job. Hollis was killed by Cross, who is also the dead man's father-in-law and former business partner. Evelyn hates her father for an earlier act of incest and, in the last scene, wants to escape the sordid web with her feeble daughter-sister, Katherine, whom Evelyn has thus far shielded from her past. Cross likewise hates Evelyn for hiding his younger "daughter" and forces Gittes to take him to the girl.

Gittes's former police partner, Lou Escobar, is the police lieutenant assigned to the case. Earlier the pair had been together on the force in Chinatown, where supervisors had discouraged them from honest police work because the corruption was too deep— hence the symbol of complete moral collapse. Escobar believes Evelyn to be the murderer, although his mind has likely been purchased by Cross. At least Escobar knows Cross to be a powerful man in city politics.

The principals all meet at night on a busy street in Chinatown. It appears that the only chance for justice to prevail is Evelyn's escape. As the scene opens:

> *Gittes is held at gunpoint by Cross and a henchman. As they walk to Evelyn's parked car, they are intercepted by Escobar and his police team. Gittes's associates, Walsh and Duffy, are also there. Gittes begins to speak, but stops short when he sees Walsh and Duffy handcuffed.*

ESCOBAR: You're under arrest, Jake.

GITTES (*relieved to be rescued from gunpoint*): Good news.

ESCOBAR: Withholding evidence, extortion, accessory after the fact!

GITTES (*protesting*): I didn't extort nothin' from nobody, Lou. This is Noah Cross, if you don't know. Evelyn's father, if you don't know. He's the bird you're after, Lou. I can explain everything if you just give me five minutes . . .

ESCOBAR: Shut up!

GITTES: Five minutes is all I need. He's rich, you understand?

ESCOBAR (*yelling*): Shut up! (*Now whispering*) Shut up or I'm going to lock you to the wheel of that car.

CROSS: Lieutenant, I am rich. I am Noah Cross. Evelyn Mulwray is my daughter—

GITTES: He's crazy, Lou. He killed Mulwray because of the water thing. If you'll just listen to me for five minutes . . .

ESCOBAR (*to a subordinate*): Lock him to the car.

GITTES (*being moved away*): Lou, you don't know what's going on here, I'm telling you.

Evelyn and Katherine rush past the crowd, heading for her car. Cross approaches.

CROSS: Katherine! I . . . I am your . . . your . . . grandfather.

Evelyn blocks his approach.

EVELYN: Get away from her! Get away!

CROSS: Evelyn . . . please, please be reasonable. How many years have I got? She's mine, too!

EVELYN (*angrily*): She's never going to know that!

Evelyn draws a small pistol. Cross backs away.

CROSS: Evelyn, you're a disturbed woman. You cannot hope to provide—

GITTES (*from off camera*): Evelyn, put that gun away. Let the police handle this.

EVELYN (*irate but under control*): He owns the police!

Evelyn circles the car to the driver's side, while Cross approaches again.

EVELYN: Get away from her!

CROSS: You'll have to kill me first.

EVELYN: Get away! Get—

Evelyn fires at Cross. He clutches his arm. Evelyn enters car, shouts to Katherine in back seat.

EVELYN (*frantically*): Katherine, close the door.

Evelyn behind the wheel, the car takes off down the street.

ESCOBAR (*yelling*): Halt!

He fires twice at the car, missing. A third shot is deflected by Gittes, who grabs his arm. Another detective steps up, takes aim, fires three shots. The car, now a hundred yards away, stops in the middle of the street, the horn blaring. All the men—police, Gittes, Cross—run toward the vehicle. Katherine screams.

Escobar arrives first and opens the driver's door. Evelyn's body falls away from the horn to reveal blood streaming from her left eye. The men are stunned. Meanwhile, Cross has opened the passenger door and is comforting the hysterical Katherine in a grandfatherly manner. He cups his hand over her mouth and leads her away from the scene. Escobar, recovering his senses, turns to a uniformed policeman.

ESCOBAR: Turn 'em loose, turn 'em all loose.
Handcuffs are released.
ESCOBAR (*to Walsh and Duffy*): You want to do your partner a big favor? Take him home.
The men are too stunned to move.
ESCOBAR (*yells*): Take him home! Just get the hell out of here!
DUFFY (*whispering, trying to coax Gittes from the scene*): Come on, Jake.
ESCOBAR (*whispering*): Go home, Jake. I'm doin' you a favor.
DUFFY: Come on, Jake.
WALSH (*as he, Duffy, and Gittes move slowly away from the car*): Forget it, Jake, it's Chinatown.

The crowd disperses as the camera pans the street and a policeman is heard yelling, "All right, come on, clear the area, get on the sidewalk, clear the street. . . ."

(Adapted script from *Chinatown*, Paramount Pictures.)

Back in the good old days of the 1930s, 1940s, and 1950s, American films were characterized by their happy endings, writes film critic John Simon.[8] So buoyant and optimistic were Hollywood's productions that a neologism appeared in several European languages: "happyend." It meant a "joyous resolution of complicated intrigues and overwhelming problems, allowing the hero and heroine, in the last shot, and against all probability, to fall into each other's arms and live, by implication, happily ever after."

The "happyend" formula was well stated in an interview with the late Lucille Ball, who first appeared in movies in 1934. Said Miss Ball:

I hate all the graphic violence and sex in movies and on TV. I miss the big, beautiful musicals and nice love stories. Now it's hard to find stories or stars who could do the marvelous,

glamorous movies . . . that let audiences dream and fantas-
ize. What television and movies give you is glaring red, running blood and foul words, and it leaves everybody without
hope. Poverty and sickness and psychos and wierdos are
coming out of the closet—and doing it all on television. I
think that comedy and drama ought to let us have a little
escape from our troubles. . . . There's no difficulty understanding my shows. They always had a beginning, a middle,
and a happy ending.[9]

Simon notes that the tide of films began to change in the 1960s,
and the tidal wave of change came in the 1970s. What troubles him is
not that former optimism was challenged by present realism, but that
the new tide merely replaces fake happy endings with fake unhappy
ones.

Consider the neofascist genre in which the armed hero virtuously
kills off his opponents in the name of justice. "You may be sheriff, but
I'm the law out here," John Rambo tells the sole survivor of an ill-
fated posse. Or consider Axel Foley's (the Beverly Hills cop) one-man
crusade to bring his partner's slayer to justice. Observes Simon: "In
an indiscriminately vicious world, the only release and relief comes
from beating up or killing, from taking the law into one's own hands
and becoming Superman, Superblack, Superwhatever. In the old days,
it was the victory of the forces of right over those of wrong; now,
however, it is I (or my alter ego) against everyone else."

Or consider the cinema of unbeatable darkness. In *The French
Connection, Serpico, The Godfather I* and *II*, and *Chinatown*, there
are only losers in the end. Old bad values have given way to a new bad
value: total despair effected by contrived, manipulative endings such
as *Chinatown*'s, where the villain is lightly wounded at close range
while the heroine, in a car speeding away from a nervous cop, takes a
bullet between the eyes.

Or consider the films of political and social commentary. American filmmakers barely scratch the surface of tough, complex problems.
An individual politician may be corrupt, but the system as a whole is
okay. A war may be vile and pointless as long as the enemy is also
cruel and immoral.

Do American films accurately reflect our society? "No," Simon
answers, "if you mean honestly coming to grips with the difficulties
we face, the insufficiencies of the society that we have fashioned and
that in turn, molds us."[10]

If cultural literacy is a value we seek to develop, entertainment programming must do more to unravel the complexities before us.

Community values are the constant background of cases such as this. Would Jake's problem be as intense and mysterious if the water crisis happened in Omaha? Urban enclaves typically retain native language, cuisine, temples or churches, and sometimes schools, but also dramatized perceptions of stealth, cunning, betrayal, power, and lust. *The Godfather* and its sequels created perceptions not altogether cheery about Italian-American communities. The *Jaws* phenomenon tells us something about resort towns, however misleading. In *Chinatown*, the problem is even more subtle since neither Chinese-Americans nor their culture figure in the plot, except as a setting where justice is normally thwarted by a preponderance of mystery and evil.

Scriptwriters might be culpable if we assume that even entertainment programs should contain something of educational value, something to illuminate the paradoxes we humans face or something to aid us in solving them. To conclude that no solutions are available— or that virtuous solutions are impossible because nothing good can happen in *this* part of town—may be to abrogate a crucial responsibility and to discourage the kind of painful problem solving that humans must undertake to work through troubling problems. On the other extreme, denouements that fail to grapple at all with complex problems, choosing instead to wish one's troubles away in a scene of superficial merriment, seem equally to miss the mark of educating viewers toward responsible living.

Thus, enlightened discussion of the happy–unhappy motif centers largely on step two in the Potter Box, where underlying values are exposed and debated. Beyond that, appealing to an ethical principle, the Aristotelian mean could be used to call media producers to realistic drama. Many examples, from *Gandhi* to *Tender Mercies* to dramatic television epics such as "The Autobiography of Miss Jane Pittman," suggest that stirring drama and the honest portrayal of human problem solving need not be mutually exclusive. Hollywood's *Born on The Fourth of July* and Dustin Hoffman's hit *Rain Man* are signs of cinematic progress—honesty, criticism, and drama.

76. DREAMING OURSELVES INTO MIDDLE-CLASS COMFORT

"Fabulous prizes" yells the announcer to open a popular television game show in which a lot of chance and a bit of consumer knowledge combine with cutthroat tactics against other contestants to win entry to games featuring bigger prizes—mostly household items in the $500 to $1,000 price range.

The pace is quick. Contestants are on their way from studio seats to the front before the host is introduced. "Come on, down," yells the announcer off camera as each of four names is called. The audience cheers enthusiastically.

The first contestant, a nicely dressed black woman, wins a grandfather clock. The camera catches the happy reaction of her family in the audience. "I came to win, I came to win," she yells on stage to celebrate her good fortune. "I want you to win," the host assures her.

To the next contestant the host says. "Ours has been described as the most exciting show on television. Don't you think it would be exciting if you should win that!" Curtains open to reveal a sparkling red sports car, adorned with a female model who could make an army jeep sparkle. The car is worth $19,800, the contestant is told, and to win it she must answer a couple of questions and putt a golf ball into a hole. She misses. She turns to the host to say "Thank you," but the host is speaking to the audience and does not hear her. Someone in the orchestra lets go with a trombone groan.

The chance games include a simulated bank safe, the combination to which opens the door to the "fabulous prizes." Contestants guess for correct numbers while the studio audience yells their hunches. The host, jovial yet paternal, calls the crowd fickle for groaning when their guesses miss the mark. His chiding is all part of the fun.

The next contestant races to the front. "I even dreamt about you last night," she tells the host. His reply: "What were we doing?" She hardly caught the nuance. "I had to spin that big wheel and I was so small you had to hold me," she said. The host retorts quickly, "If you get up here, baby, I'll hold you." The audience cheers.

Not everyone wins, of course. Losers retreat graciously and quickly to their seats. Winners cup their hands in disbelief and anticipation. The chance for immediate possession of expensive furnishings is a rare moment—the dream of yuppiedom come true.

What social benefits accrue from the television game shows? Do they serve as an outlet for people who like to gamble a little for fun? Or are they entertainment programs pure and simple with no social benefits required?

In a society where gambling is becoming more and more acceptable (most states now allow some form of it), it may seem academic to discuss the merits of television shows that play to those risk-taking drives. Yet critics challenge this prevailing ethos. A sociologist at the University of Colorado has suggested that television game shows perpetuate irresponsible expectations of economic and social ladder climbing.[11]

The show's message seems to be that have-nots wish they had; middle-class people seek upper-middle; everyone wishes he or she had more. Expensive toys and the equipment of leisure are class-defined comforts that never bow to alternative visions. When was the last game show that enabled a winner to learn, to enjoy, or to create culture (a violin or banjo with lessons from a master, a printing press, or a season at the Lincoln Center)? What game show helped a winner get a business loan or led to a graduate degree and a career doing productive work in the sciences or arts? Rather, success is having a rich, upper-class lifestyle, and the achievement of it is shown to ride on the winds of chance. No greater counterpoint to the Puritan work ethic could be imagined.

"Where do we draw the line between social entertainment and more serious activities that lead to pathological behavior such as compulsive gambling?" the Colorado researcher asks. Perhaps in a system of limited resources, the greatest good for the greatest number precludes bankrolling benefits for the very few. But utilitarianism would object to these games of chance only if the cost of losing outweighs the value of winning. Contestants on game shows (and certainly viewers) put up no ante (except their time) and pay no penalty for losing. As long as the competition is voluntary and all contestants have an equal chance at winning, the game remains a game, more public than playing Monopoly or PacMan, but still just a whimsy and a dream.

77. Bigotry as Debate

"Black Perspectives on the News" was typically a 30-minute talk show produced for distribution on the Public Broadcasting Service by WHYY in Philadelphia. The show scheduled for the last week in September, however, was not the ordinary half-hour.

Bring together the head of the American Nazi Party and the

Imperial Wizard of the Ku Klux Klan. Cast them with three black interviewers. Result: 60 minutes of largely uncontrolled, rambling conversation that included several sharply anti-Semitic remarks.

When word of the show leaked out, many viewers in Philadelphia were upset that a publicly funded station would produce such a diatribe. Three Nazi prison camp survivors living in the city filed suit to prevent the station from putting the show on the air. A local judge ruled in their favor on the day the broadcast was scheduled, and only a reversal from the state's Superior Court kept the 9 P.M. program on schedule. Even then, about 2,000 Jewish, Polish, and black demonstrators protested outside the studio that evening.

The Jewish community was not about to sit by while shades of the Third Reich danced on the screens of the nation's television sets. At WNET in New York, the American Jewish Congress (AJC) was especially active in protesting the upcoming show: A letter of protest was written accusing the station management of gross irresponsibility.

When the AJC letter was released to the press, WNET perceived it as a claim by the AJC that it had won cancellation of the show. Now the station was in a dilemma. Said one executive: "If we are perceived as yielding to the wishes of one pressure group, we'll be asked to give in to others and there'll be no end to it."[12] WNET's final decision: The station would produce its own version of the show, to be called "The Extremists: American Nazis and the K.K.K.," and this revised version would include about a half-hour from the original "Black Perspectives" production. "We almost had no choice," said the WNET executive.

Two sides were lined up for battle. The AJC vigorously denied that it had claimed credit for a programming decision at WNET. However, it would not retract its belief that the show was reprehensible and that its cancellation was the only right decision. In Cleveland the AJC protested: "There is no legal or democratic necessity to publicize falsehood." A *New York Times* critic, pondering the role of the public in media decisions, commented: "The American Jewish Congress is only one of many groups in this country which knows itself to be in possession of the truth, and if television producers did not resist the constant pressures, the world of television would be an even blander place than it is. One group's falsehood is another's truth."[13]

WHYY felt deserted. Only 105 of the 207 PBS stations aired the program, even when WHYY tacked on a 30-minute follow-up featuring spokespeople from the American Jewish Committee, the National Jewish Community Relations Advisory Council, and the Pennsylvania Human Relations Commission. James Karayn, president of WHYY, criticized PBS affiliates for succumbing to pressure: "I thought the whole reason for public television was to air public issues that commercial TV wouldn't. . . . Even if our judgment was wrong in this case, the station broadcasts over 5,000 hours of programming a year, and we are not going to allow a few people who object to one program to destroy the whole thing."[14]

The American Civil Liberties Union (ACLU) fully supported the position of WHYY. "The danger of prior censorship by pressure is greater than the danger of irresponsibility by the press," said the ACLU.[15]

On what moral grounds could the AJC object to "Black Perspectives" being aired in New York City? Perhaps a closer look at the letter sent from Naomi Levine, executive director of the AJC, to WNET management will cast light on the reasoning involved:

What is involved here is Channel 13's program judgment—not censorship. Obviously TV and radio stations have the right to decide what shows they believe are worthy of public viewing. . . . The community . . . has an equal right to question the wisdom of their decisions.

In this instance we believe that any decision by Channel 13 to broadcast a program admittedly racist and anti-Semitic in content, a discussion which has been described by . . . the station which originated it . . . as containing "contradictory and factually inaccurate" statements, would be an act of irresponsible journalism and wretched program judgment.

We do not object to this program because its subject matter is controversial. We do not believe there is anything "controversial" about racial and religious hatred. . . .

We are confident that Channel 13 is not so bankrupt in

program ideas that it must give precious air time to a program that projects racial and religious hatred and whose only
result can be to inflame interracial and interreligious relations in our city. We recognize your right and authority to
decide upon your own programs; we are grateful that in the
exercise of that judgment you have understood that carrying
this program would be an irresponsible act and a serious
abuse of public trust.[16]

The AJC seems to be arguing that the content of the show is so
demeaning that it does not deserve the protection normally accorded
to controversial debate. The content is especially demeaning to the
AJC and its constituency, of course. Others might find the racial slurs
naughty but not intolerable. Indeed, considering the debaters, some
harsh language should be expected. Yet the AJC might press its argument that when humans become the subject of racial hatred, speech
has passed into the purely destructive zone. One vital need of any
culture is survival, and racial hatred never serves that end. Certainly
the Judeo-Christian ethic of persons as ends plays a large role in AJC
strategy.

But nearly all other ethical foundations can be brought to bear
on the AJC's case as well. The golden mean might argue that vigorous
programming should avoid the extreme of inflammatory demagoguery,
especially the kind that our century has seen explode so violently and
brutally. Utility could claim that no one is served by bigotry, and that
the aims of groups like the Klan are so contrary to long-term benefits
for all that it has, by its own devices, forfeited all rights to the public
soapbox. The categorical imperative could never allow racism as a universal good, and the veil of ignorance would equalize the power of a
national network and the relative smallness of a religious-cultural protest group.

WNET's response to the AJC points to an underlying adversity
between media producers and public interest groups. The assumed
right of professionals to determine their own standards and set their
own agenda is an important and hard-won privilege. But all doctors
are accountable to other doctors; no surgeon cuts her own idiosyncratic
incision. In this case, it seems, the community of media professionals
has strongly questioned WHYY's wisdom, yet WHYY continues to
assert its "professional" independence. Perhaps with more time to
prove its case, WHYY could move its colleagues toward a negotiated

settlement, but the station can hardly claim that the AJC is encroaching. Public opinion is the business of everyone. The two parties should work toward mutually acceptable principles that would provide the groundwork for future cooperation.

78. A NEW GROUP OF LONG-STANDING MEMBERS DEMANDS RESPECT

The Gray Panthers' Media Watch asks volunteer television monitors to evaluate a program's "ageism." The following reproduces the Media Watch's criteria for evaluation:

Stereotypes

Any oversimplification or generalization of the characteristics and images of old age that demean or ridicule older people. Examples:

1. Appearance: Face always blank or expressionless; body always bent over and infirm.
2. Clothing: Men's baggy and unpressed; women's frumpy and ill fitting.
3. Speech: Halting and high pitched.
4. Personality: Stubborn, rigid, forgetful.
5. In comparison to others, are older people depicted as less capable? Do they have less to contribute? Are their ideas usually old-fashioned? Is the rocking chair image predominant?

Distortions

The use of myth or outright falsehoods to depict old age as either an idyllic or moribund stage of life. Examples:

1. Are old people depicted as intruders or meddlers in the relationships of others?
2. Are old people ridiculed when they show sexual feelings?
3. When there is an age difference in romantic relationships, are older women accorded the same respect as older men?
4. Are older people patronized and treated as children?

Omissions
The exclusion of avoidance of older people, of their life concerns, and of the positive aspects of aging. Examples:

1. Are the oppressive conditions under which older people must live in society analyzed? Are alternatives to existing conditions presented?
2. In any discussion of social and economic issues, are the perspectives of older people included?
3. Are older people directly involved in writing, directing, and producing the program?
4. How about the acting? Are there valid reasons for young actors to play the roles of older people?[17]

Comedian Johnny Carson has done a skit portraying a doddering old lady, Aunt Blabby. The semi-soap "Mary Hartman, Mary Hartman" featured a secondary character called the Fernwood Flasher, who took up the perversion in his elderly years. In a survey of 300 newspapers, feature stories were found to be "festooned with stereotypes about old age and analogies about youth." Older men were "spry," women were "tough."[18] Countless television dramas have portrayed post-65ers as soft-headed, dependent, impotent, decrepit, and sentimental. Whether in humor or in serious drama, the portrayals share a common flaw: ageism, or "discrimination on the basis of chronological age."

The Media Watch is determined, vocal, and not without success. A comedy segment performed by Carol Burnett portrayed the elderly as cranky, stubborn, crumbling human beings, according to the Gray Panthers. Their complaints eventually reached the ears of the National Association of Broadcasters, which recommended that age be handled with the same sensitivity accorded race, sex, and creed.

Professional codes notwithstanding, however, the elderly may be television's most stereotyped demographic group. A major study conducted by the Annenberg School of Communications at the University of Pennsylvania found that heavy television viewing

makes a consistently negative contribution to the public's image of the personal characteristics of the elderly, and the quality of their lives. We did not find watching television to be associated with *any* positive images of older people.

Heavy viewers believe that the elderly are unhealthy, in worse shape financially, not active sexually, closed-minded, not good at getting things done, and so on.[19]

The study concluded that these patterns of social stereotyping are the "creation of a system of broadcasting and of storytelling with deep historical, cultural, and commercial roots. This system allows very few degrees of freedom" in which producers and directors can work.

An earlier study found that characterizations of successful persons decrease with age, just as the number of personal failures on television increase with age. "Aging in prime-time drama is thus associated with increasing evil, failure, and unhappiness. In a world of generally positive and happy endings, only 40 percent of older males and even fewer female characters are seen as successful, happy, and good," the study claims.[20]

While the goals of the Gray Panthers may appear commendable and the findings of social scientists deplorable, not all television decision makers are enthusiastic about the implications of either. The concerns of the Panthers constitute a potential danger to free expression, some media people contend. A director for the Mary Tyler Moore company said about the problem of ageism on television: "I have heard a lot of complaints. I understand how these people feel. But I came away wondering if they aren't really after creative control. I'm not going to have any group tell me what I can do. I won't let any pressure group tell me how to be creative."[21]

Such responses are not unlike the sentiments of some free press advocates of the 1930s, a decade when pressure groups were particularly successful in influencing the content of popular entertainment. Newspaper editor Ralph Ingersoll said in 1941:

All pressure groups and special interests . . . are antagonistic to the whole truth and nothing but the truth. Quite legitimately, for their own purposes, but still hostile to the objectives of a really free press. . . . No pressure group regards itself as an enemy of truth . . . and I'm not thinking of greedy monopolists with paid lobbies in Washington, but of wholly respectable and sincere organizations such as labor unions, churches, *people over sixty*, of people who fought in the last war. Yet from the journalist's point of view they are all enemies, because they try to impose their orientation of the facts.[22]

Perhaps the Gray Panthers are too thin-skinned when they object to exaggerated depictions of the elderly on the Carson or Burnett shows. Humor lives on exaggeration of human foibles and exploitation of stereotypical behavior. If we cannot laugh at ourselves, are we taking ourselves too seriously? One possible answer: We do not violate the dignity of another person or group until we are unable to convince them that our depictions are innocent and without malice. When the butt of the joke can no longer be persuaded that the depiction is sympathetic, then we have cause to reexamine the message. Use of Rawls's principle in this case finally hinges on the importance of possible personal offense compared to the need for a free, unrestrained drama industry.

And perhaps the Gray Panthers' efforts are paying off. Who has more fun these days on prime-time television than the post-50 set in "Golden Girls"?

79. THE FATHER KNOWS BEST

Ralph McInerny is among the most prolific of modern philosophers, but not only in academia. As a hobby, mental exercise, and just for fun, he began writing fiction in 1964 and published his third novel, *Priest*, in 1973. The success of this novel prompted his agent to suggest that he develop a mystery series. Hence Father Roger Dowling entered the literary world.

Father Dowling works at a parish west of Chicago in Fox River, Illinois. But his parishioners and contacts are anything but laid-back hayseed types. Dowling is surrounded by thieves, murderers, conspirators, addicts, corrupted or jaundiced police, ambitious and greedy entrepreneurs, shady Mafia types, and clever attorneys—the stuff of mystery.

In such a setting, one might expect Father Dowling to be an Indiana Jones with a collar—placid in the classroom or church but irrepressible in the field. Instead, Dowling is a rather conservative churchman who worries about trendiness and the loss of piety in the modern world. His mode of solving a crime is to listen with the intensity of a Sherlock Holmes, act with the collegiality of a Barney Fife, and then let those who are not so clever take the credit for the case while he returns to ordinary parish tasks, the responsibilities of his calling.

The Father Dowling Mysteries sell about 10,000 copies each, many to libraries. They have a loyal following despite modest numbers. That loyalty was enough to attract the interest of NBC in 1988, when its Friday night prime time took the Dowling character (played by Tom Bosley) and gave it a life on the screen.

With some changes, of course.

"Roger" might be a nice name for a cowboy or a rabbit, but not for a detective priest. Frank fits better. And a lone priest today would be like a Ranger without Tonto of yesteryear. Add Sister Steve, a streetwise nun who, for all her feminist wisdom, still wears a habit. The Fox River setting is a tad dry, too. Put the good Reverend in Chicago, where he can find some action. Add one murder and one car chase per episode. The result, well. . . .

TV Guide offered a stern review of "Father Dowling" just before NBC called it quits. Merrill Panitt observed that the "long rubber arm of coincidence has never been stretched so far." Somewhere between the book version and the screen, executive producers Fred Silverman and Dean Hargrove "forgot to bless the stories, which follow a set pattern and create an impression of having been turned out by a computer."[23] McInerny himself does not watch television, but from reports he has heard, he wonders whether the TV Dowling reflects anything of the parish calling that characterizes his priest. The network had purchased the name of his gumshoe clergyman, but none of the TV stories followed any of the book plots.

Can television translate the nuances of a fully developed literary narrative in its 30- and 60-minute packages? Notable achievements by Hallmark aside, have prime-time serials or made-for-TV movies fared as well? The popular literary landscape seems riddled with writers who saw their narratives so radically altered by TV scripting that questions of integrity and credibility persisted despite the financial windfall. Joseph Wambaugh told one interviewer about his fight to keep "Police Story" honest:

They pay me a lot of money to use my name and be a consultant and all that business, but they're not listening to me.

I'm trying to tell them what a police show should be about, what police life is all about. And so far they are giving me cops-and-robbers stories. What I've gone through with television has been unreal. They brought me in to give them the first true-life television shows about police. Good drama, strong in plot, strong in character, adult shows. And I sit there . . . and they nod their heads and say "Yes, but there's the real world and then there's the real world of television. The folks like lots of shooting and chase scenes." And I keep telling them, that is not what I'm here for. But they can't really free themselves from that misconception yet, and I was terribly naive to think that they could.[24]

McInerny's dilemma was similar, yet for television more densely complex. Wambaugh's turf was the police department. He had worked on the Los Angeles force. His tape-recorded interviews which formed the basis of successful novels such as *The New Centurions* and *The Blue Knight* were stories of real people he knew. His own honor was at stake in the network version. But police drama was a natural for television. Cops and robbers (and worse) have been ducking TV bullets for years. How could television, with so much experience at it, trivialize a cop story?

Not so for McInerny. His character was not a Magnum P.I.-type. Father Dowdy might have been an appropriate name for this flatfoot. The Dowling persona is not a progressivist, activist, Father Berrigan clone. Rather, Dowling as written is religiously sensitive, sympathetic to tradition, mindful of the past, and reluctant—not unwilling—to accommodate cultural trends. He seems to want his people to experience peace of soul as much as restitution of righteousness and proper administration of justice. Can television provide nourishment to such a character?

Some church-based groups readily argue that television stereotyping is never more superficial than in its portrayal of religious life. Donald Wildmon's American Family Association includes that category along with violence, sex, and profanity in its watchdogging efforts. Yet Martin Marty of the University of Chicago issued public calls for more religion in prime time. Why? That dimension of life, he claims, has been radically exorcised from the screen.[25] A full picture of the harmony of life in any community or ethnic conclave needs the middle C of faith, hope, and love most frequently found in religious faith and institutions.

Given television's track record, Wambaugh had reason to worry about the metamorphosis of his characters, and McInerny had more reason still. Perhaps unwittingly, each surrendered some loyalty to their readers when they sold rights to TV networks. Perhaps McInerny should have written a tougher bargain and retained a share of control. Yet Wambaugh illustrates how difficult that can be even for a street-wise negotiator.

Finally the issue must revolve around the purpose of the creative material. If McInerny writes simply to sell books and build royalties, then the more lucrative the television contract, the better the deal. Among those who stress personal happiness, such a monetary approach to the creative arts could be justified provided no unnecessary harm is done to others. But McInerny does not situate his own goals in these terms, nor his sense of purpose as a writer. Indeed, we contend that writers owe primary loyalty to the art, the craft, the expression of human mind and spirit that generates our mythology and narrative. Fidelity to characterization, with all the nuances of behavior and belief that make Father Dowling a rare-breed crime fighter, become a necessary condition to the opening of new markets and media channels. Television purchased rights to the Dowling persona but used the last name and vocation only, essentially creating a new character. Fidelity to the craft, we contend, should suggest a completely new name as a more honest move by the small screen artists.

Good literary writers also need to become good readers of the fine print of television-rights contracts. Selling rights for reasonable profits should not become a game in which wealthy media companies determine our cultural and mythological agendas. There may indeed be room in our imaginations for a great new crime-fighter called "Wimpman," but must he wear an "S" on his chest and a cape on his back?

NOTES

1. For an excellent discussion on ethnic diversity, see the September 1988 issue of *Media & Values* (No. 43).
2. Louis Brandeis, with Samuel Warren, "The Right to Privacy," *Harvard Law Review* 4 (15 December 1890): 196.
3. Quotations taken from *Time*, 9 January 1989, pp. 57–59. Swislow's review was published in *Quill*, March 1989, p. 21.
4. *TV Guide*, 20 April 1985, p. 5.
5. Tom Shales reported on and reviewed "Baby M." His column appeared in the *DuPage Daily Journal*, 20 May 1988.
6. M. Scott Peck, *People of the Lie* (New York: Simon and Shuster, 1985).

7. *Quill*, March 1989, pp. 24–26.
8. John Simon, "From Fake Happyendings to Fake Unhappyendings," *New York Times Magazine*, 8 June 1975, pp. 17–19.
9. Quoted in *U.S. News and World Report*, 26 September 1977, p. 58.
10. Simon, "From Fake Happyendings," p. 35.
11. Tomás Martinez, "Gambling, Goods, and Game Shows," *Society*, September/October 1977, pp. 79–81.
12. Quoted in Les Brown, "7 PBS Stations Reject Klansman and Nazi Interview," *New York Times*, 1 October 1977, p. 48.
13. Walter Goodman, "How Should Public TV Handle the Inflammatory?" *New York Times*, 11 December 1977, sec. 2, p. 39; and Goodman's reply to a letter, *New York Times*, 25 December 1977, sec. 2, p. 35.
14. Quoted in Goodman, "How Should Public TV," sec. 2, p. 39; and in Brown, "7 PBS Stations," p. 48.
15. Quoted in Brown, "7 PBS Stations," p. 48.
16. Undated press release issued by the American Jewish Congress, headed: "New York's Public TV Station Won't Share Panel Discussion with Nazi, Ku Klux Klansman."
17. "Media Watch Criteria" was sent to the authors by Lydia Bragger, national media coordinator for the Gray Panthers.
18. Carole Rich, "Don't call them 'Spry'", *Quill*, February 1989, pp. 12–13.
19. George Gerbner, Larry Gross, Nancy Signorielli, and Michael Morgan, "Aging with Television: Images on Television Drama and Conceptions of Social Reality," *Journal of Communication* 30 (Winter 1980): 47.
20. Craig Aronoff, "Old Age in Prime Time," *Journal of Communication* 24 (Autumn 1974): 86.
21. Jay Sandrich, as quoted in "Nobody (in TV) Loves You When You're Old and Gray," *New York Times*, 24 July 1977, sec. 2, p. 21.
22. Ralph Ingersoll, "A Free Press—For What?" in *Freedom of the Press Today*, ed. Harold L. Ickes (New York: Vanguard Press, 1941), p. 142.
23. Merrill Panitt, "Father Dowling Mysteries," *TV Guide*, 1–7 April, 1989, p. 39. The production company for the Dowling mysteries, Viacom, succeeded in selling eleven new episodes to ABC after the NBC cancellation. Those episodes were aired in the first quarter of 1990. The future of the series is uncertain at this time. Ralph McInerny said in an interview with the authors that he is as distant from the ABC series as he was from the NBC one, and in fact only the network changed, not the storyline, cast, or conception.
24. Quoted in Steven V. Roberts, "Cop of the Year," *Esquire*, December 1973, p. 153.
25. Martin Marty, "We Need More Religion in Our Sit-coms," *TV Guide*, 24 December 1983, pp. 2–8.

CHAPTER 16

Censorship

"Censorship," one of the ugly words of the English language, speaks of the repression that democratic beliefs officially and inexorably condemn. It warns of the consequences of state tyranny, church tyranny, union tyranny, corporation tyranny—the strong hand of any institution silencing the dissenting voice. "Liberty," on the other hand, provokes cherished feelings that resonate with our deepest human longings—an elusive goal, perhaps, but eminently worth the sacrifice required for each step in its advance.

So by our ideals we set the stage for the great paradox of democratic theory: liberty can never be absolute, censorship can never be absent. Liberty requires constraints at every level—speech, sex, movement, health care, business, religious practice—in order for people to create an ordered society. That which we prize most must be taken in measured portions.

Few of our essential constraints partake of the spirit of Star Chamber repression in seventeenth-century England. The jailing and hanging of writers no longer occurs at the whim of the monarch. Yet many contemporary restrictions are nonetheless called censorship. One of our fundamental questions, then, is where to draw the lines—a question of ethics.

At the end of World War II, the Hutchins Commision on Freedom of the Press struggled over this question as they deliberated toward a theory of press freedom that would promote social responsibility as a new and important concept in media studies. All of the commission members were ardent democrats; some might even be called dreamy-eyed in their praise of democratic virtues. True liberals in the historic sense, they held free inquiry to be a paramount ideal. Yet they wrestled with the question of censorship. The chief philosopher of the commission, William Ernest Hocking of Harvard, captured the dilemma poignantly in an essay written as plans for the commission were being laid:

> Are . . . thoughts all equally worthy of protection? Are there no ideas unfit for expression, insane, obscene, destructive? Are all hypotheses on the same level, each one, however vile or silly, to be taken with the same mock reverence because some academic jackass brings it forth? Is non-censorship so great a virtue that it can denounce all censorship as lacking in human liberality?[1]

The cases in this section attempt to point out a few of the dimensions of those questions. The first case, "Skin at the Grocery Store," probes the role of agencies that assume guardianship over the morals of a large constituency, and hence indirectly over the public as a whole. The next case, *"Death Wish,"* asks if television poses ethical problems specific to that pervasive medium. The third case, *"Cruising,"* approaches the problem from the viewpoint of a countercultural programming.

The fourth case, *"High Times,"* ponders the difference between words and actions: do legal distinctions cloud the common moral claims? "The Cable Is Blue" (the fifth case) points to our greater technical ability to channel programs to specific markets. Assuming the consent of the buyer, should choices abound?

"The Artist Censors Himself," the sixth case, looks at the influence of ideology on free communication from a personal perspective. Finally, the last case, *"Show Me,"* moves the debate into the public library, a community institution whose honored name has only recently been challenged.

While the reader puzzles with us over these democratic conundrums, we may be encouraged in the knowledge that to do so—to read this book and think about these questions—is testimony that we are at least on the way to answers. In too many societies, the range of permissible media is tightly defined by a power elite. At least we can claim the advantage of a bias toward latitude: Censorship must be justified. In these cases we ask whether modern censors have demonstrated their case for building dikes against the flow.

80. SKIN AT THE GROCERY STORE

For Frank Hudock, Jr., manager at a suburban Chicago 7-Eleven
store, the magazines behind the counter meant $6,000 in monthly
sales revenue. Like most of the other 7-Eleven managers around
the country (Southland Corporation operates and franchises about
7,400 such stores), Hudock kept the adult magazines partially
covered and out of the hands of juveniles.

A block from Hudock's store on Main Street in Wheaton rests
the First Baptist Church. In the late summer of 1984 the pastors
and youth of the First Baptist Church began an action that created
a brief media storm and led to a new career for Hudock.

The issues were clear-cut. Southland Corporation's policy was
to carry three adult magazines (*Playboy, Penthouse,* and *Forum*)
and to keep them hidden until a customer inquired. Hudock carried 70 titles or so, some of them pornographic by any definition,
and sometimes the covers were visible. The church was doing
what moral guardians have done through the centuries: a little
moral suasion to keep smut out of the neighborhood. As pastor
David Murdock put it, "If we can't write laws to keep these things
off the shelves, at least we could boycott them. Each community
has a responsibility to itself."

The boycott began in October. Pastors Murdock and Steve
French had tried to persuade Hudock in person, without success.
Then teenagers from the church, carrying placards and marching
peaceably, let their opposition to lewd literature be known. Before
long the *Chicago Tribune* and *Chicago Sun-Times,* and television
journalist John Callaway, were reporting and examining the prospect of church boycotts threatening the free speech rights of publishers and the distribution rights of private businesses. A televised debate between French and the special counsel for Playboy
Enterprises was the highest forum the issue achieved. Southland
declined to be represented there.

By early December Frank Hudock had endured enough. The
girlie mags were going off the shelves and out of the store. "It's
like a ghost town," he said. "It's been very slow." A week later,
citing heavy losses, Hudock surrendered his store to the parent
corporation, which immediately returned the three best sellers
to the shelves. In a brief published statement entitled "Freedom
of Choice," Southland appealed to its "restrictive policy" for the

right to sell these publications: "We believe this policy is fair.
Every day 7 million customers have the freedom to choose what
they want at 7-Eleven."

This action by a Baptist church against magazines that cater to las-
civious interests is a drama played innumerable times in this God-
fearing land of pleasure seekers. Among media practitioners, such action is dismissed as reactionary, rural, and fairly inconsequential. But
leaders of this boycott were signalling what they perceived as their
right, as one institution against a commercial magazine publisher and
its local distributor, to determine what media their community would
accept and what it would deny. And not all such campaigns by moral
guardians have been so lackluster in winning their point.

Moral guardians have been wary of the motion picture industry
ever since John C. Rice administered a prolonged kiss to Mary Irwin
in 1896, a dramatic moment that gave the International Reform Bureau
initial steam. But the largely Protestant protest lacked central authority and failed to develop a comprehensive moral argument.

When the Catholic church stepped into a major guardianship role
in the 1930s, it suffered no such handicaps. Through the Legion of
Decency, the church mustered the most vigorous and populous protest
against cinema fare (and media fare in general) of this century. Catholic
thinking was at the foundation of the Motion Picture Production Code
of 1930 and much of the Hays Office's effort to enforce self-regulation
for the industry. For instance, a Catholic layperson was given charge
of the Production Code Administration, the industry's own script review and code enforcement bureau.

The Catholic apology for intervention in the nation's entertainment business was delivered most cogently by a Jesuit priest in *Catholic Viewpoint on Censorship*. Harold C. Gardiner placed the Legion's
guardianship role in the context of Catholic political philosophy which
viewed the state as a natural (meaning God-ordained) institution and
therefore to be respected. Yet custom and tradition are also important
social forces and these are the domain of the many groups that comprise the larger nation. While law serves as a final arbiter in civil disputes, the first court of appeal is the informal constraint of group customs and values. This primary arbitrating and civilizing force needs
protection.

Given Gardiner's portrait of the state, individual freedom can never be merely doing as one pleases. True freedom is freedom to act as one ought: "The fundamental 'oughtness' under which a man can alone act with full freedom is . . . an 'oughtness' that is handed to man by the faculty of his reason." The Legion, argued Gardiner, is not a censoring agency able to coerce behavior, but a guide to the reasoned "formation of public opinion, and whatever suppression of material (films or books) follows as a result of the formed opinion is secondary and accidental to their main purpose." Here is a kind of control, but in the open marketplace apart from legal constraints and dependent on the support of a significant public. Any attempt to suppress the Legion "is an attempt to shut off the channels of free opinion and debate that make for a socially, intellectually, and morally stronger America."[2]

Catholics may censor a film, but no one is required to join the church. First Baptist Church may urge a boycott, but even its members can disagree with the demonstrators and cross the line of placards to buy a loaf of bread. The voluntary nature of these guardian agencies allows for much individual discretion.

Though no champion of the church, C. Wright Mills laments the modern trend toward mass society and finds the decline of the "voluntary association as a genuine instrument of the public" to be one of the most important structural causes of the trend. Modern power, he writes, is in the hands of the "the huge corporation, the inaccessible government, the grim military establishment." Between these institutions (which contradict notions of traditional democratic pluralism by their bureaucratic control over formerly active "publics") and the primary institutions of family and community, there are no "intermediate associations" for the coalescence of socially responsible public opinion. Mass media have "helped less to enlarge and animate the discussions of primary publics than to transform them into a set of media markets in mass-like society."[3]

Doubtless Mills would have taken serious issue with many of the guardians' position. Nevertheless, his concern for the recovery of community-level publics able to speak powerfully to their political and social milieu raises the right questions. When churches and PTAs and nearly every parent in Chicago began to fume over TV ads for a new film featuring a killer dressed as Santa, the networks courteously pulled their ads while theaters quickly changed their bookings. Who could complain?

In the end, Southland bit the bullet. In April 1986, corporation president Jere W. Thompson said his company would respond to "growing public awareness and concern over a possible connection between adult magazines and crime, violence, and child abuse" by pulling from all company-owned stores the three disputed magazines. But a speaker for Southland was quick to note that protests from antipornography groups "did not enter into our decision."[4]

81. DEATH WISH AND TELEVISION VIOLENCE

A telex message was sent to ail CBS affiliates:

> WE HAVE JUST VIEWED THE EDITED VERSION OF DEATH WISH AND BELIEVE THAT ITS THEME OF VIGILANTE REVENGE, TOGETHER WITH THE SCENES OF BRUTALITY AND VIOLENCE, IS AN INCITEMENT TO INHUMAN BEHAVIOR AND SOCIAL TERRORISM. EACH CBS AFFILIATE HAS THE LEGAL AND MORAL OBLIGATION TO DETERMINE WHETHER THIS FILM SHOULD BE BROADCAST INTO THE LIVING ROOMS OF ITS SERVICE AREA. WE BELIEVE IT SHOULD NOT. HOPE YOU AGREE AND WILL DRAW THE LINE HERE.

REV. PATRICK J. SULLIVAN, S.J.   REV. WILLIAM F. FORE
DEPARTMENT OF   COMMUNICATION COMMISSION
    COMMUNICATION   NATIONAL COUNCIL OF
U.S. CATHOLIC CONFERENCE   CHURCHES (NCC)
    (USCC)   475 RIVERSIDE DRIVE, N.Y., N.Y.
1011 FIRST AVE., N.Y., N.Y.

In a joint statement issued the same day as the telex message, the agencies explained their mutual action:

> *Death Wish* is a blatant and cynical example of television's constantly escalating lesson to young and old that violence is the acceptable solution to most problems: a view we reject. We reject it as Christians and as citizens of a nation that is struggling to maintain its principles of democracy and the value of the individual in a world that increasingly violates those principles.
>
> We believe that a decision on the part of the CBS network and its affiliates to broadcast the film *Death Wish* is immoral. In addition to the many moments of brutality and violence, the greatest problem is that the theme of the film teaches violence: the solution to brutality is even

more brutality and the taking of the law into one's own
hands. This theme is socially irresponsible, and when it
is portrayed in an exciting way as a model for others to
follow, and then is made available to virtually every home
in America, it becomes an incitement to the worst kind
of inhuman behavior and social terrorism.

We do not question the right of the CBS network and
local stations to decide to broadcast *Death Wish*. We do
question the morality and the social responsibility of the
decision. We have asked CBS not to show the film. We
commend those stations which already have refused to
carry it, and we encourage others to join them.

In the 1960s, Catholics abandoned the effort to censor or boycott films,
opting instead for a strategy of film education and, at the same time,
expanding considerably the tolerance limits for approving a film. The
change in tactics was not a full-scale surrender in the battle for morality in media. Neither Protestants nor Catholics were suggesting that
dehumanizing, gratuitous sex and violence were now acceptable cinematic themes; rather, they were insisting that the proper and only
place to register protest against cultural products in a free society was
at the box office: Individuals should not pay to view bad movies.

Then came the problem of morally objectionable motion pictures
appearing on television. The theater is one thing—away from home,
an admission price to discourage the indifferent, a ratings system to
provide some warning of potential problems. But television is that
lackadaisical box in the center of the home, available to children and
adults for nothing more than a flick of a switch. Apparently this difference prompted the National Council of Churches and the U.S. Catholic Conference to act.

Few stations acknowledged receipt of the telex communiqué.
Four stations had already decided not to take the feed, but none can-
celed *Death Wish* because of the NCC/USCC request. William Fore
explained that the "main value of protest was to call attention to the
public that television was moving into ever-increasing violence."[5]

Guardian agencies are not fussing over media fare to broaden their
profit margin. Rather, they seem to be motivated by something akin
to Rawls's principle that finds justice done by decisions made in the
best interests of (or at least acceptable to) the politically weakest par-

ticipant. In the producer-distributor-sponsor-viewer matrix, the weakest link (in terms of determining which shows are aired) is the viewer. While some might argue that viewers are ultimately in control, we ask whether minority values must always suffer the preeminence of market-researched majority tastes. What if decisions about television programming were made in a room where negotiators shared equal voting power and did not know which of the four principal roles (producer, distributor, sponsor, viewer) they would assume upon leaving the room. Around such a table, delivering markets to advertisers might be less important than in our current commercial system. Protecting the right of the distributor to make a free decision would still be vital, but responsiveness to community values might increase without tipping TV into blandness and naiveté.

82. CRUISING FOR SURVIVAL

During the summer of 1979, film director William Friedkin brought a crew to Manhattan's gay district to do location shots for a film depicting the sadomasochistic leather fringe of the homosexual subculture. Entitled *Cruising*, the film starred Al Pacino as an undercover detective out to find a sadistic killer. While investigating, Pacino's character becomes confused about his own sexual identity and finally, maybe, commits a murder in the same bloody mode used by the man he stalked. Scenes from the film show torture, mutilated genitals, men urinating on other men as a kind of erotic exercise, and several murders of gays by gays.

Soon after Friedkin arrived in New York, *Village Voice* writer Arthur Bell obtained a copy of the screenplay and reacted with a column that urged gays to stop the filming at once by whatever means necessary. The film, claimed Bell, was dangerous to the homosexual community: It would inspire brutality from oppressive straights; it would legitimize violence against gays.

Homosexuals in New York took the warning. Several hundred conducted nightly protest marches, often where film crews were working. Gay bars that had contracted with Friedkin to be used for location shots were damaged; many cancelled their contracts. Friedkin and his staff were targets of cans, bottles, and Gay Rights Task Force pressure.[6]

This pressure began on July 25 when representatives of the National Gay Rights Task Force (NGRTF) asked New York's Mayor

Edward I. Koch to withdraw Friedkin's film permit. Ethan Geto, a spokesperson for the NGRTF, insisted that his group was not advocating censorship, only that "the mayor respond to a large segment of his constituency and withdraw the support of the city."[7]

On July 26 Mayor Koch rejected the demand for a license cancellation. "To do otherwise would involve censorship," Koch explained. "It is the business of this city's administration to encourage the return of film making to New York City by cooperating to whatever extent feasible with film makers. . . . Whether it is a group that seeks to make the gay life exciting or to make it negative, it's not our job to look into that, and we are not going to do it."[8] Koch's statement drew a thousand demonstrators into Greenwich Village, blocking traffic on the Avenue of the Americas. Police arrested two people.

Charges and countercharges came from the filmmakers, the gays, and the press. Geto likened the film to the Ku Klux Klan "making a movie about the black community on 125th Street in Harlem." Film producer Jerry Weintraub argued that *Cruising* was a true depiction: "what is really there."[9] The *New York Times* editorialized on July 28: "We understand the fears of the demonstrators but think they erred in seeking any official discrimination against the film. Anyone has the right to try to embarrass or boycott another's speech. But to enlist government in the protest invites unacceptable censorship. Those who are often denied their rights by official action ought to appreciate that better than most."[10]

On August 6, after a week of loud protest to "raise the consciousness" of Friedkin and Weintraub, the Gay Task Force withdrew its demand that the city revoke the film license. The demand, they admitted, smacked of censorship.

However, street demonstrations kept the matter of self-censorship alive. On August 20 nearly one hundred police were called out to restrain the demonstrators after Weintraub was hit by a bottle. Pickets followed the film crew to most of their 80 locations throughout the city, using whistles and noisemakers to try to disrupt filming. Efforts to establish dialogue between the two sides repeatedly failed, each claiming that the other was simply out to parade its self-interested position.

General Cinema Corporation cancelled 33 bookings, claiming that the film should have been rated "X." After location shooting was finished, Friedkin stated: "I don't make a film because I'm against something. For that matter, I don't make a film because I'm for something—I don't make propaganda. If anything, all the films I've made are enormously ambiguous."[11] The Gay Task Force responded to Friedkin's disclaimers in a letter to the *Times*: Demonstrators, much more peaceful than if blacks or Jews had been the subject of a bigoted film, hope they have shown the need "for our inclusion in the system of industry self-censorship that is now applied to all other minorities."[12] The public was fascinated. *Cruising* led *Variety*'s list of top-grossing films for six weeks.

In the two previous cases, "Skin" and "*Death Wish*," traditional and broadly accepted pressure groups had sought, unsuccessfully, to stem what they considered detrimental magazine and film fare. For *Cruising*, however, the group was a minority based on broadly disputed sexual preferences.

Nevertheless, it was a group, not a lone crusader, which saw in the movie the potential for harmful effects. And the effects it foresaw were ones involving actual physical harm, not merely psychological or moral perturbation. The Gay Task Force considered *Cruising* a direct physical threat. In retrospect, we might regard those perceptions as overly reactive, but a group responding to a crisis cannot be held accountable to every even-minded rationalization that, from our own vantage point, seems the wiser path of action. (As it happened, of course, cooler heads in the Task Force eventually prevailed and the demonstrations subsided.)

The ethicist's task is to evaluate the moral claims advanced by the Task Force (which held the welfare of its public uppermost), the mayor of New York (who must make political decisions based on the interests of the city as a whole), and the filmmakers (who feel responsible for creative and artistic integrity).

The Task Force can hardly object to the film merely because it exposes the distasteful, violent side of one of its fringe subcultures. Initially, the gay community felt that Friedkin was creating a sensationalized version of truth, but eventually these objections were waived. Indeed, a public examination of any culture—whether the deviant brutishness of sadomasochism or the redemptive idealism of Boys Town—is fair game for the movie industry. Dramatization of cultures should be true to the spirit of the group under examination, and if the film is critical, the criticism should be fair, not based on wild exaggerations or naive stereotypes. In the case of *Cruising*, the jury was divided. *Time* argued that the film genuinely reflected the violence of homosexual homocide.[13] *New Yorker* film critic Robert Angel called *Cruising* a "slovenly, bruising sort of movie. . . . It scares us in a dishonest way."[14]

New York's mayor seemed to base his argument on the utilitarian principle. A healthy city budget serves the interests of all the people, and film licenses contribute to that end. The moral content of the film is not the city's concern. While the prospect of a city official censoring a filmmaker's work is ominous and unacceptable, neither can the mayor's confusion of means and ends stand up to ethical scrutiny. A healthy city budget is indeed laudable, but not at the expense of common decency. For example, a city would be condemned for importing and selling slaves in order to raise revenue. Slavery is understood to be a demeaning, inhumane condition, and no amount of benefit justifies slavery today. Sadomasochism per se, though it involves supposedly consenting adults, partakes of the same kind of moral condemnation and should not be a means of public revenue-making. Can films about S-M barbarity claim immunity from the same moral charges?

A case similar in issue, if not in setting, arose when director Peter Weir took a movie production crew to Lancaster County, Pennsylvania, to shoot the murder mystery *Witness*. In the film, Philadelphia detective John Book (Harrison Ford) seeks refuge on an Amish farm and falls in love with a young widow (Kelly McGillis). The Pennsylvania Bureau of Motion Pictures has been among the nation's most aggressive promotional units, and their success in attracting Weir and Paramount was the result of hard work and effort. But the Amish were not happy. Their problem was not the likelihood of minor misrepresentations or even the prospect of increased tourism disturbing their lifestyle. Their complaints were fundamental to a world view that regards mediated reality an objectification of culture that leads to alienation. Drama is wrong, their bishops argued, because it obscures appearance and reality; it deceives. Violence is also wrong, and to watch dramatic violence is irrational. They also resented the intrusion of Paramount on fairness grounds. "We have done nothing against these people (Paramount). How would they like for us to come and invade their privacy and expose their way of living to the whole world?"[15]

The filmmaker's concern for integrity and freedom is a social value that needs jealous guarding. Artistic freedom has been a long time in coming, and its legal status today is reasonably secure. Its moral status is more difficult to evaluate, simply because it enjoys legal sanction. Friedkin's arguments focus on the purpose of art. At a minimum, one could argue that the purpose of art is to explore the meaning of humanness, its qualities and ambiguities, in such a way as to move the quest for meaning toward an ethically justifiable goal. This restriction excludes art for the sake of exploiting an audience; it even argues against art for the sole end of profit making. Friedkin and others may quarrel with the "in such a way" clause, but an ethicist would insist that all creative effort is goal directed. Friedkin should make his true goals a part of his defense.

83. HIGH TIMES *MAGAZINE AND* DRUG MARKET *INFORMATION*
The promotional blurb read:

> 7,000,000,000 JOINTS! Yes, it has been estimated by the government that over 7 billion joints will be rolled in the United States this year. That's the equivalent of thirty joints for every man, woman, and child in the country. Of course, there are lots of highs, legal, semilegal, and illegal. Everything from herbs to meditation, and laughing gas to mushrooms.
> *High Times* is written for that High Society.
> With its authoritative columns, timely news and reviews, fascinating features, and beautiful appearance, *High Times* is a magazine that people read, take seriously, show their friends, and keep around a long, long time.

High Times is one of those magazines that goes under the rubric "underground press." Despite the label, it has a slick, aboveground appearance, evidence that a lot of people are buying. Articles range from the kinky Christmas wishes of the late Truman Capote to life histories of the gurus of punk rock and pot. A regular feature gives market quotations on drugs from Madrid, Melbourne, Moscow, and other worldwide trading posts. Printed on every two-page market spread: "The TransHigh Market Quotations are intended solely for comparative purposes and in no way are meant as an inducement to illegal activity, nor as an endorsement of any drug usage or trafficking."

Ads are mostly for paraphernalia, but occasionally even these take an exotic turn. A full-color page shows the handles of two umbrellas, with the caption: "Better Smoked Than Soaked. Nosy narcs will change their minds, if they have any left, after they sustain a cranial impact equal to eight g's from the flexible metal blackjack on this hand-carved wooden handle. Only $150."[16]

A parent from a Chicago suburb wrote about *High Times* to a *Chicago Tribune* columnist:

> We tell our children that drugs are dangerous, and this magazine tells them how to grow them. How can drugs be illegal and yet a magazine like this be sold? Is there no limit to freedom of the press? It's strange that this junk is protected by the courts, but when we try to raise our children to be good and decent, and they wind up in court, then it's the parents' fault. We need help.[17]

In response, the columnist spoke with the chairperson of the department of psychiatry at a Chicago medical school. The doctor commented: "All kinds of people market the youth culture. There is a natural experimenting with what you can do with your body, and if they want to feel goofy, they can feel goofy. You'll never be able to control your child."[18]

If the psychiatrist is right, we should give up and return to the caves. His comment, of course, hinges on the meaning of "control." We agree that parents (or surrogate parents) cannot *determine* the behavior or value system of children, but enlightened guidance is something different. Upon the possibility of careful direction rests, in fact, the whole point of ethical analysis: Reasonable beings can know the good, and knowing, should follow it. So to swallow the psychiatrist's advice is to opt for the "terrain of anarchy" which was called an unacceptable extreme at the outset of this chapter.

The problem of *High Times* is the difficulty of cultural inconsistency. What the society declares to be illegal in deed is not illegal in print. Words are protected and free; behavior is constrained. It is a rare problem, given humankind's history of intolerance, and perhaps it is a problem that could only occur in a literate culture where the stream of oral delivery is mollified by the passivity of print.

The same arguments opposing *High Times* would also militate against *Soldier of Fortune, Eagle, Gung-Ho,* and *New Breed.* How can civilized people live in peace with armed mercenaries running about eager to bring the Rambo character to life? For that matter, if everyone were suddenly to regard *TV Guide* as a *summa theologica,* devoting every waking hour to television viewing, civilization truly would recede to the Dark Ages.

The golden mean, a consensus-seeking principle, suggests the existence of extremes. At the moral frontier of any free culture will be advocates whose ideas, if widely accepted, would subvert moral order. The mean's strength is in its persuasive appeal to rational control, not in elimination of the extremes themselves. In this case, rational control rightly begins with family units and progressively relaxes as it proceeds through larger social institutions.

84. The Cable Is Blue

Academy Cablevision (pseudonym) began service in a midwestern city of a half million in the mid-1970s. A year later they began to offer "Telecinema." For a monthly fee of three dollars customers could get a converter box with a key enabling them to pick up four extra channels: one a children's channel, two offering neighborhood cinematic fare, and Channel F, described by Academy's program director as their "R-rated service."

"It was pretty soft stuff," said Debra MacDonald, who reviews and purchases movies for Channel F. "Nudity and innuendos, nothing more. Our policy was to show no graphic or oral sex, no penetration, and no male frontal nudity or erections. Those were the guidelines our lawyers advised, and the city's police vice squad went along with it. Sure, they monitored us. And if the vice officers didn't like a movie, we pulled it." That happened only once, said MacDonald.[19] A movie called *Cartoon* featuring animated characters and explicit sexual material drew a phone call from the vice squad after it had been on the wire for three days. Academy dropped the movie without protest.

"Our typical titles were things like *Campus Playmates* and *Swinging Playmates,* the stuff you might see at a drive-in. We definitely stayed away from the movies shown in art theaters, although several of our customers actually wanted more males and more explicit sex. I remember a letter from a 65-year-old woman who said that she and her husband enjoyed the adult movies, but they would like to see more male frontal nudity. So we had all kinds of people watching, but many of them wouldn't have been caught dead walking into an adult movie house," said MacDonald.

Because Telecinema used a converter box with a key, parents could control family viewing. Children could not inadvertently (or purposefully) tune in adult movies. But the main reason for the box and key was not protection of children, said MacDonald. It was the protection of the customer's monthly bill. "Our subscribers didn't want a babysitter coming over and rolling up a twenty dollar bill on Telecinema," she explained. If a parent really wanted to protect the children, they had the option of getting a filter on the box that would eliminate Channel F altogether. But no one ever requested that, said MacDonald.

Academy stirred up a little community reaction when Telecinema was first offered, but according to Debra it was positive, not critical. Even when the city became troubled about a local skin magazine, there was no spillover of antiporn sentiment to Academy.

Unfortunately for Academy's owners, the lack of community reaction showed up on the company's ledger, and Telecinema was dropped after five years on the wire. "We were losing money on that part of our operation," said Debra, "though Channel F accounted for about 50 percent of our Telecinema income. Our two [cable television] competitors in this area still offer blue movies, but they don't like to talk about it. One of them is trying to get franchises in the South where skin flicks would not be accepted.

"We don't talk about it a lot, either. It was part of our service for a while. When we cancelled, some people complained. We still get letters asking when the service will resume. And we might do it again under a one-time monthly charge system. Under the pay-as-you-watch system, we had people spending $100 to $200 a month on Channel F, but not enough of them to make it go."

An ethicist might initially ask whether the viewing of such programs by informed adults constitutes a genuine dilemma at all. If the blue channel is properly controlled and the viewer sufficiently informed, there should be no unconsenting viewers.

Control and information become two key elements in the ethicist's approach to the question. Unlike a movie house, cable television has no brightly colored marquees alerting every passerby to the promiscuity of the product. But cable is more intrusive than a movie theater, more accessible, less ritualistic; watching cable requires less of a commitment from its viewers than going to a theater. Control of the product so only those who want it get it (and then after certain other minimal conditions such as age or parental supervision are met) is satisfied here.

An ethicist might also argue that a cable company issue a specific policy regarding its blue channel. How blue is blue? A stated policy would alert viewers to the product, permitting many to use other entertainments, and would allow some the freedom of informed choice.

No ethical framework except hedonism would advocate that the values portrayed in the skin flicks become the social norm. And hedonism, because it focuses on greed and denies the individual's responsibility to the social whole, is not a moral option. Under any moral framework, control and information become minimum conditions for blues on the air.

While a viewer's personal ethics may argue rigorously against sexual brutishness, imposing a sex ethic on the public raises other concerns. Our society permits prostitution and gambling—business ventures that make no claim to moral foundations. These we regulate, recognizing that to permit them the same freedom of enterprise we give to ice cream shops would be to expose ourselves to dangerous and destructive impulses. If we cordon off a red-light district, can we not by the same logic give moral sanction to blue movies on the tube, assuming there is sufficient control and information to protect the unsuspecting viewer?

Perhaps the greatest good for the greatest number is a principle that would allow us this option. If viewers are consenting and informed adults, and if nonviewers are not being intimidated, let the buyer beware. The golden mean might also justify a blue movie, after safeguards are observed. Some might argue that scintillating R-movies are a reasonable compromise between the truly obscene and the altogether sexless.

The television is less adept, perhaps even negligent, at developing sexually mature drama that respects the persons-as-ends principle.

Here is where the ultimate test is rendered. Movies without a responsible sex ethic may pose little public menace, but the viewer is the loser; the one who feeds an appetite for brutality is the tragic victim. The persons-as-ends principle, or "do unto others," assumes that the self also be well cared for. The principle cannot condone self-injury, even if the self wills it and no one other than the self is intimidated.

85. THE ARTIST CENSORS HIMSELF

Eric Hurlbert, a respected playwright from Western Europe and a recognized voice of the New Left, was a student of countries that had undergone popular revolutions. His own intuition was that social change happens only through forceful confrontation, and that populist movements carry the greatest likelihood of translating confrontation into real social gains. Cuba held special interest for him, for here was a revolutionary movement in the backyard of a powerful ideological and economic adversary. How had the revolutionary movement changed the landscape and lifestyle of Cuba? Hurlbert determined to find out.

His trip through Cuba was intense. For three months he visited local leaders, ate with common people, worked alongside farmers and laborers, and visited every conceivable cultural setting Cuba had to offer, from Havana saloons to back-country folk festivals. Eric did not conduct any public seminars or give public lectures while in Cuba. He had made no commitments to editors or producers for material following his trip. He was not financed by any interested party. He had gone to learn, not to further an international career.

All this was fortunate from Eric's viewpoint, for the trip revealed much that he had not anticipated. In a word, he had become disillusioned. The agrarian reforms had not raised farmers' living standards; no vital intellectual movement undergirded the people's crusade; tradition and culture had suffered under the standardizing influence of bureaucracy and a weak national economy. Eric had found the country poor and the people lethargic, their government riddled with patronage and impervious to citizens' needs. Regrettably, Eric could see little difference between present-day Cuba and life there before the revolution except that military uniforms were simpler and the political rhetoric was of a different ideological hue.

When Eric's trip was over, he struggled for weeks about how, or even whether, to give literary expression to his impressions and feelings. As a serious writer, he felt obligated to tell an honest story—not to gloss over the revolution's imperfections. At the same time, he was identified with and emotionally committed to the ideology behind the Cuban regime. How would an honest dramatic description be interpreted?

After much soul-searching, Eric decided not to write his play or any other piece for publication. His reason: Such a piece could be used polemically by the Right.

In this case, we presume that no official coloration of the facts distorted Eric's literary judgment, that he had succeeded in exploring Cuban society as it is lived by the natives, and that Eric was indebted to no party for favorable results. The pressure to censor his creativity was internal—a felt pressure not to speak lest his words be distorted or misused.

Hurlbert's motives were internal, yet he cannot be automatically cleared of moral blame. Consider the point raised by Archibald MacLeish, a prolific writer who was never accused of pulling punches: "No writer worthy of the name ever refused to make his position clear for fear that position might be of service to others than himself. The further truth is that the man who refuses to defend his convictions for fear he may defend them in the wrong company has no convictions."[20] Writer André Gide has likewise been criticized for his decision to stay mute about abuses he had observed in the Soviet Union. A strong, public stand by a respected man of letters could have influenced public opinion, and might even have saved lives.

On the other hand, Hurlbert reckoned that a creator of literary or visual art has the liberty to decide whether or not to create. One can hardly be faulted for a personal decision to not produce. Judgment can be rendered only on what exists, not on images and intuitions still in the creator's mind. Partly on this basis, Hurlbert had decided to lay aside his pen.

The question could easily be situated at most every level of media work—writer, editor, producer, cinematographer. Is ideological commitment a sufficient reason to withhold a work of art that might add perspective and depth to the human pursuit of meaning and value? Is the possibility of distortion by one's ideological opponents sufficient cause for censoring entertainment material?

Hurlbert's struggle was with his own conscience. His actions had direct influence only on his own creative work. As in the case of Gide, Hurlbert's writing might have aided some people, and if it was within his power to provide aid, he would have been obliged to do so. But in this case he had no constituents pleading for his writing, no innocent victims begging that their untold suffering get a hearing. We cannot presume that Hurlbert could identify any specific persons or groups who would suffer loss for his silence. He did not snatch bread from starving children by his decision to not write.

Since no one was directly injured by Hurlbert's decision, no moral blame is involved. But we might accuse Hurlbert of failure of nerve; we might insist that he get out of the writing business if he can no longer "tell it like it is." Certainly his subsequent writings, whatever they might be, will be less powerful if the public discovers the reasons for his silence on Cuba. Hurlbert has traded away some of his independence and some of his critical edge by sparing his ideological colleagues an incisive public exposure. As a creative writer, Hurlbert will have to be on guard that his writings do not degenerate into mere propaganda. Hurlbert himself could not ethically wish that all writers with an ideology become publicists, for that would result in just the sort of deconscientization which has frustrated him about the so-called free world.

86. SHOW ME AND PRESSURES ON LIBRARIES

Folks in Oak Lawn, a south Chicago suburb, were incensed. The book *Show Me* was now available in the local public libraries and, worse, it was being read by teenagers.

Show Me is a picture book. Full-page photos of teenagers in various sexual acts—masturbation, oral sex, and so forth—are used to teach reproduction and anatomy. Younger models are shown exploring each other's genitals. Photos of erections and insertions teach the joys of sexual exploration. A commentary by Dr. Helga Fleischhauer-Hardt explains that parents should use the book with children as part of the process of teaching kids about their sexuality. "In no way can looking at the pictures damage a child, even if he or she does not yet understand them," she writes.

According to protesting parents, the actual use being made of the book by its mostly younger readers had little to do with academic physiology. Children were observed giggling over its contents, perhaps enjoying a salacious moment not intended by the author. Indeed, when librarian James O'Brien responded to the first wave of protests, he discovered that both copies were "absent from the library without benefit of check-out."

But the books' disappearance did not quiet the protest. State Representative Jane Barnes joined a group of concerned residents who claimed *Show Me* was obscene and pornographic. O'Brien was ordered by the Village Library Board to investigate the allegations.

During the weeks that followed, the media turned out for board meetings as never before. So did townspeople. Security guards and the fire marshall got involved in crowd control, and a referendum to increase the library's tax base was soundly defeated.

Finally the Oak Lawn Library agreed to place *Show Me* in the office of the children's librarian and to lend it only to adults and parents. Nonetheless, Representative Barnes pushed a bill through an Illinois House Committee that would have held librarians liable for criminal prosecution under obscenity laws, while State Senator Jeremiah Joyce did the same in the Senate. Neither bill passed.[21]

Response from professional librarians and others concerned about censorship was understandably strong. Judith Krug, executive director of the American Library Association's Office of Intellectual Freedom, claimed that the bill would have a "chilling effect" on librarians' rights.[22] The *Chicago Sun-Times* called Joyce's efforts a "stupid bill . . . insidious. . . . It lets book-banners bare their fangs and it could intimidate librarians and library boards into censoring good literature."[23]

The issues surrounding book censorship have a long and complicated history. The liberal reaction in seventeenth-century England was against book censorship primarily. Limiting the reproduction and distribution of heretical books was, long before that, the domain of established religious bodies. Many contemporary political regimes exercise a censorship over books that is as vicious and complete as the most tightly controlled monastery ever was. So the battle still rages between an unrestrained freedom of expression, full-fledged censorship, and a middle ground wherein freedom is given wide berth but restricted for reasons that appear to be in a community's public interest.

Pragmatists would ask about the value of Fleischhauer-Hardt's thesis, but psychological literature does not support it. A national survey conducted by the Family Research Council showed higher teenage pregnancy rates among those who participated in programs at family-planning clinics, linking information with unwanted pregnancies. In a study on AIDS-related information programs, researchers found that use of condoms by teens actually diminished after exposure to information. Of the teens who did change behavior, only one in five altered behavior in effective ways. Summarizing several tests of the efficacy of sex education, researchers reported in *American Psychologist* that neither positive nor negative effects, such as measurable behavioral change, have been demonstrated.[24] Should controls on sex information therefore be stronger, lighter, or unchanged?

When professional librarians are asked for an opinion, the debate often turns acrimonious. Feelings are strong and accusations are not always helpful in moving toward principled answers. An article in the *Library Journal*, for example, uses *ad hominem* tactics to explain the rationale of those who would keep certain books from general circulation. The article suggests that a censor is a person with "some suppressed impulses which he often wishes others to suppress also."[25] Modern-day censors keep alive the spirit of Puritan New England, with its oppressive tangle of dark, subliminal, masochistic drives, the writer states.

The American Library Association (ALA) has been extremely cautious over the influence of groups like Citizens United for Responsible Education and the National Congress for Academic Excellence. The ALA has characterized such public interest groups as right-wing do-gooders who seek to encroach on the librarians' professional domain. Said the ALA: "The crucial point is that these educational pressure groups, like other right-of-center pressure groups, view 'the others'—be they professional educators, students, women—as unable to reason, unable to choose from the bewildering array of often contradictory material on a given issue. They seem to see themselves as the guardians and proponents of the correct idea."[26]

The pressure groups hold that professionals have imported liberal values not indigenous to the communities they serve. To return control of educational and library facilities to parents and communities seems to them a reasonable demand, however threatening it may be to the outside professional.

A socially responsible public library system cannot be oblivious to the tastes and sensitivities of its community of patrons. To claim that professional privilege or expertise should dominate library policy decisions is to circumvent Rawls's rule that justice is approached only in negotiations that have excluded the social differences factor. That principle might be implemented by asking a third party to negotiate between competing value groups. Such third parties could well be professional persons such as teachers, social workers, clergy, or librarians themselves. Third-party groups might be more successful in finding ways to offer reading material that challenges traditional ideas without subverting deeply held values.

Certainly books on sexual practice for adults are considered legitimate for most community libraries. However, youngsters receiving first training in the meaning of sexuality need to inherit values that many parents still make it their goal to provide. Public libraries should not write their mission so broadly as to compete against the value systems of families in this delicate matter. *Show Me* is such a book. It cannot provide the moral framework for sexual instruction that a family can. The book, like sex itself, should not be a matter of idle and superficial curiosity, available to any youngster who knows of its presence. The persons-as-ends principle is not upheld when the sexual imagination turns exploitative, and no reasonable person could wish that all youngsters (the Kantian imperative) imitate the apparent freedom of the models used in *Show Me*.

NOTES

1. William Ernest Hocking, "The Meaning of Liberalism: An Essay in Definition," in *Liberal Theology: An Appraisal*, ed. David E. Roberts and Henry P. Van Dusen (New York: Charles Scribner's Sons, 1942), pp. 54–55.
2. Harold C. Gardiner, *Catholic Viewpoint in Censorship* (New York: Hanover House, 1958), pp. 106–107.
3. C. Wright Mills, *The Power Elite* (New York: Oxford University Press, 1956; Galaxy Books, 1959), pp. 306–311.
4. Quoted in *Chicago Tribune*, 11 April 1986, sec. 3, pp. 1, 4.
5. William Fore, personal letter, 10 July 1980.
6. "Protesters Call the Film 'Cruising' Antihomosexual," *New York Times*, 26 July 1979, p. B7.

7. Quoted in Les Ledbetter, "1000 in 'Village' Renew Protest Against Movie on Homosexuals," *New York Times*, 27 July 1979, p. B2.
8. Ibid.
9. Quoted in "Protestors Call the Film 'Cruising' Antihomosexual," p. B7.
10. "Between Expression and Suppression," *New York Times*, 28 July 1979, p. 16.
11. Quoted in Janet Maslin, "Friedkin Defends His "Cruising," *New York Times*, 18 September 1979, p. C12.
12. Letter to Editor, *New York Times*, 27 September 1979, p. A18.
13. Frank Rich, "Cop-Out in a Dark Demimonde," *Time*, 18 February 1980, p. 67.
14. Robert Angel, "Mean Streets," *The New Yorker*, 18 February 1980. pp. 126, 128.
15. John Hostetler and Donald Kraybill, "Hollywood Markets the Amish," in *Image Ethics*, ed. Larry Gross et al. (New York: Oxford University Press, 1988), pp. 226–235.
16. Quoted in Jack Mabley, "Magazine Pushes the Drug Culture," *Chicago Tribune*, 3 September 1976, sec. 1, p. 4.
17. Ibid.
18. Ibid.
19. This case is based on an interview with a cable company official who wished to remain unidentified, along with her company. Names used in this case study are fictitious.
20. Archibald MacLeish, "Communists, Writers, and the Spanish War," in *A Time to Speak* (Boston: Houghton, Mifflin, 1940), p. 99.
21. In addition to press reports cited in notes 22–23 and 25–26 below, material for this case was drawn from a mimeographed paper by James M. O'Brien, head librarian, Oak Lawn Public Library, "A Chronological History of a Censorship Challenge," n.d.
22 Quoted in Karen Koshner, "Librarian Obscenity Law Asked," *Chicago Sun-Times*, 3 December 1980, p. 16.
23. "A Stupid Boost for Book-Banners," *Chicago Sun-Times*, 5 December 1980, p. 51.
24. Joseph A. Olsen and Stan E. Weed, "Effects of Family Planning Programs for Teenagers on Adolescent Birth and Pregnancy Rates," *Family Perspective* 20 (Fall 1986): 153–195. Also see June A. Flora and Carl E. Thoresen, "Reducing the Risk of AIDS in Adolescents," *American Psychologist* 43 (November 1988): 965; and Jeanne Brooks-Gunn and Frank F. Furstenberg Jr., "Adolescent Sexual Behavior," *American Psychologist* 44 (February 1989): 249.
25. Eli M. Oboler, "Paternalistic Morality and Censorship," *Library Journal*, 1 September 1973, p. 2397.
26. American Library Association statement quoted in Susan Wagner, "Right-of-Center Censorship Increasing, ALA Finds," *Publishers Weekly*, 13 February 1978, p. 58.

CHAPTER 17

Epilogue

Questions of social ethics have always been the subtext of news stories, advertising messages, and entertainment programs—street crime and its victims, political deals, beauty and power, the society column with all its pseudodrama—but the last generation of newspaper readers and television viewers has come to discover that ethics of the media (in all its many forms) is a big news story too. A financial reporter is nabbed for passing corporate secrets to eager investors, and news columns wonder about other press perks. A network news host asks two young adults—one a convicted rapist and the other his former accuser—if they care to embrace, and the nation groans in disdain. The stories go on.

The approach to media ethics argued in the cases and commentaries in this book links itself strongly to a notion concerning media and public life called social responsibility theory. Social responsibility has been a marketplace theme since the Greek Peripatetics. Revived in nineteenth-century England as a trumpet call for prison and legal reform, it was applied to the press in the report of Robert Hutchins and his woebegone commission of twelve scholars in 1947. *A Free and Responsible Press* aptly captured the two sides of the classical liberal dilemma: A press free of all constraints could easily run amuck in its own drive for power and profit; a press too constrained by the power of the state would fail to achieve its lofty mission—informing citizens—and would turn the clock back to the dreaded Star Chamber. But free of state control and responsible to the public for essential democratic services, the press could flourish and the peoples' delicate experiment in democracy could mature. "Social responsibility" became an appeal to the ethics of telling the truth over making profits, telling all the truth over exposing special interests, and practicing truthtelling with the flinty eye of fairness that recognizes how hard it is to hit the truth dead center.

For all its potential, the social responsibility theory of the media has had a stadium of detractors for every player on the field. The press itself was scornful of Hutchins's work. (The commission's benefactor, Henry Luce, graded its output "a gentleman's 'C' and no better.") Academics have challenged its misty appeal to broad coverage and public involvement. One recent and astute critic argued that the theory "reaffirms the existing social order while at the same time providing the cloak of moral rectitude for those who claim to follow the doctrine."[1] Needless to say, to be powerful an idea cannot be mere garmentry.

A socially responsible press is a medium in tension, conscious of its obligations to enlighten readers and viewers and all too aware of its deadlines and competitors. No real news event follows a textbook case study. Each time a reporter goes out or an ad agent begins a campaign, something new is happening. In this frenzied world, how can "obligation to truth" or "comprehensive coverage of minority groups" hope to hold its own against "get the quote" and "shoot the tear-jerking photo"? How can truthtelling be allowed to give a competitor an advertising edge? How can respect for the elderly be written into television comedy? Somewhere in the sorting out of these media imperatives, a practitioner must begin to assign priorities and then live by them. That process is called moral reasoning. We contend that journalists, advertising executives, public relations practitioners, and entertainment programmers should be among the best trained moral thinkers in the land.

In a recent address to journalism educators on terrorism and the media, Fred W. Friendly urged that clever investigative techniques are not enough: "We need to make journalists *think*." The thrill of the craft—"getting the goods on the bad guys"—must be linked to the satisfaction of achieving a professional's "insight and discipline."[2] Friendly was echoing the concerns of a print media colleague, Charles Sieb, former *Washington Post* ombudsman, who urged less emphasis on such skills as copy editing, editorial writing, even newswriting, and "more emphasis on more basic matters, personal integrity, the making of ethical judgment. . . . Ethical quandaries are much more significant aspects of the journalist's real world . . . and much more difficult matters" than journalism schools have realized.[3]

The media serve a broad purpose in democratic life. As our technological society becomes increasingly complex, we expect the press to inform us fully on all issues. We need accounts of our common public life, enlightened consumer information, and entertainment programs with redeeming value. Newspapers, videotext, magazines, interactive cable, network television and the now ubiquitous personal computer all together form a paramount social institution, so deeply embedded that we label our present era "the information age." In order to measure and critique this social enterprise meaningfully, we have operated in this volume from the perspective of social ethics. With the Potter Box as a springboard, we have advocated a wide-angled type of moral reasoning compatible with the media's informational and entertainment missions.

Increasing interest in professional ethics—ethical reasoning concerning job-related questions—has not always led to a deepening of ethical reflection and a broadening of moral concern. Some conversations about sources, truthtelling, and privacy are short indeed. It is important to understand why journalists and professionals in persuasion alternately care about and resist turning the moral spotlight on their work. Nobody likes to be told what to do or think, least of all the press. But that objection aside, following are some common responses to questions of professional conduct, elaborated in terms of what those responses mean to many people in communications industries.

1. *If I don't hurt anyone, I've done okay.*

    Meaning: I have an important job to perform that demands skill with words, shapes, colors, graphics, and continuity. I want to do the best I can as an artist, and as long as nobody is deliberately harmed by what I do, the moral element is satisfied. All other considerations are questions of esthetics.

    Comment: The moral quest that seeks to bring no harm to people is honorable but insufficient. While it avoids adding to the considerable weight of human suffering in the world, it is less aggressive in identifying and resolving problems already there. Morality requires beneficence—that we do certain things and not merely avoid the hurtful. Morality also requires that we look at motivations and intentions, which are not always expressed in behaviors. The minimalist appeal to "cause no harm" is sometimes blind to what sociologist Robert Bellah calls the "habits of the heart."

Journalists who use this approach to ethical reasoning usually mean something different than do advertising, public relations, and entertainment professionals. Most journalists understand that many of their stories will hurt someone in some way, so in the minds of journalists, this inclination to cause no harm is qualified to mean: cause no harm unnecessary to the public's need to know what is happening. This is an important qualification, but it still falls short of stipulating the media's positive duties. Nor does it indicate when harm may be necessary. This qualified statement also assumes a lot about the phenomenon called "the public," and we need to know more about why public information is deemed so important.

2.   *If I do what I feel is right, that's all a person can be expected to do.*

Meaning: The world is full of competing moral systems and contradictory assertions about what is right and wrong. Arguing over these competing claims only leads to frustration. The point of morality is that each person has to do what he or she believes is right. Beyond that, you are imposing your answers on me, and that is wrong.

Comment: No moral system would suggest that people violate their conscience. In that sense, doing what feels right is an important and probably universal moral guide. But it is not enough. First of all, our feelings can experience wild fluctuations not always within our control. During periods of disappointment, feelings toward the self vary widely. Or we may be brainwashed or drunk; feelings at those times would be disastrous guides for moral action. More important, the appeal to feelings isolates each person into an autonomous, self-enclosed moral system. While some visions of the human person may point to this kind of individualism, this book insists that humans are accountable to each other, interdependent and not isolated selves. To lodge our ultimate moral appeal inside ourselves is to risk deception and isolation.

3.   *The Code of Ethics sits on my desk and hangs on the wall. I go strictly by the book.*

Meaning: Test my conduct against an objective standard, and I'll smell like roses. If the Code doesn't outlaw it, don't bother me. I respect the profession I'm in, but I don't have patience with introspective moral gnat-chasers who want all my internal vibrations to resonate with the angels. Let me do my job and judge me by the standards of the profession.

Comment: Taking professional codes seriously is a much needed antidote to the kind of ethical individualism that creates Lone Rangers but no Texas Rangers. Adjusting to commonly held standards generates an ethos of accountability that overcomes the deficits of egoism and holds open the possibility of ethical debate from a base of community givens. But a simple appeal to codes on desk tops may be a shield against tough moral inquiry from outside the profession. Doctors alone do not create standards for doctors, nor lawyers for lawyers, and, thankfully, neither do politicians alone create moral standards for politicians. Professions need dialogue with each other, with citizens, and with wider communities of concern in order to inhibit a professional privilege that begins to detach itself from all other jurisdictions. In worst case situations, the appeal to codes can be a ruse for business-as-usual. The mere fact that Shaka could command the immediate execution of any of his subjects, a social code commonly understood, does not make ancient Zulu law necessarily moral. Organizations are too prone to self-interest to accept the notion that all codes are genuinely inspired by disinterested ethical concerns.

4. *Honesty demands that we cease all this hype about ethics and get to the heart of the matter: You get the story as best you can, write as fast as you can, and the rest is history. We have a job to do.*

Meaning: My career is top priority.

Comment: Honest careerism may be a more virtuous path than feigning concern over the moral imagination but neglecting the duties that such reflection imposes. Careerism is not to be quickly despised, since it does have the benefit of directing a titanic wave of energy into a profession that cannot be satiated. As an alternative to lethargy or corruption, careerism has many attractive plusses, not the least of which are the personal rewards of meeting important goals and receiving acclaim for one's talents. Many professionals would find this fourth statement closest to their own disposition.

Yet we come back to the inadequacy of conducting one's life as though only the self and its needs mattered. In formal ethical theory, such an approach is called hedonism. While the word suggests images of wild extravagance, it means simply that in a calculus of pleasure, only elements that promote the self's happiness get counted. Such an approach, if widely shared, would likely spell the end of responsible media practice and revive the era of hucksterism. If Dr. Buckley's goat gland formula was a farce and a con, who could object to Buckley's seeking his best interests?

Perhaps this response points with keenest hindsight to the strategic problem of grounding our moral inquiry in norms. Apart from norms, ethics is a guess, a majority vote, or a personal choice. Norms give ethics a foundation and make moral claims obligatory. Norms eliminate the "every person for herself" modality as quickly as they question the professionalization motif that seeks autonomy from outsiders. Norms become the bedrock of ethical behavior and thinking, the sounding board and center point of dispute resolution. Norms also make claims on us which cannot be dismissed, only submerged or suppressed.

Our use of the Potter Box in the preceding cases involves grappling with norms. In the southeast quadrant, below loyalties and adjacent to professional and cultural values, rest norms. Why should the demands of social justice overrule some institutional concerns for profit? Norms become the substance of our appeal. Why should librarians exercise caution over displaying controversial books? Ultimately norms become the center of the argument.

Norms concern our picture of what reality is like—how everything got here and what the meaning of our lives is. If existence has mostly instrumental meaning, then norms concerning one's right to life, to medical or educational enhancements, will be based on one's productivity—that is, on one's instrumental value to others. If existence has intrinsic meaning, norms would carry different obligations and be based on different foundations.

Of course, not everyone agrees on how reality is constituted and thus we also disagree on what norms reflect the reality in which we live. Because we want belief to be voluntarily adopted (not coerced), we hold freedom of speech and conscience to be a guiding social norm. But even this statement requires that we explain why beliefs ought not be forced on everyone. Some cultures obviously believe they should be.

In a pluralistic culture, many harmonies compete for adoption, and the cacophony sometimes discourages us from attaching ourselves to any of them. Intellectual detachment is said to provide the distance a communicator needs in order to see the world and its complexities objectively. In fact, all of us need some detachment in order to develop critical knowledge about our own intellectual commitments. On the other hand, living in perpetual detachment is impossible, for choices

must be made and the grounds for making choices must be acknowledged. So our many harmonies co-exist, competing for expression in
public policy and appealing as best they can to the needs and aspirations
of both true believers and skeptics. Pluralism, if you will, is God's gift
to heretics.

In the Introduction, we selected five normative proposals with
profound impact on Western civilization. In the cases, we suggested
how those ethical norms might effect a morally justified conclusion
to a genuine dilemma. For some cases, we worked with more than one
norm. For others, we found common ground between two norms. At
times we merely pointed to the normative dimension but were not
explicit.

Journalism is a profession in search of norms. Advertising, public
relations, and entertainment professionals are right there with news
reporters in the hunt for foundations to moral claims. The search is
complicated by the reality that most public communication projects
need to respect a variety of responsible visions of truth and even to
represent them to some degree in their pages or through air time. Yet
media ethics languishes in a potpourri. Is there a recipe besides veg-
etable stew that a media institution can adopt to provide normative
grounding and pluralistic freedom?

We believe that helpful directions lie in the recovery of a fuller
notion of the human person as a communal being. Enlightened ra-
tionalism was a triumphal notion in the era of divine-right monarchy,
but its emphasis on individual autonomy has tended to obscure the
social and communal nature of the human person. One cannot read
far into the writings of Hutchins commissioners like Hocking, Niebuhr, Shuster, or Hutchins himself without finding explicit reference
to persons in community as a core element, an irreducible essential.
Human beings are not in fact autonomous and isolated. Neither do
bonds of community submerge the person in the soup of statism or
tribalism, disallowing moral choice and replacing conscience with Lev-
iathan. Rather, "persons in community" reflects the essential social
bonds that define human life and acknowledges that persons are truly
moral agents. The five normative principles woven through this book
are, in a sense, alternative explanations of the person–community connection, with varying implications on how that connection ought to
be expressed in the professions of culture formation.

Are these implications crystal clear and airtight? Any professional
will describe the dangers. Looming from one side is the threat of pru-
dery and its consequence: programming that portrays a false sense of

innocence about human affairs. On the other side is moral anarchy, the abandonment of all moral principle except that of absolute freedom. Responsible media can ill afford the danger of either terrain. Society is not served by the mindless dumping of its moral traditions; nor do we explore the moral life intelligently through casuistry or naiveté.

Our cases, therefore, present one of the most perplexing issues for a pluralistic culture: how to achieve moral continuity and, at the same time, moral exploration. If "culture" means anything, it means a common ground of moral understanding ordering the lives of diverse people. Media should both respect and challenge that common ground.

Especially in convoluted and stressful times, a continuing stream of questions and debates will catch news, advertising, public relations, and entertainment in its wake. As long as law-bending, stereotyping, and violence subvert our democratic experiment, media will find themselves in the storm center. Understanding communication ethics may be hard work with few direct incentives and no immediate material gains, but the media professional whose career includes its probing is serving the audience well: doing the good work of building a socially responsible press. On that premise this book is offered. Toward that end this book is only a short installment.

NOTES

1. Herbert Altschull, *Agents of Power* (White Plains, N.Y.: Longman, 1984), p. 304.
2. From the report of a speech at the AEJMC annual meetings, Memphis, Tenn., August 1985.
3. Speech to the Association for Education in Journalism, East Lansing, Mich., 11 August 1981.

Cases by Medium

BOOKS
69. Corporate Takeovers of Media Companies
70. The Book That Squeaked
71. The Purpose Is Profit
73. Super Strip
79. The Father Knows Best
85. The Artist Censors Himself
86. *Show Me* and Pressures on Libraries

MAGAZINES
1. The Time Warner Colossus
32. The Market Illiterate
33. A Magazine and Its Audience
37. A Minuscule (and Tasteless) Difference
52. The Media Subsidy
68. Comic Capers
80. Skin at the Grocery Store
83. *High Times* Magazine and Drug Market Information

MOTION PICTURES
1. The Time Warner Colossus
48. The Captive Audience
65. *Papillon* and Prescreening
72. Deep Trouble for Harry
74. History Burning
75. Are Fake Unhappy Endings Any Better Than Fake Happy Ones?
82. *Cruising* for Survival
84. The Cable Is Blue

NEWSPAPERS

PHOTOGRAPHY

RADIO

RECORDS

TELEVISION

3. Ownership of Cable Television
16. A Television Reporter as Family Friend
17. Presidential Commission on World Hunger
19. The Homeless Story
21. Ten Weeks at Wounded Knee
27. Fantasy for Selling
28. Animated Sales Catalogs Masquerading as Entertainment
29. Saying "No" Too Often
35. The 30-Second Candidate
36. Feminine Hygiene in the Living Room
41. Gun for Hire?
42. Larger than Life
49. Never Have So Few Scared So Many
55. Regal Holding Company
62. Spin Doctors
63. Pesticide Panic
64. Hear It, Feel It, Do It
66. "Holocaust" and Television's Limits as a Medium
67. "The Storyteller"
74. History Burning
76. Dreaming Ourselves into Middle-Class Comfort
77. Bigotry as Debate
78. A New Group of Longstanding Members Demands Respect
79. The Father Knows Best
81. *Death Wish* and Television Violence
84. The Cable Is Blue

VIDEO

1. The Time Warner Colossus

Cases by Issue

CENSORSHIP

CHILDREN

CONFIDENTIALITY

MINORITIES AND THE ELDERLY

PRIVACY

SENSATIONALISM

STEREOTYPING

VIOLENCE

INTRODUCTORY

Bayles, Michael. *Professional Ethics.* Belmont, Calif: Wadsworth, 1981.
 An overview, for upper-level undergraduates, of ethical issues faced by professions as a whole. Bayles examines the meaning of professional obligation and challenges the traditional norms that usually go unquestioned.

Bowie, Norman E. *Making Ethical Decisions.* New York: McGraw-Hill, 1985.
 An anthology of classical and contemporary writers, organized around such important issues as relativism, respect for principles, morality, rights, virtue and justice, and equality. An effective companion text for courses in media ethics.

Callahan, Daniel, and Sissela Bok. *Ethics Teaching in Higher Education.* New York: Plenum, 1980.
 Essays prepared for the Hastings Center Project on the Teaching of Ethics. Includes important chapters on the goals of ethics instruction, whistle-blowing, and the history of ethics in university curricula.

Dyck, Arthur, J. *On Human Care: An Introduction to Ethics.* Nashville, Tenn.: Abingdon, 1977.
 Uses the Potter Box to introduce ethical questions regarding world populations and the environment. In the process of dealing with issues in the medical profession, readers are confronted with the basic problems in ethical theory.

Frankena, William K. *Ethics.* Englewood Cliffs, N.J.: Prentice-Hall, 1963.
 A summary of ethical theory for general readers. This familiar classic, though brief, is a virtual encyclopedia of major concepts and thinkers in philosophical ethics.

Gert, Bernard. *The Moral Rules.* New York: Harper Torchbooks, 1973.
 Addressed primarily to the ordinary reader, Gert nonetheless develops a sophisticated theory of moral obligation. The heart of the book is a set of ten moral rules that can be justified for all rational persons, rules such as don't kill, don't deceive, don't deprive of pleasure, and so forth.

Goldman, Alan H. *The Moral Foundations of Professional Ethics.* Totowa, N.J.: Rowman & Littlefield, 1980.
Intelligent and careful defense of a rights-based theory of professional ethics in the liberal tradition. Focuses on the key issue—whether professions are governed by special moral principles that differ from our common moral framework.

Johannesen, Richard L. *Ethics in Human Communication.* 3d ed. Prospect Heights, Ill.: Waveland Press, 1990.
Places ethical responsibility in the context of political philosophy and communication theory. Includes cases and analysis of ethics codes.

Kultgen, John. *Ethics and Professionalism.* Philadelphia: University of Pennsylvania Press, 1988.
From a pragmatist perspective, examines institutional practices and rules in such areas as confidentiality, professional paternalism, social action, and the workplace.

Lebacqz, Karen. *Professional Ethics: Power and Paradox.* Nashville, Tenn.: Abingdon Press, 1985.
A skillful blend of theory and practice examining rule morality, virtue and character, and professional structures.

MacIntyre, Alasdair. *A Short History of Ethics.* New York: Macmillan, 1966.
Outlines in a readable manner the history of moral philosophy in the Western tradition, from Homer in ancient Greece to twentieth-century ethicists.

Rogers, Jack B., and Forrest E. Baird. *Introduction to Philosophy: A Case Method Approach.* San Francisco: Harper and Row, 1981.
A textbook introducing twelve major philosophers from Socrates to Wittgenstein through simulated cases, role playing, questions, and a contemporary response.

Taylor, Paul W. *Principles of Ethics: An Introduction.* Encino, Calif.: Dickensen Publishing Co., 1975.
Well-written chapters for beginners. Provides excellent definitions of ethics, morals, and values. A good overview of utilitarian and Kantian ethics.

NEWS

Christians, Clifford G., and Catherine L. Covert. *Teaching Ethics in Journalism Education.* New York: Hastings Center Monograph, 1980.
Survey of ethics teaching and substantive issues in journalism ethics today. Outlines four instructional objectives.

Cooper, Thomas W. *Communication Ethics and Global Change.* New York: Longman, 1989.
Essays from sixteen countries on the important issues in media ethics. Overview chapters on the important international issues are included in sections I and III. Codes of Ethics included in the Appendix.

Elliott, Deni T., ed. *Responsible Journalism.* Beverly Hills, Calif: Sage, 1986.

Nine essays by academics, examining issues in press theory and social responsibility.

Goodwin, H. Eugene. *Groping for Ethics in Journalism.* 2d ed. Ames: Iowa State University Press, 1987.
Explores a variety of issues: conflicts of interest, deception, misrepresentation, privacy, sources, and incompetence. Based on interviews with a wide-ranging sample of professionals and academics, and a review of the media codes and literature.

Hulteng, John L. *The Messenger's Motives: Ethical Problems of the News Media.* 2d ed. Englewood Cliffs, N.J.: Prentice-Hall, 1985.
Built on a series of cases and illustrations that show how the media operate. Questions how successfully they live up to contemporary codes of ethics.

Klaidman, Stephen, and Tom L. Beauchamp. *The Virtuous Journalist.* New York: Oxford University Press, 1987.
Built around real-life cases, this volume describes the character traits and professional virtues needed for fair, truthful, and competent journalism.

Lambeth, Edmund B. *Committed Journalism: An Ethic for the Profession.* Bloomington: Indiana University Press, 1986.
Outlines a framework for ethical journalism from the codes, ideals, and best practice in the field.

Merrill, John C. *The Dialectic in Journalism: Toward a Responsible Use of Press Freedom.* Baton Rouge: Louisiana State University Press, 1989.
Examines the tension between responsible action and freedom in the context of the Western intellectual tradition.

Pippert, Wesley G. *An Ethics of News: A Reporter's Search for Truth.* Washington, D.C.: Georgetown University Press, 1989.
Analysis of ethical issues in news, based on author's personal experiences. Focuses on the issue of truthtelling.

Rivers, William L., Wilbur Schramm, and Clifford Christians. *Responsibility in Mass Communication.* 3d ed. New York: Harper and Row, 1980.
A classic text on media ethics that argues for the social responsibility option.

Schmuhl, Robert, ed. *The Responsibilities of Journalists.* Notre Dame, Ind.: University of Notre Dame Press, 1984.
Papers and speeches presented at a Notre Dame conference. Papers written by a mixture of professionals, journalism educators, and ethicists.

ADVERTISING

Baum, Robert J., Norman E. Bowie, and Deborah G. Johnson, eds. *Business and Professional Ethics Journal* 3, Spring/Summer 1984.
Special double issue in which advertising professionals, educators, and philosophers discuss important topics: manipulative advertising, professional advertising content, and children as consumers.

Beauchamp, Thomas L., and Norman E. Bowie. "Ethical Issues in Advertising."

In *Ethical Theory and Business*. 2d ed. Englewood Cliffs, N.J.: Prentice-Hall, 1983.
Case studies, legal opinions, and essays on such ethical issues as deception and creating consumer demand.

Capitman, William. "Morality in Advertising—A Public Imperative," *MSU Business Topics*, Spring 1971.
A reply to Theodore Levitt.

Chonko, Lawrence B., Shelby D. Hunt, and Roy D. Howell, "Ethics and the American Advertising Federation Principles," *International Journal of Advertising*, October 1987, pp. 255–274.
An important study examining the effectiveness of recent American Advertising Federation principles.

Cone, Fairfax. *With All Its Faults*. Boston: Little, Brown & Co., 1969.
A sensitive practitioner looks at his business from the vantage point of 40 years experience.

Gossage, Howard. *Is Advertising Worth Saving?* Urbana: University of Illinois Press, 1986.
A renowned practitioner and perceptive critic examines the philosophies and practices of his business and finds them wanting.

Jugenheimer, Donald W., Dean M. Krugman, Vincent P. Norris, and Kim B. Rotzoll. *Working Papers on Advertising and Ethics*. Papers presented at the AAAA Convention. Department of Advertising *Working Paper*, University of Illinois at Urbana, May 1982.
Suggests principles to guide advertising ethics and applies them to advertising organizations, the audience, and teaching.

Kottman, E. John. "The Parity Product—Advertising's Achilles Heel," *Journal of Advertising* 6:4(1977), 34–39.
An examination of one of advertising's enduring ethical areas.

Levitt, Theodore. "The Morality (?) of Advertising," *Harvard Business Review*, July-August 1970.
A provocative positioning of advertising as a form of "alleviating imagery."

Mander, Jerry. "Four Arguments for the Elimination of Advertising." In *Advertising and the Public*, ed. Kim Rotzoll. Urbana: University of Illinois Department of Advertising, 1979.
A major attack on four presumably inherent dimensions of the advertising process.

Modic, Stanley J. "Forget Ethics—And Succeed?" *Industry Week*, October 19, 1987, pp. 17–18.
A 1987 survey among Industry Week *readers reveals that many felt business ethics were lower than two years earlier.*

Ogilvy, David. *Confessions of an Advertising Man*. New York: Atheneum, 1963.
A literate statement of how advertising should be practiced, by a most influential modern practitioner.

Palmer, Edward, and Aimee Dorr, eds. *Children and the Faces of Television.* New York: Academic Press, 1980, chaps. 15–21.
Seven authors examine the behavioral, political, and ethical dimensions of advertising to children.

Rotfeld, Herbert J., and Patrick R. Parsons, "Self Regulation and Magazine Advertising," *Journal of Advertising*, no. 4 (1989), 33–41.
A major survey of magazines examines their acceptance policies.

Rotzoll, Kim, and Clifford Christians. "Advertising Agency Practitioners' Perceptions of Ethical Decisions," *Journalism Quarterly* 57 (Autumn 1980), 425–431.
On the basis of research reflected in this book, the authors examine key ethical dimensions of advertising agency practice, as seen by the practitioners.

Rotzoll, Kim, James Haefner, and Charles Sandage. *Advertising in Contemporary Society.* 2nd ed. Cincinnati: South-Western Publishing, 1990, chaps. 1–4.
An explanation of advertising's roots in the market and the world view of classical liberalism; visions of advertising as an institution; the strains on advertising under the neo-liberal world view.

Terkel, Studs. *Working.* New York: Avon Books, 1975, pp. 112–147.
Among others, Terkel interviews six people involved in the advertising business.

Zanot, Eric. "Unseen but Effective Advertising Regulation: The Clearance Process, *Journal of Advertising*, no. 4 (1985), 44–51.
Traces clearance procedures normally followed by major advertisers, agencies, and media.

CODES, GUIDELINES

The advertising business involves a wide array of guidelines, codes, and standards dealing with the legal and ethical dimensions of the process. These are some of the more important sources:

Council of Better Business Bureaus, Inc.
845 Third Avenue
New York, NY 10022

American Advertising Federation
1225 Connecticut Ave., NW
Washington, DC 20036

National Association of Broadcasters
1771 N Street, NW
Washington, DC 20036

Association of National Advertisers
155 East 44th Street
New York, NY 10017

PUBLIC RELATIONS

Bernays, Edward L. *Crystallizing Public Opinion.* New York: Boni and Live Right, 1923; *Biography of an Idea: Memoirs of Public Relations Council Edward L. Bernays.* New York: Simon and Schuster, 1965.

Bernays makes it clear how much the world depends on the proper formation of public attitudes.

Bivins, Thomas H. "Applying Ethical Theory to Public Relations," *Journal of Business Ethics* 6 (1987): 195–200; "Professional Advocacy in Public Relations," *Business and Professional Ethics Journal* 6:1 (1988): 82–91; "Ethical Implications of the Relationship of Purpose to Role and Function in Public Relations," *Journal of Business Ethics* 8(1989): 65–73.
Examines public relations as a professional domain, and connects those features of its social role to the relevant ethical theories.

Creedon, Pamela J. *Women in Mass Communication: Challenging Gender Values.* Beverly Hills, Calif.: Sage Publications, 1989.
A book accounting for the increased number of women in mass media occupations, with several chapters contributed by public relations scholars.

Ellul, Jacques. *Propaganda.* New York, Vintage, 1973.
Always innovative, Ellul explores public attitude formation as part of the larger social issue surrounding la technique.

Grunig, Larissa A. "Toward the Philosophy of Public Relations." In Elizabeth Lance Toth and Robert L. Heath, eds., *Rhetorical and Critical Approaches to Public Relations.* Hillsdale, N.J.: Lawrence Erlbaum Associates, in press.
First major attempt to construct a conceptual framework for studying public relations ethics. Influenced by a feminist perspective, and argues that public relations involves not persuasion but an exchange of information.

Hiebert, Roy Eldon. *Courtier to the Crowd: The Story of Ivy Lee and the Development of Public Relations.* Ames, Iowa: State University Press, 1966.
The story of one of the founding geniuses.

Kruckeberg, Dean and Kenneth Starck. *Public Relations and Community: A Reconstructed Theory.* New York: Praeger, 1988.
Explores the social responsibility of public relations practitioners in contemporary American society.

Lippmann, Walter. *Public Opinion.* New York: MacMillan, 1922.
This book sets the agenda for much of twentieth century thinking on media in general and public relations in particular.

Miller, Debra A. and Barbara A. Hines, eds. *Ethical Trends and Issues in Public Relations Education.* Proceedings from the 1984 and 1985 Educators Workshops. International Association of Business Communicators, District 3, May 1986.
A summary of workshops in Baltimore, Maryland and Alexandria, Virginia on the subject of priority ethical issues for public relations educators.

Olasky, Marvin N. *Corporate Public Relations: A New Historical Perspective.* Hillsdale, N.J.: Lawrence Erlbaum Associates, 1987.
How public relations has contributed to our understanding of industry, from railroads to the movie business.

Sinclair, Upton. *The Brass Check.* Pasadena: Author, 1920.

No advocate of the profession of public relations, Sinclair was one of the first to tell us why we should be watchful.

ENTERTAINMENT

Alley, Robert S. *Television: Ethics for Hire?* Nashville Tenn.: Abingdon, 1977.
Interviews with Norman Lear, Alan Alda, Earl Hamner, and others give insight into the aims and ethics of industry pace setters.

Casebier, Allan, and Janet Casebier, eds. *Social Responsibilities of the Mass Media.* Washington, D.C.: University Press of America, 1978.
Part Three of this collection of essays deals with entertainment programming: pro- and antisocial images, controversial content, rights and obligations of producers. Included is a discussion of the issues by conference delegates.

Christians, Clifford, and Kim Rotzoll. "Ethical Issues in the Film Industry." In Bruce Austin, ed., *Current Research in Film, Volume 2.* Norwood, N.J.: Ablex, 1985, pp. 225–237.
Jacques Ellul's "la technique" is applied to an understanding of the organizational culture of cinema—especially finance, production and sales.

Clor, Harry M. *Obscenity and Public Morality: Censorship in a Liberal Society.* Chicago: University of Chicago Press. 1969.
A reasoned moral argument for restricting certain kinds of communication in a liberal democracy. Legal and ethical issues are integrated in this critique of laissez-faire *freedom.*

Cooper, Thomas W. *Television and Ethics: A Bibliography.* Boston: G. K. Hall and Co., 1988.
1,170 sources are cited—many of them annotated—on all aspects of television and ethics.

Does Television Change History? Proceedings of the Second National Conference on Television and Ethics, 6 March 1987, Boston, Mass. Boston: Emerson College, 1987.
Attempts to distinguish documentary and docudrama, and evaluates the issues involved in ethically producing the latter.

Ellul, Jacques. *Propaganda: The Formation of Men's Attitudes.* Trans. Konrad Keller and Jean Lerner. New York: Vintage Books, 1965.
An expansive critique of modern symbols and their threat to democratic freedom.

Final Report of the Attorney General's Commission on Pornography. Nashville, Tenn.: Rutledge Hill Press, 1986.
An attempt by experts summoned during the Reagan administration to speak definitively on the dangers of pornography.

Gross, Larry, John Stuart Katz, and Jay Ruby, eds. *Images Ethics: The Moral Rights of Subjects in Photographs, Film, and Television.* New York: Oxford University Press, 1988.

Original essays on the ethics of representation which view moral questions in terms of the subject rather than the rights of producers and filmmakers.

Mander, Jerry. *Four Arguments for the Elimination of Television.* New York: Morrow, 1978.
Some ideas are harmed by their treatment on television, says the author. Four provocative chapters and a radical conclusion.

Newcomb, Horace, and Robert Alley, *The Producer's Medium: Conversations with Creators of American TV.* New York: Oxford University Press, 1983.
Interviews with notable producers (Norman Lear, Richard Levinson, William Link, and Garry Marshall, for example) about the values they express as artists.

Phelan, John M. *Disenchantment: Meaning and Morality in the Media.* New York: Hastings House, 1980.
Proposing that a public philosophy arises from the humanities, Phelan addresses the problems of new technology and cultural freedom.

Schwartz, Tony. *The Responsive Chord.* New York: Anchor/Doubleday, 1973.
A resonance theory of communication is the framework for exploring the ethics of television and radio. Advertising and news functions are also part of this discussion.

Thayer, Lee, ed. *Ethics Morality and the Media.* New York: Hastings House, 1980.
Twenty-seven essays and speeches—most by practitioners—on the current status of media ethics, with a long introduction ("Notes on American Culture") by the editor.

Clifford G. Christians is a professor of communications at the University of Illinois, Urbana-Champaign, where he directs the doctoral program in communications and heads the media studies unit. He has a B.A. in classics, a B.D. and Th.M. in theology, an M.A. in sociolinguistics from Southern California, and a Ph.D. in communications from Illinois. He has been a visiting scholar in philosophical ethics at Princeton University and in social ethics at the University of Chicago. He has published essays on various aspects of mass communication (including ethics) in *Journalism Monographs, Journal of Broadcasting, Journalism History, Journal of Communication, Journal of Mass Media Ethics, Communication,* and *International Journal of Mass Communication Research.* He has completed a third edition of Rivers and Schramm's *Responsibility in Mass Communication,* has co-authored *Jacques Ellul: Interpretive Essays* with Jay Van Hook, and has written *Teaching Ethics in Journalism Education* with Catherine Covert. He contributed the article "Media Ethics" to the *International Encyclopedia of Communications.*

Kim B. Rotzoll is a professor of advertising and head of the Department of Advertising at the University of Illinois, Urbana-Champaign. He holds a B.A. in advertising, an M.A. in journalism, and a Ph.D. in sociology from The Pennsylvania State University. He is the senior author of *Advertising in Contemporary Society* and an author of *Advertising Theory and Practice.* He has published articles in *Journal of Advertising, Journal of Advertising Research, Journal of Consumer Affairs, Journalism Quarterly, Christian Century, Journalism Educator, Journal of Advertising History,* and several anthologies. His teaching and speaking interests concern advertising as a social and economic institution and advertising ethics as well as advertising history. He has been a guest lecturer in China, Denmark, and Bahrain.

Mark Fackler is associate professor of communication at Wheaton (Ill.) College. He holds an A.B. in philosophy, an M.A. in communications, an M.A. in theology, and a Ph.D. in communications from the University of Illinois. His professional experience includes writing for magazines and radio, audiovisual production, graphics, and public relations. He has been guest lecturer at the Poynter Institute for Media Studies. He teaches courses in communication theory, ethics, and law.